The Nature and Development of the Modern State

D0113184

Also by Graeme Gill

Democracy and Post-Communism
Elites and Leadership in Russian Politics (ed.)
Peasants and Government in the Russian Revolution
Power in the Party (with Roderick Pitty)
Russia's Stillborn Democracy? (with Roger D. Markwick)
Stalinism
The Collapse of a Single-Party System
The Dynamics of Democratization
The Origins of the Stalinist Political System
The Politics of Transition (with Stephen White and Darrell Slider)
The Rules of the Communist Party of the Soviet Union
Twentieth-Century Russia

The Nature and Development of the Modern State

Graeme Gill
School of Economics and Political Science
The University of Sydney

First published 2003 by
PALGRAVE MACMILLAN
Houndmills, Basingstoke, Hampshire RG21 6XS and
175 Fifth Avenue, New York, N.Y. 10010
Companies and representatives throughout the world

PALGRAVE MACMILLAN is the global academic imprint of the Palgrave Macmillan division of St. Martin's Press, LLC and of Palgrave Macmillan Ltd. Macmillan® is a registered trademark in the United States, United Kingdom and other countries. Palgrave is a registered trademark in the European Union and other countries.

ISBN 0–333–80449–X hardback
ISBN 0–333–80450–3 paperback

This book is printed on paper suitable for recycling and made from fully managed and sustained forest sources.

A catalogue record for this book is available from the British Library.

A catalog record for this book is available from the Library of Congress.

10   9   8   7   6   5   4   3   2   1
12 11 10 09 08 07 06 05 04 03

Printed in China

Contents

List of Tables   vii

Preface   ix

1   The Modern State   **1**

What is the State?   2
Perspectives on the Role of the State   8
State Autonomy and Interdependence   12
State Capacity   22
The Role of Power   24

2   The Ancient State   **33**

The Ancient City-State   35
The Ancient Empires   47
The Ancient State and Institutional Interdependence   58
The Ancient State   68

3   The Feudal and Early Modern State   **73**

The Feudal System   74
The Consolidation and Centralization of   80
   Administrative Power
Absolutism and Constitutionalism   97
Institutional Interdependence?   104

4   The State, Capitalism and Industrialization   **115**

The State and Industrialism   117
The 'Late Developers'   124
Industrialization and the Development of   127
   State Infrastructure
The Social Embedding of the State   139

5   The Western State and the Outside World   **149**

War and the State   152
National Identity   158

The Wider World 160
The Asian State 169
The Uniqueness of the Western State? 185
Colonial Globalization? 191

6 The Twentieth Century: The State Embedded? 194

Welfare Capitalism 194
The Communist Challenge 210
Capitalist Success, Communist Failure? 222
No Third Way 224

7 State Capacity in a Globalized World 226

Economic Globalization 227
Political Globalization 230
Cultural/Ideological Globalization 234
The Limits of Globalization 239
The State and Globalization 246
The *Longue Durée* of the State 255

Notes and References 257

Index 297

List of Tables

4.1   Railway development in Europe   128
4.2   State employment of civilian personnel   130
4.3   Total state revenue   131
4.4   Achievement of the suffrage   143

Preface

On seeing this book, readers may well ask: why yet another book on the nature of the state? In the last part of the twentieth century, the political science literature literally exploded with books about the state. Authors focused on issues such as the structure, role and functions of the contemporary state, the state's historical development, the part the state plays in economic development, the philosophical meaning of the state, and state origins. There were studies of different types of governments – democratic, authoritarian, dictatorial, single-party, populist, presidential, parliamentary, monarchical, republican, federal, unitary – with authors pointing to the various types of institutional arrangements to distinguish between different polities. There were also innumerable studies of individual political systems. Although this common fare of comparative politics generally focused upon regimes rather than states, implicit in it was often an assumption that the states were different: for example, the communist state was seen to be very different from that of liberal democracy. In the face of such an array of scholarship, what can yet another book hope to contribute?

Given the centrality of the state for the conduct of life in the twentieth century, it is not surprising that it should be the subject of substantial scholarship or that there has been a diversity of approaches to it. What is perhaps more surprising is that there has been little explicit study of that which is central to the state's survival and functioning, state capacity. State capacity is what enables the state as an institution not just to survive and carry out rudimentary functions, but to make and implement policies throughout the territory over which it claims sovereignty. It is state capacity that enables the modern state to intervene in all walks of life, and it is the nature and extent of that capacity that distinguishes the modern state from its predecessors. The analysis of state capacity must therefore be at the heart of our understanding of the state, what it does and how it does it.

The main aim of this book is analysis of the nature and development, over time, of state capacity. Its essential argument is that what distinguishes the modern state from its earlier forebears is the much enhanced capacity of the modern state to achieve its goals. Despite differences in institutional configurations (e.g. between American presidentialism and British parliamentarism) and national histories and traditions, the modern state is conceived of as a single type of political formation that is distinguished from its earlier counterparts by the extent of its capacity. It is the nature and extent of state capacity that defines a state as modern. This capacity results from a combination of the internal discipline and centralization of the state structure (the state's bureaucratic infrastructure), and the type of relationship that is developed between the state and society, including economy, classes and elites (the state's embeddedness). It is the following through of the development of state capacity that constitutes both the backbone of this book and the principal focus of the explanation for the changing nature of the state over time.

There are many studies of the way state structures have emerged. These studies focus principally upon the organs of central government, tracing the development of bureaucracy, legislature and judiciary and charting the struggle between crown and nobility in an attempt to explain the emergence of the modern state form. But what is central to this process, and something that most studies largely ignore, is the development of state capacity over time. The history of the development of the state is not one of continued, unbroken growth in state capacity. Rather, the development of this has occurred in fits and starts, with setbacks in some cases more common than advances; witness the cases of the breakdown of central power in the national histories of most states. This means that an attempt to chart the nature and growth of state capacity does not require a detailed study of all aspects of particular states' national histories. Rather what is needed is a focus upon those periods when state capacity made the greatest advances: in the ancient states when for the first time established polities sought the systematic expansion of state capacity, the feudal and early modern period when the slow process of statebuilding led to the gradual accretion of state capacity, and industrialization which created the infrastructure and social relationships to enable the massive expansion of that capacity. And rather than detailed national histories of states during these periods, what we need to understand is the dynamic of the shaping of the course of state capacity. We do not need to study all states to understand the development of state capacity. While the book draws on a wide range of examples from the development of different states, it makes no attempt to be a comprehensive or exhaustive comparative study. Rather, it deploys examples to illuminate similarities and differences, for example Britain as the first modern state in terms of the extent and character of its capacity, and Russia as a case of the transformation from backwater to superpower.

Chapter 1 sets out the conception of the state that is being used in this book. Emphasizing the bureaucratic nature of the state's structure, its centralization and internal differentiation, its sovereignty and its territoriality, the chapter outlines various views of the role the state plays in society. This is directly related to notions of state autonomy and to the interdependence of the state with society. Such interdependence and the forms it takes are central to the subsequent analysis, because it is the balance of types of interdependence, especially between organic and institutional interdependence, that is important for the embeddedness of the state in society and the development of state capacity. Such capacity is also linked to infrastructural power, to the ability to penetrate and work with society through regularized institutional procedures.

High-level capacity is central to an effective, modern, state, but it is not essential to the existence of the state itself. As Chapter 2 shows, the early states – including the most long-lasting state in history (Egypt) – were not characterized by high levels of state capacity. While formally the level of centralization was very high in all of these polities, in practice central control was much more episodic and segmental, and reliant upon the cooperation of locally based elites. However, the extent of interdependence with society was very limited. These characteristics reflected the underdeveloped nature of the bureaucratic structure and the regime's socially exclusivist cast. The ancient states should thus be seen as attempts at the administrative control of society rather than interdependent cooperation with it. But they do show how states can survive for long periods without being firmly embedded in the society as a whole and without having highly developed capacity.

Chapter 3 shows how the feudal and early modern state sought to overcome the infrastructural weakness of the ancient state. The focus of this chapter is upon the development of the capacity of the state, principally through the development of the bureaucratic apparatus of the state's structure, the centralization of its authority, and the growth of organic and institutional interdependence. Two development paths are evident among the Western states that were to be the forebears of two of the first modern states, France and Britain. France pursued an overarching path of state-building, attempting to unite the diverse lands of France through a centralized, professional bureaucratic structure. Little attempt was made at legislative interdependence through the promotion of broadly based parliamentary institutions. Britain pursued an organic path of state-building, relying heavily upon local elites for the projection of state power, but drawing those elites into the state structure through parliamentary involvement. The former path created a large central state apparatus, but one which lacked the infrastructural means to ensure regularized central control. The latter led to a smaller central apparatus with reliance upon the integration of local notables rather than a bureaucratic structure as the means of administering the country. On the eve of industrialization, the state remained an organization whose central institutions were weakly embedded in society and whose capacity was limited.

The great breakthrough in state capacity came about as a result of industrialization and the increased scope for institutional reach that this created. This process is discussed in Chapter 4. Industrialization and many of the social changes that went with it created the means for the projection of central power more effectively into the lower reaches of society and for the expansion of state–society interdependence. This enabled increased effectiveness of bureaucratic states like the French and stimulated the development of a larger bureaucratized state in Britain. Industrialization strengthened state infrastructure, while the social developments accompanying it expanded popular involvement in public life and thereby the scope for interdependence between state and society. The state's bureaucratic reach became more extended, the state itself became more embedded in society, and thereby its capacity increased. Along with this went a major expansion in the spheres of activity within which the state became involved.

Like industrialization, warfare has been seen as a major factor in the growth of state capacity, and the arguments about this are explored in Chapter 5. But warfare is only one way in which external factors are believed to have shaped domestic developments. The growth of the capacity of the Western state needs to be seen in its broader geopolitical context. Throughout the period of the growth of state capacity, Western Europe was interacting with a much broader geographical area. Eastern Europe was a significant partner in this regard, but more important in the view of established scholarship has been the wider world. One way of conceptualizing this has been through world system theory, and this is analysed in this chapter.

One question that this broader perspective raises is that of the claimed uniqueness and superiority of the Western state form. Assumptions about the Western state's uniqueness and superiority rest upon the fact that industrialization became the principal mode for organizing society initially in the West, and that Western states were able to extend their political control across the globe through colonial expansion. However, analysis of the leading Asian states suggests that the Western state was certainly not unique, and therefore was not superior as a type of political formation to those emerging elsewhere.

Chapter 6 looks at the modern state, contrasting the welfare state with its chief competitor, communism. The twentieth century saw the sphere of state interest expand to its greatest limits under the guise of the Western welfare state and communism. These were the great ideological competitors for much of the twentieth century, but they shared a view that state action could positively improve society while differing over the extent of such state activity. The welfare state sought to shape the market economy through participation in it (although the forms whereby this was achieved differed significantly between states) while the communist state sought through administrative control to direct the course of economic development. In the welfare state, all aspects of interdependence were expanded, while under communism the infrastructure of interdependence was weak; the state sought control rather than cooperation with society. The corresponding low levels of interdependence were an important factor in the collapse of communism. Despite the failure of the communist model and the late twentieth-century rollback of the welfare state, at the end of that century the state was still more solidly embedded in society than it had been at any time in the past except for the decades immediately following the Second World War.

By the late twentieth-century the state had become the dominant political form on the globe, and with the growth of the welfare state, its competence seemed to be unchallenged. However in the last decades of that century, globalization seemed to cast a doubt over the future of the state. This is the focus of Chapter 7. Globalization seemed to threaten substantially to reduce state autonomy and even to eliminate the need for the state altogether. However, in practice the state has not been so easily brushed aside. The combination of effective bureaucratic infrastructure and broad-based interdependence that underpinned the success of the welfare state and the collapse of the communist is also the key to the state continuing to play a central role in the face of the challenge posed by globalization. Thus it is expanded state capacity, resting upon developed bureaucratic infrastructure and extensive interdependence, that not only distinguishes the modern state from its forebears, but ensures that the state will continue to play a leading role into the future.

This book has its origins in a fourth-year honours course taught jointly with Linda Weiss in the Department of Government and Public Administration at the University of Sydney during the early 1990s. It concentrated my attention and forced me to do some disciplined reading on a concept that had for long intrigued me but the treatment of which in the scholarly literature had always seemed to be unsatisfying. In particular, the attempts to understand the development of the state historically either seemed to lose themselves in the historical detail or to amount to a simple categorization of forms of state. The modern state seemed to be little but the agglomeration of bits from the past. I have tried to show, analytically, both how the modern state differs from its forebears and also how the principal distinguishing factor, state capacity, was developed over time. This argument owes much to the participants in those seminars of the early 1990s, and I give them my belated thanks. In an earlier draft, the manuscript was read by Linda Weiss and John Hobson, and I thank them for the comments and apologize for not taking all of their well-made points into account. Final thanks also go to Steven Kennedy at Palgrave, without whose dogged pursuit of this manuscript, this book would probably never have seen the light of day

GRAEME GILL

1

The Modern State

The role of the state was paramount during the twentieth century. The conditions within which millions of people lived were shaped by the state, the role it sought to pursue, and the ability it had to pursue that role. The centrality of the state is evident as soon as we look at some of the most important developments of that century. In the communist countries, states forced through rapidly-paced programmes of societal transformation that turned (in one case) a backward, partly industrialized society into a nuclear superpower within 40 years. In the capitalist West, the post-war long boom characterized by the highest and most sustained living standards ever achieved by large populations was underpinned by state expenditure policies and the construction of the welfare state. In parts of the Third World, weak states – and in some cases kleptocratic states – were instrumental in the continuation of widespread poverty, disease, low living standards, violence and war. More than in any other century, people's lives everywhere on the globe were affected by the successes and failings of states.

The state, its power and its capacity were for a long time the central focus of many of those who thought seriously about politics. In part reflecting the origins of political science in constitutional law, this approach projected the state directly into the centre of the concern to understand political life. In contemporary society of the time, the power of the state seemed to loom large in the lives of its subjects. However, in the period following the Second World War, at least in the English-speaking world, the state seemed to go out of fashion. This may in part have been a response to recent and contemporary history, with the Nazi experience in Germany being seen as a case of overweening state power at the expense of the citizenry, and the communist threat being conceived in the same way. But it was also a function of the way in which political science developed as an independent discipline, spreading the intellectual net to embrace things other than formal institutional structures. Throughout the 1950s and 1960s the changing intellectual fashion, reflected in the prominence in the discipline of methodologies such as behaviouralism and functionalism and the direction of interest towards social actors broadly conceived, squeezed the state out of the centre of concern. However, with the growing calls in the 1980s to 'bring the state back in',[1] this relative neglect of the state by English-speaking scholars[2] was well and truly reversed. The size of the literature on the state and its future expanded enormously and shows little sign of diminishing. This is merely recognition of the important role the state plays in contemporary life. But what do we mean by the state? Where does it come from? And what does it do?

What is the State?

While most definitions of the state will differ in some details, the core is widely accepted. An early and influential view of the state is provided by Max Weber:

> The primary formal characteristics of the modern state are as follows: it possesses an administrative and legal order subject to change by legislation, to which the organized activities of the administrative staff, which are also controlled by regulations, are oriented. This system of order claims binding authority, not only over the members of the state, the citizens, most of whom have obtained membership by birth, but also to a very large extent over all action taking place in the area of its jurisdiction. It is thus a compulsory organization with a territorial basis. Furthermore, today, the use of force is regarded as legitimate only in so far as it is either permitted by the state or prescribed by it ... The claim of the modern state to monopolize the use of force is as essential to it as its character of compulsory jurisdiction and of continuous operation.[3]

Weber's definition is complex and elliptical, but suggestive of a vision of the modern state comprising a number of elements. These are a centralized and bureaucratically organized administrative and legal order run by an administrative staff, binding authority over what occurs within its area of jurisdiction, a territorial basis, and a monopoly of the use of force. These elements form the core of most subsequent definitions of the modern state. These elements need to be broken down and elaborated upon, because much that is implicit in Weber's definition is explicit in the views of contemporary scholars.

Central to the generally accepted view of the modern state is a bureaucratic form of organization.[4] The offices, and many of the institutions of which the state consists, are structured in a formal hierarchy with clear lines of direction and accountability. This formal hierarchy, and the rules of direction and obedience intrinsic to it, is essential for the central state authorities to project their power and authority into the society and across the territory over which they have jurisdiction. The bureaucratic nature of the organization means that it is run by formal rules designed to ensure its efficient functioning. Objective rules and standards are meant to prevail in all decision-making, thereby eliminating personal or partial considerations from the process. Advancement through the bureaucratic structure is based on merit, measured in terms of the acquisition of qualifications and performance on the job, and offices are filled by professional, full-time officials. There is regularized communication up and down the structure and a high level of discipline and obedience to instructions from above. In the modern state (with the exception of city-states such as Monaco), bureaucrats and the structures in which they work will be divided into a central state apparatus, usually located in the national capital, and a regional apparatus which conducts the administration in the areas outside the capital. Both parts of the state structure should run along bureaucratic lines.

This bureaucratic structure is characterized by specialization and organizational differentiation from other bodies. This means that the hierarchical structure of offices and institutions that forms the physical manifestation of the modern state is distinct from all other organizations and bodies found within the society. In practice, of course, no organization is totally distinct from other structures in society. They are linked together by numerous bonds (personal, institutional and ideological). In contemporary Western democracies, the state is connected to institutions such as political parties, pressure groups, non-governmental organizations (NGOs) and businesses, and through these, to the society as a whole. As will be argued later, this is crucial to state survival. But what is essential is that the state is distinguished from these other groups by the nature of its primary concerns and responsibilities: the state focuses upon political affairs with its sphere of concern ranging across all aspects of political life.

In this sense, the modern state is much more wide-ranging than other political organizations such as parties and interest groups. Furthermore, the notion of what is political and within the sphere of state concerns has expanded considerably, as will be shown in this book. Areas as diverse as environmentalism, welfare, safety at work and childcare have become the concern of the state because of their importance for the ordering of life in contemporary society. And in the secular sphere, this is the state's primary role: the regulation and ordering of community life.[5] The modern state is thus a distinct institution, separated from others by this overarching responsibility. Also important is what has been called the autonomy of the state. The state is independent of the control of other organizations or social groups within the society, and able to pursue its own aims and objectives differently from those of other parts of the society. This notion of autonomy will be discussed further below.

The modern state is both centralized and internally organizationally differentiated. The bureaucratic structure that is the state is not a monolithic machine, but a congeries of institutions, agencies, organizations and bodies. It is functionally organized into executive, legislative and judicial arms, while each of these (in particular the executive) is further divided into distinct parts. For example, the bureaucratic administrative machine consists of a range of distinct government departments, agencies and organizations, many of which have branches throughout the regions as well as a central office. Similarly, there will be a hierarchy of judicial and perhaps legislative organs spreading across the territory. The state structure is therefore highly differentiated. However, it is bound together by ties of centralism. All of the discrete parts of the state machine are linked to their counterparts at different levels by organizational rules, regulations and procedures, and by the range of informal relationships and practices which enable any bureaucratic structure to function. The ties between these different parts bind them all into a hierarchical structure where the central offices of state exercise overall directive and administrative power. These different parts do not exercise authority on their own behalf, but only that authority which flows to them as part of the state. In this sense, the state is both highly differentiated and strongly centralized. It is this that enables it to carry out its central, unique, function, the centralized coordination of power on a territorial basis.

The modern state is sovereign, or the ultimate source of authority within the territory under its jurisdiction. There are two aspects of this, the internal and the external. Internally, it means that there are no authorities higher than the state. The citizen cannot appeal against the state to any other authority; the state is supreme, and its will cannot be countermanded. While the appeal to conscience is today accepted in many states as a valid claim against state authority, this is not generally seen as a vitiation of the state's claim to sovereignty because in most instances the state does not seek to enter the moral realm. Externally, state sovereignty means that other states recognize the authority of a state within its borders and accept that that state can speak for its citizens in international affairs. External sovereignty is therefore the international recognition of the domestic sovereignty of a particular state. Sovereignty is crucial to the state because it is this that elevates the state to a position of superiority in the society and constitutes the recognition of its right to make binding decisions upon those who live within its bounds. In essence, this is the focus of the state's role: its right to make binding decisions upon its citizens and upon those who enter its territory. This right is the key to its power and role, and although at times the sovereignty of individual states may be vitiated (e.g., by voluntary cession through international treaty or involuntarily through the action of other states), as a principle for defining the state, sovereignty remains central.

The right to exercise authority must be backed up by the capacity to do so, and this is where a further characteristic of the modern state is important: the monopoly over the legitimate use of force. The state has at its disposal a preponderance of coercion within the society. Institutionally manifested in the armed forces, police and paramilitary forces, this preponderance of force is important for the maintenance of state supremacy although, in terms of the daily course of political life, such force is usually secondary. It is there to back up the state's legitimacy if it is called into question and to ensure the observance of laws and the maintenance of order when these are infringed. As well as this preponderance of force, what sets the state apart from other entities that might use coercion is that the state possesses a monopoly of the *legitimate* use of such coercion. Only the state has the right to use organized coercion to get its way. This is intrinsic to state sovereignty and essential for the state to be able to achieve what many see as its basic purpose, the security of its citizens through the maintenance of law and order.

The modern state is territorially-based and bounded. The state exercises its authority within territorial boundaries which are clearly defined and acknowledged internationally. It possesses no authority outside those boundaries, just as no other state possesses authority within another state's boundaries. The state's territorial basis distinguishes it from most other types of organization or association, whose power and authority tend to be functionally-based rather than geographically defined. It is this territorial basis that injects an element of ambiguity into the notion of the state. In English, but not in many other languages, the same word, 'state', is used both for the administrative apparatus that runs a country, and the territorial formation of which that country consists. In this book, it is the former which is the focus of attention.

Some point to one further characteristic of the modern state, the existence of a popular feeling of identity with and attachment to it, or what Finer calls, 'a community of feeling'.[6] This community of feeling is often held to rest upon assumptions about shared ethnic identity and to be manifested in a common language, culture and history. Many states have had populations who have shared such feelings, and this has given rise to the term 'nation state'. Yet the vast majority of states are not characterized by a coincidence between a particular geopolitical unit and a single ethnic group; most states have within their boundaries a variety of ethnic groups, and many ethnic groups are to be found spread across state boundaries. So insofar as the term 'nation state' implies a coincidence between state and ethnic nation, it is a misnomer. Nevertheless, it is true that states generally have sought to engender in their populace a sense of identity with the state, to bring about feelings of attachment and identification with the state. Such an endeavour has been an essential part of state-building, from the granting of citizenship to all inhabitants of the Roman Empire after AD 212 to 'the invention of tradition'[7] by states in the nineteenth century. But although the development of such an attachment occurs in most states, it is not a definitional quality of the state.

These characteristics stemming from the Weberian conception of the state – a centralized and bureaucratically organized administrative and legal order run by an administrative staff, sovereignty, territoriality, and a monopoly of the legitimate use of force – are the central elements of the modern state. The nature of the regime (i.e., the system of rule or government) is not relevant to whether a particular formation is a modern state or not. The characteristics noted above may be present in states run by liberal democratic parties, by a single party, by the military and even by a single dictator. The definition of a state is not dependent upon the nature of the regime. The state as defined by those characteristics can be used by a regime to achieve its ends. Indeed, it is the capabilities implicit in those characteristics that enable the state to be used in this way.

These characteristics of the modern state are individually shared by many other organizations, but no other organization shares all of them. Particularly distinctive is the combination of sovereignty and territoriality, because while many organizations claim sovereignty, in no other type of organization apart from the state is this defined territorially; in other organizations, such as the church or business concerns, this is defined functionally or on the basis of the personal attachment of people to that entity (e.g., through employment). It is this combination of factors that sets the state apart, and it is this that enables the state through the formalization of its enactments in law and the projection of them through its institutional structure to bring about both the depersonalization of power and its transformation into a continuing public force. The power of the state is impersonal, much of it exercised through bureaucratic channels, and unrelenting. In a quotation where the word 'state' could easily be substituted for 'government', a scholar of medieval France has said: 'What distinguishes government from personal control is its unremitting character. To be governed is to be subjected to the regular pressure of an authority operating according to fixed rules. In the full sense of the word, it is arguable that nobody was governed before the later nineteenth century.'[8] To the extent that the state can be said to have an essence, it is the continuing projection of public power in the pursuit of its aims. It does this in a particular territory through acceptance of its sovereignty, its bureaucratic structure and the monopoly of coercion.

The projection of public power does not mean that that power is necessarily used for the best interests of the society as a whole, although that clearly is the basis upon which the modern state is legitimized. This is reflected in the view that the principal responsibility of the state is to create the conditions for secure and civilized life, a responsibility realized through the oft-quoted view that the state's role is to ensure law and order. The use of public power to serve social interests is the fundamental rationale of the modern state, especially in its democratic variants. But this simple assertion of the perceived purpose of the state leaves open the role the state actually plays in contemporary life. This role has been conceived in a number of ways, each of which is associated with a different perspective on the nature of the state. These perspectives turn upon the interests that the state seeks to realize and its relationship with other forces in society.

Perspectives on the Role of the State

The State as Partisan

The 'partisan' model[9] sees the state as pursuing its own institutional interests or those of the officials who work within it. The state is seen as acting on its own behalf rather than in the interests of any other group. This assumes that the state is autonomous from other forces in society (see below), but does not necessarily imply that the state is all-powerful. In pursuing its own interests, the state may simply be able to override any opposition to it from within society, but in the contemporary world it is more likely that the state must work with other forces in society to achieve its aims. This may require bargaining and compromise, enabling others to achieve some of their aims in return for being able to gain some of the state's. State aims may also often coincide with the aims of other groups, so the state may be able to get its way without much opposition, or at least with significant social support. In any event, the key factor is that the state pursues its own interests regardless of the views of other social forces.

The partisan model of the state is consistent with the Weberian view of the state outlined through the characteristics noted above. Although the usual view of the Weberian model emphasizes the rationality, and hence objectivity, of bureaucratic performance, such a concern for rationality and the adherence to bureaucratic norms effectively represents an assertion of the interests of the state. Demanding that life be conducted according to bureaucratic norms automatically moves it on to the ground where the state is most dominant. In this way, the independent entity of the state acts to realize its interests. This view of the state is also consistent with a school that has been so important in the study of international relations: realism. Realism sees the state as a unitary actor relentlessly pursuing its interests in the international sphere, and although this view has come under considerable criticism, it remains prominent in the international relations literature.[10]

The State as Guardian

In this view, the state acts not to advance its own interests but to stabilize the system overall. This conceives of the state as 'an autonomous institutional force capable of rebalancing the social pressures upon it'.[11] The state is seen as keeping in view the best interests of the system as a whole and reacting to developments to ensure that that system does not become destabilized. For some, it is the state managers and bureaucrats who decide what is in the best interests of the system, using their professional knowledge and skills to determine the policies which will maintain the status quo. For those who see the predominance of certain interests in society (e.g., the capitalist class, big business, business–trade union corporatist arrangements), the state is seen as working with them to stabilize the system from which those interests benefit; one strand in Marxism has this view (see below). Some of those who adopt a more pluralist approach, seeing policy-making as much more a function of the inter-play between different social forces and groups, see the state as main-taining a balance between these groups to ensure that none gains the sort of primacy that might upset the whole structure. In this view, the state may be seen as an arena within which different forces, groups and individuals struggle for supremacy to implement their ideas. In any event, the state is essentially neutral, seeking to stabilize the sys-tem and teaming up with various social forces in order to do so.

This view of the state is consistent with the liberal view of the state which sees it as remaining neutral in domestic affairs while acting to protect the individual rights of those who constitute the commu-nity.[12] This view has also been prominent among those who have studied the origins of the state. For Service,[13] the state provided a range of benefits for all; Carneiro[14] saw the state emerging in order to combat a serious challenge confronting the community as a whole; while Wittfogel[15] saw it as essential for the construction and mainte-nance of large-scale irrigation projects upon which the community depended. Otto Hintze[16] argued that military challenge from without encouraged military centralization within, which became consoli-dated into the state form. In all of these views, the state's role was guardian of the interests of the community.

The State as Instrument

In this view, the state is conceived as a pliable instrument which is controlled by forces outside it to achieve their ends. There is little sense of state autonomy or room for independent action by state actors, and the impression of the state is that it is largely monolithic.

The state is captured and turned to the ends sought by those who capture it. Elite theorists tend to see the state in this light.[17] This view may also be held by pluralists who argue that the democratic electoral process is the means whereby different groups compete for control of the state, with the victor being determined by the levels of popular support the contestants achieve.[18] Among students of state origins, the instrumental view of the state was prominent. For Fried,[19] the state was a means of consolidating control by a leading kin group, while those who saw the state as resulting from external conquest saw it as the means of rule by the conquerors.[20]

However, the most influential theory in which the instrumental view of the state has been prominent has been Marxism, an approach which takes no account of institutional structures (and is therefore in striking contrast to Weber) and which focuses purely upon the role of the state. This view is most clearly reflected in Marx's comment that 'The executive of the modern state is but a committee for managing the common affairs of the whole bourgeoisie.'[21] In this view, the state is explicitly the instrument of rule by the dominant class. This view is also clear in Engels' work on the origin of the state,[22] where the state is clearly shown as emerging to institutionalize the dominance of the economically exploitative class. However, this crude, directly instrumental approach is not the only one within Marxism. Some theorists have adopted a guardian perspective on the state, seeing its role as protecting the interests of the capitalist class generally despite the ramifications this may have for individual capitalists and regardless of the direct political role played by members of this class.[23] In some of his writings, Marx also suggested that the state could play an arbitrating role between balanced social classes (see below), but it has been the instrumental and guardian approaches that have been most influential.

***

All of these perspectives see the state's role to be in part the guaranteeing of the established social order. Even when the state is used as an instrument to bring about substantial social change, it acts as guarantor of the new social order which it has helped to bring about. As part of this, the state guarantees property relations, which is a crucial aspect of the power structure, defence from outside challenges, and domestic order. This involves providing for (or at least facilitating and regulating) the conditions of at least minimal subsistence on the part of those who live under it. In turn, this provokes disagreement among political observers about the degree to which the state should be involved in society. These disagreements are essentially ideological, based on the preferences of their holders rather than any objective analysis of what the state actually does.

The essential point about the degree of involvement in society turns on whether the state is seen as a positive or a negative force. In most of the English-speaking world in the last decades of the twentieth century, the latter evaluation predominated. But this was not an original position; it had its roots much earlier in the perception that the state infringed personal liberty. In this view, individuals are best able to prosecute their own affairs without restriction from higher-standing authorities. As a result, the state should play a minimalist role in society. It should ensure law and order and perhaps provide a minimal infrastructure, but beyond that it should withdraw from the social sphere. State action is seen as crowding out private individual activity and as imposing unnecessary limits upon people's freedom. Rarely do proponents of this view argue that the state has absolutely no role to play. Rather than an activist state, they see the state as essentially performing a nightwatchman function, maintaining nothing but a watching brief over society and ensuring, through minimal action, the maintenance of order and security.

In contrast, a more positive view of the state sees it as providing real benefits to society through adopting an activist role. Views differ on how activist the state should be. The position underpinning the communist-ruled states of the twentieth century was that the state should be maximally involved in all aspects of life. Through its involvement the state could not only direct the development and growth of society, but ensure that that society is characterized by freedom, equality and the good life for all. The Western welfare state assumed a less extensive state role, but nevertheless one in which the state did more than simply provide a basic infrastructure of support for its people. The state was directly responsible for undergirding people's lives through the provision of a wide range of services at minimal or no direct cost to the consumer, with the aim of ensuring social development that benefited all, not just the wealthy. Even in those Western countries where the welfare state was very limited, for much of the twentieth century state involvement at some level above the bare minimum was seen as desirable and encouraged.

These contrasting views of the role of the state and its involvement in public life are central to the shape the modern state has taken in various countries, but they do not directly impinge upon the definition of the modern state. Where they are relevant is in the growth of state capacity that enabled the development of the welfare state. This is one factor about the modern state that clearly distinguishes it from its predecessors: it has a much greater capacity to intervene in society at large than any of its predecessors had. But it is also relevant to the question of state autonomy.

State Autonomy and Interdependence

There has been a tendency in much of the theorizing about the state to conceive of the state in an epiphenomenal way. The state is seen as not having an existence in and of itself, but as being merely a representation of other social forces. This is the view taken by proponents of the instrumental and some of the guardian models of the state noted above. The liberal approach to the state views it as an arena within which a variety of social forces struggle for supremacy, within a context of a broad value consensus which underpins the legitimate authority of the whole process. In this view, the state does not exist independently of the interactions of these social groups; it is their relationships which give the state its meaning and purpose. This epiphenomenal approach to the state is also evident in Marxism. In this view, the state is the means whereby the exercise and consolidation of the control of the dominant class is brought about. The state has no existence, purpose or interests independent of those of the dominant class. It is thereby a product of class interest rather than an organization with any independent standing or purpose.

However, this epiphenomenal approach, reducing the state to a manifestation of deeper social forces, is misleading. Certainly there will be instances when the state is used by other groups for their own ends. The state can be captured by particular groups and their agenda imposed upon it; but this does not happen all the time. The state as an institution does possess the potential for autonomy, the potential for pursuing policies that are in its own interests as an institution, that are in the personal interests of those who work in the state, or that are in the interests of the society as a whole as perceived by state officials. This is the partisan view of the state. It assumes that the state is not automatically the representation of other social forces, but has an existence and a set of interests that are different from and potentially in conflict with those of other social forces. Once we conceive of the state as a set of institutional structures, primarily administrative and coercive, it follows that those structures and the people who work in them will have their own interests arising from the state's very existence. At minimum, these will include maintenance of the state structure and protection of its integrity against outside forces. By extension this will also embrace the maintenance of order in society, since the existence of widespread conflict and dissent is destructive of the state itself. Thus even without implying any idealistic feelings or aspirations on the part of the state, its concern for its own survival will dictate that it has an independent interest in the way in which society is ordered. Given that the state also has to participate in international geopolitics by interacting with, *inter alia*, other entities like itself, the quest for survival will lead it to pursue policies in the international arena as well as the domestic.

If the very existence of the state as an institutional structure generates a set of interests centred around its maintenance and survival, this will lead to overlap with the interests of the dominant classes in society. State survival requires domestic peace and order, and this is best achieved through the guaranteeing of the existing power structure, including as expressed through property relations. Clearly the dominant classes share this aim, wishing to bolster their predominance against possible challenge from below. In this sense, the state is normally concerned to defend the status quo, an aim which coincides with that of the dominant classes. However, the state's desire for maintenance and survival also generates a point of tension with the dominant classes in society. Central to the state's survival is its ability to collect sufficient resources to sustain its operations, but in this it is in competition with the dominant classes. Both state and class seek to extract resources from the populace, thereby generating the tax–rent trade-off; the more the people have to pay in taxes, the less landowners can extract in the form of rent, and vice versa. This tension is present in the relationship between all states and dominant classes and, unless it is stabilized, the relationship between the two is likely to be difficult. Furthermore, the state may actively pursue policies at variance with those preferred by the dominant classes. The state's quest for order and domestic peace may encourage it to make concessions to lower classes at the expense of dominant classes, while its desire for external security may lead it into policies which have a negative impact upon the wealth of members of the dominant class or may even lead it to seek to restructure domestic society, the better to compete internationally. Thus state and class interests do not always coincide, and it is the capacity of the state to maintain its autonomy that enables it to pursue its interests in this situation. But what enables the state to establish and maintain its autonomy?

There have been a number of answers to this question. Marx provided one in his discussion of mid-nineteenth-century France when he referred to Bonapartism.[24] In this conception, a broad balance of social forces in which none gained a primary or dominant position enabled the state to escape from control and pursue a course guided by its own perceptions. The Bonapartist leader, relying upon the state bureaucratic and coercive infrastructure, was able for a time to override social interests and pursue his own course of action without constraint. The problem with this conception of the state and its autonomy is that it continues to see the state in terms of the other social forces in the society. What enables the state to gain autonomy is nothing about the state itself, but the nature of the broader class relationships within society as a whole. Of course in practice state autonomy is linked to the nature of class relations; but to define state autonomy purely as a function of those relations is once again to reduce the state to epiphenomenal status. State autonomy has been better explained in other ways.

One approach to this question is to focus upon the nature of state personnel.[25] In this view, state autonomy depends upon the holders of high civil and military posts not being recruited from the dominant classes and not developing close relations with those classes once in office. It is thus the personal origins and associations of state officials that are seen to be central. In Trimberger's view, when officials retain ties to dominant elites, reform may be possible, but revolution from above can only come about when the state elite is free of such ties. Thus this view sees state autonomy as being the same as the state having few direct relations with the society as a whole. This implies that state power is best conceived of as a zero sum game, to be exercised over the society rather than through it. State autonomy is thus a product of the insulation of the state from society. The problem with this approach is that it conceives of the state acting autonomously only against the will of society. This is because it has focused upon those major cases when the state has stepped in to fundamentally re-organize society in the form of a revolution from above. Such an effort clearly provoked opposition from within society, and the state has been able to overcome that through the mobilization of coercive capacity. But it is not clear that this way of viewing the problem assists in our understanding of how the state administers the society in an ongoing fashion. When the focus is upon humdrum day-to-day administration, the view of the state arising from periods of large-scale state-induced societal transformation is not necessarily the most useful. Such an approach emphasizes the disconnection of state from society, which is precisely the reverse of the situation that prevails in looking at normal administration.

Another approach is to see the state as a distinctive sort of organization operating in a sphere that no other organization fully occupies, although many will impinge on it.[26] The state is seen as the only type of institution that projects power throughout an area defined in territorial terms; autonomy stems from 'the state's unique ability to provide a territorially *centralized form* of organization'.[27] It combines this territorial focus with an institutional structure attuned to the needs and demands of a territorial unit. This implies a combination of administrative capacity and coercive potential, and is underpinned by recognition of the need to use power as a means rather than it being an end. But what is important about this territorial focus is that the state is the only body which may be defined in terms of exercising political power (as opposed to economic or ideological: see below) over that territory. As such, the state has a unique role to play in a sphere conceptually autonomous from other spheres of activity. The state is, therefore, in principle autonomous, and it remains so unless it is captured by forces operating in the other spheres of power. Thus, in this view, state autonomy arises from the distinctiveness of the state as an organization, from the fact that it and it alone can perform certain functions. This general proposition requires greater specificity before we can use this notion of the source of autonomy to analyse the changing role of the state.

One view which builds upon this sees state autonomy as arising from the fact that the state as an institution is located at the intersection of the international and the domestic arenas.[28] Having responsibilities in both arenas, for defence and the pursuit of interests abroad and for the ordering and security of life at home, the state is able to escape the control of potential captors. It is able to play off different groups against one another, balancing between the two arenas of activity, and is also able to use them to blunt challenges to its continuing position. What is central to this view of the basis of state autonomy is the function of the state, and the fact that that function must be carried out within two distinct policy arenas. Rooted in both but restricted to neither, the state is thereby able to maintain its autonomy from all of those groups whose interests are limited in the way that its interests are not. This is a persuasive explanation of state autonomy, emphasizing as it does the duality of the state's role and therefore the importance of the often ignored external arena. But as it currently stands, it underestimates the complexity of both the state and the context within which the state acts.

Neither external nor internal arena is monolithic; each is divided into numerous discrete but individually overlapping spheres, each of which is populated by a diversity of actors. In the international arena, a state will be concerned with a range of issues, including military security, economic security and welfare, international regulation, trade, people movements, terrorism, cultural relations and maybe human rights. In each of these policy spheres, it will have to interact with a different set of actors: other states, official and unofficial international organizations of various sorts, and even individuals and small groups may be relevant. In the domestic arena, the range of different spheres in which the state is active is much larger. All areas of life are potentially areas of policy concern, from those dealing with individuals' personal lives all the way through to major issues such as the structure and functioning of the polity itself. In every one of these policy spheres, a diversity of actors is to be found, ranging from individual political activists through to highly organized formal associations. The sheer number of spheres and actors and the range of their concerns, and the fact that the state is involved in them all (some episodically, others continuously), of itself means that the state is able to maintain its autonomy should those who run it desire to do so. The competing interests of its potential clients, for that is what those operating in the various policy spheres effectively are given that they are seeking state support to get their way on a particular issue, inhibit the creation of the sorts of coalitions necessary for establishing stable and continuing control over the state. State autonomy thus rests on the multiplicity of interests seeking to gain its support.

The situation is actually more complex than this because the state itself is not a monolith. The state is internally differentiated into a variety of institutional structures. These are divided vertically by function, horizontally by geography. The vertical divisions roughly correspond to the major spheres within which both the multitudinous interests noted above are active and the state must take an interest. Within the state, these are viewed as policy areas (and constituencies), and are signified by the presence in states of civil service departments devoted to particular policy areas, such as health, transport, education, law and order and consumer affairs. The horizontal divisions correspond to the spatial organization of the polity: whether it is a federal or unitary state, the jurisdiction of local and regional government. Many of the vertically defined segments of the state, the civil service departments, will be divided horizontally as well. The legislative arm of the state may also be divided horizontally, as in a federation. What is important about these vertical divisions is the relationship that develops between these segments of the state and the political activists and forces active within the broader social spheres and policy constituencies. The more these segments sink their roots into their constituencies, the more firmly rooted the state will be in the society. But, in addition, the more diverse are the constituencies within which the state is thereby rooted, the more secure the state as an institution is from seizure by a particular group. The conflicting demands generated from within these constituencies in their total effect will normally ensure that no constituency becomes dominant, and therefore will liberate the central state apparatus from external control. If those constituencies were to come together and thereby form stable coalitions, the likelihood of capture of central state organs would increase. But given the maintenance of normal political conditions, the diversity of groups and demands will ensure that this does not occur, and therefore should sustain the continuing autonomy of the state.

The reverse is also important, however. By becoming closely connected with these policy constituencies, the arms of the state also open themselves up to penetration by those constituencies. No arm of the state, be it government department, agency or statutory authority, can remain completely immune to (and separated in a watertight container from) those constituencies if it wishes to be effective in its policy-making and administrative endeavours. In order to carry out its functions, to make and implement policy and to conduct the rule-making which is the state's role in society, it needs the cooperation of these relevant constituencies and the organizations of which they consist. In exchange, state bodies must allow their own partial penetration by those constituencies. In institutional terms, this may take the form of discussion, bargaining and negotiation, maybe the cooption of members of these constituencies into the workings of the state body, and the inclusion of members of the former in policy drafting and implementation. There are also more informal links: personal contacts between people working in the same policy sector, personal favours, inducements and other forms of influence-peddling.

Whatever form it takes, the penetration of state bodies by these constituencies is central to the former's functioning.

This penetration seems to call into question state autonomy. It seems to be exactly the scenario envisaged by those who argue that the state is captured by particular groups and therefore acts purely as an instrument of those groups. However, the situation is not so simple. Two factors, together, enable the state to maintain its autonomy even in a situation of such penetration. The effect of the penetration of state organs on state autonomy is counterbalanced by both the nature of the policy spheres and the nature of the state. In terms of policy spheres, in contemporary Western society, policies are usually the object of conflict between different groups within society, with the result that in a particular policy area, the state is rarely confronted by a single dominant interest group. State bodies must inevitably interact with a range of groups, and therefore are less likely to fall under the control of one unchallenged group. In terms of the nature of the state, penetration may be offset by both the bulk of the state itself and by its centralization. The capacity of individual state bodies in the policy spheres is heavily reliant upon the state as a whole. They can do nothing without the authority and the resources provided by the state as a whole; they are but a part of the larger enterprise. Furthermore, this is an enterprise that is run on centralized lines, in the sense that ultimate authority lies at the centre and there are rules and norms that bind the whole together under the overall direction of central state organs. Such rules and norms are crucial to the overall operation of the state organization and provide the rationale for those who work within it.

Moreover, the state's central organs will seek to limit any loss of control over non-central organs that may be threatened by penetration of lower-level organs by constituencies within society. Thus despite penetration at the local level, lower-level state organizations are not necessarily captured or lose their autonomy. And certainly it does not mean that the state as a whole has lost its autonomy, even if a large number of its lower-level organs have been penetrated. By the nature of the policy constituencies, those arms of the state that have been penetrated will have been penetrated by different groups whose interests will not always coincide. Individual state bodies interact with different policy constituencies, with the result that penetration is achieved by a mosaic of different actors, which enables the state overall to balance upon these and retain its autonomy. In this sense, the state can be seen as an arena within which these actors can compete for the achievement of their aims, but the very diversity of those actors ensures the state's autonomy.

This constitutes a process of the embedding of the state in particular policy constituencies and in the society more generally while maintaining state autonomy. This may be called 'institutional interdependence',[29] reflecting the interactive nature of the relationship. The principal site of institutional interdependence is the economic sphere, broadly conceived, but given that this term refers to the existence of a cooperative working relationship between state body and organized groups or associations within society, it can exist in any sphere of life. This is a form of institutional embedding of the state in the organizational structures of the society. This type of embedding is paralleled by another. This may be called 'organic interdependence', and consists chiefly of the way in which different segments of society (usually seen in terms of classes, but other conceptualizations are possible) find representation in state organs. With the exception of pure conquest states, and then only for a very short time, state machines usually are staffed by people living in the regions over which the state rules. Usually those people come overwhelmingly from particular classes, maintaining those class links even while they serve as state officials. Even in cases such as the traditional Chinese where state officials adopt an ethos and outlook closely identified with their functional positions in the state machine, residual ties with their social origins (e.g., at their most basic, with their families) rarely were completely eliminated. This means both that the state machine gains vital links into the class structure as a whole, and that within officialdom there is likely to be a tension between those linkages and the pull of the bureaucratic ideology which is meant specifically to eliminate those ties and turn the officials into loyal and dedicated servants of the state. While the ties with the social constituency from which state officials come can influence the shaping of state policy, the effect of bureaucratic ideology and, at least in some cases, of the diversity of backgrounds from which officials come, limits the possibility of the state machine being captured by this broad social constituency. All states are characterized by this sort of bureaucratic organic interdependence, and all states are therefore rooted to some degree in their societies. How much will depend upon the strength of the continuing social ties compared with the bureaucratic ideology, and the breadth of the constituencies from which officials come.

However, there is another form of organic interdependence which not all states have shared: the legislative. The development of a legislative arm (where the chief executive is separate from the legislature, as in a pure presidential system, that chief executive is included here) is another way of embedding the state in society because it provides a means for various sectors of society to gain representation in the state and to play a part in authoritative decision-making at the highest level. Through representatives, various sectors of society are effectively coopted into the state's activities and, in contrast to the situation for state officials, their role in the state organ is meant to reflect the continuing nature of their ties with their social constituency. In other words, these people are not meant to take on a new guise as officials of the state, but to continue to represent their social constituencies inside the state structure. Clearly not all who entered the parliamentary chambers saw themselves as consciously representing defined social constituencies in the population, but structurally that is what they were doing. Their presence in state legislative bodies effectively rooted the state in the broader society while at the same time being a potent source of legitimacy for the state.

Such legislative organic interdependence could be important for state autonomy in three ways. First, the more diverse in social terms the membership of such bodies was, the less the likelihood that this could be a channel whereby the state could be controlled by one particular segment of society. Second, the interests of the state and of the social classes represented in state organs (and who historically have dominated the legislature) do not always coincide. Rather there is usually a tension between them, and the chief form this takes is the argument over tax. The state usually seeks to increase its level of revenue acquisition through taxation. Dominant classes seek to increase their take of revenue through exploitation in one form or another of other class groups. This is the classic stand-off between taxes and rents; the more rent peasants pay to the landowners, the less tax they can pay, and vice versa. This tension may also be present in other areas, and creates a relationship between state and upper classes characterized by competition and cooperation: they compete for revenue and sometimes on other policy issues, but need to cooperate to achieve their ends. This sort of relationship itself fosters autonomy. Third, the mere presence of a legislative arm of the state creates a tension within the state itself because the interests and perspectives of the legislative arm do not always coincide with those of the executive. A dynamic tension emerges whereby both seek to enjoy and usually, if possible, expand, their privileges, power and room for manoeuvre. Historically this often led to clashes, but even when such clashes have not been overt, the relationship between legislative and executive arms has been competitive as well as cooperative. Such a relationship makes the capture of both legislative and executive arms by social forces more difficult, and it also can lead to both arms seeking partners in society at large. The result is that legislative organic interdependence enhances state autonomy while at the same time rooting the state in a social constituency which may be broad or narrow depending upon the social composition of the legislators.

Where institutional and both types of organic interdependence are well-developed, the state is more firmly embedded in and penetrative of the society than where these are underdeveloped. It is also usually more effective than where such interdependencies are missing or weak. It is more soundly rooted not only because its attachment to social forces enables it better to implement effective policy, but also because that attachment creates incentives for the social forces to seek to work through the existing structure to achieve their ends rather than go outside it. This means that the state's connections with society help to stabilize the whole situation and lock many of the more important social forces into a position of supporting the status quo. If those social forces can achieve some of their aims through the relationship with the state, and the corresponding power structure, they will be more likely to support it, including in times of difficulty. In this sense, the stability and survivability of the state depends upon the degree to which it is rooted in society at large.

Returning to the three perspectives of the state discussed above (partisan, guardian and instrumental), the subsequent discussion has explained how the state has its own interests and how it can maintain its autonomy to pursue those interests. This does not mean that the other perspectives on the state are always and inevitably wrong. Clearly the state is able to pursue its own goals on the basis of the autonomy it is able to win. But there can also be situations when the state acts as more of an arbiter between competing groups rather than pursuing its own policy. Indeed, the state often acts in this way, and this perspective is quite consistent with that of the partisan state; the state may pursue its own aims sometimes and act more as an arbiter at others. This is probably the normal, or most common, situation. But similarly there can be situations when the state is captured by a particular group within society and then turned to the achievement of that group's ends. In such situations of capture, the state loses its autonomy and becomes an instrument of its captors. Over time, of course, with the construction of a new social reality as a result of the exertion of state power, that autonomy may return as state and former captors' aims come together. State autonomy is probably best seen not as the exception, but as the norm.

State Capacity

This rooting of the state in diverse policy and social constituencies through institutional and organic interdependence not only enables state autonomy, but can facilitate the development of state capacity. Too often, scholars have tended to see state capacity in zero sum terms, as power which the state exercised over society. As noted above when discussing the revolution from the above paradigm, there are times when the state does exercise power over society and an expansion of state power can be interpreted as a decline in societal power. But in the normal course of events, the state does not exercise power against society, but through it. The state must administer society, it must ensure law and order and a tolerable degree of security, it must ensure that the processes essential to collective life function in a regular fashion. All of these things require the state to cooperate with other social forces, to work with them in achieving the aims which the state has and which many of those forces share. Similarly, in the more limited policy spheres, the state must seek the cooperation of the particular constituencies and groups which inhabit those spheres. The state will achieve more of its aims if it works in partnership with the groups that are active in whatever sphere is relevant than if it ignores them. It is likely both to formulate more effective policy and ensure its implementation if it cooperates with those groups most directly affected by it.

This sort of relationship involves the maintenance of state autonomy combined with a connectedness to policy and social constituencies. Through this connectedness, state organs are able to mobilize social forces for their aims, even if in the process it may mean that the state also accedes to some of the demands of those with whom they are working. In this way, this relationship enables state and policy and social forces to achieve some of their goals in partnership. But it also means that the state is, through the diversity of these, able to maintain its autonomy and, through the connectedness it constitutes, expand and sustain state capacity. Such capacity may not be well developed in all sectors of national life, but may differ between sectors: for example, a state powerfully connected to the welfare sector may be weakly connected to the industrial sector. The sectoral nature of capacity highlights the differentiation within the state, with different sections of the state structure connected with different social sectors to different degrees. It is the links between these social constituencies and the different parts of the state that constitute the mosaic of state capacity. It is important to note that the question of which sections of the state are most closely linked into their respective social constituencies is often a result of the political choices made by state elites. In this sense, capacity is not intrinsic to the state structure. It must be constructed and maintained, and this involves state officials working with members of their particular sectoral constituencies.

The notion of state capacity is linked to the distinction between two types of state power, infrastructural and despotic.[30] Infrastructural power is defined as 'the capacity of the state actually to penetrate civil society, and to implement logistically political decisions throughout the realm', or 'to penetrate and centrally coordinate the activities of civil society through its own infrastructure'; it is 'the logistics of political control'. Despotic power is 'the range of actions which the elite is empowered to undertake without routine, institutionalized negotiation with civil society groups'. The essential difference between these types of power is the presence or absence of an institutionalized means to 'negotiate' with groups in society. In practice, what this means is the presence or absence of a routinized set of procedures operated by the state and accepted by society through which discussion, bargaining and negotiation can occur and decisions can be made and implemented. This assumes both an effective state bureaucratic structure and a high level of interdependence with society. Where institutional and organic interdependence are well developed, infrastructural power can be wielded, because they are the crucial struts of infrastructural power. Where such interdependence is absent (and this may be a geographical region or a policy sphere), the state must use extraordinary, non-routinized means, or despotic power. For example, the difference between a state collecting taxes by means of automatic withdrawals on the part of the employer before employees receive their pay, or by means of episodic visits by military detachments, is a distinction between infrastructural and despotic power. The more infrastructural the state's power and the less despotic, the greater the level of interdependence characteristic of the state–society relationship, and the greater the capacity the state will enjoy. The more the state's power is despotic, the lower the level of state–society interdependence will be, the less efficient it will be at administering the society and the more problematic its capacity.

The Role of Power

Crucial to capacity is power. The state is, par excellence, the means for concentrating power, but power is itself a diversified concept. There is not merely one type of power, and neither is there one means through which power can be expressed or projected. There is a wide diversity of the latter and there is a range of different types of power. In his magisterial work,[31] Michael Mann refers to sources of power rather than types of power. He believes there are four such sources: ideological, economic, political and military, and that these sources of power offer alternative organizational means of social control over people, material and territories. In terms of the state, this would mean that different states would be able to mobilize these different sources of power to different degrees; one may rely more upon political, military and ideological power than upon economic, and vice versa. Mann's theory therefore provides a very useful way of seeing different states in terms of the power maps they use to establish and project their control. But it is important to recognize that these sources of power are open not only to states, but to those who would challenge individual states. There can be no monopoly over these sources of power, and they can be used just as easily by, for example, marcher lords or nomadic tribesmen, as they can by central state authorities. So these sources of power may be seen as arenas of struggle whereby state authorities seek to establish their primacy over would-be challengers. Historically such struggles are endemic. The principal dynamic is one whereby state authorities try to build up the state's power in these different areas, to establish central control over the sources of power and their manifestation, and thereby to deny to potential challengers an edge in these areas. Given that power is not zero sum, and that a state can never totally monopolize any form of power, the situation is always shifting and potentially unstable.

Mann distinguishes between four sources of power, but we can be more parsimonious in our analysis by reducing this to three: ideological, economic and political. Mann's military power can be collapsed into political power. But what do these mean? And why is military power best seen as a component of political?

Ideological Power

Ideological power is essentially the power of ideas. It involves the construction of intellectual arguments which are aimed at justifying a particular conception of social or political arrangements. Such arguments have at their base the intent to persuade hearers of their truth, although belief in them does not always depend upon personal conviction. In practice, it may rely upon blind faith, custom or tradition, but even so its essential rationale involves a logic stemming from certain fundamental beliefs about society and how it should be structured. The detail of these beliefs will differ from case to case, but there are in principle two types: ascendant and descendant. The ascendant principle has historically been the less common of the two types, rooting a justification for political and social arrangements in the society itself, usually conceived in terms of the populace. The most common form of ascendant belief has been the modern ideology of democracy, but in practice this has been a dominant paradigm for the organization of society only over the last 200 years of a history of organized political society stretching back over 5,000 years. The descendant principle nests the justification for political and social arrangements in some conception of the gods. Society is seen as in some sense a divinely-inspired order, with religion being a major prop to, and justification of, schemes for the organization of society. An important difference between the ascendant and descendant forms is that the former is much more open to change by society and the people in it than the latter, where any change may call into question the fundament of religious belief which underpins that society.

To say that ideological power is the justification of sets of social and political arrangements puts a bland face upon one aspect of this, the justification of power relationships. Power relationships, the way in which certain groups dominate others in society through the structure of that society itself, are themselves justified ideologically. Generally this is seen in terms of the legitimation of the political system and is a crucial element in the structuring of any society. The rulers must be seen to be legitimate, to have the right to rule rather than simply relying upon brute force to maintain their position.

Ideological power is thus the means of establishing authority on the part of the rulers. But ideological power is also a means of establishing social solidarity within the community. It helps to define the social unit by specifying the qualities which mark it off from its neighbours. This is usually done in terms of the presentation of a pseudo-historical or mythological vision which provides a sense of a common past for the community based upon common experiences and common beliefs. A sense of normative solidarity, of belonging together as a natural unit, is thus also linked with ideological power.

What this means is that ideological power is the means of defining both the nature of the community and the power relations that hold sway within it. It is therefore a very potent form of power because the more a single ideological message dominates the community, the more secure the arrangements legitimated by that message should be, and therefore the less the rulers should have to rely upon force to maintain themselves in power. This ability to define what is right and wrong, what is acceptable and unacceptable, is fundamental to the occupation of ruling office. But this also makes ideological power an arena for vigorous conflict. If an alternative vision can displace that which rules in a particular society, those political forces connected to this alternative will be strongly placed to displace the existing rulers. Control over ideological power is therefore always something that is contested. The chief form in which this takes place is the contest of ideas, but this is usually linked to the capture of certain normative institutions in the society whose task it is to generate, project and protect ideological power. Throughout much of human history, the main such institution has been the priesthood and the temple. Law-givers have been another important actor in this regard, although there has often been a close relationship between religious and legal functionaries. These have provided the normative underpinning for the society and any shift in that normative basis has usually required a change in personnel among religious leaders. This is not always the case, but normative shifts have usually involved personnel changes as well. It is control of such institutions and the rituals which are associated with the normative belief system and embedded in those institutions that is the key to ideological power.

Economic Power

Economic power stems essentially from the physical need for survival, but because the societies with which we are concerned were not at the purely subsistence level, economic power involves the capacity to determine the economic conditions under which people live. When large numbers of people come together, individual subsistence economies can no longer operate because there is a need for a section of the populace to be engaged in work other than food production. Division of labour must occur if the community is to be anything other than a transitory phenomenon. This means that there must be social organization of economic life. This involves the three central elements of economic life: production, distribution and exchange. The way that these are structured determines the life chances and the life style of the populace. For example, a mechanism designed to ensure the equal distribution of all goods produced in the society would create a very different sort of social structure and society from a mechanism designed to direct most goods to a privileged few while leaving the majority with access only to those goods they produce themselves. It is this relationship between economic activity on the one hand and life chances and life style on the other which gives economics a generative role in the development of social class, and therefore in the structuring of the society as a whole.

The key to economic power is the extent of control over economic activity which the rulers can exercise. In principle there are two extremes, neither ever having been achieved. The first is the full market economy where political authorities play no role at all. The second is the totalitarian system where political authorities control all aspects of economic activity. Both extremes are impossible in practice; all societies fall somewhere in between. The issue is where on this continuum a society is located, or how much control the rulers can exercise over economic life, and what means they use to try to exercise that control. How much control rulers are able to exercise is, of course, something specific to each case, and it may also change over time; but the means through which rulers seek to exercise such control are much more standard. There are two principal means of achieving this: first, direct involvement in economic activity. This may take the form of state monopolies of certain types of activity whereby competition to the state is formally prohibited and enforced by state penalties, but it may also take the form of the more limited entry of the state into economic activity through the establishment of state agencies to act in competition with non-state bodies in particular spheres of activity, or state action in intervening in the market to achieve certain limited but particular goals. The mass purchase of grain to ensure an adequate food supply to the urban poor is an example of this. The second means of achieving control is through regulation. The rulers may generate a wide range of rules, laws and regulations designed to structure economic activity. Such measures will range from broad laws relating to the general conduct of economic life to quite specific measures about particular aspects of economic activity; but what is crucial is the capacity of the rulers to enforce these measures. This depends upon political power, as discussed below.

Like ideological power, economic power is an arena of conflict, but it is usually a different form of conflict from that evident in the ideological sphere. Rarely is there a direct clash between two opposed coherent forces seeking radically different ways of organizing the economy and its relationship with political authorities. This does occur, as the industrial revolution of the eighteenth and nineteenth centuries and the capitalism versus communism clash of the twentieth century demonstrate, but these are unusual. More usual is the conduct of continuing struggle at the micro level. Economic actors are forever trying to escape or get around the rules generated by political authorities to guide their activities. Rules are denounced as onerous, as getting in the way of economic activity, as infringing freedom, and economic actors accordingly try to avoid them. But it is this third claim, that the state is infringing freedom, which is the key to this point about struggle. The attempt by economic actors to minimize the role of the state in their own particular activities constitutes an effective rejection of state control in the economy. Thus, rather than there being a direct and public conflict between rulers and economic actors, there is a continuing tug of war as the state seeks to assert its control (to whatever extent it thinks fit) while the economic actors seek, through pursuing their economic activity, to reduce the state's role. This conflict is endemic in all societies, and always calls into question the position of the state in this sphere of economic power.

There is another aspect of economic power that is important. Control over the economy, or over significant parts of it, gives the capacity both to increase the power currently held and to enrich the controllers. This does not have to take the form of the predatory regimes of people such as Mobutu in Zaire where rulers simply took what they wanted from the economy. The more usual form is the structuring of the society in such a way that particular classes gain privileged access to the goods and services that the society produces. But such a form of dominance, most clearly reflected in the wide literature on ruling class, is different from that exercised by narrow groups of political rulers. The class is broader, more differentiated and more decentralized, with the result that power is more diffused and, often, less evident. It is nevertheless there, as the class uses its economic position to entrench itself in power and privilege and to expand its economic capacity. Thus the arena of struggle for economic power is less concentrated than that for ideological power. It is also less concentrated than that for political power.

Political Power

Political power stems from the need for order, regulation and security. When large numbers of people are congregated together, for the security of all their behaviour must be regulated. Each person must be secure from those who might harm him/her, located both within the society and outside. It is this essential need for security and the possible location of threats to it both within and without the society that is the key to the combination of political and military power in the one type. While the use of military means to combat an external foe may be on a larger scale and may require more resources, the mobilization of coercive potential which this constitutes is in principle no different from the use of coercive means to secure order domestically. Mann's military power may therefore be seen as a particular form of political power.

Political power is territorially-based, in the sense that the definition of over whom power may be exercised must be expressed in territorial terms and, insofar as the state is concerned, will be centralized. This means that the focus of political power is likely to be concentrated in a central region, where direct control can be exercised over the populace, but this will be surrounded by zones in which such control is much weaker, stretching to areas over which no political control is exercised by the centre at all. The inclusion of military activity within political power also means that the scope of stabilized political power where effective control is exercised will in most cases be somewhat smaller than the episodic projection of political power outwards through military activity. In other words, the administrative reach of the political authorities will almost always be less than the military reach; an army can be sent outside the borders relatively much more easily than administrative control can be created. A concentric model of political control is useful for conceptualizing this.[32] It is important to realize that there is not necessarily a complete fit between political power on the one hand and ideological and economic power on the other. Both ideological power and economic power may be much more extensive in their reach than political power. The role of Nippur in Mesopotamia from about 2400 BC and of the Vatican throughout much of its history are examples of authorities exercising more extensive ideological than political power. In terms of economic power, the location of small states close by larger ones may mean that the economy of the former will be dominated by decisions made in the latter. Similarly domestically, political, economic and ideological power will not always coincide. Parts of a territory under a centre's political control may be ideologically heterodox and/or economically autonomous.

The form of continuing political control is administrative. Only if a centre has spread an administrative network over a territory can there be any hope of political control. In this sense, political control is much more heavily dependent upon individual people (government officials) than is either of the other two forms of power. Ideological power is vested in the ideas, the doctrines and religious beliefs of the populace, and although human agents (usually in the form of priests) are important bearers of those ideas, once they take root in the community, those human agents are less important. Economic power is vested in the processes of economic life itself, albeit an economic life in part structured by state regulation and activity, and it is this essential economic dynamic which is more important for the projection of economic power than the human actors. Of course, the human actors are important, if for no other reason than that the processes themselves could not function without them. But while the carriage of economic power is vested in part in officials (to ensure that certain sorts of regulations are obeyed), it resides overwhelmingly in the processes themselves. In contrast, administration relies fundamentally upon the officials. If the officials are not present, administrative action cannot take place. The exercise of political power through the administrative process is thus directly dependent upon the activity of government agents.[33] This is a crucial dimension of political power, but it is also one of its biggest problems.

The establishment of an effective administrative network requires a developed infrastructure, principally of communication but also of control. The problem for all governments, even contemporary ones with a highly developed infrastructure of this sort, is that its officials will disappear into society, or see their loyalties as lying rather more with the communities within which they work than with the central authorities. If this happens, the centre's capacity to continue to exercise political control over the region in which this has occurred collapses because the local official acts for that community rather than for the state. This is an intrinsic problem because if the official is to do his duty properly, he must become highly familiar with the local community and its problems. But once the official has become thus familiar, and thereby close to that community, the possibility of split loyalties is increased. While the presence of a developed communications and control infrastructure makes this less likely, or at least enables the centre to respond quickly when it does happen, it cannot prevent this type of development. States have developed a variety of ways of seeking to deal with this problem. The dispatch of plenipotentiaries from the centre to audit local officials is one method, but this is a means only of exercising episodic control. Another is the rotation of officials so that someone cannot sink roots into the local community and thereby gain the incentive to defect from the centre. But the problem with this is that if officials do not remain in one place for very long, they can never become sufficiently familiar with it to be able to act effectively in the centre's interests. So the disappearance of administrative staff is a real problem for political authorities in their quest to exercise political power. It is also a major way in which political power is contested.

Another problem, preceding that of the disappearing officials, is actually establishing effective control over regions in the first place. The establishment of states has involved the expansion of central power to encompass regions not initially under control. This has of necessity involved replacing local loyalties with loyalties to the centre, bringing local magnates under central control by eliminating their autonomy. Historically this has usually involved concentrated coercion in the form of military threat or action and has usually been resisted. This type of conflict is the clearest way in which political power is contested.

***

Ultimately, all of these types of power are linked in a variety of ways depending upon the situation. Increases in one type of power may have implications for the other two types of power. But the crucial factor for our analysis is that the aim of political authorities, both real and aspirant, has generally been to concentrate all three types of power in their hands. The aim throughout much of history has also been to monopolize those three types of power, although this has been less true of the economic and ideological spheres than of the political. State leaders have tended to see their positions as being most secure when they could concentrate these three types of power in their hands, using them in combination to overwhelm potential challengers. Normally state capacity will be most developed when all three types of power are wielded by the state.

Thus central to the modern state is its capacity to penetrate society institutionally and thereby create the conditions for the effective control over, and governance of, society. This is manifested in a bureaucratic structure in which regularized functioning through an infrastructure stretching into society enables the projection of central power far outside the capital. But crucial to the capacity of such a structure to project central power in an effective fashion is the relationship between that structure and the society within which it sits. The modern state, as reflected most fully in the liberal democratic welfare states of the West, has highly developed relations with its society. Legislative and bureaucratic organic interdependence ensure that the state is firmly rooted in the social groups which comprise the society, while institutional interdependence ensures that it is intertwined with the policy constituencies crucial to the courses of action it wants to follow. State capacity is maximized when infrastructural power is the chief form in which power is exercised. And infrastructural power is a result of the high level of regularization of process and function, including discipline, within the state bureaucracy, along with a high level of interdependence with society. It is this balance between internal centralization and discipline on the one hand and interdependence on the other that gives the state its capacity to act, and it is this that is crucial to the modern state form.

2

The Ancient State

The key to the modern state form is the capacity it possesses as a result of the combination of internal centralization and discipline on the one hand and interdependence on the other. However, such a combination has not always been in evidence, with the practical effect that where such a combination has been absent or one or both elements have been weakly developed, states have lacked capacity on the scale of the modern state. This is clearly evident if we look at the ancient state, the first form in which the state became stabilized as the dominant, continuing force in society. While the degree of institutional sophistication of individual ancient states varied considerably, all shared a weakness of capacity stemming from flawed centralization and low levels of interdependence.

When considering the ancient state, it is essential to recognize that we are dealing with extensive time spans. The clearest example is Egypt, which lasted some 3,000 years, with interruptions due to central breakdown and rule by outsiders, from its formation as a unified state around 3000 BC until its final incorporation into the Roman Empire in 30 BC. The Greek poleis survived for around 500 years, while during its thousand-year history Rome underwent a transformation from city-state to vast empire. Not all changes were as dramatic as that of Rome, but all these states underwent change over the period of their existence. More than in any other period, in analysing the structures and processes of these states, we need to bear this temporal element in mind.

One study of pre-industrial political forms[1] has identified the following types:

- patrimonial empires (e.g., Carolingian and Parthian empires)
- nomad or conquest empires (e.g., Mongols, the initial Caliphate)

- city-states (e.g., Athens, Republican Rome)
- feudal systems (e.g., medieval Europe)
- centralized, historical bureaucratic empires (e.g., Egypt, Imperial Rome)

These types of political system are not as distinct as the mere listing of them suggests. Nomad empires usually were transformed into patrimonial or centralized bureaucratic empires when the conquering nomads settled down into a sedentary existence. Centralized historical bureaucratic empires often had distinct patrimonial elements, while the erosion of imperial control in both types of empires could produce feudal-type arrangements. City-states could develop into imperial structures, as the Roman case attests. So elements of all of these types may be found in the ancient world. The survey which follows does not embrace all of the state forms of which historically we are aware. For example, the 'chariot aristocracies' of Dark Ages Greece, most of the classical Greek poleis, the range of small polities established by invaders between the Near Eastern empires, the Etruscans, Carthage and non-Western states have all been excluded. The focus is upon those polities that generally have been seen as contributing directly to the development of the Western state form: the Mesopotamian city-states and empires, Egypt, the Greek polis and Rome.

It was in Mesopotamia that the first states emerged, based on the cities of the southern plains, somewhere near the middle of the fourth century BC. These city-states were very small towns with a surrounding hinterland. There were a number of them dotted around the southern part of Sumer, some so close that they could see one another (Eridu, Ur, Uruk and Larsa[2]). Sharing a broadly common linguistic, religious and cultural milieu, these small states vigorously claimed political independence, and although at times one city was able to project its leadership over the others and there appears to have been an official called a 'Great King' who exercised nominal hegemony (but perhaps little real power) over the city-states,[3] they were not consolidated into a single state before their incorporation into the Akkadian Empire in 2334 BC. While there was frequent contact, including conflict, between these city-states, there was little interference in one another's domestic affairs.[4] Conquest by Akkad began a cycle of integration into larger empires followed by imperial disintegration and the regaining of local autonomy until the conquest of the Persian Empire by Alexander in 330 BC.[5]

Egypt was unified about 3000 BC,[6] and it retained its independent identity until incorporated into the Roman Empire in 30 BC. During this long period, stable, centralized control was interspersed by periods when that control broke down and the country became regionalized, at least in the sense that local authorities became stronger than the central rulers. But even during these periods, many elements of the centralized kingdom were maintained and, when central control was also restored, the old principles and structures (albeit sometimes with alterations) were also restored. Until Roman times, foreign conquerors also adopted the established Egyptian forms.

In Greece, the polis emerged as an independent entity in the eighth–seventh century BC and lasted until conquered by Alexander in the fourth century BC. Its classic period was the fifth–fourth century BC.[7] Like the Sumerian city-states, the Greek poleis were small, each comprising a city with a small hinterland. The city was the focus of activity, with many rural smallholders continuing to live in the city and commute daily to their farms rather than live in the countryside.[8] Many poleis were militarily weak and subject to the imperial aspirations of Athens, Sparta and Thebes. Like their Sumerian forebears, the poleis were autonomous entities within a common culture area, but their style of government was very different.

Over Rome's long history from its foundation (mythically dated to 753 BC) until its sacking and the collapse of the Western Empire in AD 476, there have been three principal types of regime: monarchy until about 509 BC, republic until 27 BC, empire thereafter. During the period of the monarchy and the early period of the Republic, Rome was a city-state. However, imperial expansion turned that city-state into an empire, with significant implications for the structuring of state power. The discussion will concentrate upon the late republican and imperial periods.

The question is: how did these states compare with their modern counterparts?

The Ancient City-State

The Structuring of Central Power

Mesopotamia. The notion of the city-state conjures up an image of a small-scale polity, usually a republic, with governance in the hands either of the populace as a whole or of the representatives of a substantial part of it. Legislative organic interdependence is high as the leading organs of the state are embedded within the people. However, this model was not widely evident in antiquity. Despite claims about some form of 'primitive democracy' at the time of the emergence of the city-states of Mesopotamia,[9] there is little hard evidence for the existence of either sovereign democratic assemblies or of developed notions of citizenship. By 2500 BC, in the view of one scholar, 'the dozen or so city-states of which we have evidence seem to have been led by a king with despotic pretensions'.[10] The emergence of kings as major figures, a process described in the Gilgamesh Epic which shows the king as the military leader who gains permanent authority because of his successes, marks this key characteristic of all Near Eastern states (except for the Jewish kingdom[11]): the absolutist nature of monarchy.

Royal absolutism initially was legitimated in terms of the local city deity, but from about 2400 BC the king claimed that he held 'his kingship by favour of Enlil, the supreme Sumerian deity'.[12] Kingship was divine in origin,[13] with its function being to ensure that humans acted in concert with the gods and their desires. The king was not seen as being an intermediary between populace and deity, but the personification of the divine.[14] By diligently performing the tasks associated with his role, the king was believed to be ensuring the welfare of the city over which he ruled.[15] There was, therefore, a fusing of the religious and the secular in the person of the monarch, with no sense of the king's accountability to the people. He was not one of them, but the extension of the divine. The sense of distance this created was increased by his use of a closed group (such as the priesthood) for administrative support. Organic interdependence was minimal.

Greece. In the Greek and Roman city-states, the structure of central power was very different, both from Mesopotamia and from each other. Legislative organic interdependence was much more extensive in both. In most cases, the classical Greek polis was a republic.[16] Although by the fifth century BC there was a significant diversity in detail of political forms,[17] the general structure was standard. There were three major political organs: magistrates, council and assembly. Much of the difference between poleis, and conflict within poleis, turned on the constituency and membership of these bodies. The following discussion focuses upon Athens.

Central to the polis and to involvement in its political life was the concept of citizenship. The polis was conceived of as an association of citizens in which all had the right to participate in the life of the state; the community of citizens had rights over the state and its actions. The issue then became who was eligible for citizenship. In most cases, citizenship was hereditary, travelling through the male line from those families deemed to have been the original members of the community. Women, children, resident foreigners and slaves were not citizens, so the citizenry was restricted to a minority of the population. But the citizenry was not class-specific; landowners, aristocrats and peasants could all be citizens, although land-holding was usually a requirement.[18] This was symbolic of the right of the citizen to a share in the state and its produce; citizens also received rights unavailable to non-citizens, including more lenient treatment in the courts.[19] But sharing also meant a share of responsibilities and, in particular, continuing interest in the affairs of state.

Citizens were expected to participate in the organs of political rule, the magistracies, councils and assemblies. This reached its apex in Athens which, from the mid-fifth century until late in the fourth century BC with two short interruptions, had what has been called a 'radical democracy'.[20] Following the reforms of Cleisthenes in 508/7, the chief organizing vehicles of political life were the ten tribes into which the citizenry formally was divided. The tribes were the basis for the organization of citizen participation in the Council and the magistracies, but were not important for the Assembly.

The Assembly was the principal decision-making body of the Athenian polity. It was essentially a mass meeting of all citizens, requiring for at least some issues a quorum of 6,000, which was charged with making decisions on all aspects of policy. The Assembly met on 40 occasions during the year plus special meetings called to deal with a sudden emergency. Attendance levels are unknown, but the body is likely to have been of shifting composition as individuals attended daily or not as their other commitments and whims dictated. From early in the fourth century BC participants received a small monetary allowance, but this would not have been enough to sustain a comfortable life style.

The Council was the most important administrative and supervisory body of the state: it controlled the agenda of the Assembly, came together daily in open meeting, and ensured the implementation of decisions of the Assembly. It was therefore the only body able to supervise the magistrates and to react quickly when needed. It consisted of 500 people, 50 from each tribe selected by lot and serving a one year term (with a maximum of two terms). Although its actions were subject to public review and as a body it was formally answerable to the Assembly, it is not clear that any notion of accountability really operated for the body as a whole, although individual officials could be answerable for perceived misdeeds. Despite the stipend that was paid to Council members from 461 BC, few but the wealthy could afford to serve on it.

The magistrates took the form of ten member boards, one from each tribe, and were the executive officers of the Council and Assembly. They were selected annually by lot or by election.[21] There was no separate civil bureaucracy, the magistrates effectively fulfilling that function. Each board oversaw a different sector of life, including maintaining the navy, running the finances of the state and organizing the festivals, under the supervision of the Council.[22] The boards generally were assisted by slaves. At the end of their terms, all magistrates had their records scrutinized and action could be brought against them for wrongdoing. The notion of the magistracy was an important innovation. It affirmed the temporary nature of rule and established the distinction between person and office. It also provided the basis for the distinction between public and private spheres and between government and ownership, with the state not seen as the property of the ruler.

Citizens were also required to serve in the juries. They were drawn from a panel of 6,000 citizens over 30 years of age, and were deployed in groups on a variety of cases throughout the year. Jury service could be quite demanding of the time of citizens, and the level of the daily payment received for service meant that the poor could not afford to be tied up in such activity for long periods. The juries affirmed a new principle: judicial power should not be in the hands of the political authorities.

In Athens the principle of the citizen soldier was strongly entrenched, but in practice this role was generally confined to the middling to wealthy peasant farmers. It was from this group that the famous armed infantryman, the hoplite, was drawn. Service in the hoplite phalanx was compulsory for all adult male citizens who met the property requirement. As a result the ordinary property owner was as important as the aristocrat, thereby symbolizing a notion of citizenship based upon equality and an organic tie between the individual and the state. However, given the cost of providing their own armour and weapons, service as a hoplite was not usually open to the lower classes, although they were able to serve in the navy. Military service was crucial for the notion of citizenship.

The very rich did not usually serve in the military, but as citizens they owed obligations to the community. One way of meeting these was the so-called liturgy, the compulsory provision of services. This began with the richest in the society carrying out various public duties for the state, such as temple construction, the provision of festivals and feasts, and the equipping of naval vessels at their own expense. This was a form of conspicuous consumption which attracted honour to the provider, but over time this ceased to be voluntary and became an expectation. This was a means of ensuring that the wealthy contributed to the well-being of the community, just as the poorer did through military service; instead of expending their labour, they spent their wealth, and in return gained honour as public benefactors. As the quest for honour escalated, so the dimensions of public benefaction rose.[23] This helped to maintain the myth of universal contribution to the community, but it also projected the wealthy symbolically into a crucial place in the community's functioning: the wealthy were essential for the continuing life of the community. This helped to legitimize their general dominance of political life and provided a symbolic underpinning for their dominance of the ruling oligarchy.

As in Mesopotamia, politics was dominated by the wealthy; they led the cliques that structured life in the Assembly and Council, and predominated in the leading offices of state. But this was a different sort of politics. It was not a politics of the palace, of decision-making behind closed doors and palace intrigues: this was a politics of the public place, a politics which required those who were to carry the day generally to argue their cases in open session and persuade people of the virtue of the positions they took. Of course this opened the way for demagogues, but it also led to the development of rhetoric and of political argument. This was almost as significant a principle of political life, differentiating the polis from its earlier Near Eastern neighbours, as was that of universal participation and rights of citizens. Furthermore, the Athenian polity was run by amateurs. The insistence on limited terms of office and regular rotation meant that it was impossible for the governing institutions to develop any sense of shared collective experience. Staffed by ordinary citizens, only in the Assembly was it possible for individuals to retain a prominent place in political life, but even that was dependent upon their capacity to capture the support of a significant number of their fellows. Political institutions did not constitute a continuing institutional basis upon which personal ambition could build in a sustained fashion.

Fundamental to the polis was the notion of citizen rule. This was a clear break with earlier modes of legitimation. Although at this time not acknowledged as a democracy, a word which had pejorative overtones,[24] this notion was the basis of the later development of democratic principles, of the notion that the organization of society and its running came not from above, but from within the community itself. This was also the basis for the much higher level of legislative organic interdependence in the Greek polis than in either Mesopotamia or Rome. The institutions of state possessed little institutional identity independent of the citizens who staffed them; they were much more embedded within the citizenry than the institutions of any other polity at this time. However, those who participated in these organs remained a minority of the population: the citizenry was far outnumbered by people living in the state who were not citizens, and only those citizens who were sufficiently wealthy could afford the time to devote to civic duties. The level of legislative organic interdependence should thus not be exaggerated despite the widespread citizen involvement in political affairs.

Rome. Like the polis, the Roman Republic rested on the principle of the community of citizens. The Roman notion of citizenship differed from that of the polis in two important ways: freed slaves of Romans were automatically incorporated into the citizen body, and whole communities of outsiders could be admitted into citizenship, especially following the so-called Social Wars of 91–87 BC. Citizenship, not the gods, was the basis of legitimacy. Given that citizenship was manifested in involvement in the political institutions of the state, like the polis Rome generated a sense of legitimation directed to the state rather than to an individual, although this was breaking down in the last century of the Republic's life. Citizenship was practically important because it gave people some protection against provincial governors, some tax advantages, and, if it was associated with the vote (which ultimately all citizens in the Republic obtained), the right to stand for election to the magistracies. All citizens had equal juridical status, at least following the extension of the suffrage to them all. However, the extension of the citizenship with the expansion of empire undermined the basis of city-state rule because it meant that it was no longer possible for all citizens to attend assembly meetings in Rome. It was clear that Rome could not remain a city-state, and even had the system not collapsed for other reasons, this would have brought about major change.

This ideal of citizen participation in the Roman republic, however, was mediated through the division of the populace into the privileged patricians and the lower-class plebeians. Although these groups were clearly seen as different in the early years of the Republic, they did not constitute firm class groups.[25] Nevertheless, the early centuries of the Republic saw a continual political struggle between these groups, and it is this struggle that shaped the development of the Republican political structure. It was further tension between the wealthy and poorer sections of society towards the end of the Republican period that contributed significantly to the collapse of the Republic and the inauguration of the Empire by Augustus.

Like its Greek predecessor, the Roman political structure comprised council, assemblies and magistrates, but in contrast to the polis and reflecting the continuing rich–poor tension, these were constructed in a way that could produce deadlock. Much of the course of the history of the Republic during its last century and a quarter was a history of conflict between various of these institutions. What drove that conflict was continuing tension and struggle between the aristocratic oligarchy that ruled Rome, and the urban poor of the capital. By the time the Republic entered its crisis phase, an impasse had been reached between the organs dominated by the aristocrats and those by the populace. Heightened levels of conflict within the aristocratic oligarchy at this time pushed this system beyond its limits and exacerbated the mutually checking nature of the institutions. This is well illustrated by Finer, when he says that the process of government in Republican Rome was complicated by four factors:

> the right of superior or equal magistrates to veto one another's actions; the existence of more than one popular Assembly; the latters' inability to act except on the initiative of a magistrate; and finally, the existence of certain officers, the tribunes, who acted as a kind of wildcard in their right to bring all public business to a stop, on the one hand, and to initiate legislation, on the other.[26]

The council in the Roman structure was the Senate. It consisted purely of ex-magistrates nominated for life by the censors,[27] it met when convened by a magistrate, and was empowered to discuss only matters brought before it (although in practice this restriction was not always observed). Its decisions were formally simply consultative, but over time this changed. By the start of the third century BC, the Senate's place as the only permanent body and the one with the most experience enabled it to gain greater control over affairs of state, including control over the state's finances, the disposition of military forces, the allocation of provinces to individual magistrates, maintenance of law and order, and relations with foreign powers. It also had the power to extend the period of a magistrate's command and, at the time of the Gracchan period, claimed the right to declare a state of emergency. Although its power waxed and waned, it was the chief organ of government until late in the Republic when the conflict with the plebeian organs and the growth of military activity in politics undermined its position. The Senate was dominated by wealthy men of aristocratic birth.[28] Senators were forbidden to participate in commerce or seek to purchase public contracts, although by at least 59 BC this latter provision seems no longer to have been operative.[29] Senators in the Republic were, however, in a position to make significant sums of money if they became provincial governors or extended loans to provincial authorities,[30] as many did.

There were two principal assemblies.[31] The Comitia Centuriata[32] formally included all adult male citizens. For the purpose of voting, it was divided into 193 centuries. Membership of these centuries was determined essentially on the basis of wealth, and the system was constructed in such a way as to advantage the wealthy over the poor.[33] Each century had one vote, and within the centuries, the voting was structured to give primacy to those over the age of 46. The rich and the old could thus outvote the poor and the young. This body elected senior magistrates (consuls, praetors and censors), could enact laws, declare war and peace, and impose the death penalty on Roman citizens. The Comitia Tributa, or tribal assembly, was divided into the 35 tribes into which the Roman people were organized[34] and therefore included both patricians and plebeians.[35] This seemingly was a more democratic mode of structuring the voting than in the Comitia Centuriata, but in fact this system discriminated against those who lived too far from Rome to play a direct part, and the urban population; urban inhabitants were concentrated in only four tribes, while rural inhabitants dominated the other 31. But many of those rural tribes were themselves dominated by larger landowners, since they were the only ones who could afford to come to Rome for the assembly's deliberations. The Comitia Tributa elected tribunes of the plebeians and aediles,[36] enacted plebiscites and conducted trials for non-capital offences.

Central to the government of Republican Rome were the magistrates, an institution that, as in the polis, emphasized the temporary nature of political power, and the distinction between person and office and government and ownership. The institution also embodied a principle of accountability since the conduct of all magistrates while in office was investigated when their terms expired. There were six different sorts of magistrate.[37] *Consuls* were the highest officers of state, the chief law-makers and the commander-in-chief of the army. Two consuls were elected annually[38] by the Comitia Centuriata, and they were formally ineligible for re-election for ten years.[39] *Censors*, of which there were two, were elected for five-year terms from among the ranks of ex-consuls, and their task was to conduct the census of the citizenry. This was a crucial political task because the role a person could play in the political life of the Republic, including participation in the assemblies and entry to the Senate, depended upon one's census class. *Praetors* (six to eight in number)[40] exercised judicial functions within the city. *Aediles* were responsible for the material needs of the city including safety, water supply, supervision of markets and prices, and food supplies. They were also responsible for the supply of games to the populace. *Quaestors*, of which there were eight, held financial responsibility, including the oversight of tax collection and the receipt of tribute and booty. There was also provision for a short-term magistrate, the *dictator*. This post was filled by nomination of a consul, usually for a brief period of time to handle a particular emergency.

In addition to these magistrates, there were the tribunes of the plebeians. These officers, of which there were ten, had a brief to defend the persons and property of the plebeians. They had the right to veto the action of any magistrate, including the consul, to call the plebeians to assembly and elicit from that meeting decisions which from 287 BC became laws binding on the whole populace, and to enforce those laws. A decision of a tribune of the plebeians could be countermanded only by another of the tribunes, with the result that if they remained solid, they could bring the whole business of government to a halt. These were therefore highly political positions, and the aristocratic oligarchy attempted to ensure that they had at least one of the tribunes to do their bidding in order to stop measures with which they disagreed.

The continuing tension between rich and poor in Rome was symbolized by the way in which the privileged sections of the population continued to dominate in those institutions not specifically designated as being associated with the plebeians. The leading magistracies were out of the reach of most plebeians. Not only were the positions honorary (although the granting of control over a province did give a magistrate access to often significant levels of wealth through tax and exploitation), but the fulfilment of the duties associated with the post often meant that the incumbent had to pay for many things out of his own pocket. The liturgies noted in Greece were also well-developed in Rome, with the expectation that magistrates would pay from their own pocket for various sorts of public works. This built on the principle of 'clientship'[41] so important in the early Republic whereby powerful nobles had peasant retainers bound to them as clients, giving them gifts in return for support, including in the assemblies in Rome. Over time this was transformed into the use of the gift for political display to attract increased support.[42] By the late Republic at least, simply to gain election could require the expenditure of considerable sums. Candidates had to spend their own money in providing evidence to the voters of their worth by providing games and entertainment, which was expensive.

The effect of this was to close out large sections of the populace from the possibility of holding political office. Political service was seen less as a public responsibility than as a source of honour to oneself and one's family. This was the source of an individual's *dignitas*, or his rank and prestige in the public sphere. Once elected, office-holders often still faced major public expense; the aediles and praetors had to put on public games, the cost of which far exceeded the subvention from the Treasury and could be ruinously expensive.[43] From early in the second century BC, the holding of the office of aedile and praetor and the consequent sponsoring of public games was almost a condition for subsequent election as consul.[44] Successive sponsors of the games sought to outdo each other, with the result that in practice occupation of high public office was not equally open to all. With only slight exaggeration, one scholar has referred to the Republic as 'an oligarchy of aristocratic families competing for the major magistracies (the consulship and the praetorship) and operating on ... a certain de facto rotation between them, dependent on their attractiveness to the popular Assembly which elected them'.[45] This oligarchy was quite narrow: 'between 232 and 133 BC the 200 consuls came from 58 aristocratic lineages (gentes), and of these, 159 came from 26 lineages, 99 from only ten lineages'.[46] Although there were scions of dominant families who did not obtain the consulship and 'new men' from outside this oligarchy who did, this oligarchy of notables generally dominated Roman public life up to the end of the Republic. Thus central power in

Republican Rome was characterized by legislative organic interdependence but, because of the domination of the Senate and the
major magistracies by those from the wealthy section of society,
politically effective interdependence was quite narrow.

The Projection of Central Power

Mesopotamia. Crucial to the ability of the central authorities to
exercise dominion over the state was the capacity to project their
power outside the capital city. This capacity differed between the
various city-states. So too did the level of bureaucratic organic interdependence achieved. Although the king in the Mesopotamian city-
state was able to subordinate the temples and priests to his will, this
does not mean that he obtained an effective bureaucratic structure
with which to run his state. None of these states developed much of
an administrative structure outside the royal palace-household, relying upon both the functionaries within that household and upon
wealthy magnates. With these functionaries effectively a separate
self-contained caste, there was limited interdependence between
these political forms and society; there was little bureaucratic
organic interdependence. Infrastructural power was weak, although
the small size of the city-state moderated this weakness.

Greece. There was no developed civil bureaucracy in the polis, so
infrastructural power was weak. In Athens, taxes were collected by
tax farmers, while the general administration of the state was in the
hands of a series of boards and commissions. These were overlapping and uncoordinated; they lacked a coherent set of administrative
structures and, being filled mainly by the wealthy, had narrow
bureaucratic organic interdependence. The rotation of the membership ensured that little expertise was built up. This was the antithesis
of a coherent, regularized, bureaucratic machine.

Rome. During the Republic, the Roman state had very little in the
way of a bureaucratic structure. Unlike in Greece where the size of
the polity ameliorated the need for an elaborate bureaucratic hierarchy, the steadily expanding Roman imperium did need a way of
projecting state power. Within the city of Rome itself, major administrative functions were carried out by small personal staffs attached
to the major magistrates. This provided no continuity and little effective penetration of society as a whole. In the provinces, initially

administration remained largely in local hands and followed local traditions as long as this arrangement did not conflict with the maintenance of order and collection of taxes.[47] Following the defeat of Carthage in the Third Punic War (149–46 BC), the provinces were ruled by a governor[48] and his own personal staff supported by a garrison of legionaries; in some cases local clients were retained, providing they became romanized. The civil administration of the Republic both at the centre and in the provinces was puny and patrimonial, in that officials provided their own staff whose loyalty clearly lay with their patron rather than the state.

Some of the functions of the state were privatized. The liturgy, as in Greece a public benefit financed by rich individuals, was one means of providing services that released the state from any obligation in this regard; but more important were the publicani, the tax farmers who were responsible for collecting taxes throughout Rome's growing domain. Usually the state auctioned the contracts for tax collection in a particular area, received the specified sum in advance of the collection, and left the publicani to then go and collect sufficient to cover the state's share and their profit. This practice, which began in the third century BC, shifted the risk from the state to the private sector. It is not clear whether this was introduced as a result of the absence of a bureaucratic means of collecting tax[49] or whether it was a conscious decision on the part of the rulers to minimize risk.[50] The public contracting-out to private companies of responsibility for such things as food supply to the army, repair of religious buildings, the supply of horses for processions and games and the feeding of the sacred geese[51] suggests that the use of such methods had its roots in the weakness of the bureaucratic apparatus. Whatever its origin, it clearly reflects the limited bureaucratic reach, low level of bureaucratic organic interdependence, and restricted potential for infrastructural power of the Roman state. The prominent role played by the army in maintaining links between Rome and its regions confirms the weakness of the civil bureaucracy.

The city-state was, in a historical sense, a dead end. If it remained small, as in Mesopotamia and Greece, it was swallowed up by a larger neighbour. If it expanded, like Rome, the city-state institutions of rule had to be transformed. The emphasis upon popular involvement through direct participation in the assembly was unsustainable when the relevant population became too large. Yet this was the essence of the Greek and Roman city-states. Both types of city-state therefore enjoyed a level of legislative organic interdependence that would be impossible for their larger successors. But given the dominance of the wealthy in politics and the restricted nature of the definition of citizenship, this interdependence remained narrowly focused. This was particularly important in the absence of bureaucratic organic interdependence, resulting principally from the underdeveloped nature of the bureaucracy. These states had no developed bureaucracy organized along specialized, functional lines and separate from the other institutions of the state, and their capacity to wield sustained infrastructural power was weak.

The Ancient Empires

The shift from city-state to empire generated significant new challenges for the polity, chiefly because of the increased size of the territory. Associated with this was usually increased social complexity. As a result, empire had to generate institutions that smaller city-states had generally been able to do without, at least if the imperial centre was effectively to run its new domains. Such institutions, ideally, would be coherently organized and embedded within the societies they administered. However, neither coherent organization nor embeddedness was realized in practice.

The Structuring of Central Power

Mesopotamia. The empires of Mesopotamia, Egypt and Rome were what Finer called palace polities.[52] This meant that authority and power, and much of the administration, was concentrated in the household of the ruler. The ruler was absolute, his household retainers dominated political and administrative positions at the centre, and there was limited development of a central bureaucracy separate from the imperial household. In Mesopotamia, an absolutist king rested upon divine or semi-divine legitimation,[53] and claimed hegemony over a large area; from the time of Akkad, the king was called the 'King of the Four Quarters' and, later, the 'King of Totality', claims reflecting at least imperial aspirations and a refusal to acknowledge neighbouring political forms as equals.[54] The government was based in the palace. Given the aspiration to rule over a large area, there was a need for greater administrative capacity at the centre. As a result, a central bureaucracy developed, but only in some of these empires (e.g., the Assyrian and the Persian) was it separate from the king's household. Central record-keeping became quite extensive, but this did not mean penetration of the society; the emergent bureaucracy remained isolated from society more broadly. The empire was a very different model of polity from the Sumerian city-states; a centralized government with an emergent record-keeping bureaucracy ruling from a single city and seeking to project its power through indirect rule over large areas was a sharp contrast to the limited horizons of the city-states, although the limited legislative organic interdependence of the earlier polities remained.

Egypt. From the time of Egyptian unification, the king[55] was the centre-piece of Egyptian life. He was the god-king[56] whose power was absolute, underpinned by the special position he held in relation to the gods. In practice, the power an individual pharaoh could wield varied, depending upon broader socio-political conditions and upon the person of the pharaoh himself. For example, the pharaohs of the third and fourth dynasties and the empire-builders of the eighteenth–twentieth dynasties were particularly powerful. But regardless of the real power of each pharaoh, the ideology of absolutism remained unchallenged. Symbolically the pharoah dominated Egypt.

The pharaoh was an important cultic figure, responsible for a range of ritual activities deemed necessary for the welfare of the kingdom. As the son and the manifestation of the god, he was the link between human society and the divine forces that ruled the world. He was clearly set apart from his people. Through the performance of established rituals, he had to ensure both the well-being of the country and the order of the universe. He was also responsible for the maintenance of existing temples and the construction of new ones, the building of public works (but not irrigation), and for maintaining the funerary cults of his predecessors. The pharaoh was also a war leader, responsible for the protection of the kingdom from outside enemies, especially in the New Kingdom period of Egyptian expansion. But he also had a central role in the governance of the country. The law does not appear to have been codified but was an expression of the king's will, while the central administrative bureaucracy was an extension of royal power. During most of the Old Kingdom, the administration was literally an extension of the pharaoh's household.[57] Details of this central bureaucracy are scant, although individual ministers seem to have had a variety of functions while the departments into which the bureaucracy was divided were more specialized.[58] During the New Kingdom, the central administration was bifurcated between the royal household officialdom and the civil bureaucracy,[59] and it was at this time that tension between pharaoh and officials was most likely.[60] The civil bureaucracy was headed by a vizier, who had oversight over the whole range of administrative activity. Access to the bureaucracy was in theory open to all people of talent, but in practice this was linked to social status; the sons of scribes and prominent officials tended to dominate administrative ranks, with scions of the aristocracy filling many of the top posts. Many of these top posts became virtually hereditary. The organic interdependence of the bureaucracy was therefore very narrow, and infrastructural power weak.

Rome. The establishment of the Roman Empire by Augustus instituted a revolution in Roman government. The essence of Augustus' changes was to shift power away from the comitia, the Senate and the consuls and locate it firmly in the hands of the princeps (first man in the state), the unofficial title he took for himself. The princeps was the commander-in-chief of the armies, had the power of appointment of governors in imperial provinces, was able to override all other office-holders, nominated candidates for election to official posts, decided peace and war, convened and presided over the Senate, promoted legislation in the Senate, could issue edicts with binding force, could preside over any judicial case he wished, and was the supreme priest, the Pontifex Maximus. The treasury was under his control,[61] and he dominated the new imperial system of government. The Senate retained a role. It could issue decisions that gained the force of law only with the approval of the princeps, appoint governors to senatorial provinces (usually without armies, in contrast to those in imperial provinces), exercise some judicial functions, and advise on foreign affairs. The comitia lost all independent legislative power and the capacity to choose magistrates. The genius of Augustus' reorganization is that he fundamentally shifted the locus of power in the Roman system, concentrating it in the person of the emperor, while retaining most of the forms of the Republic. This meant that much of the rhetoric of legitimation also remained unchanged, with the emperor's power formally stemming from conferral of it upon him by the Senate and the comitia. This changed over time, when the emperor came to be seen as a god.[62]

The emperor remained central to the politico-administrative structure created by Augustus throughout the life of the Empire, although as in all systems where supreme power is held by one person, the power an emperor could wield varied depending upon the personality of the emperor and prevailing conditions.[63] The emperor had to deal with the Senate and, although there was no prospect of this body displacing the emperor and restoring some form of republican rule, it was still an institution with influence, staffed by experienced people, able to reproduce itself, and conscious of its own importance. Indeed, during the first and second centuries AD, most emperors sought to present themselves as constitutional rulers, abiding by the Republican constitution, and therefore accorded the Senate significant formal authority. However, the Senate's waning importance was reflected in the imperial succession of Macrinus (217–18), the first emperor not to have been in the Senate, and by the acknowledgement early in the third century of the emperor as the sole legislator in the state. In the troubled third century, the Senate sometimes opposed the army in proposing candidates for the position of emperor in a series of succession struggles and wars; and as this office itself declined in vigour, independence and importance in the fourth and fifth centuries in the West, the Senate remained as a cornerstone of the Western Roman Empire. But the Senate did not constitute a political vehicle available to all of the populace; it remained throughout the preserve of the privileged and clearly acted with a view to preserving the position of that section of the population. It was this power and position of the members of the Senate individually that persuaded emperors to treat the body with some consideration. In contrast, the vehicles that had made some provision for popular involvement in the Republic, the comitia and the tribunes of the plebeians, atrophied; the comitia retained a nominal existence until the third century, but we know of no exercise of legislative or judicial function after the first century.[64]

The main potential restriction on the emperor came from the army. With Augustus' establishment of the praetorian guard in 27 BC and the stationing of three of the nine cohorts in Rome, for the first time an armed military force under the direct control of a leading state official was allowed to be stationed within the city's walls; under the Republic, armed troops were not allowed to cross the boundary into the city except for celebration of a triumph. In AD 23 Tiberius concentrated these guards in one camp in the capital, thereby increasing their cohesion and capacity for action. This also increased their potential to exercise influence in cases of succession; the prefect of the guard was instrumental in enabling Caligula to accede to the throne alone in AD 37 and, following his murder in AD 41, they placed Claudius on the throne. Also important was the army more broadly, especially during the third century when the legions were active in overthrowing emperors and placing their own candidates on the throne. Recognizing this potential power, all emperors beginning with Augustus at accession gave monetary payments (the donativum) to the military in an endeavour to gain their loyalty.[65] From Septimius Severus (193–211) on, these donativa became what one author has called 'a systematic purchase of military fidelity'.[66] However, as the currency devalued, successive emperors found they had to supplement this with the free distribution of rations, clothing and raw materials for arms to the troops.

The expanded role of the military diminished somewhat the position of emperor. Another development which contributed to this was the practice of sharing the imperial position. In the reign of Marcus Aurelius (161–80), the concept of shared rule was introduced. Marcus ruled jointly with Lucius Verus until the latter's death eight years after ascending the throne. This arrangement was repeated when Septimius Severus died in 211, with Caracalla and his brother Geta ruling as co-emperors until the latter's murder by Caracalla that same year. With the restoration of stability following the middle 40 years of the third century AD when there were 20 emperors, many of whom met a violent end and were placed on the throne by the army, Diocletian proclaimed a co-emperor in Maximian, another soldier. In 293 Diocletian established the tetrarchy, an arrangement whereby the two emperors were shadowed by two junior rulers who were to succeed to the supreme positions when one of the joint emperors died or resigned. Just as the joint emperors had operated in different parts of the empire (both at the head of armies defending the frontiers), so each of the tetrarchs was allocated a different part of the empire to administer. As the senior figure, Diocletian made the most important decisions. From his death until the collapse of the Empire, and especially following Constantine's establishment of a capital at Constantinople in 324, the Empire was either wracked by civil war or ruled by two or more sovereign emperors. The virtue of consolidated power in a single figure demonstrated in the earlier periods of imperial history, and even the success of a joint arrangement as demonstrated by the ability of the tetrarchy to work together to push back barbarian incursions on the borders, was lost as the system of joint rule simply collapsed under the increasing barbarian pressure on the borders and the ambitions of many of the rulers. By the end of the third century, the Western and Eastern halves of the Empire were going their own ways.

Emperors remained cut off from the broad ranks of society at large. Surrounded by personal councillors, supporters and cronies,[67] the emperor generally remained ensconced in his palaces, isolated from the mass of the population. Those who possessed military origins and sought to lead the armies in defence of the Empire were just as isolated from the populace. The position of emperor lacked legislative organic interdependence.

Throughout the life of the Empire, the central bureaucracy remained limited in size and scope, even following its expansion under the later emperors. Most of the administrative work was carried out by unpaid magistrates, city councillors and the army, with only a very small bureaucratic structure in the capital. Significant work was done in the emperor's household by slaves and freedmen[68] rather than in a separate civil administrative structure, although there was greater regularization of the latter during the second century AD under the Antonine emperors.[69] Under Diocletian, the civil bureaucracy expanded considerably, building upon the increased autonomy it had been able to achieve during the succession of weak emperors in the third century. Nevertheless, throughout this period the central administrative structure was not large,[70] and given that entry to it usually involved connections and work in it required literacy, its membership was drawn from a narrow section of society.

The Projection of Central Power

Mesopotamia. In order for rule to be effective, the power concentrated at the centre had to be projected over the territory as a whole. But in the ancient empires, the development of bureaucratic structures to do this was very limited. In the Mesopotamian empires, the reliance on local magnates with local loyalties and perspectives, be they former local kings acting as clients or landowners who may have recently moved in as colonists,[71] severely restricted the capacity of the king to exert close control over his empire. In the Assyrian Empire, local officials actually stayed at the royal court and administered their territories from there.[72] Such local officials in the Assyrian Empire ran their regions as 'profit-making concerns' and the governorships could be inherited.[73] Local officials were completely at the mercy of the monarch; their wealth and power were a direct gift from him, reflecting the patrimonial nature of the administration. While the army could be used to project royal power, this was not an effective way of administering the state.

The position of the people in the structure of Mesopotamian rule is not clear. Although there were developed lists of laws,[74] the king's absolutism was not restricted by theories about limited government, citizenship, or human or natural rights. Under the Assyrian and Persian Empires, for example, all of the subjects were acknowledged as the 'slaves' of the monarch and were liable for regular service to the state through corvée, or forced, labour.[75] Indeed, such labour was probably common throughout the polities of this region given the apparent absence of widespread slavery and the scale of some of the public buildings that were erected. Many of the rural labourers were probably also tied to the land.[76] Certainly the people exercised no control over their rulers and there was little interdependence.

Egypt. The physical circumstances of the Egyptian state made the problem of controlling local officials less significant than it was in the Near Eastern empires. Egypt was the classic case of Mann's caged civilization. The state stretched along the Nile River, a narrow band of cultivable earth (made so by the annual Nile flood) bounded to the east and west by inhospitable desert. This meant not only that there was really nowhere for people to escape the projection of central power, but also there were no neighbouring hostile powers or marcher lords with which internal dissidents could link up.[77] Neither were there trading partners easily accessible and able to act as a magnet for Egyptian regions, drawing them away from the unified kingdom. Furthermore, the Nile provided a perfect means for communication and projection of power; the current flowed north, the prevailing winds blew south, so travel either way was relatively effortless. Access to irrigation water was not an issue except perhaps at the very local level,[78] and therefore this was not an issue that obstructed national unity. These conditions facilitated the establishment and maintenance (with some breaks) of central control over a prolonged period, but the problem of localization remained.

Initially in the Old Kingdom, the nobility was a service nobility, owing its status and wealth to the pharaoh. Such nobles usually occupied an official position in the administrative structure. However, over time, this service aspect became more attenuated. Egypt's economy was a moneyless economy. Consequently, in order to reward local officials, the pharaoh usually gave them land or the revenue from landed estates. Up to the end of the Fifth Dynasty, the centre relied principally upon palace-based supervisory officials who visited the regions at intervals to assert central control over local affairs. By the Sixth Dynasty, records show nobles holding land in their own right separate from that received from the pharaoh in return for service. By the late Old Kingdom–early Middle Kingdom, there was a nobility that possessed hereditary landed estates, wealth and status and they were able to exercise significant power over local inhabitants of all ranks. This situation was strengthened by the regularization of the administrative structure through the establishment of a governor resident in each nome (or province), although Lower Egypt (essentially the Nile delta area) may have continued to be ruled from the capital, Memphis, until the Middle Kingdom. This system seems to have lasted through the Middle Kingdom and into the New Kingdom.

What really enabled these local magnates to strengthen their local control was the First Intermediate Period. It was at this time that local elites became unambiguously the dominant forces in their regions,[79] a primacy they were able to carry forward into the Middle Kingdom, albeit with greater royal oversight.[80] With the establishment of the Middle Kingdom, it was from the ranks of these magnates that local officials were drawn. But it is important to recognize that, with the establishment of this hierarchical system of authority, there was no division of functions. The governor and his administration carried out many of the same functions as the central bureaucracy: he was the commander-in-chief of the nome army (which became part of the royal army if required), collected taxes, maintained order and justice, stored food and oversaw irrigation and, at least from the First Intermediate Period, was also the chief priest in the local temple. He had his own treasury, granaries, military command and household officials. According to Finer, 'His court was the pharaoh's court in miniature.'[81] The governor remained beholden to the pharaoh, owing direct allegiance to him and dependent upon royal favours. Following the central weakness of the Second Intermediate Period, when the New Kingdom was established local autonomy was restricted; in those areas outside Egypt which became part of the empire (Nubia, Palestine and Syria) where local rulers were left *in situ*, members of their families were often taken as hostages to Egypt to ensure continuing loyalty.[82] Generally local autonomy was restricted in the New Kingdom under strong pharaohs, and it was only when less able individuals took the throne after the first two pharaohs of the twentieth dynasty that local officials regained greater autonomy.

Rome. The Roman emperor had to project his power over a much larger geographical area than any of his predecessors, but he faced similar limitations. As one author argues, the Empire was a 'myriad of self-governing cities'; basically a 'superstructure for coordination and control' where high policy decisions were made, 'but the dynamics of workaday life came from the cities'.[83] City officials received no formal payment, although they were in a position to reap financial gain from their appointment. The lack of payment and the expectation that they would meet some of the costs of office from their own pockets was one factor in ensuring that power in the cities tended to be concentrated in the hands of the rich, who also commonly came to possess Roman citizenship. In Veyne's words, the cities 'were governed by notables, by a class or order of rich and prestigious individuals who saw politics as a state duty rather than as a profession or vocation'.[84] Unlike the governors, city councillors and magistrates were generally locals. In the third century the degree of city autonomy was eroded by central expansion, both in the form of closer supervision of the identity of the local leaders and denial of their right to issue currency. The sinews of central control resided in the means whereby the centre retained power over the governors and city councillors, who were the real rulers of the local cells of which the Empire consisted.

There were three main means whereby the centre maintained control over its agents throughout the Empire. First, the right of appointment of governors was concentrated in the emperor and the Senate; the former appointed those whose posts meant that they needed to command legions, the latter only a small body of troops.[85] Most governors were of senatorial rank, and therefore part of the Roman 'establishment'. The governor was a salaried official with only a very small personal staff to run the province, but (often of greater importance) he was also in a position to exploit his position for personal gain. However, the development of a relatively sophisticated legal system with provision for protection of the individual meant that throughout the Empire individuals had the right to bring suits against officials. At the end of their period of office (usually three years for imperial and one year for Senatorial appointments), governors could be prosecuted for corruption or extortion. At least in principle this provided an extra potential avenue of reportage to the centre about misdeeds of the local elites, and could constitute a check upon the power of the governors. In practice, it was difficult to get a conviction against former governors; members of the Senate tended to stick together. However, under the Principate, governors were brought more tightly under central control than they had been during the Republic.[86]

Second, the army played a crucial role in the administration of the empire. Augustus created a fully professional standing army, incorporated non-citizen auxiliaries into the military structure and apportioned legions and auxiliaries as permanent garrisons of individual provinces. The legions not only played a pacifying and defensive role, but they were also responsible for the construction of much of the infrastructure essential for imperial administration. Many of the major public works, especially roads and aqueducts, were constructed by the army. When they were not fighting, the soldiers constituted a vast labour force which the state used to develop its transport and communications infrastructure. The net-work of roads that criss-crossed the Empire facilitated not only trade, but the rapid movement of both officials and the military itself.[87] Given the stationing of significant numbers of troops throughout the provinces,[88] and given the emperor's formal position as commander-in-chief, the army constituted an arm of the administration that could be independent of local elites and therefore a check upon them. However, as pressure mounted on the Empire's borders from the second century, military demands increased. The rise of such challenges placed immense military and economic strains on the Empire, while the involvement of the army throughout much of the third century in the internecine warfare surrounding imperial succession struggles further weakened the Empire's capacity to cope with these challenges. The standard of the troops fell and increased reliance was had on foreign mercenaries and barbarian tribesmen. By the end of the fourth century, the army was led by foreign generals, foreign mercenaries dominated, the quality of the troops was low, and the civil authorities had lost control over their military forces. Given the decline in the vigour of civilian political institutions in the face of the expansion of the emperor's power, the erosion of the military as a cohesive unit subordinate to the emperor was a critical blow to the capacity of the Empire to survive. The early role of the military as an agent of romanization ceased to have much importance as it became itself less and less like the model of Roman citizenship it had been initially.

The third method was the generation and spread of Roman culture. One of the characteristics of the Empire is that a common Roman culture became diffused across it. Resting overwhelmingly upon literacy and fostered through the ideals of education and public service, generalized commitment to a set of Roman values became embedded in the citizenry, especially its higher levels. The effect was that the Empire was not seen as Romans ruling over others, but as Romans from diverse backgrounds sharing the rule of a common enterprise. In a concrete sense this was manifested in the way in which both membership of the Senate and individual emperors came from different parts of the Empire. By the time of Septimius Severus (193–211), Italians probably constituted less than 50 per cent of the Senate.[89] Turning to the emperors, Trajan and Marcus Aurelius were born in Spain, Septimius Severus came from North Africa, Macrinus was from Mauretania, and Diocletian came from Dalmatia, to name only a few. The result was the development of a ruling class culture uniting those who ruled the Empire. While this did not ensure complete obedience to the centre at all times, it did assist in the task of imperial administration.

Roman administration generally rested lightly upon the population, at least until the late second century AD. The prominent role of amateur notables ensured an absence of coherence and long term policy. The administrative weight of the state increased markedly in the Late Empire as the centre's needs for extra resources to fund the army and to deal with external challenge and internal disruption grew (see below). Government throughout the Empire, including at the city level, remained oligarchic, with the populace playing little direct role. Legislative organic interdependence was thus even narrower in the Empire than it had been in the Republic.

The ancient empires were therefore palace polities with power at the centre overwhelmingly concentrated in the king and his household. In both Egypt and Rome a distinct central bureaucracy was slow to emerge and was never able to develop as a powerful entity separate from the monarch. The projection of central power remained reliant upon the cooperation of local notables, even when central functionaries were despatched into the provinces, because of the continuing weakness of the infrastructural means for the exertion of central power. This reliance upon local notables does not represent bureaucratic organic interdependence; rather it is a case of the weakness of the state meaning that society itself had to take on part of the administrative load.

Only the wealthy were able to gain positions in the emergent bureaucracy, while in the only assembly that remained in action throughout the imperial period, the Roman Senate, the source of its membership remained socially narrow. There was therefore limited organic interdependence in the empires.

The Ancient State and Institutional Interdependence

Institutional interdependence is based principally in the economic sphere, and requires the state to enter an interactive and mutually supporting relationship with autonomous economic actors. This sort of relationship barely existed in the ancient world. None of these polities had integrated economies in the modern sense of that word. Economic life was organized and conducted overwhelmingly at the local and regional levels. It was based on the hamlet, the village, or even the household. All the states were dependent upon contacts through trade or tribute with sources of the goods which they needed from outside the region. The hamlets, villages and towns, while primarily locally-focused, were thereby locked into a larger set of commercial relations upon which their urban life style depended.[90] But even in the Egyptian and Roman empires, where there was a greater attempt to integrate these cellular modes of economic life into a more overarching system, economic life remained overwhelmingly locally/regionally focused. What role did the state play in the ancient economy?

Mesopotamia

The Mesopotamian city-state has been seen as an *oikos* (household),[91] concerned to produce goods for its members and satisfy its own needs rather than to trade with others, and as having a state-dominated redistributive economy; some argued that all of the land was owned by the temples/states, with the people working in a purely dependent relationship.[92] Certainly the king and his private domains were an important part in the overall production enterprise, while the temples played an important redistributive role, collecting grain surpluses for distribution in times of difficulty.[93] But beside this state sector there was also production by private households on estates and small farms[94] whose surpluses went into the central storehouses and granaries for redistribution in times of need and for the king to use as gifts. Marketplaces existed for the exchange of goods, especially those that could not be produced within the city-state (such as stone, timber and wood). The status of other land is not certain, but it may have been provided to officials as part of their formal positions (and was therefore lost when that ended) or leased out to tenants by the state. Indeed, sources suggest that there was extensive private property of land during this early period, although it seems to have played little economic role in southern Mesopotamia.[95] Most land-holders were probably in a dependent relationship with the state. There was private activity in trade,[96] contracting work done for building and other sorts of similar activities, but the private sphere remained dependent upon state patronage.

When the city-states were replaced by empires, both the same sort of economic structure based on independent nuclei and the dominance of the state through the royal and temple complexes continued to prevail.[97] But what the empire did and the city-state did not was try to exploit those nuclei (the villages and cities and their irrigated hinterlands) in a more systematic fashion, moving resources from these peripheral areas into the imperial core. Principally through taxes and tribute, the imperial overlords sought to utilize the conquered regions for economic gain. Their capacity to do this was restricted by the weakness of the administrative infrastructure and the propensity of local magnates to identify more with their local regions than with the centre. Nevertheless, with a standing army, the centre could mobilize coercion in its attempt to reap economic gain, but this was limited and episodic. Control over merchants, traders and artisans within the towns was more likely, because it was here that imperial officials were located, but even then the problem of local identification was relevant. Throughout the period many merchants conducted independent trading activities, although many also seem to have acted as agents for the palace or temple.[98] In Mann's view, this attempt at integrating economic activity through administrative/military pressure constituted 'compulsory cooperation',[99] and while it strengthened the state through expediting the flow of resources to it, it also strengthened those decentralized elites upon whom the centre relied to implement its programmes. Economic integration was therefore highly problematic and institutional interdependence effectively non-existent.

Egypt

State predominance was also evident in Egypt. Egypt was essentially a localized, subsistence economy resting on small-scale agricultural production and barter with householders seeking to supply their own needs rather than producing for a larger market. The evidence deriving from formal inscriptions makes no mention of private economic activity in the Old and Middle Kingdoms, although private land ownership did exist.[100] Productive land seems to have been of three types: royal estates owned by the crown, tax-exempt land belonging to pious foundations (the most important were those relating to the pharaoh's afterlife), and private land which was subject to tax. Major estates usually relied on serf labour. The surpluses that they produced as a result of the alluvial agriculture in which they were engaged was collected by the state to sustain the elite and for redistribution in times of difficulty.[101] The state held all parts of the economic activity of Egypt together. It collected the surplus grain, distributed it to its employees and stored it for times of need; it controlled the mining of precious metals and the conduct of foreign trade[102] upon which the community was reliant for a wide range of its needs; and it organized corvée labour for the construction of the great temples and tombs. Taxation was levied on the basis of an annual census and was paid in kind (usually grain) into state depots where it was retained until needed for payment to state beneficiaries or servants or to offset the effect of a poor harvest. Egypt was, in the words of one study:

> a classic example of the storage and redistribution type [of economy]. The palace was, amongst other things, an institution responsible for organizing the entire economy, collecting and storing wealth produced inside the country, acquiring foreign produce, and then filtering it back through the system as it was required. The assignment of substantial estates to temples and officials created secondary storage and redistribution centres, but these were always closely enmeshed with that of the palace and formed an integral part of it.[103]

Indeed the temples, which in the New Kingdom possessed about 33 per cent of Egypt's cultivable land and 20 per cent of its population,[104] and which had their own specialized administrative staff, artisans and labourers, were part of the state economic network.[105]

State control was most marked in the New Kingdom.[106] Taxes were extensive and foreign trade was a government monopoly, although private merchants still seem to have been present at least for some of this time.[107] The poorer part of the population was subject to corvée labour, both for special projects and continuing maintenance of infrastructure. Most agricultural workers on royal and temple estates worked in a servile condition with little effective legal protection. Direct state enterprise was widespread, including the construction of funerary buildings (the archaeological record does not have much evidence of public buildings), the establishment and construction of entire towns, and the management of redistributional activities through the state storage facilities. Given the absence of money, all public employees were paid in rations. This is a picture of an economy in which the state clearly plays the dominant role, but it is a role that is performed through administrative rather than market or money means. In Finer's words, Egypt was a 'state-*owned* economy … run, on a command basis' (emphasis in original)[108] with all wealth and revenue symbolically the property of the pharaoh. The personal domain of the New Kingdom pharaoh was huge, reflecting the way that the eighteenth dynasty had come to power by conquest, including seizing the estates of many regional notables. Furthermore, as the empire expanded, the flow of trade, tribute and booty greatly expanded the pharaoh's coffers. Such wealth was used both to consolidate the army's loyalty and to fulfil the manifold obligations to gift-giving that were the pharaoh's lot.[109]

Was there no private economic activity? A provincial landed nobility had emerged at least as early as the sixth dynasty and pursued its own economic activity[110] subject to state taxation. With many of these nobles doubling as state officials, the line between state and non-state activity was blurred. Individual artisans clearly did exist, but they do not appear to have been a large part of the population. There is no mention of professional merchants in Egyptian texts before 1000 BC.[111] Egypt was a country in which the state dominated economic life, and economic integration was achieved principally by administrative means rather than through institutional interdependence.

Greece

A very different form of economic organization occurred in the Greek polis. If the polis was the first political form in which large numbers of citizens could become involved in political life, this was because the cities were rich enough to be able to afford such a leisured class.[112] Most of the work was done by free peasants, dependent tenants and artisans, with slavery constituting a significant component of the city's labour force. Private ownership of land

and productive resources was the backbone of economic life, and the state did not play anything like the redistributive role so important in the palace and temple polities of the Near East.

The state played little role in economic life. The state was not directly involved in trade, except for some inter-polis regulation of it,[113] or in the regulation of employment or the resolution of labour disputes. The state did not follow a conscious economic policy, as opposed to making ad hoc decisions that had economic implications, and apart from a monopoly on mineral resources, other monopolies were rare.[114] The Athenian state's role in mining is clear evidence of its limited part in the economy; although it asserted ownership of the mines, exploitation was left to private citizens with the state exacting income for the leases and royalties on the produce.[115] There was little concern for the welfare of the poor, although in most poleis the authorities tried to ensure adequate food supplies for the city. Taxation was limited;[116] it was not levied on land, which was a clear privilege for the citizenry, while the absence of a growth in productivity denied the state the possibility of growing revenues from indirect taxation. The absence of an extensive central state infrastructure meant that this shortage of ready capital was not a major continuing problem, but it did become acute when sustained military activity was needed. While there was private activity in commercial, artisanal and financial (banking) spheres,[117] this barely intersected with state concerns and did not constitute a market economy.[118] The state's lack of engagement with the economy is shown by the fact that although it claimed the monopoly of the minting of coinage, it did not accept any obligation to ensure that there was sufficient available. Thus the Athenian state played little direct part in economic life.

Rome

The Roman economy, like that of Greece, was based primarily upon private ownership. The state was directly involved in some areas of activity, including the minting of the coinage, armaments factories and mines, but there were also significant areas of state activity that were privatized; the tax farming system of the Republic is a good instance, while the working of the mines, exploitation of the forests and fisheries and supply of salt could be contracted out to the publicani.[119] Trade was generally conducted by freedmen and foreigners while most manufacturing was carried on by small artisans and workmen, often formally slaves but able to act as if they were freedmen. Much of this activity was conducted through guilds or corporations authorized (and for many by the end of the third century, directed) by the state. By the time of Diocletian (AD 284–305), individuals could not prosper unless they belonged to a corporation. Throughout both the Republic and the Empire, agricultural production was dominated by a combination of small-scale free farmers and larger, usually absentee, landowners[120] whose land was worked by dependent labour.[121] Some 80–90 per cent of people worked on the land, with the bulk of the produce going into local markets; most of the economy was localized, and therefore cellular in nature. In the words of one scholar, rather than an economic system there was 'an enormous conglomeration of interdependent markets'.[122] Most activity was small-scale and local in provenance, with little evidence of money-lending for business purposes. There was, however, long distance trade in a whole range of goods, including luxury goods from China. The improved infrastructure provided by the Roman road system and the greater safety of navigation because of the elimination of piracy facilitated such trade. Similarly a single monetary system and the extension and enforcement of Roman law by the legions created a single economic area much more developed than any that had existed before. But the resultant Empire-wide trade was the surface layer on an economic network that was much more a congeries of local networks than a highly integrated Empire-wide economic system.[123]

Despite the basis of private ownership, economic life in the empire was not capitalist.[124] This is because the structuring of life chances and access to wealth were not market determined but largely shaped by the state. During the extension of empire under the Republic, the conquest of the future provinces was a major source of wealth. Substantial quantities of booty[125] went to the state to finance public works in the late Republic, but a significant amount also went into the hands of the conquering generals, although they were expected to use much of this to erect a public building for the community. But more important than the booty from conquest was the continuing right senior Roman officials had to gain tribute and wealth from the provinces, a right that was particularly important given the prejudice held by the ruling aristocracy against wealth gained through business activities and the prohibition on senators engaging in commerce.[126] One scholar has argued that, under the Republic, more of the profits from the provinces flowed into the pockets of the Roman upper class than into the state treasury.[127] The Senate accorded to particular consuls the right of rule over particular provinces for the tenure of their consulship. Being given a rich province ensured that the consul would be well set up financially at the end of his tenure; being given a poor province was likely to be a major handicap to the accumulation of wealth. With a similar process in train under the Empire, this meant that significant amounts of wealth and resources generated from the provinces remained outside any market system; they were determined administratively by the state. While the extent of this differed from time to time, its dimensions, especially cumulatively, were significant.

An important non-market aspect of the place of wealth in Roman society is reflected in its use in politics in the late Republic. During this period there was a clear link between political success and the ability to use financial resources both to bribe officials and voters and to put on major public displays, usually in the form of games. The periods leading up to elections for major positions were always ones in which rivals sought to put on the best public displays in order to win over the allegiance of the voters.[128] This conspicuous consumption had become central to the conduct of politics, and while it may have had short-term stimulatory effects on the urban economy, generally it was not an economically productive use of resources. It led to high levels of indebtedness to money-lenders among those noble families who dominated the search for office at this time. This was a major reason why successful election as a consul was so important; access to the resources of the province over which one was given imperium was often necessary to defray the costs of election. When the Empire replaced the Republic, the complex of gift-giving and conspicuous consumption (called *euergetism*, or 'the economy of the gift'[129]) was taken over by the emperor. With the wealth of the Empire at his disposal, he used the construction of public buildings and facilities and the provision of bread and circuses to buttress his position in the minds of the citizens of Rome and to fulfil the sense of obligation that was broadly seen to attach to the possession of wealth. Only the emperor could make gifts to the Roman state.[130] Spending in this way was therefore not undertaken for economic reasons, but from a sense of honour and obligation embedded in the community and to advance their political aspirations.[131] Such gift-giving was not viewed as corruption, but as part of the normal process of life throughout both Republic and Empire.

Much of the stimulus for trade was provided, albeit indirectly, by the state. The extent of central taxation, of the administrative redirection of wealth away from the provinces and into the centre, meant that if local elites were to survive, they too had to extract wealth from the localities. Trade was one means of doing this. Furthermore the levels of economic activity were also related to the availability of coin and, given the absence of fiduciary instruments, this meant that economic life was dependent upon the state's willingness to mint enough coin for all needs. But the minting of coin was a by-product of the state's administrative needs, not a response to economic requirements, and therefore the failure to produce sufficient hard currency by the state, followed from the mid–late first century AD by the progressive devaluation of the currency through official debasement of the coinage,[132] constituted a brake on the development of economic life.

Much state income was spent on maintenance of the army, expenditure which did have an economic dimension. The army was a significant stimulus to economic activity in the areas in which it was quartered, which for much of the life of the Empire was in the poorer and economically underdeveloped border provinces such as Britain, the Rhineland, and the Danube area. Not only did the army stimulate economic activity by its role in pacification and in the building of infrastructure, but its presence also created a major source of demand for the local economy. This 'legionary economy'[133] was a major element in economic life across the Empire. But again this meant that local economic development was at the mercy, in large part, of administrative decision.

The functioning of a market was also undermined by state action. An important aspect of this was the state's role in acquiring large quantities of grain to ensure that the poor of Rome did not go hungry. The extent of state acquisition was significant, and so was its means: it was mostly gained not through the activities of merchants (although some was purchased), but by taxation or requisition implemented through local officials, or it was produced on public and imperial estates.[134] This posed a serious obstacle to the emergence of a genuine grain market in the Empire,[135] even had there been the levels of information flow between centres of production and consumption to enable market forces. In any case, the operation of this massive system of state supply of grain also reflects the failure of private suppliers to supply the required quantity of grain to the populace at a realistic price; transport costs were too high to enable private traders to supply enough grain to meet popular needs. Generally state reliance upon its own administrative structure and upon labour corvée rather than entering into commercial transactions meant that it overshadowed private enterprise.[136] For example, its reliance upon requisition to ensure the supply of foodstuffs to the army during the third century meant that a significant part of the produce was removed from the market by state administrative action. Individual state decisions also disrupted the functioning of markets, such as the second century BC decision prohibiting the production of wine and oil in Gaul which would have competed with Italian production.

Although state action shaped economic activity, the state had no clear and consistent economic policy,[137] except perhaps under Diocletian. Decisions were made on the basis of the information available to the centre, but there was little attempt to generate an overall policy for the economy. Unlike the Greek polis, the state did attempt to exercise some control over interest rates legislatively, with some success.[138] The centre did have a sense of income and expenditure, and of the need to have currency available to meet its needs, but there was no overall policy. Initially the state relied for its funds on conquest, booty, tribute, tax and bribes (which enabled the Roman wealthy to avoid having to bear too heavy a burden for the sustenance of the state). After the Empire reached its territorial maximum, and the aim of the emperor was to maintain it rather than expand it, the centre relied overwhelmingly upon taxation.[139] The principal prop to state coffers was the tax on land, a tax inevitably passed on to the poor and middle classes while the wealthy escaped much of the financial burden.[140] But the problem was that, given the relative absence of innovation in production techniques over the life of the Empire, this was not a growing source of income. This meant that in times of crisis when extra funds were needed, the regular system was inadequate. With no means of borrowing large amounts of money, other ways had to be found; Marcus Aurelius sold public property while Domitian, Septimius Severus, Caracalla and Maximinus all confiscated personal possessions. The overwhelming reliance upon local notables for tax collection following the demise of the tax farming system and the centre's inability to exercise effective control over them also restricted the centre's access to what tax funds there were. This occurred in a time when, from the late second century, the demands for defence in the face of barbarian pressure were rising and therefore even greater funds were needed. Furthermore, given that there was virtually no distinction between the funds of the state and those of the emperor,[141] and all funds were administered by the emperor, the continued funding of state activity was precarious.

The state did become more directly involved in economic life at various times. For example, under Trajan (98–117) the state moved 'towards completer control of the national economy and revenue through more stringent assessment and enforcement of taxation, increased direction or compulsion of labour, compulsory state leases, and armies of officials to enforce these requirements'.[142] State regulation reached its peak under Diocletian (284–305). Compulsory labour was intensified and measures were introduced seeking to lock people into the guilds and essential professions (including government service) and on to the land.[143] Exactions in kind were regularized into a formal system based upon a detailed census, thereby providing some indication of future state revenues, which was one step towards a state budget. In an attempt to stem the inflation fuelled by the progressive devaluation of the currency, Diocletian issued an edict that sought to fix maximum prices for all goods and maximum wages for all workers in all parts of the Empire. The size of the state bureaucracy grew and, with the increased danger from without, extra resources had to be directed into the military sphere. The resulting increased 'use of taxes in kind and levies for other supplies for the military, as well as for the court and bureaucracy, limited the sphere of activities of private traders and cut into their profits'.[144] This constituted an attempt at massive state intervention in the economy which, despite failing to achieve its aims, 'declares the official death of the world of free exchange and uncontrolled laissez-faire economic activity.'[145] In the third century the state became the largest landed proprietor, the biggest owner of mines and quarries and the most important industrial producer.[146] But even given the increased state role, this did not become a fully state-run economy: state activity in industry was directed more towards controlling the organization and fulfilment of the workers' responsibilities than in directly controlling their role in production; the state was directly concerned only in the production of goods it needed and was less concerned about broader issues of consumer supply; and the private trade sector retained a degree of autonomy and importance. Thus even when the Roman state was most involved in economic life, its real concerns were quite narrow and did not embrace the entirety of economic activity.

In the ancient world, even when the state played a major part in economic activity, its role was essentially administrative. It sought to ensure the exploitation of economic activity and resources rather than to participate in their growth and development. It did not generally seek to cooperate with autonomous actors to structure economic activity, but to organize the flow of resources into state coffers. There was almost no institutional interdependence; rather there was attempted administrative organization as the state sought to ensure its capacity to tax. But this aspiration was continually frustrated by the weakness of infrastructural power at the state's disposal.

The Ancient State

Despite their differences, the ancient states shared a number of common features, although this is less true of the Greek poleis and the Roman Republic than of the other polities surveyed. These states were all based on cities, which is in sharp contrast to the communities which surrounded them. Political authority was rooted strongly in the beliefs fostered by the state and shared, to different degrees, by the population. In the Near East and Egypt, the position of the ruler was explicitly legitimized by reference to the doctrinal principles of the major belief system. In Greece and Republican Rome, the political arrangements were based on assumptions of a more secular nature, related directly to the form of the state and the notion of citizenship, while during the Roman Empire these principles became overlaid with elements of a more sacral kind. Except in the Greek poleis and Republican Rome, politics was structured around an individual ruler and was conducted primarily within the bounds of the royal palace. The symbolic merging of state and emperor was common. Except in the city-states, there was continuing tug of war between the ruler and his personal entourage and an emergent civil bureaucracy. In all cases, but especially in the larger states, the weakness of the infrastructure of administration ensured that central control remained remote and episodic rather than continuing and close. State penetration of society was weak and arbitrary, organic interdependence brittle and narrow, and the flow of information into the centre uncertain. These agrarian states relied overwhelmingly upon the land-owning elite for basic administration throughout the countryside. The state sat at the top of society, rooted only in the upper classes and possessing little real penetrative power. It had greater capacity to prevent things from happening than to instigate and carry them through.[147]

The state's relationship with the populace was attenuated. Not only did distance and undeveloped infrastructure hinder the growth of a tight link, but generally many of the populace looked upon the state with distrust and suspicion. When agents of the state appeared, it was usually in the form of the tax gatherer or the soldier, and in both cases local inhabitants usually had to surrender some of their resources. So the state appeared arbitrary, predatory and exploitative, and was therefore distrusted.[148]

In the economic sphere, there was no developed market system or even an integrated economic system functioning in any of these polities. The economy was local and cellular, with the people interacting economically with those in the immediate vicinity. Certainly their produce was taken farther afield, but this was more often through acquisition by or on behalf of the state rather than through long distance trade in which independent local producers were involved. The elite were involved in longer distance trade, at least in the sense that they bought luxury items which often came from regions far distant, but this was a very thin layer of economic activity compared with economic life as a whole. Production surpluses were taken by the elite through the state to sustain their style of life based upon conspicuous consumption. For these elite, the main aim of economic life was not the generation of capital for productive investment but the accumulation of wealth for status, prestige and consumption. Although there was an underlay of private enterprise and initiative, in all polities except the polis, states played a major driving role in economic life. But their role was chiefly administrative and organizational rather than interdependent and productive; they were less actors in an economic milieu along with other actors than the primary organizers of economic activity at the national level. State activity was not directed systematically at building up the power of the state in the form the mercantilists were to advocate many centuries later, but at sustaining the army, keeping the population pacified, and maintaining the elite life style.

There are also systematic differences between the different types of state, however. There are clear distinctions between the city-states of Sumer, Athens and Republican Rome on the one hand, and the imperial monarchies of the Near East and Imperial Rome on the other.[149] The city-states (except for Sumer) differed from the empires in the rooting of legitimacy in the state and citizenship rather than in the gods. They were the source of the republican tradition and, by extension, the democratic principles that were to become so important more than a millennium and a half later. Furthermore, Athens and Republican Rome recognized the separation between the person and political office, with authority stemming from the latter rather than the former. They recognized that government was different from ownership and that the ruler should not treat the state as if it was his personal property. In the monarchies, the principle of rule was patrimonial, with resources belonging to the emperor. But despite this reliance upon an ascendant notion of legitimation, and the corresponding principle of reliance upon the citizenry as a whole for the conduct of affairs of state, the city-states still lacked the infrastructure to be able to establish and maintain continuing administrative control over the territory. Being smaller, the city-states could get by without an extensive bureaucracy and, although it would be an exaggeration to say that the monarchies possessed such a structure, their bureaucracies were more complex and developed. Despite commonality of citizenship and ideological integration, continuing control was beyond these states. The lower level of bureaucratization of the city-state and its reliance upon a citizen army, rather than a standing army as in the monarchies (at least at their highest form of development), meant that the need for taxes was less and state financing could be more ad hoc. There was little systematization in the monarchies. The city-states also differed from the monarchies in that they saw themselves as part of international systems of other city-states whereas the monarchies did not accept other actors as equals, preferring to see them simply as 'barbarians'. Finally, the state sought to play a much more intrusive role generally in economic affairs in the monarchies than in the city-states (again with the exception of those in Sumer).

Clearly the ancient states did not have in a developed form any of the characteristics of the modern state. There was no clear separation between specialized institutions of government and administration. The city-states lacked a separate central bureaucracy altogether, while the bureaucracies of the monarchical empires were overwhelmingly patrimonial in nature and lacked the rationalized specialization and internal differentiation characteristic of their modern counterparts. Central authorities in all of these states claimed to be sovereign without using that word, but given the infrastructural weakness from which they all suffered, they had difficulty in projecting this across the territory they claimed to rule. This was reflected in practice in the fact that the central authorities often lacked a monopoly of legitimate force; for example, nome governors in Egypt and local commanders in Imperial Rome were also able to demand the loyalty of state armed forces. The problems with projecting central power and question marks over the precise location of borders, indeed perhaps even the replacement of clear borders by the existence of ambiguous semi-contested zones, compromised the notion of territorial boundaries of the ancient states, even if the focus of these states was clearly territorial. Thus while these states may have had a high degree of centralization of political authority in the centre, in practice as geographical entities they were much more loosely held together.

In terms of relationship with society too, the ancient states were very different from their modern counterparts. Interdependence was weakly developed in all of the ancient states. Through the various assemblies in the city-states there was a link of legislative organic interdependence between the state and sections of the populace, but this was with a minority of the people. In the Greek polis, the restriction of participation to citizens meant that the state lacked connection with most of those who lived under its rule, while in Rome the assemblies were dominated by those who lived in the city itself, with the result that those who lived elsewhere in the growing empire were not organically connected to the state. Organic bureaucratic interdependence was also weakly developed. The extent to which emergent bureaucratic structures were dominated by members drawn from narrow social constituencies (rulers' household, aristocrats, priests), added to the propensity of these to turn themselves into semi-closed castes, attenuated any connections these people would have had with the wider society. The reliance upon local magnates for regional control and administration potentially gave the central state a channel of connection with the society more broadly, but the effectiveness of this was limited by the propensity of such magnates to give primary loyalty to the locality rather than the centre. This could, of course, be offset by the reliance of the magnates upon the centre for things such as prestige, position and resources, thereby establishing a sense of interdependence, but this was not reinforced and strengthened by bureaucratic links. The relative disconnection of ancient states from society means that the principal form of integration of society and state was ideological and military–administrative rather than economic. State and society were held together by administrative links, but because these did not penetrate very deeply into society, they may have tied the upper levels of society to the state while leaving the lower levels less well-integrated into the structure. This means that the infrastructural power of these states was weak and their capacity limited; the state lacked the capacity administratively to project political, economic and ideological power in a routine fashion into the lower levels of society. It was these weaknesses that the feudal and early modern states sought to overcome.

3

The Feudal and Early Modern State

The ancient state remained infrastructurally weak and possessing limited capacity. These characteristics were principally because of the limited development of a coherent, well-organized bureaucratic infrastructure and the narrow basis of organic interdependence enjoyed by the state. In feudal and early modern times, major attempts were made to overcome these weaknesses as the national state developed as the principal political form in Western Europe. There were two basic models of state-building in the most successful states: organic and overarching.

With the fall of the Roman Empire, the development of state capacity generally atrophied in the West. The territorial disintegration of the former imperial domains and associated breakdown of centralized rule led to the emergence of a large number of small political units in which political development was retarded. It was the later dynamic between feudalism and the emergent national state structure that stimulated the development of state capacity, but such a development was by no means certain. One scholar has argued that in the thirteenth century there were a number of possible alternative courses of development open to the polities of Europe:[1]

- the national state which actually emerged from about 1500
- a political federation or empire controlled loosely from a single centre, such as the Holy Roman Empire or the Habsburg Empire
- a theocratic federation held together by the structure of the Church, such as the Papal States
- an intensive trading network without large-scale political organization, such as the Hanseatic League based on towns or the northern Italian city-states
- persistence of the feudal structure

This list of possibilities is another way of saying that relations between people and communities during feudalism were based on a variety of different principles:

1 Territorial – the sharing of a common territory.
2 Personal – ties of mutual obligation linking individuals in a series of dyadic relationships. This was the essence of the feudal structure.
3 Ideological – the presence of a common culture that united most closely the nobility but also extended to the ordinary people. It was reflected in the use of Latin as a common elite language, but was most strongly evident in the hold Christianity had on the population, a hold given concrete form by the role of the Church centred in Rome. Indeed, the Church constituted an alternative basis of affiliation uniting believers and providing them with an hierarchical structure which gave form and substance to their religious convictions.
4 Commercial – links between communities based upon their involvement in common trading networks. Such networks could be localized, in which case they were vulnerable to the extension of territorial control, or long distance (as in the Hanseatic League).

For the national state to emerge supreme, the territorial principle had to become the dominant form of organizing large-scale society. This had to be combined with the centralization of power and authority within that territory. It is this process, the centralization of power and authority on a territorial basis, which led to the emergence of the national state and its dominance in Western Europe. The core areas of the first modern states (and those which provided the model for others to copy) were to be found, in those areas where feudalism was strongest, southeast England, the Paris basin and Castile.[2] How did feudalism provide a basis for modern state development, especially given that its personalist essence seems so far removed from that of the state? Indeed, in the words of two scholars, tenth- and eleventh-century feudalism 'was the very opposite of the modern concept of the state'.[3]

The Feudal System

The heart of feudalism was the set of mutual obligations between vassal and lord. At its simplest, the king gave to his vassals rights over the land and appurtenances and jurisdiction over the peasants who lived on that land. This benefice was not a grant of ownership over the land, but one of conditional tenure whereby the vassal retained control over the land as long as he provided military support to the king when the latter needed it. If the vassal should die, the land in theory reverted to the king, who could confirm a new vassal in possession of it. The effect of this system was to give local magnates control over their lands and all that happened on them. The peasants were serfs and the magnate was able to exploit their labour in order to generate a surplus to sustain his own life style, including building up his military means. The magnate also had the right to exercise judicial control over this area, meting out justice to his own vassals and serfs. The magnate was the focus of local government and administration, taking decisions upon all of those issues to do with local life that were brought before him. He was responsible for the maintenance of order and the collection of taxes; a fief gave jurisdiction and government over the population of that land 'to the exclusion of the granting authority'.[4] This means that both the local economy and local governance were in the hands of the local magnate. But the public office performed by the magnate was a result of his private obligations to his lord. In this sense, the private and public were inextricably intertwined. Public duty became 'a form of rent paid for the use of land and enforced by a private contract'.[5] The magnate could also enfeoff some of the lands he held from the king to his own vassals, again in return for services rendered, usually of a military type. Thus while the king may have been at the top of the feudal hierarchy, real rule lay with territorial magnates whose principal profession was that of bearing arms and who constituted, in the words of one scholar, a '*consortium* of landholding warriors'.[6] But even at this level rule was indirect, exercised through vassals. The essence of this was personal obligation; feudalism was rule over people, not land.

Formally, the king was considered to be the owner of all the enfeoffed land in the country; it was his patrimony. This was why he was able to pass part of his land into the hands of the magnates. But in doing so, the king's control over the land became indirect. His authority over the mass of the population was mediated through the magnates, and it was they who exercised practical control on the ground. If a magnate enfeoffed some of his vassals, those vassals owed obligations to that magnate, not to the king. The king's capacity to control the magnates was, initially, quite restricted. If the magnate refused to respond to the king's summons to lend military support, in theory the king could deprive that magnate of his holdings, but in practice this was not easy. The magnate possessed his own armed force and, if it came to conflict, there was no guarantee that the king would prevail. The bargain between lord and vassal had rights and responsibilities on both sides. If the vassal believed that the lord had not met his responsibilities, he could legally end the relationship; if the lord believed a vassal was in default of his obligations, he could formally terminate the tenancy. Both outcomes would probably have to be supported by force. The feudal state was thus comprised of layers of actors who were autonomous in practice but who owed fealty to others. Rule, such as it was, was indirect, exercised through vassals. In the words of one scholar, the ruler's powers were:

> feeble and indirect. His ritual functions and the infrastructure of literacy for his bureaucracy were controlled by a transnational church; his juridical authority was shared with church and local manorial courts; his military leadership was exercised only at times of crisis and over retainers of other lords; and he had virtually no fiscal or economically redistributive powers.[7]

The capacity of the feudal state to exercise central power was even lower than that of many ancient states. For the mass of the populace, affairs at court were of little direct consequence; their world was local, and the principal forces within it were local also.

The essence of this structure was the personal nature of the tie between lords and vassals. Each vassal owed personal obligations to the lord, with the land being symbolic of that tie. The political structure that emerged on this basis was therefore not territorial in nature, although its physical expression was reflected in land-holding. It was a structure that relied upon personal ties regardless of geographical location. The lands of one lord's vassals could be scattered among the lands of another lord's vassals, creating a geographical mosaic of personal dyadic ties. This situation could be further complicated if a person was the vassal of two lords, holding different parcels of land from each of them. If those two lords came into conflict and both sought to mobilize the support of their vassals, that common vassal was faced with a problem: either carry out one set of his obligations by supporting one of the protagonists, or break both by supporting neither. Kings were not immune from this problem. With the Norman invasion of England in 1066, the English king effectively became a vassal of the French king for those lands he held on the continent, including those lands that were part of the later Angevin empire in western France.[8]

This situation, where individuals of noble birth (be they kings or local magnates) controlled territories in return for giving military support to their superiors, has been called one of 'parcellized sovereignty'.[9] This decentralized structure seems to be a poor breeding ground for the emergence of the more centralized, integrated modern state. The feudal king exercised little direct power. In England, which had been unified in 954 under Eadred and where centralizing policies had been followed by some of his successors,[10] a strong monarchy was set in place by the Normans, but even here the king needed to tread carefully in his dealings with his noble magnates: John fought against his barons and finally had the Magna Carta forced upon him, Henry III and Edward II had to face open challenges from the nobles with the latter being forced to abdicate, while Richard II was deposed in a coup. In France, where regional magnates were stronger than in England,[11] the king was forced to negotiate with his nobles over all issues of importance. The king could command but, if his vassals refused to comply, there was little that he could do short of going to war against them. And to do this, he needed the support of at least some of those vassals since his personal forces were often no greater than those of his vassals. In effect this meant that there was no accepted centre of sovereignty. Worse, effective power was shifted down the hierarchy as the only people who could bring about direct effects upon those below them were the magnates upon the serfs. All other relationships, based as they were upon personal ties, were practically unenforceable. The complexity of the structure (different vassals could have different sets of obligations to the same lord) meant that everything had to be individually negotiated. Furthermore, because of the presence of sub-vassals where land had been enfeoffed by a vassal to one of his own vassals, some of those negotiations involved three or more partners. This was a structure, disarticulated, decentralized and cellular, which could not survive intact. It dispersed and fragmented power, creating a situation of what one scholar has termed 'feudal entropy'.[12] If left to develop in accord with its own dynamic, it could only lead to fragmentation. How, then, did it contribute to the emergence of the modern state?

An important aspect of feudalism was its law-governed nature. Under feudalism there was no distinctive corpus of law laid down by an independent authority which all obeyed, but the system was itself governed by rules and agreements which were considered to be binding. People had an acknowledged status in the overall structure, and with that status went certain rights and obligations. If those rights and obligations were infringed, the wronged party had the right of redress, even if in practice it was difficult to realise this. This principle had three implications for political authority and its exercise. First, the structure of rights and obligations implied a hierarchy with the king at the top. Without the fiction that all of the land belonged to the king which he could then pass to vassals in return for service, the whole structure of mutual rights and obligations running through society and ultimately tying everyone to the centre had no intellectual underpinning. Thus although in practice these rights and obligations tended to promote centrifugal tendencies, they implied an overall system with the king at the top. In this sense, feudal law created a 'material and ideological framework for political cohesiveness' that was absent in non-feudal areas.[13] Second, it provided a justification for opposition to the wrongful exercise of power by political authorities, thereby laying a basis for notions of limited government. Third, these rights and obligations existed independently of formal political authority. They rested on the principle of dyadic personal relations, and although this particular basis of rules was to disappear, this constituted recognition of the principle that rules could have an existence independent of the supreme political authority; law did not have to be a political tool of the ruler. This also established the principle that the basis upon which differences should be resolved and disputes settled was the rights and obligations embedded in the system.

The rules embedded in the stronger feudal states also aided states' development in two other ways. First, feudal law and custom prevented the sale and division of land-holdings, thereby contributing to the consolidation of such holdings and the creation of larger units.[14] Where laws of primogeniture did not prevail, as in Russia, land-holdings were subject to continuing division as generation succeeded generation, with the result that the local units became successively smaller. Such fragmentation did not apply in the more strongly feudal areas where the larger units could make better building blocks for broader unity, if the people in control of them could be subdued (see below). Second, dyadic ties often linked the possessors of fiefs in different regions, thereby creating ties of obligation which cut across territorial divisions. Although these were personal in nature, they did tie together different parts of the countryside that otherwise would have been seen as definably different units. In this sense, they created a basis for the development of a sense of identity broader than a lord's own immediate area.

Feudal arrangements were undercut by a series of developments:

1 The centrifugal tendencies inherent in the feudal structure also created significant pressures towards the centralization of rule. Important here were implications of the place of law and of rules noted above. The underpinning of this system by recognition of the primacy of the king fuelled in the monarch aspirations to turn that ideological primacy into practical rule, and although similar aspirations may have been harboured by some of the nobles, ultimately centralization was brought about under royal auspices. Furthermore, although it was all very well to accept that disputes should be resolved according to the rules, to make this practicable there was a need for a locus of sovereignty which could pass down judgement.

2 The transformation of fiefs into inheritable property.[15] The longer a particular fief was held by one family, the greater the propensity on all sides to consider it private property. This transformation from conditional to absolute tenure robbed feudalism of its essential axis and eroded the power and position of the monarch.

3 The growing commercialization of the economy in the eleventh century,[16] including its monetization, undercut the principle of in kind fulfilment of obligations and made the supply of military force by the magnates to the king redundant. Rather than providing knights, many chose to pay the king in cash to discharge their obligations. Payment rather than service became the norm.[17]

4 This was linked to the tendency of kings increasingly during the 1200s to turn to mercenaries rather than the feudal levy to conduct their wars. This change was prompted by the commercialization of the economy, the limitations on the availability of feudal levies (e.g., they generally were available only for periods of 40 days, and there was always uncertainty as to whether they would actually turn up to support the king), the extent of warfare, and the new availability of soldiers for rent.

5 The commercialization of the economy stimulated the development of towns as centres of independent activity. Utilizing the parcellized sovereignty of feudalism to create some autonomy

for themselves from both royal and noble control, the burghers in the towns became a new element in the socio-political equation and one that did not fit into the feudal pattern.[18]

6   The development of functional corporate communities, which by the fourteenth century had taken the form of estates or orders. These combined people of the same status position – nobles, clergy, burghers – and accorded to them collectively their own privileges, rights and obligations. The growth of these collective bodies, and ultimately their representation in assemblies, undercut the principle of the feudal dyadic relationship.

Against the background of these developments, the kings in England and France set out on a course that was to end in the emergence of the national state. They sought to centralize power and authority in their hands within a broadly, if vaguely, defined territory. This process necessitated beating off the challenge to royal sovereignty posed by external actors, and reducing the rights and prerogatives possessed by the landed nobility. The chief means of doing this was the consolidation and centralization of administrative power. There were two different models of this process of state-building: an organic model in England and an overarching model in France.

The Consolidation and Centralization of Administrative Power

It is important to avoid a teleological approach to the subject of state development. Not all state builders set out with the conscious intent of building up the sort of state that existed on the eve of the French Revolution, let alone today. The growth of the state may, as Mann has observed, have been 'less the result of conscious power aggrandizement than of desperate searches for temporary expedients to stave off fiscal disaster',[19] but this does not mean that the kings did not pursue a course of expanding their power at the expense of those who stood in the way of this. Mann's 'fiscal disaster' may at times have been the result of ostentatious life style, but it was just as likely to be a function of the attempt to project royal authority. The principal mechanisms for state construction were territorial consolidation and the centralization of power and authority through the construction of a central bureaucratic apparatus. Implicit in both of these processes was overcoming the autonomous power wielded by other actors in the society.

A first step here was the rejection of the aspirations to temporal control possessed by the Church. The Church was the only translocal organization which, by 1000, bridged the Continent. But it did so by claiming not territorial jurisdiction, but ideological primacy. It provided the ideological normative system of Christianity which unified the multitude of cellular communities that constituted the feudal landscape.[20] In the eleventh and early twelfth centuries, the clash between king and pope increased in scope and intensity, but from this point the Church's power began to wane, finally being broken at the time of the Reformation. The rolling-back of Church aspirations marked the end of the transnational challenge and the ascendancy of the nation state as the dominant form in Western Europe.[21] It also substantially strengthened the state's capacity to wield ideological power, even if this continued to be shared with the Church.

The elimination of the power of the Church as a challenger to secular state power was a crucial step on the way to the development of a separate state administrative structure and, ultimately, to the modern state. But crucial also was the structuring of domestic power and the breakdown of feudal relations. The consolidation and centralization of power had two major aspects: the development of infrastructural power through growth of royal machinery of government and administration (essentially the construction of a royal bureaucracy), and the winding-back of the rights and prerogatives of the local magnates or nobles. These were two sides of the one coin, because the extension of central bureaucratic control constituted a revocation of many of the rights and privileges enjoyed by the regional magnates. At the outset of this process, there was a clear distinction between the royal domains and those of the regional magnates. The income from each of these supported different things. The royal domains provided most of the material resources for the sustenance of the king and his household; most of the expenses of the royal court initially were derived from this source, along with fines imposed by the royal courts, dues owed by his vassals, and taxes imposed on the movement of goods through specific points such as ports and bridges. That is why, to the extent that one can talk of a national government in the feudal period, the description of it as a patrimony is close to the truth. The very existence of the court relied overwhelmingly upon the lands held by the king in person. Similarly in the regions, the power and position of the local magnate depended upon the resources he could exploit from the lands under his control. This was part of the feudal bargain. But given that the magnate had responsibility for general law and order within his region, local government was also patrimonial, but it was the patrimony of people different from the king. This patchwork of patrimonies constituted a major barrier to the growth of the modern national state. If the regional patrimonies were left intact or if they were strengthened, they could prove formidable obstacles for any leader seeking to weld them into a more coherent and integrated political unit. This was the story of the Holy Roman Empire. By the same token, if a king wished to build a national state, he had to break down those patrimonies and replace them with his own rule. But to do so, he had to create a bureaucratic structure to project his rule. This is what the English and French kings in the eleventh and twelfth centuries began to do.

The attempt to consolidate royal power began from very different starting points in England and France, and this profoundly affected the pattern of developments in each country. The Norman conquerors found in England a unified kingdom[22] divided into sub-units, the shires and counties, in each of which, as well as a noble landowner, there was a royal official (the shire reeve) and a form of local government involving the free male population. This high level of local involvement in matters such as dispensing justice, maintaining order and organizing local defence and revenue collection[23] undercut the position of the local magnate compared with his counterparts on much of the Continent. It therefore weakened him *vis-à-vis* the Crown when the king sought to strengthen central power. Furthermore, the unified kingdom meant that the superiority of a single ruler was widely recognized and the territorial integrity of the English (not British) state was not in question. The king ruled the land with the assistance of the nobles.

The Normans were thus faced with a centralized kingdom with a tradition of local government that neither coincided with nor relied upon the personal obligations between king and nobles. When the Normans came to power under William I in 1066, they instituted a strengthened kingship[24] established through conquest and resting on powerful traditions of Norman rulership[25] and they maintained the earlier administrative system,[26] simply substituting the existing Anglo-Saxon nobles with those of Norman extraction who accompanied the Conqueror. However, in distributing those lands, William ensured that parcels of land were not concentrated, so that by 1100 no noble was in the position of being able to establish a consolidated administration. Furthermore, from 1086 all land-holders, not just the king's own vassals, owed fealty to the king, even against their own lords.[27] The Norman kings also inherited a number of traditions from Anglo-Saxon times: the principle of a national military force, the absence of the right present in France for local magnates to wage private war, and the right of the king to levy national taxation.[28] The Norman feudal system was thus grafted on to the older structure, retaining significant elements of it.

In contrast, when the Capetian dynasty came to power in the Île de France around Paris in 987, the country that was to be France comprised a large number of principalities, and the position of king itself was elected (reflecting the Carolingian tradition). The regional magnates were much more powerful than their English counterparts; vassals owed fidelity only to their immediate overlords and they retained the right to engage in private warfare. This was not ended until the fifteenth century. The dynasty had therefore both to establish its own suzerainty based on descent and to widen its control over regions that had not been united in a close political form for many years. France was not a centralized kingdom with a structure of local government under a central administrative hub; rather, it was a territory that was politically structured by the lines of personal obligation to feudal lords. This difference was to be crucial in a number of respects:

1 In England, differences between king and vassals did not constitute arguments about the territorial integrity of the state but about relative rights and obligations within that state. In France, such differences called the very state into question. English differences legitimated divisions within the political entity, while in France they questioned whether there should be a single entity.

2 The notion of a centralized kingdom, added to the tradition of royal consultation with the nobles, established the principle of the involvement of the nobles in the government of the territorially-defined kingdom, not simply in the working through of feudal obligations. With the issue of the state not in question in England, feudal obligations could be transformed into rights against the ruler. When the state was in question and the territorial issue was defined in feudal terms, as in France, there was less basis for noble involvement in governmental affairs because their concerns could be cast purely in terms of the personal relationships of feudalism.

3 The presence in England of a local administration wider than the nobility gave a broader basis for government in the countryside,

and strengthened pressures for broader representation in consultative councils at the centre, and more deeply rooted administration in society.

The obstacles faced by the French monarchs were therefore much more significant than those of their counterparts in England, and much more characteristic of the situation elsewhere on the Continent. In this sense, the English path to state-building was unique.

Organic State-Building

The construction of central power, its projection across the country and the reduction of the power of the barons were all part of the one process. In England, the struggle with the barons stretched until the power of the landed magnates was shattered by the Wars of the Roses (1455–85); this marked the end of the magnates' military attempts to determine who could sit on the throne. Before this, both the identity of the king and influence over him were the subject of incessant manoeuvring and scheming among the magnates; Magna Carta (1215) and de Montfort's rebellion (1258–65) are two celebrated instances of this. But despite the conflict and tension between Crown and aristocracy evident in such developments, this was primarily a dispute about the disposition of power within the country, not an attempt to break away from the centralized kingdom by the magnates. Given this acceptance of the national entity, even if there was considerable vagueness and ambiguity about its precise dimensions, and despite the tensions, Crown and aristocracy supported one another in the sense that both realized that they needed the other to sustain their power. The magnates relied upon the Crown to regulate their affairs peacefully and thereby enable them to exploit the peasants. The Crown relied upon the magnates for some aspects of local administration and for funding. They shared interests and preferences with the result that the relationship was basically a cooperative one, albeit one with times of tension and dispute.[29]

The development of a central administrative structure took the form of a struggle to create institutions separate from the king's private household and yet not under the control of the magnates.[30] Initially the structure built upon the king's household. The first steps towards centralization of control grew out of management of the royal domains. In the words of Strayer, 'in most countries central financial institutions grew out of the work of local estate-managers'[31] because the job of these people was to consolidate the revenues from the royal lands and put them at the disposal of the king. In order to achieve this, they had to engage in record- and account-keeping, thereby constituting the beginnings of a larger and more developed bureaucratic structure. It was the search for financial revenues which most propelled the development of a central administrative apparatus around the king. This was crucial for his relationship with the landed magnates since the development of such a structure potentially gave the Crown the capacity to tax the populace independent of the local nobility. In its early form, this central state power comprised three types of institutions: a chancery to coordinate the work of all officials and handle foreign relations, a treasury to deal with revenue collection, and a high court to mete out justice.

The implementation of justice was one of the principal means whereby the English king was able to centralize rule and reduce the importance of the regional magnates.[32] By claiming jurisdiction over various types of behaviour, the king could intervene in areas where he had no land and no rights, even in relations between vassals and lord. Given that the king had passed out the lands, his court was the logical place in which disputes could be resolved. This did not translate immediately into his acquisition of wide-ranging judicial powers, but it did underpin the gradual extension of royal justice and the growth of the royal court. The king's reliance in part on revenue generated by fines his courts imposed also meant that this increased the income flow into the centre. The initial means of expanding royal authority in this area were through the building-up of the king's court at the centre and the establishment of itinerant judges, a development which also stimulated the emergence of juries, and therefore further local participation in the activities of governance. Royal justice expanded significantly under Henry II (1154–89), and by the thirteenth century all important cases were heard by the king's judges;[33] by the time of Edward I (1272–1307), the king's courts had replaced other courts as the courts of first instance for most litigants,[34] and the leading judicial figure in the localities, the justice of the peace, was appointed by the Crown from among the local notables.[35] The expansion of royal justice was important not only in a practical sense, in that it extended royal reach at the expense of local magnates, but also ideologically. It was a positive assertion of royal sovereignty over local particularism; what counted was the king's laws enforced through royal institutions, not the decisions of a local magnate. But these laws were not simply handed down from on high. The customary law which had structured much local life for centuries continued to be applied, with the juries a major means of doing this.

Also crucial to the process of centralization in England was the power to tax. Control over revenue was central to the capacity of the king to expand his power. Institution-building required money, and the control the king had over receipts from his domain,[36] fines, tolls and customs dues was insufficient to build such a structure. He had to gain access to the populace at large, but to do this he initially needed the acquiescence of the magnates. This need opened the way for the development of Parliament, to be discussed further below. In practice, Parliament provided a means for the king to obtain the assent of the magnates for the levying of taxes. Once it was agreed that a tax should be imposed, the king had the right to determine its nature, how it was to be collected, and who should be exempt. The access to tax revenues this provided gave the king a much larger financial basis upon which to rest his growing administration. Initially fiscal matters were concentrated in the king's household, but over the twelfth century a specialized treasury, the Exchequer, developed as an independent body. That this was not sufficient for all that he wished to do is reflected in the frequent state of indebtedness within which the Crown found itself, but the access to the populace that it reflected was an important avenue for the future raising of revenue; the end of the twelfth century saw the first instance of the imposition of a direct tax on the entire realm in order to meet the crises of the time, including the third crusade, Richard's incarceration and the need to ransom him, and war with France.[37] The gaining of taxing powers also stimulated the development of state administrative institutions including a financial apparatus. By the end of the twelfth century the state could run itself without the presence of the king, as reflected in its performance during the prolonged absence of Richard I (1189–99). But it was hardly efficient; one scholar claims that while England may have been the best organized kingdom in Europe in the thirteenth century, 'it was by any modern standard quite appallingly incoherent, clumsy, crime-ridden, and corrupt'.[38]

While the institutions of the central state subsequently developed and became more complex, there were strong pressures toward the personal appropriation of office. Initially in the post-twelfth-century period, most positions in the bureaucracy were held by clerics, on a pleasure tenure (i.e., at the pleasure of the king), and with minimal salaries. Their income came from Church benefices, an effective ecclesiastical subsidy to public administration. The large-scale switch to lay administrators came about in the first half of the fifteenth century,[39] and with this came the replacement of pleasure tenure by life tenure, plus the scope for fulfilling one's duties through a deputy. This enabled office-holders to continue to hold office without fulfilling the functions of such office, which were carried out by the said deputy. By the end of the fifteenth century, life tenure, allied to the English common law, enabled office-holders to claim that their offices were freehold property. This further enabled officials who resigned their offices to claim financial compensation from a successor, thereby entrenching the principle of bureaucratic patrimonialism. However, the situation was not as fluid as it was in France: although an official could sell his office, he was not able to name his successor without higher (often royal) approval, and the Crown could not multiply offices by dividing them. Over time, the bureaucratic structure of central state institutions outside the king's household became more regularized, routinized and differentiated, and increasingly separate from that household. This was a prolonged process, despite the description of part of it as a 'Tudor revolution in government'.[40] But even this process did not immediately eliminate the patrimonial aspects of the bureaucracy. Patronage remained crucial in bureaucratic life; in the words of one scholar, by the second half of the fifteenth century, most important administrative positions (including the great offices of state) were held by 'lay proprietary officeholders who collected the bulk of their income in the form of fees and gratuities. Pluralism, the appointment of deputies, and the granting of reversions were all common, as was the traffic in offices among private individuals.'[41] This fiscal basis of the bureaucracy increased its independence from the Crown and ensured that bureaucratic organic interdependence remained socially very narrow.

The reach of the state at this time remained limited. Well into the seventeenth century, the state remained small and weak, beginning to grow significantly only under the Commonwealth and Protectorate (1649–60). The struggle to develop effective central organs was matched by the absence at lower levels of routinized bodies answerable to the centre. Much of the local administration and governance remained substantially in the hands of local notables whose allegiance to the centre was not buttressed by firm bureaucratic supports ensuring its continuity and maintenance, even though the individuals owed feudal obligations directly to the king. It was in the interests of local notables to remain associated with the state and royal power because this gave access to prestige, patronage and wealth. The system continued to be plagued by overlapping jurisdictions, weak links between centre and localities, the propensity of local notables to put parochial concerns above larger needs, and the farming of many taxing functions.[42] The continuing reliance overwhelmingly upon local notables for the conduct of local administration meant that the professional state machine which was emerging at the centre did not extend far into the depths of society. Local and regional communities by and large governed themselves. This means that emergent national administration was clearly bifurcated between the growing professional machine at the centre and the continuing amateur ranks at the lower levels, with the contacts between them improving only slowly. But in the sort of situation that prevailed, where the infra-structural contacts between apex and base were very weak and central officials did not seek to exercise close monitoring of what occurred at local levels, having a local administration that was rooted soundly in the local community and did not seek to reject central power was not a disadvantage compared with its French counterpart, a central bureaucracy seeking to reach into the localities but not succeeding very well. This was particularly the case given that these local notables were tied into the centre not only through the developing administrative web, but importantly through the Parliament as well (see below). Indeed, it was the local gentry whose power was consolidated as that of the territorial magnates waned.[43] Through their role as the lower levels of the administration, the gentry became the linchpin for the whole English state.[44]

Crucial in this development was the Parliament. In Europe, assemblies were propelled into political prominence by the king's need for taxation revenue, especially to conduct military activities. Advisory bodies, usually consisting of magnates and/or leading members of the king's retinue, had been in existence from early feudal times, where the model of the monarchy, especially in England, had been consultatory. However, their role was purely advisory; except in times of very weak kings, they exercised no mandatory power over the king and were summoned and functioned at his pleasure. They were, in effect, extensions of the royal court. In addition, in some countries (England, Scandinavia, Poland and Hungary) assemblies functioned at the local level to provide overall governance of the region, carrying out those functions with the aid of royal officials.[45] These local assemblies united the freemen of the region in a form of self-government that, in its most developed form in England, constituted the basis of the administrative structure discussed above.

The development of more independent representative assemblies at the upper level occurred in the twelfth century and accelerated across the continent in the 1250–1350 period.[46] They differed from the earlier councils by being regular rather than ad hoc and by claiming to represent the whole population. In the feudal bodies, individuals were present on the basis of their personal links to the ruler, whereas in the representative assemblies they represented broader corporate groups. This notion of representation was new.

The genesis of these representative assemblies was the increasing need for taxation experienced by the Crown at this time. The existing fiscal base of the monarchy had to be supplemented by new sources of revenue, but the principle that was applied was that any new sources had to be approved by those who were to bear the burden.[47] Consequently monarchs began to call into existence assemblies of notables from around the country to validate their tax plans. This was a means of seeking to coordinate rule through the representatives of the lower-level political authorities. Although such assemblies were often ultimately to turn into restraints upon the king, initially they were viewed with distrust by the magnates because they were seen as occasions upon which the king was going to make demands for resources which they could hardly resist. But their basis lay in the terms of the feudal contract whereby the nobles who had traditionally been called upon to give counsel to the king now saw this as a right to give advice, and one upon which they vigorously insisted. The structure of such assemblies was generally based upon the theory of estates. The formation of estates had received royal encouragement because they were seen as corporate entities which could form assemblies which the ruler could use to gain consent, and thereby gain access to the tax revenues held by their members.[48] This view received a kind of formal legitimation through the theory of feudal rule elaborated by churchmen in the tenth and eleventh centuries whereby the king ruled over a hierarchy of estates below him. The estate assemblies[49] generally had three houses, one for each estate: nobility, clergy and burghers. However, in those countries that had assemblies at the local level, the pattern of representation in the higher-level assembly was different: an upper house combined representatives of the nobility and clergy, while a lower house had representatives of the lower organs of government, both rural and urban.

The latter type of assembly was structurally more powerful than the former. In the estate-based assemblies, where the divisions between estates were reflected in divisions between chambers, the king could play on the differences between estates to disrupt the functioning of the chambers, and thereby undercut their effectiveness as institutions. Where those divisions did not coincide, the mixed membership of the chambers created fewer openings for the king to broker separate deals with individual groups of citizens, and thereby contributed to the overall integrity and coherence of the institution as a whole. Furthermore, the territorial basis of these non-estate-based assemblies, with representatives coming from the different regions, gave them access to the financial resources of the local communities they represented of the sort which the king did not enjoy. This was particularly important given the burgeoning wealth of some of the towns. This implied a notion of rule by consent, and reflects the way in which such assemblies were the means for the exchange of rights for revenue.

In England, both the Magna Carta and the de Montfort rebellion had strengthened the powers of the advisory assembly, the Great Council, and this was gradually transformed into a bicameral Parliament with, by 1330, a relatively fixed composition: the upper house, or Lords, comprised the clergy and nobility, and the lower house, or Commons, the representatives of the shires and boroughs.[50] The following centuries saw a continuing struggle between king and Parliament for supremacy, a struggle powered by the Crown's continuing attempts to expand its taxing and legislative power against the resistance of the Parliament.[51] In this struggle, the Parliament's roots in the local communities and the administrative arrangements that ran them was crucial. This gave the Parliament control over local resources through the local notables who combined their roles as members of Parliament with local prominence. By the fifteenth century, the Crown was dependent upon the Commons for most of its income because this was the mechanism through which local taxes were negotiated.[52] Particularly important in this was the increasing power of urban commercial elements in the late Middle Ages who saw the Parliament as a means of expanding room for their economic activities.[53] Ultimately the civil war and the subsequent acts of settlement established Parliamentary supremacy and judicial independence and prevented the establishment in England of an absolutist monarchy.

The importance of the Parliament for this model of state development lies not only in the power it vested in local authorities compared with the Crown, but also in the way in which it tied all parts of the political structure together. With local administration in the hands of local notables rather than members of a central bureaucracy, the danger was that the state would simply disappear into society. That it did not is due to the strength of the conception of the country as a united kingdom under central rule, and the role of the Parliament in tying local powers into a single structure. The notion of the 'Crown in Parliament' and the representation of these local powers at the centre, reflected the highly developed level of legislative organic interdependence characteristic of the English state. Both ideologically and practically the local authorities were tied to the centre, but not through a professional bureaucratic machine. While the absence of such a machine gave the appearance of a weak state with little infrastructural power, the role of Parliament as the locus of negotiation between centre and localities made up for this. The royal court and the emergent professional bureaucracy may have been characterized by narrow interdependence with society, but this was not the case with the bulk of the administration of the country. Such interdependence is at the core of the organic model of state development.

Overarching State-Building

In France, where the regional divisions were deeper and the monarchy initially weaker, the principal means of seeking to extend royal power were also justice and finance, but the institutions generated were simpler and less formalized.[54] By the time of Philip IV (1285–1315), there was an emergent central administrative structure consisting of an inner council, a series of specialized departments including an accounting office, and the Parlement de Paris which was a judicial organ.[55] But this structure was very different from the institutions in England. Rather than the court and main offices of state being dominated by the nobles, these were dominated mainly by lawyers trained in Roman law, by clerks and people from non-noble backgrounds who were prone to push royal power against feudal prerogatives. The inner council contained some landed magnates, but also royal knights (many of whom were from non-noble houses); there was rivalry and distrust between these two groups.[56] The territorial magnates were in a much less powerful position in the central institutions of the French state than their English counterparts and therefore, unlike the latter, were less able to change their feudal obligations into rights against the king, although they remained prominent forces in the provincial administrations. The focus of government under Philip was the Grand Council, which moved around the country with him and was separate from the broader royal administration which remained in Paris. The king did seek the counsel of the magnates through the Estates-General, but this was more ad hoc and unsystematic than in England.

In France, the assembly that emerged was based on the estates. It had three houses, each representing a definably different social interest, and therefore lacking the unity to be able to enforce its will on the monarch. Over time, rulers were able to marginalize this body, relying upon a more developed bureaucratic structure directly to penetrate society and extract the resources they needed. Charles VII (1422–61) claimed a monopoly of taxing powers, including the right to do this without convening the Estates-General or asking the magnates. The French Estates-General declined after 1440, and did not meet between 1614 and 1789. This was due in part to the fact that, given the continuing strength of local authorities, it was more sensible for the king to negotiate tax issues with them rather than with the central Estates-General, leaving the latter without the leverage over the monarch enjoyed by the English Parliament.

The centralization of power was a more uneven process than it was in England, with royal power virtually collapsing during the Hundred Years War (1337–1453) and waxing and waning subsequently, although the king was firmly in control by the seventeenth and eighteenth centuries.[57] Until the thirteenth century, royal power was virtually restricted to the Île de France, where the Capets were the direct feudal lords. Elsewhere in the territory that was to become France, power was vested in individual feudal lords who generally lacked the corporate sense of unity evident among their counterparts in England[58] but were intent upon defending their feudal rights against erosion by the king. During the thirteenth century the larger principalities were added to the royal holdings, principally through war, marriage and inheritance; most principalities were linked to the king by the dyadic ties of feudal law. The newly-gained regions were permitted to retain their own customs and institutions, but all important offices were filled by officials despatched from Paris. There was thus no insistence on the uniformity of laws and institutions as in England, but there was a greater reliance upon central functionaries than local notables for administration. In France there was continuing distrust of local figures, and therefore a perceived need to build the royal bureaucracy as quickly as possible. Given the regional variations in France and the continued strength of local traditions including the often prominent role in local affairs played by the magnates, such a bureaucracy was vital to holding the country together.

As this bureaucracy developed through the despatch of central officials into the localities, it was initially characterized by a network of overlapping jurisdictions, resulting in frequent conflicts and ambiguity in the exercise of power.[59] Nevertheless over time the bureaucracy, comprised of paid professional administrators, began to become more specialized in function and efficient in performance.[60] This is despite the increasingly patrimonial nature acquired by the bureaucracy. Between the early sixteenth century and the mid-seventeenth century, in part in response to the king's shortage of funds, proprietary office-holding (i.e., officials holding office as their property) became common.[61] The king was considered to have proprietorial rights over the bureaucracy, a fact reflected in his capacity to dispose of official office almost as he saw fit. He had the power to appoint people to leading office, but he was also able to sell that office and thereby increase the revenue flow into his coffers. This practice expanded throughout the state apparatus; in 1515 there were 4,041 venal officials, while by 1600 this had risen to 11,000; between 1570 and 1576, 10–15 per cent of state revenue came from the sale of office.[62] From 1604 payment of an annual fee ensured that the office could be inherited, a practice that gave office-holders a patrimonial claim to their offices and the king a regular source of income.[63]

Such venality undermined the reality of royal control and possibly also bureaucratic efficiency. It undermined the former by placing part of the bureaucratic machine in the hands of officials whose link with the monarch became purely pecuniary,[64] and the latter by turning official position into property that could be used to generate income. It could also mean a reduction in tax revenues for the king because the holders of venal office sought to use that to line their own pockets, and therefore retained a significant share of what they collected.[65] The absence of any form of monitoring of the performance of such officials, including financial officials, meant that much of the state machine was effectively outside royal control; with regard to finances, one scholar has referred to 'private enterprise in royal finance'.[66] Despite such venality and the consequent fusing of public power with private property, which remained common right up until the Revolution, during the seventeenth and eighteenth centuries the royal bureaucracy increasingly was staffed by professional civil servants, with ministries emerging during the latter century. In the words of one scholar, 'Departments were strictly organized, the size of their staffs enumerated, appointments and salaries regulated, and expenses monitored.'[67] Patrimonialism and bureaucratic differentiation were therefore not incompatible but, as in England, patrimonialism was instrumental in ensuring that bureaucratic organic interdependence remained socially very narrow.

The development of a state bureaucracy did not create a uniform administrative structure. From the thirteenth century, the king's sovereignty was spread across the regional divisions, but without eliminating them. He was not strong enough to eliminate the existing divisions, but just strong enough to project his authority over the top of them. The expansion of royal power had usually involved a guarantee of the traditional rights and privileges of the region, thereby ensuring a degree of decentralization, a lack of uniformity,[68] and continuing local bases of power. The king could, in Finer's words, 'aggregate a kingdom of the Franks rather than homogenize a "France"'.[69] He was by this time acknowledged as the temporal sovereign, although his capacity to make rules with universal application was in practice more restricted than his formal rights. There was also general acknowledgement of his right to tax his subjects, although in practice there was some haggling with the magnates over the tax levels and some sharing of the proceeds.[70] The Crown's capacity to take advantage of this was restricted by the more limited development of a financial infrastructure at the centre and by the problems in negotiating makeshift arrangements with individual regions.

Indeed, much of the course of governance at this time was characterized by negotiation and compromise between the king and magnates and, whenever royal power waned, regional authorities were all too willing to take advantage of it.[71] This was facilitated by the fact that just as the king was trying to develop and systematize a bureaucratic structure to project his power, the same process was occurring within many of the fiefs. By the mid-sixteenth century, central control was established across most of modern France, something achieved principally through the operation of feudal ties which enabled the king to resume control over lands once the current occupier had died, and through the centralizing measures of Francis I (1515–47).[72] But this did not create an integrated kingdom. The king had a standing army, but parts of it were commanded by the magnates, and there was still little uniformity of government, administration or law across the country. In the words of one author:

France was still a welter of diverse authorities, particularisms, and immunities. Its centralization consisted of a multitude of individual contracts between the Crown, as the one universally recognized political superior, and the provincial Estates, the towns with their charters, the commercial guilds, and the ecclesiastical establishments. The regime was a web-work of dyadic ties.[73]

Central control collapsed again with the Wars of Religion (1562–98), and only under Louis XIII (1610–43) and the ministry of Richelieu (1624–42) was the Crown able to regain significant control.[74] An important aspect of this was the introduction of a network of officials appointed by (and loyal to) the Crown to run the fiscal apparatus and to regularize tax assessment and collection. This effectively took control over revenues out of the hands of permanent officials and put it under officials directly answerable to and removable by the Crown,[75] even if in practice this capacity to control finances was limited by the continued ability of magnates and venal officials to play a part in the collection process. Effective centralization remained blocked by the diversity of local conditions and jurisdictions. It was not until the time of Mazarin and Louis XIV (1643–1715) that officials sent to the regions tended not to fall under the control of the local magnates.[76] In France, the attempted solution to the problem of local administration was therefore very different from that of the English: instead of continuing to rely upon local notables, the French king sought to undercut them by the attempted projection of bureaucratic power.

Thus the emergent French state, in the form of an expanding professional bureaucracy, did not create a uniform administrative structure firmly rooted in local society. Its levels of both bureaucratic and legislative organic interdependence were low; it arched over the society rather than being firmly embedded within it. The existence of local diversity and magnate power in France had encouraged the king to seek the development of a centralized bureaucratic structure to overcome these divisions. In contrast, in England, the tradition of unity undercut parcellized sovereignty and enabled the Crown to continue to rely for local administration on local notables. This was a form of social interdependence, in contrast to the organizational basis the French state sought to extend to the regions.

The processes of administrative regularization and centralization and of legislative development therefore were fundamentally shaped by the essential differences between English and French feudalism and the inheritances each received from the pre-feudal era. In England, the pre-Norman kingdom was already centralized with authority concentrated in the person of the king, while local administration was carried out by a cross-section of local notables. As a result, when William I sought to impose his feudal rule upon the kingdom, he built on top of this structure: local power remained outside the exclusive control of large land-owning magnates, and all vassals owed a direct obligation to him rather than one mediated through local magnates. The political dynamism was thus three-fold: king, magnates and local notables. Despite their obligations to the Crown, English local notables shared with the magnates a basis in local society and therefore a set of interests that overlapped with those of the magnates. The three groups were thus tied together in a relationship which, in institutional terms, was played out in the Parliament. It was the combined strength of the magnates and notables which ensured that the king was gradually brought under Parliamentary oversight, at least in financial terms, and which ultimately locked them together in ruling the kingdom. This did not occur without differences and conflicts, but these were not disputes over the integrity of the kingdom: a centralized English state was taken as given. Furthermore, to the extent that taxation was processed through Parliament, it was the case of Crown, nobility and notables imposing it together.

However, if the English king sought to extend his powers through expansion of the tradition of centralized kingship, this was not an option for his French counterpart who had to rely upon the extension of his feudal rights to expand his power. The conflict between Crown and nobles was much more over the nature of the French state and the question of whether feudal rights and privileges could be maintained as a bulwark against royal power. Here the rent-versus-tax conflict was acute and open, as magnates sought to limit the flow of taxes to the centre and maximize the flow of rents and dues into their own pockets and therefore consolidate their local power against the centre. Furthermore, because of the absence of a tradition of local administration by notables owing direct allegiance to the king, early French kings sought to administer the country through the injection of royal officials from above into the regions. Regional administration was therefore in principle more highly centralized than in England, but in practice less effective at linking the regions with the centre. The continuing autonomy and power of local legislatures and authorities undercut the ability of a central French legislature to emerge as a potent constraint upon the monarch because he could achieve more of what he wanted by dealing with those regional authorities. The contrast is summarized by Wood:

> The early emergence of a unitary national Parliament and the traditional formula of 'the Crown in Parliament', testify to the process of state-formation which so sharply distinguished the English monarchical state from the French, with its fragmented jurisdictions and representative institutions vertically and horizontally divided by class and region.[77]

This difference in both administrative and legislative structures, in the very much narrower dimensions of interdependence in France than in England, would shape the political outcomes of the shift from a feudal state, absolutism or constitutionalism.[78]

Absolutism and Constitutionalism

By the sixteenth century a different sort of political structure was emerging. The parcellized sovereignty of feudalism had gone and, although there were still significant question marks over the penetration of society and the centre's capacity to control developments at the periphery, there was less dispute about the principle of the centralized national state, despite the conflicts of the second half of the sixteenth century.[79] Indeed, the conception of the state was much clearer under absolutism than it had been before because of the absence of overlapping feudal rights; these had been largely destroyed by the consolidation of the state. The sovereignty of the centre, however its institutional relations were configured, was broadly accepted and the sense of there being a territorial state was established. This did not mean that the king could automatically exercise effective continuing control over the magnates. Across Europe, magnates were bought off through the elaboration of a ritualized and hierarchical court society,[80] plus in France the skilful manipulation of patronage by Louis XIV (1643–1715). Louis was able to extend the control of his officials at the expense of the nobles and affirm that the basis of nobility lay in a royal grant.[81] But whereas in feudal times the magnates were important as individuals, in the post-feudal epoch they were important as a class. And increasingly many of them came to play a more routinized part in the institutions of state. They gained representation in the national assemblies and in the army, not as independent sub-contractors as in feudal times, but as officers in the new national armies. Lesser nobility also used the practice of the sale of office to enter the bureaucracy.

In England, which by 1600 had become a cultural and linguistic unit (although the British state had not yet been consolidated), the symbolism of the 'Crown in Parliament' reflected not only the consolidation of the notion of the national state, but also of the unity of Crown and propertied classes.[82] But in all territorial states that were emerging, control of the periphery by the centre remained problematic. By the sixteenth and seventeenth centuries in most western kingdoms, the centre would buy the support of local notables, ignore some local non-conformity, and use force as an example where necessary, a combination usually sufficient to ensure the broad implementation of central commands.[83] The early modern state legislated much more often and in more fields than its medieval predecessor, was able to make more of those decisions stick, and the laws it adopted were generally more impersonal and applied to the population as a whole without particular exclusions for rank, but it remained detached from society as a whole. The administrative structure of states, right up until the French Revolution, remained 'just barely adequate ... every new internal or external crisis strained [it] severely'.[84]

The distinction between absolutist rule and constitutionalism is significant, but it should not be exaggerated. This was not a distinction between autocracy/authoritarian rule and democracy, because in neither system was there a place for popular sovereignty. The essential difference lay in the structuring of political rule at the top and the avenues of access into the political process for those below what had become the national level of a consolidated territorial state.

The absolutist state involved a significantly different set of political arrangements from those that had applied under feudalism. The balance that had existed between king and magnates had been destroyed, and the position of the latter had been undermined. This does not mean that the landed nobility were powerless under absolutist rule: indeed, the whole structure relied upon their continuing support, and therefore absolutism in the sense of the all-powerful nature of the king was a myth. However, the position of the nobility at the centre had been transformed. With the expansion of the royal court and the efforts made to project the majesty of the king by intensifying its glamour and expanding its public role,[85] the nobility were reduced to the status of courtiers. Their position at court was now almost wholly dependent upon the king's favour, their aim being to integrate themselves more securely into his good graces because therein lay the path to prosperity; this also weakened their regional roots.[86] The king's word was law, with the result that rather than law being seen as emerging out of the community and posing a restraint upon the monarch, it appeared as the instrument of his rule. And as an instrument of royal rule, it could no longer bind the monarch. Government continued to be conducted through a series of councils, formed at the king's pleasure and at the head of a range of state departments. The bureaucracy retained much of its patrimonial character, with the sale of office being a major means whereby noble families sought to bolster their positions in the changing circumstances.[87]

The state's reach into society had lengthened; in the late eighteenth century, there were some 300,000 officials in France compared with 16,000 in Britain.[88] However, the sale of office effectively removed large sections of the bureaucracy from central control, rendering it segmental in form with some of those segments operating largely on the basis of the drive for personal enrichment. By the 1770s in France, there were only about 50,000 salaried, removable officials in the state bureaucracy,[89] and given that, unlike in England which still relied overwhelmingly on local notables, the French sought to administer the countryside by paid civil servants, this was a significant weakness. The state remained 'riddled with private and corporate property rights';[90] French kings still relied heavily on personal patronage for the administration of their realm and tax farming remained prominent. A tension remained between the informal chains of patronage and the growth of a more rationalist bureaucracy within the administrative structure. Thus even though its reach had improved, in absolutist France the control the centre exercised over the countryside remained weak and episodic with local magnates often remaining prominent.

Like the absolutist state, the English constitutionalist state had a king at its head (except in 1649–60) and rested on a bureaucracy that may have been little less patrimonial in nature than that of France. However, in contrast to France, the king's powers had been curbed by Parliament. By the late seventeenth century the balance had tipped firmly in favour of the Parliamentary forces, with the monarch increasingly restricted to a role approaching that of the constitutional monarchs of today; as early as the sixteenth century a strong king such as Henry VIII, who had a re-organized and more effective central bureaucracy than his predecessors as well as a powerful office at its heart, and therefore better coordinating capacity than any of his predecessors, could neither tax nor legislate without Parliament, while his powers were themselves the subject of Parliamentary statute. Law was emerging as supreme, binding upon both people and government, but this was increasingly the law of the legislature administered by courts independent of both monarch and assembly.

However, it is important to note that despite the increased role of the legislature compared with absolutist regimes, in neither did society at large play a part in government. The mass of the population remained excluded from systematic and routine participation in politics. Society remained something to be ruled over rather than something having a part in the ruling. Similar to absolutism, the power of the nobility had been transformed. The rise of urban merchants and entrepreneurs had created a new class of wealthy citizens whose collective presence helped to counteract the dominance the feudal nobility formerly had exercised. Furthermore, that nobility itself had undergone a change. With the disappearance of its unique military role under feudalism and its concomitant central place in the structure of power relations, it was transformed into a land-owning class whose primary function was to lend stability to the social structure, and thereby the political structure. The nobility was also important in terms of taxation, and the difference between constitutional and absolutist regimes was important here. In England taxation was levied on both the landed and trading rich with their consent expressed through their respective Parliamentary assemblies. In France the landed nobility was exempt. This was an important factor both in the ability of absolutist kings to do away with representative assemblies[91] and in the greater capacity of constitutional states to extract taxation in times of war.

This is a significant difference in social basis between the two types of states and it had implications for their future development. The nobility were partly integrated into the constitutional state in a way they were not under absolutism. Their participation in a representative assembly, and therefore in the state fiscal chain of acquisition reflected in the tax system, meant that they were intrinsically part of the political structure. Under absolutism their presence outside that fiscal chain and the absence of a representative assembly made them more marginal to the political system. This was reflected in their role at court, where their position and even presence was dependent upon the king's favour. The presence of this crucial group, inside or outside the fiscal system, had implications for the centre's ability routinely to generate high levels of tax revenue, and therefore for its capacity both to compete in war and to develop its own central organs; in 1654 in France, 63 per cent of all tax income came from extraordinary taxes.[92] These different locations were also important for the future development of class relations. The inclusion of the nobility in the fiscal chain helped to facilitate the merging of landed and commercial interests, thereby laying the basis for a future capitalist class and a sound basis of state revenue. In contrast, the exclusion of the nobility under absolutism hindered the unity of landed property and commercial wealth.[93]

Although in constitutional England the king was more constrained by institutions than in France, there is no evidence that the administrative system was much more rational in its operation. In both types of system, some higher-level offices were functionally specialized, formal rules and hierarchical supervision applied, and the distinction between state office and private property was partially institutionalized.[94] Increasingly the central bureaucracy was coming to function along standardized lines, with the bureaucracy developing a sense of identity and *esprit de corps* separate from the monarch. A crucial development was the stabilization of the state's financial apparatus. The earlier reliance upon the private initiative of tax collectors, financiers, and the holders of offices that had been purchased was overcome in England by reforms in the late seventeenth and early eighteenth century. Customs and excise were brought under central control in 1671 and 1683 respectively, salaried tax collectors replaced tax farmers in 1692, in 1714 a permanent treasury board was established to supervise the movement of revenue to the Exchequer, and in the mid-eighteenth century the Bank of England was taken over.[95] These measures effectively constituted the nationalization of English public finance, and enabled the state to restructure its debt. Only the interest had to be repaid as long as the chief lenders (the London business world and the Dutch) retained confidence in the state's ability to continue to gain access to funds, while short-term credit now rested on broad-based public investment rather than cliques of financiers. This gave the English state an enormously flexible financial instrument, something lacking in France where state finance was never effectively centralized under the monarchy.[96]

Local administration remained in the hands of local notables autonomous from the growing bureaucratic structure of the central state. Patronage continued to be central to the way in which both administrative and legislative spheres operated, receiving an important boost in the first half of the seventeenth century when the Crown ran into financial difficulties and resorted to such methods as the farming of the customs collection and reliance upon officials who would raise money on their own account to pay for state functions.[97] Although the civil war broke up these patronage networks and the Commonwealth and Protectorate took measures to eliminate patrimonialism, such practices made a comeback with the Restoration. Despite the emergence of a more rationalized and efficient bureaucratic machine, 'Old Corruption' remained a central issue into the nineteenth century, both in the administrative structure and Parliamentary politics; personal patronage remained an indispensable key to career success. It was during this period too that the state acquired a monopoly of legitimate force. The chief form this took was the emergence of a national, standing army, subject to continuing military discipline and separated off from society at large. The introduction of uniforms plus the development of weaponry created a military force that was distinct from the population it was supposed to protect, and provided the state with a weapon not just for external defence, but for the maintenance of internal order as well. The contrast with feudalism, where the local basis of military detachments robbed the centre of the monopoly of coercion, is stark.

What also began to emerge during the late feudal–early modern period was a sense of national unity shared by wide sections of the populace. What this amounts to is the growth of a feeling of being part of a national community, of Anderson's 'imagined community'[98] defined roughly in terms of state borders. This marks the shift from dynastic realm to national state. It is not clear when such a vision began to take hold, and the time clearly differs for different countries and different segments of the population. For Strayer,[99] there were some signs of this in England, France and Spain in the seventeenth century, but it is likely that this developed earlier. Among the nobility it is probable that some sense of this was present in the wars of the sixteenth century, when it was clear that conflict was not over feudal rights and obligations. Indeed, the earlier ejection of English power from France may be the starting point for this. For the English monarchy it was openly manifest with Henry VIII's break from Rome. The operation of mercantilist policies in the sixteenth century (see below) is an indication that the state elite was beginning to see things in this way.[100] This was a significant change of perspective, but in the early modern period it was restricted to the elite levels of society. It is doubtful that the mass of the populace shared such a conception or, if they did, it was only weakly developed and was unlikely to be a spur to action. This was to change in coming centuries.

Associated with this was the development of a sense of the state as separate from the person of the ruler with legitimation resting in the institutions of the state.[101] This is linked to notions of divine right and the claim for royal authority as a God-given mandate unlimited by secular law. The king's authority was absolute because it came from God. Jean Bodin in the sixteenth century was the first systematically to argue that the king had the sovereign capacity to create new law and to impose unquestioning obedience to it rather than merely to exercise traditional justice. As the image of God on earth, he was bound only by natural law, which limited his ability to levy taxes at will and arbitrarily seize another's goods. But Bodin's importance also lay in the notion of sovereignty he espoused. Sovereignty, which was indivisible, was seen to reside in the king, but he was also seen as 'a personalized expression of a secularized administrative entity'.[102] In this sense, sovereignty applied to the state structure as a whole, and assumed a 'co-ordinated system of administrative rule',[103] and in this way was directly relevant to the constitutional regime of Britain. But it was that other aspect of feudal kingship, the principle that people had a right to be consulted on matters which affected them, that was the basis upon which the power of assemblies was built and a new mode of legitimation emerged. In the sixteenth century, a new mode of arguing became prominent, social contract theory. This assumed that the political entity had been created on the basis of a contract between its members, and therefore political authority came from that contract rather than from God. Authority was thereby vested, effectively, in the community rather than in the monarch, who became merely the representative of that community. Although there were a variety of different contract theories with different political implications for the position of the monarch compared with the people, all based legitimation in popular consent. This was the beginning of the sorts of notions that would underpin the modern state.

By the time of the French Revolution, Western Europe mainly comprised national territorial states with a central power resting on a professional bureaucracy and a standing army.[104] The outlines of the modern state were visible in both the absolutist and constitutional versions of the contemporary polity. The territorially consolidated national state had emerged as the most powerful type of polity in the region. The German states remained disunited and cut across by the commercial Hanseatic League, with the power of the German king (the Holy Roman Emperor) restricted by the continuing aspirations of the princes who ran the states. The Italian city-states also remained divided, with none attaining a position from which they could dominate their neighbours.[105] These types of political forms could not compete with the national state. In the latter, centralized authority with its growing monopoly of coercion and the alliance with commercial interests based on a broad coincidence of interests[106] was better able to mobilize resources and to prevent the sorts of freeriding that were common in confederal arrangements than in those polities where sovereignty remained under question. Once these successful models were established, ambitious politicians elsewhere sought to follow their lead, forsaking other possible models of political authority. The shaping of these states, or at least their early exemplars (France and England), lay in the feudal milieu. It was the reaction to the disintegrative forces in the feudal structure itself plus the disintegrative effects upon that structure of the commercialization of economic life and the impact of military competition and technology (see Chapter 5) that led to the erosion of feudalism and its replacement by a more centralized form of political authority.

With the emergence of these new forms, the state's capacity for infrastructural power increased, although it was not until the nineteenth century that a quantum leap in state capacity was evident. While the institutions of the state were becoming increasingly complex, the means whereby central power was projected remained weak; local areas continued largely to govern themselves. Bureaucratic patrimonialism ensured that bureaucratic organic interdependence remained narrowly drawn in both the immediate post-feudal and the early modern absolutist and constitutional states. It also placed severe limits upon central control within the bureaucracy and upon the development of norms of bureaucratic procedure. And while at all times the monarchy remained relatively insulated from society, in England the Parliament closely tied the administrative but weakly bureaucratized arm of the state into society more broadly; not, of course, into the poor strata of the community, but certainly into its wealthy and middling sections. Such interdependence was crucial for the state to survive given its relatively undeveloped bureaucratic nature.

Institutional Interdependence?

The relationship between the state and economic activity changed fundamentally in the shift from the feudal state to the early modern.

Indeed, it was during this period that the very notion of 'the economy' emerged. One of the characteristics of feudalism is seen to be the merging of the political and economic spheres. This refers to the way in which the locus of most economic activity was the manor, and these were run by the nobles whose position was defined in terms of their formal relations with their superiors, and ultimately the monarch. The manors were often almost self-contained little worlds of their own, producing most of what they needed through a combination of peasants working on their own and their lords' land. Goods were taken to market, and thereby the non-productive sectors of society were fed, but the bulk of economic activity occurred within the bounds of the manors. Most economic activity was local. The logic of this arrangement derived from the feudal obligations that bound vassals and suzerains together. The local noble possessed the manor as a result of his relationship with his suzerain, and his ability to meet his obligations depended overwhelmingly upon that possession of the manor. In this sense, the economic aspects of life were intrinsically tied to the political; one made no sense without the other. But this does not mean the state was closely intertwined with the economy. Those landed notables upon which feudalism rested did have their roots strongly within the local communities and the economic activities in which they engaged, but given that these notables did not constitute an integrated state apparatus, they did not closely tie the state into those economic activities. The tie was decentralized and personalized, not national and institutional.

This is reflected in the position of the monarch. Like the other nobles, the ruler was a major landowner who used the proceeds from his estate to manage his affairs. The ruler ran his household, and therefore the nascent state machine, from the proceeds of his estates like any other feudal lord. Like the other lords, the ruler benefited from the feudal obligations that adhered to the position he held: rents, dues and commuted services on his estates, the proceeds from monopolies he granted to local artisans and merchants, forest rights, fines and fees generated by the court system, and even profits skimmed off from the minting of coins were all major sources of income for the ruler.[107] The ruler could also supplement the funds he had available in ways which the other lords could not by special levies designed to meet a particular exigency, usually a war. In classic feudalism, the ruler was personally tied into economic activity, but the state was not. This was to begin to change with the commercialization and increased prosperity accompanying the economic expansion beginning in the eleventh century.

The revival and expansion of economic activity beginning in the eleventh century, involving the increased monetization of the economy, the expanding commercialization of retail and trade activity, the growth of mining, manufacturing and agriculture, the development of credit facilities, and the revival of long distance trade in luxury items, had a significant effect on feudal society. The gradual replacement of financial payments for feudal obligations has been noted above. But also important was the opportunity created for expanded sources of state income. As economic activity grew and wealth expanded, rulers increasingly saw the solution to their economic problems to lie not in the produce from their own lands, but in the exploitation of the economic activity of others. The seigneurial basis of royal power gradually was displaced by exploitation of broader economic activity. However, until the seventeenth century, generally the ruler's approach to the exploitation of economic life reflected short-term expedients rather than any coherent longer-term policy. Intervention in economic life generally was motivated by a desire to increase the revenue flows into the royal coffers rather than to improve economic performance: for example, the tolls imposed on domestic commerce rarely were used to improve the roads for which purpose they had been levied,[108] and duties were imposed on the export of goods. Funds were required to meet various pressing needs, especially in times of war. There was no sense of a general balance between income and expenditure in the ruler's household,[109] with revenue often being directed almost immediately into the meeting of one of the ruler's financial commitments. Furthermore, all of the funds collected were usually expended, with little concern to build up financial resources to meet later demands. In this sense, there was no consolidated revenue, only a fluctuating balance of cash in hand backed up by whatever credit the ruler could organize. There were, therefore, no regularized finances of the state and, indeed, not even a notion of public finance separate from the personal finances of the ruler.[110]

The economic revival was important in helping to change this, because it was the attempt by rulers to enlarge the revenue flow from economic activity into their own pockets that stimulated stronger resistance from within society. In England, this was part of the strengthening of Parliament discussed above. In all countries (although in some much quicker than others), such resistance forced some regularization of financial affairs and a separation of the finances of the ruler from the state. Taxation, the right to levy it and the purposes to which it was to be directed, was the principal form that this took and, as noted above, a major stimulus to this was war. In France geopolitical tensions were common as the king sought to enlarge his realm at the expense of the other lords, while the drive to expand English control over the Scots and Welsh and the attempt to defend the empire in France confronted the king with frequent military demands; in the twelfth, thirteenth and fourteenth centuries in particular, the military demands were heavy. By 1200 the English monarchy was already shifting away from reliance upon the royal domains toward a more general system of revenue-raising based upon the growing strength of the assumption that the ruler had a right to exact revenue from the general body of his subjects. In contrast in France, royal revenue-raising remained rooted in seigneurial rights and the produce of the domain; French nobles continued to reject non-feudal taxation up until the fourteenth century, with 1360 being the first time annual taxes could be levied across the realm in peace-time.[111] It was this generalized acceptance of the principle that rulers had the right to tax their subjects ostensibly for the general welfare – in England an acceptance that became bound up with the rise of Parliament, in France without such strengthening of an assembly's power – that marked the change from the personalized power of the feudal monarch to the institutional power of the state.

As the reliance upon taxation grew,[112] the forms tax took reflected the limits of state capacity. Throughout much of both the feudal and early modern periods, the principal form of taxation was indirect.[113] Taxes were imposed upon exports and imports, excises were imposed upon domestically-produced and consumed goods, tolls existed on means of transportation. Monopolies were established whereby individuals or groups were given exclusive right to manu-facture or trade in certain items in return for regular payments. Direct taxes were also used, including the hearth tax in England[114] and the taille (or land tax) in France,[115] but the collection of indirect taxes was simpler because it involved fewer collection points and less arbi-trariness in calculating tax liability levels. It did not need a tax gath-erer to visit every household in the realm. But regardless of the balance between direct and indirect taxes upon which different rulers relied at different times, throughout this period tax collection remained a haphazard operation, often reliant on tax farmers for its completion. Generally tax incomes were used by the state to support its own activities rather than to promote economic or social develop-ment, and tax levels were therefore directly related to its own needs rather than economic conditions. In this regard, the English state was better placed than the French: the reliance of English administration on local notables meant that less was needed in taxation to finance it than in France.

Taxation was not the only way in which political authorities were involved in economic life, however; economic activity had always been subject to attempts by political authorities to regulate and control. Much of this control was exercised from local levels rather than the putative national ruler. The fairs, which were such an important arena of commerce in feudal times, relied upon the local lord for the security of merchants travelling there (usually this was in conjunction with the lord's feudal superior, who was often the king) and for the system of justice and regulation within the fairs.[116] In twelfth-century England, most regulation of trade was at the local level.[117] However, the would-be ruler also sought to regulate economic activity. The central licensing of fairs and markets began in England with William I, but it was another century before this right was generally acknowledged, and it was not until the thirteenth century that the king claimed the right to close a market operating without a licence.[118] Some early royal charters of towns had provisions regulating commercial activity within them.[119] A standardized coinage was introduced into England in the 1160s and in France in 1262.[120] In 1290 in England, the king ordered all toll-owners to use those moneys to maintain the roads they controlled, and gradually through royal action internal customs barriers (although not road tolls) were abolished; by the end of the Middle Ages they were insignificant, with the only check on the movement of goods being at the border. Such a situation was not achieved until much later on the Continent: Austria in 1775, France 1790 and Venice 1794.[121] And kings often sought to enact regulations relating to some aspect of economic activity (e.g., an excise duty on wool and hides imposed in England in 1275), but for the most part these were ineffective. Royal intervention was episodic and not closely connected to what was happening on the ground.

As royal bureaucracies became better established, attempts at royal intervention in economic life became more sustained. In the fourteenth and fifteenth centuries, a string of measures introduced by successive monarchs sought to regulate foreign trade through protective measures designed to defend English industry and commerce from foreign competition. These included prohibition on the export and import of certain sorts of items, the restriction to English ships of the carriage of English goods, and the establishment of local trading companies. In France, especially during the reign of Louis XI (1461–83), similar sorts of measures were undertaken to protect domestic industry and attract foreign craftsmen. But such measures were not underpinned by a conscious conception of a policy designed to promote national economic development. These were still partial measures designed to meet specific difficulties. It was not until the sixteenth century that there emerged coherent thinking that conceived of something like a national economy[122] and that saw a link between the power of a state and the development of its economy.

These developments marked the transition from the feudal state to the early modern state, with an accompanying increased state interest in economic involvement. By this time the bulk of the state and its activities in pursuing its own development were themselves important factors in structuring economic activity. The early modern state was generally the largest single actor on the economic stage; it was the largest receiver of income, the largest spender, and the largest employer.[123] Its needs stimulated economic activity. A considerable proportion of the state's income in the early modern period was spent on conspicuous consumption, principally in the form of the projection of an image of the royal court as glorious and all-powerful. This stimulated certain sorts of production by providing a guaranteed market for its products. States also became directly involved in production. Many courts had small workshops lodged on to their flanks to provide the goods they required. States fostered building projects, which stimulated local industry; the extension and subsequent rebuilding of Hampton Court in England and Versailles in France are two prominent examples of this, but perhaps of more continuing importance was the creation of new ports. Of course much of the funding for such projects was derived from borrowing, and large-scale state borrowing could also have a destabilizing effect. It could drain funds from more directly economic activity, lead to bankruptcies, and force up interest rates. But it could also stimulate economic activity; indeed, the development of borrowing and the banking system itself was shaped by the state's need for credit.[124] Thus even when the state did not set out to implement specifically economic policy, its activities helped to shape economic development.

By the middle of the sixteenth century, with a well-established international credit market operating, leading financial officials in Europe had a sense of a national balance of payments, even if the term was not yet in use.[125] Despite the fact that by the end of that century taxation was generally accepted as the only means of funding a state, states did not have annual budgets.[126] The management of state finances remained disjointed, yet it was during this century that both in England and France the state made a renewed push to regulate economic life. The position of the French king seemed to be stronger than that of the English in this regard. Not only did he have a more extensive state bureaucracy, but he also had more untrammelled access to economic life because he possessed rights which for his counterpart were problematic:[127]

1   The French king claimed the right to administer all economic enterprises that were deemed necessary for the defence of the realm. The rights of the English Crown in this regard were contested by Parliament.
2   The French king had the right to dispose of some natural products, most especially ores, minerals and salt, even when these were found in privately-owned lands. In England, possession of underground resources (except gold and silver) lay with the landowner.
3   The French king claimed the right to establish a monopoly of certain branches of manufacturing in particular towns or provinces, and to endow this upon individuals. In England, this encountered Parliamentary and local resistance from urban authorities; in 1640 Parliament ended nearly all industrial monopolies.

The attempts by the French kings to increase their regulatory control over the economy were more successful in the century leading up to the English civil war than were those of the English monarchs. The monarchs of both countries over this century introduced similar sorts of measures. They attempted to strengthen the craft guilds in the towns and to use them to regulate production and relations between masters and workers. Attempts were made to fix wages and prices,[128] to guarantee the quality of products produced. The state sought to play a role in ensuring food supplies, although in England this was mainly left to local authorities.[129] Royal monopolies were established over weapons production, in what was a trend across the Continent,[130] although they were much less successful in England than in France. Such monopolies covered the production of saltpetre, gunpowder, shot, cannon balls, muskets and artillery pieces in France, whose king was also able to establish a monopoly on mining and on the production of salt.

In France, encouragement was also given to inventors through the allocation of patents, to foreign craftsmen through the granting of special privileges, and some royal workshops were also established to produce artistic and luxury items. Restrictions were placed on imports to help manufacturers, incentives were provided to producers, state workshops were established to produce some luxury goods, and monopoly rights were granted for the production of other goods. In terms of foreign trade, the import of raw materials was tax free while manufactured goods were taxed, French exports were subsidized, and from 1673 foreign ships were excluded from colonial trade. Overseas trading companies were largely state controlled and their economic activities were meant to be subordinated to state interests. In the sixteenth–seventeenth century, the English state also acted to defend its domestic economy. The wool trade had long been protected, reflecting its long-standing importance for royal revenues.[131] Italian merchant bankers were expelled and the Hanseatic merchants stripped of their privileges, the predecessor of the Royal Exchange was founded in the mid-1560s, high duties were placed on foreign products, and the Navigation Act of 1651 restricted the use of foreign shipping in bringing goods to England. Private trading companies were launched, usually with a monopoly franchise granted by the Crown, to dominate trade with the expanding empire. In contrast to the French, the English state did not seek to control these companies, instead being content to facilitate their operations, to bolster their monopoly at home and use them as a source of revenue through taxes and loans. From the early 1700s, English grain exports were underpinned by bounties. Although state control was much more extensive in France than in England, because of the continuing divisions within the country, the French were further than the English from having a national economy.[132]

While the attempted expansion of royal regulation constituted a new phase in the relationship between state and economic life,[133] it is not clear that the aim was to facilitate economic development. The attempts to regulate relations between masters and workers, to fix wages and prices, and guarantee the quality of goods were aimed as much at ensuring social peace as anything else. Similarly the monopolies over salt and many other products were designed to ensure continuing levels of state income, while those over armaments were directed at improving the state's capacity for defence. But although the advantages of such measures were not generally seen in economic terms, they were seen in terms of strengthening the state, albeit sometimes indirectly. This outlook was consistent with the thinking that was emerging in the seventeenth century that saw state resources as a weapon in geopolitical conflict and therefore sought ways of comparing the resources possessed by the different states.[134] It was a short step from this to mercantilism.

Mercantilism was a loose set of assumptions rather than a coherent system, but its essence was the following: 'the wealth of the kingdom could be increased through manufactures, whose export would sustain the necessary imports of precious metals and other scarce commodities, while measures should be taken to minimize the export of bullion and the importation of expensive luxury goods'.[135] This meant that there was seen to be a direct relationship between economic growth, the prosperity of the populace and the growth in the state's fiscal and military power.[136] Mercantilism represents the first conscious enunciation of a principle of structuring national economic life in a way that would benefit both the populace and the state. In Braudel's words, mercantilism was 'the transfer of control of economic activity from the local community to the state'.[137] This tying of the state and its power to the regulation of the economy marks a complete contrast with the feudal situation, where the perspective was essentially personalist. It marks the state as an independent actor in the conceptions of political elites, and emphasizes the importance for state power and survival of economic policy. It came to the fore about the time the English state adopted virtually sole responsibility for funding national defence (just after the Restoration),[138] and when the first sustained joint use of economic power in a war occurred.[139] The most enthusiastic supporter of mercantilism has usually been considered to be French finance minister Jean-Baptiste Colbert (1661–83), who pursued an economically interventionist policy designed to build state power, but his successes were limited.[140] The policy also operated in England, where there was a significant increase in the share of income taken by the state in the late seventeenth century.[141] But while mercantilism was clearly an important change in the state's attitude to the economy, it could not of itself overcome the continuing weakness in the state's institutional interdependence. There were not well-developed ties between the state and economic actors which would enable sustained cooperation in policy-making and implementation.

***

Despite the limitations of mercantilism as a doctrine, its emergence clearly reflects the changed conception of the state possessed by political elites. The administrative construction arising out of the feudal state transformed the early modern state into an entity very different from its feudal roots. The personalized nature of feudal political arrangements was transformed into an institutional structure that had many of the characteristics of the modern state in embryonic form, and was clearly a major advance upon its feudal parent in terms of the administrative machinery and the regularity with which it worked. Similarly, although less so in many of the absolutist states, legitimation no longer rested upon either a religious basis or claims related to personal lineage. And a state that was seeking actively to intervene in the economy, and which now possessed some instruments to do so, clearly contrasts with its feudal forebear; the capacity of the early modern state far surpassed that of its feudal predecessor. Thus it was during this period that the state as an identifiable and distinct entity emerged. Authority became more depersonalized, being vested in offices rather than individuals, more regularized, and more differentiated from other spheres of life. The state bureaucracy was becoming more specialized and claims to a central monopoly of force more realistic. But the state was also looking at becoming more interventionist in many sectors of life, reflecting an increase in its infrastructural power.

This also reflects the fact that, as its bulk grew and its capacities increased, the state began to shift from being a taxing body intent on garnering resources to itself largely simply to maintain itself, into a body with a broader vision of its role in society. The move away from the feudal personalist base and the strengthening of infrastructural capacity transformed the state from a weak adjunct of the ruler's household into a more substantial bureaucratic structure whose impact upon society could be significant. But that impact, and the state's connection with society, was profoundly influenced by the way the state developed during the feudal period. In France, where the centre relied principally upon the extension of bureaucratic reach to penetrate society and overcome the legacy of strong local autonomy, the result was an attempted hyper-centralization in absolutism. But up until the Revolution the state remained very weakly anchored in what would be French society. The state's organic interdependence, both bureaucratic and legislative, was narrow and shallow.

The English state was more solidly embedded in its society. This was because the combination of pre-feudal centralized tradition and local administration meant that the centre relied less on the extension of a centralized bureaucracy into the lower reaches of society than upon the continued cooperation of local notables for the administration of the country. These lower-level notables did not disappear into society and thereby leave the central state apparatus free floating because they were tied in to the state through its legislative arm. Thus in England, narrowly-based bureaucratic organic interdependence was substantially supplemented by a well-developed legislative organic interdependence. It was this reliance upon both administrative and legislative arms that enabled the state to become firmly embedded in society and, despite its smaller size, to operate more effectively than its absolutist French counterpart, but state capacity remained restricted in both countries. The infrastructure did not exist to extend effective political power into the lowest reaches of society, state policy was still not grounded in a cooperative relationship with forces in the society, and ideological power remained shared with the Church. Central government rarely extended into the localities, which throughout this period largely governed themselves.

Nevertheless, by the end of the eighteenth century there was a clear difference between the English and French states, and this was a difference rooted in the feudal period. Despite the difference, both states were clearly much more developed institutionally than they had been at any time in the past but, given their continuing infrastructural weakness, both states remained pre-modern in nature.

4

The State, Capitalism and Industrialization

By the second half of the eighteenth century, despite the continued presence of the Russian, Habsburg and Ottoman empires in Eastern Europe and the diversity of small states in what would become Germany and Italy, the territorial state was becoming the dominant political actor in Europe. Increasingly central government was becoming more complex, especially in the non-absolutist states where the Court played a much more restricted role. However, the state's capacity to project central rule into the localities remained limited. The infrastructure did not exist to enable the construction of a bureaucratic hierarchy extending deep into society. Similarly, in constitutional England, where central rule relied upon the cooperation of local notables tied to the centre by ideology and the Parliament, the institutional means did not exist for the exercise of intrusive controls by the centre or for a coherent process of interdependence between state and society. In the nineteenth century the means that would enable both of these would begin to be built. This was associated with the rise of industrialization.

Much of the discussion of the relationship between the state and its emergence on the one hand and capitalism on the other has been confused by a tendency to merge capitalism with industrialization. Perhaps in part seduced by the Marxist notion of the transition from feudalism to capitalism, many writers have been prone to see capitalism only in terms of industrial capitalism. However, it is clear that if we acknowledge the important role played by mercantile and financial capital in the economic development of much of Europe, capitalism at least in some sectors predated the industrial surge of the late-eighteenth and nineteenth centuries.[1] In her discussion of the economic activities of city states in the thirteenth century, Janet

Abu-Lughod argues that because of the feudal form of social organization that still prevailed, the merchants should be considered 'pre-capitalist' and the cities 'almost capitalist'.[2] What this means is that before capitalism became established as the dominant socio-economic structure in individual countries and in the Continent more generally, capitalist processes and principles dominated in particular sectors of economic life.

Similarly, there has been significant debate about the relationship between absolutist rule and capitalism. For one school of thought, reflected in the work of Perry Anderson, absolutism was the form of state fashioned by the feudal nobility when their power was ebbing, in an attempt to bolster their traditional position by using state power to keep the peasantry in check. The absolutist state was thus a 'redeployed and recharged apparatus of feudal domination', 'the new political carapace of a threatened nobility', and the final throw of 'the feudal nobility in the epoch of transition to capitalism'.[3] However, for others, the absolutist state was the strong state that was necessary to legitimize the capitalist social revolution and to provide the protection that the construction of capitalism and the extension of its political power needed.[4] Thus rather than being the shell of a renewed feudal nobility, absolutism became the vehicle of an emergent capitalism. A third view saw the absolutist state as the tool neither of the feudal aristocracy nor the emergent bourgeoisie, but as an autonomous actor in itself, either temporarily as bourgeoisie and aristocracy balanced each other[5] or more permanently as autonomous state elites were able to boost state extraction from their subjects and strengthen state power.[6] There has been considerable dispute over these interpretations of the nature of absolutism but, regardless of their differences, all agree on one point: capitalist forces were operating in Europe well before the industrial development of the late eighteenth and nineteenth centuries. Thus the issue that is the focus of this chapter is not the relationship between the emergent state and capitalism, but between the state and capitalist industrialism,[7] which is when capitalism became the dominant mode of economic production and social organization.

The debate about the nature of absolutism turns on the issue of its relationship with the rise of capitalist industrialism. For those who see absolutism as central to the emergence of capitalist industrialism, three factors usually are identified as being crucial:

- territoral centralization and the creation of a single economic space governed by common principles backed up by the force of the state

- the re-introduction of Roman Law, and with it the sense of private property
- mercantilist policies directed at increasing the power of the state by structuring economic matters in particular ways

Each of these points will be discussed below, but it is important to recognize that there is no necessity about absolutist rule as a precursor to, or incubator of, capitalist industrialism. The earliest development of capitalist industrialism occurred in Britain and, as argued in the preceding chapter, Britain was not an absolutist power. Certainly in terms of the relationship between state and society, following 1688 the state's power seemed substantial; there was no armed force in the kingdom that could stand against the political authorities should the latter choose to flex their military muscles. However, the state itself was not monolithic, and the monarchy was far from the position acquired by its absolutist cousins in France and Spain. Balanced by the Parliament, and indeed from 1688 effectively limited by the Parliament, the monarch increasingly came to rule under the banner of a constitutional regime. Far from capitalist industrialism stemming from absolutism, it actually grew out of a constitutionalist regime. Furthermore, this regime was one which fostered the unity of property-owning classes by subjecting all to fiscal extraction measures while continuing to rely on local notables for administrative functions, in contrast to absolutism which sought to strengthen the feudal distinctions between different types of property.[8] However, although not absolutist, this regime 'was a firm and centrally focused system which provided the security and uniformity upon which trade and industry could be based'.[9]

The State and Industrialism

The state played a crucial role in the blossoming of capitalist industrialism. This role had two principal elements: first, the by-product of actions taken by the state which were not designed to have an economic impact but which did facilitate capitalist industrial development; second, measures that were designed to have a direct economic impact, and that therefore show the state playing a conscious and active role in economic affairs.[10] Both types of action were crucial in fostering capitalist industrialism, and show the way the state had moved by this time into a position whereby it could not just affect the economy from the side, but could actually reshape it through state action. We will look at this question by concentrating on Britain, the first industrializer of the modern period and the country where the state has traditionally been seen as having played little role in industrialization.

One of the most critical factors facilitating the emergence of capitalist industrialism was one aspect of the process of state development itself, the territorial consolidation of the state. Territorial consolidation involved both the extension of the power and authority of a single centre over the national territory, a development involving the elimination of autonomous centres of power which sought to challenge the centre, and the delineation of national boundaries as lines establishing the limits of that centre's authority. This was important economically because what it did was to create a single economic space defined politically.[11] Such a development could encourage cultural and linguistic unity, and thereby the development of a single cultural unit, a status England had gained by about 1600.[12] The assertion of political authority, even if at times more ad hoc and intermittent than systematic and regularized, imposed upon society a series of restraints which acted to structure and facilitate economic activity. One of the most important of these was the establishment of law and order. While the development of a consistent code of legislation was not something that came quickly or easily to states, the elimination of rival centres of power within the national state ensured that at least only one such code prevailed. The regularization of this code was important because it reflected a growing predictability of life and security of activity, including commerce. It created the environment within which trust could develop, something upon which large-scale economic activity relied. The primacy of the law, and the willingness and capacity of the state to enforce it, created a much more secure environment. It enabled entrepreneurs to take risks and extend their economic activity, providing them with the guarantee that even if all risk could not be eliminated, certain types could be reduced by the threat of state retribution. This increased security not only against banditry on the roads, but also against breach of contract in business dealings; contract law gave a stable underpinning to economic exchange. The emergence of the state as a potential arbiter in this regard greatly enhanced the prospects for expanded economic activity.

The development of a codified legal system applying across the territory was also important because of what it enshrined, the concept of private ownership.[13] In Britain this was rooted not in a revived

Roman Law (as it was in France), but in the common law tradition growing out of pre-Conquest times. The importance of this lay less in the form of law in which it was embodied than in what it embraced. Private property came to be recognized not just in land and material property, but also in patents and inventions. The extension of the principle of private ownership was important because it gave increased security to those seeking to engage in economic life as well as providing them with legal title to the resources which they could then mobilize in productive ways to increase their wealth. In this way it provided a solid underpinning to the growth of the private economy. The extension of this to patents encouraged both invention and investment, and therefore stimulated economic development. Thus while law was important for capitalist economic development, that law did not have to be Roman in origin.

As well as legal regulation, the extension of central power involved a shift towards the standardization of the currency and the establishment of common systems of weights and measures. These provided a consistent and standard medium of exchange, thereby facilitating increased economic interaction. Combined with the increased security stemming from the state enforcement of the legal system, the development of such measures not only facilitated economic interaction, but also helped to break down the isolation of the local market systems which had been the hallmark of economic life in feudal times. Increased commerce could gradually draw the diverse regions closer together, while the introduction of standardized means of exchange helped to break down the barriers separating them. In this sense, these measures helped to create the conditions for the emergence of a national economic space which transcended the localist particularisms so characteristic of feudalism. The effect of this was reinforced by the state's pursuit of mercantilist policies, including the elimination of internal tolls and trade barriers and the systematic imposition of tariffs on foreign goods. State action was thus crucial for defining the boundaries of the economic area: it broke down many of the localist boundaries within state borders and reinforced those external borders through the imposition of economic controls. Indeed the whole process of internal colonialization involving the absorption of the Scots, Welsh and Irish into the British state and the state-fostered opening-up of these regions to economic exploitation (e.g., the Highland clearances) was an important element in the creation of such an entity. The definition of the single national economic space was thus a function of state action.

Another way the state assisted in overcoming internal local boundaries to economic activity was the support it gave to the construction of modes of transport, especially the railways and canals. Although state involvement was more substantial and direct on the Continent than in Britain, even in Britain the state was crucial to the construction of such infrastructure; parliamentary support for these private endeavours was crucial, while national regulation underpinned the growing networks' operation.

Another aspect of state development was significant for the fostering of economic development. The role of geopolitical competition and war in state development will be discussed more fully below, but this could also be important for economic stimulation. State involvement in war, preparation for war and the maintenance of a powerful international profile all involved increased expenditure on armaments and weapons production. This sort of industrial production had a number of spin-offs. First, military conflict and the need to supply the troops increased the consumption of iron and textiles, thereby providing a direct stimulus to these sectors of the economy. In the nineteenth century (in some countries at least) it also stimulated the development of railways, something which had clear ramifications for subsequent economic development. Second, military demand for large quantities of particular items in a hurry stimulated the deepening and concentration of production. Cottage industries could not provide the military wherewithal in the amounts and with the precision needed, thereby encouraging the development of larger production centres. Third, military exigencies created demand in the economy, and could therefore help to substitute for a lack of demand arising from the civilian sector. And fourth, because of the importance of this sort of enterprise, states frequently became directly involved in the production of the means of waging war. The establishment of state arsenals (e.g., in Venice as early as 1104) and of state monopolies in textiles, iron foundries and arms factories[14] was a common response to international geopolitical uncertainty. More generally, then, military concerns encouraged states in the eighteenth and nineteenth centuries to seek to introduce industrial policies. In these ways, state involvement in military activity could act as a stimulant to economic development. By the nineteenth century, this was a stimulant to industrial production, at least in Britain and France, while it may also be argued that the long period of intense war in which Britain was involved in the eighteenth century made the government receptive to the sort of measures that would stimulate industrial development in the nineteenth century.[15] It is striking that in the main period of British industrialization, the state incurred very high levels of state expenditure.[16]

The British state was also instrumental in developing the funding basis upon which industrialization rested, although not primarily through direct investment. Through its involvement in military activity and the associated need to borrow in order to sustain this effort, the state stimulated the development of a domestic money market, preferring to borrow at home through the Bank of England (established 1694). With the national debt concentrated principally in the City of London, it was upon this secure base that the financial market developed, thereby providing a source of funds for the industrial growth that occurred in the eighteenth and nineteenth centuries. The strong development of British financial capital rested upon this basis.[17] The position of capital was further buttressed by the tax system and the interest rate policy pursued by successive governments which had the effect of diverting income into the hands of those elements of the population who were both in a position and felt disposed to invest in economic development.[18] In addition, until 1846, Britain maintained high tariff walls behind which the early industrial spurts could take place[19] and which facilitated its early competitive advantage. Such a policy clearly advantaged economic development, and was in part motivated precisely by that aim.

The state's role in fostering the growth of capitalist industrialism is also evident in what we may call its pacificatory role. Reference has been made above to one form of pacification: the destruction of potential alternative authoritative power centres and the consequent creation of a single economic space within which the state enforced law and order. But also important was the state's role in creating the structures of discipline and coercion which were so important for the emergence of an urban working class. As capitalist industrialism grew, it relied upon the creation of a docile labour force. The state played a crucial role in this. The creation of the Metropolitan Police in 1829 in direct response to the popular disorder of the preceding decades was the public symbol of this role. It emerged openly as a disciplinary organ, with a brief to maintain public order (for a fuller discussion, see below) including the disciplining of the work force. The state introduced a range of measures to bring about labour control, including the revised Poor Law system and the prohibition on the emigration of skilled workers and the export of machinery in 1795, and the Anti-Combination Acts of 1799. But as well as the stick of coercion, the state also sought popular pacification through the growing provision of a range of services to the burgeoning urban working-class population. The introduction of such things as sewerage, paved roads and street lighting, the growth of regulation in housing and the gradual emergence of public transport were all designed to improve the quality of urban life, and given that an increasing proportion of urban inhabitants worked in the new factories and mills, they improved the life of the working class. The development of a disciplined and passive working class, while never fully achieved, was therefore a result in part of the intervention of the British state in the conditions of urban life.

Through these means the British state established the basis upon which capitalist industrialism could grow. While some of these were by-products of state development, the state also introduced measures aiming to foster economic development. The elimination of some of the constraints of the feudal period, such as the power of the guilds and sumptuary laws, and the enclosure of agricultural land,[20] were important in creating an environment in which capitalist industrialism could prosper. More immediate were mercantilist measures, including changing policy related to protection and free trade. Early British industrial development occurred behind protectionist tariff walls and mercantilist policies designed specifically to foster economic growth. Once Britain had achieved the leading position internationally, and being the first to industrialize this was not difficult, international protectionism was seen as being economically disadvantageous. Accordingly, in the first half of the nineteenth century, the main elements of mercantilism were wound back. By the mid-nineteenth century, British policy was as close to laissez-faire as it would get;[21] except for the mint, some armaments establishments and some building, the state was no longer involved in direct production. But even during the laissez-faire period, state involvement in the economy at some level remained essential. There was still the need for the regulation of commercial activities, the oversight of economic and transport infrastructure, and stabilization of financial and currency matters.

Thus when the official policy of laissez-faire was overturned in the face of increasing competition from elsewhere in Europe in the last quarter of the nineteenth century, there was a basis of state involvement in the economy from which this could grow. Britain was part of a Europe-wide trend whereby, in the words of one scholar, 'the state moved to tackle the economic and social problems of growth, to salvage railways [*sic*] systems, to bolster weak sections of the economy, and to ameliorate the increasingly apparent social tensions and problems of urban and industrial maturity, which demanded more welfare legislation and social reform'.[22] In Britain, government loans to enterprises, mainly in the armaments and communications sectors, increased from zero before 1870 to about £50 million just before 1914, enlarged social welfare provisions were enacted, and government intervention in the labour market (including fixing wage rates and involvement in labour disputes) became accepted.[23]

The policy leading to the creation of empire was also relevant here. While imperial ambition was partly driven by the aspiration to state glorification, economic motives were always present.[24] Indeed, the imperial system of commerce was designed specifically to benefit the home market and its emergent industrial basis. This was an important source of wealth underpinning British economic development. The state was never simply motivated by the desire to promote economic development, but this was always one part of its intention as it expanded its sphere of competence, especially during the nineteenth century (see below). But it is important to recognize that the British state's role in the development of capitalist industrialism was essentially facilitatory. The main impetus for industrial development came from non-state sources, principally from the emergent capitalist class which used the opportunities and openings in part provided by the state to establish their enterprises and pursue their profits.

The British state at the national level was never simply the instrument of the industrialists; indeed, it was much closer to financial circles in the City than it was to the emergent industrial establishment.[25] However, the linkage between industrialists and the state at lower levels was often much closer. In the new industrial towns, industrialists often entered the local councils and urban authorities, prompted in part by the fact that it was these bodies that exercised the planning and licensing powers fundamental to the operation of local industry. Indeed, it was usually the municipal councils that were behind the provision of the sorts of urban service noted above. But also significant was the high level of amateurism at the lower levels of the English state.[26] As indicated in the last chapter, a large number of offices at the lower levels of English administration were filled not by full-time salaried civil servants, but by members of the local gentry acting in an unpaid, essentially amateur capacity. The best example of this is the Justice of the Peace who, although an amateur, acted 'within a strict framework of statutory regulation, in which they were personally liable for maladministration'.[27] Local landowners were also prominent in parliamentary representation. They therefore played a substantial role in running local affairs. This was important for the issue at hand because of the coming together of the traditional landed interests and the emergent industrial and financial interests. The prominent role in local government and administration played by the gentry, added to the connections between this group and emergent capitalists, meant that the bases of the English state were more intimately connected with the impulse to capitalist industrialism than was the case for states elsewhere. This meant that, although the national leaders of the state may initially have been wary of the potential effects and consequences of the development of industrialism, there was much more sympathy for this development at the lower levels of the state, and the state was a more willing partner in it than might have been expected. Nevertheless, the primary impetus for capitalist industrialism came from the industrialists themselves.

The 'Late Developers'

The nature of the role played by the British state, primarily facilitatory rather than generative,[28] reflects the circumstances of British industrialization. Being the first state to industrialize on a large scale, not only did the British state have no models to follow, it had no direct competitor against which to measure its performance. State elites were aware of some of the implications industrialization could have for geopolitical competition and especially for the honing of the war machine. However, because Britain had no immediate challenger in the industrialization stakes and because the process of industrialization itself was new and therefore little understood, there was little incentive for the state to become a direct force in driving industrialization. State elites could afford to let industrialization broadly take its course without trying to use the state to propel it forward at a rate faster than, or in a direction other than, that which it would have taken without such intervention. This luxury was not available to those who came to industrialization somewhat later.

The situation of the so-called 'late developers' and their use of the state to accelerate the course of development has been recognized for some time.[29] The essence of this argument is that state elites perceive their country to be at a disadvantage because of the higher levels of industrialization already achieved by other states, most importantly Britain. Recognizing that in their own countries the sort of bourgeoisie that was the primary force for industrial development in Britain was weak, those elites seek to use the state as a 'surrogate entrepreneur' to drive through a programme of full-scale industrialization. Rather than playing a limited facilitatory role, the state is a major force generating industrial development and expansion, both through direct investment and a wide range of other policy initiatives.

The primary examples of this are said to be Tsarist Russia and Germany.[30] In both countries, the state pursued active policies designed to stimulate economic growth and thereby strengthen both the state and the regime; it was not a conscious policy to foster capitalist industrial development because the emergence of independent capitalist entrepreneurs was frustrated, but an attempt to strengthen political rule. In Russia, especially in the 1890s when Sergei Witte was Finance Minister, the state pursued a policy of stimulating heavy industrial development, principally through using railway construction as a stimulus. This was accompanied by high tariff protection which was aimed not just at protecting domestic industry from foreign competition, but at generating a balance of payments surplus. This was designed to bring about the accumulation of gold, which would enable the shifting of the currency on to the gold standard and thereby facilitate foreign investment. In addition, industry was to be assisted through state subsidies and guaranteed supply contracts, while heavy taxation levels would bring about a shift of resources from the peasant population into the industrial sector.[31] In Germany in the latter part of the nineteenth century, state policy was also directed at stimulating domestic development. High tariff walls,[32] railway construction (although this began before the main period of industrial development, it accelerated significantly after German unification in 1871 ushered in the main period of industrial growth), welcoming foreign capital, financial support to industry[33] and the encouragement of mergers and cartels to assist investment and competition were all designed to assist German industrialization and to reinforce the highly cartelized form this took.

John Hobson has criticized the late developer thesis.[34] He has argued that this thesis:

- exaggerates the 'economic rationality' of the state by underplaying the fiscal and geopolitical motives of the state, which often cut across more purely economic factors

- underestimates the extent to which state policy was motivated by short-term considerations rather than long-term perspectives on economic policy
- assumes a coherence in the state which is belied by the conflict that ensued between different bureaucratic departments
- assumes that states were seeking full industrialization when this was by no means necessarily the case
- underplays the importance of geopolitical imperatives, in particular the inter-state military system
- assumes that states were important only in cases of late development

These points are well made with regard to the logic of the Gerschenkron late developer thesis. However, they are less relevant to the phenomenon at the heart of that thesis: the increased role played by the state in the direct sponsoring of industrial development. It is clear that these states played a similar role to that of Britain in creating much of the infrastructure for industrial growth: a national economic space, common means of exchange and property rights. But, in addition, they were directly involved in shaping the course of industrial development through the measures they took to promote that development. Regardless of whether this was prompted by short-term geopolitical concerns or longer-term economic goals, it clearly constituted a higher level of intervention into the economic process than was evident in Britain. This does not mean that it was more effective,[35] but it was certainly larger in scale and different in contour.

The state had always had an impact upon economic life even when it did not consciously seek to do so. A decision to go to war in feudal times could stimulate those regions where the production of military wherewithal was conducted and adversely affect those from which large numbers of men were withdrawn to fight. Resort to the printing press in order to finance military activity could lead to inflation in some parts of the country or in that section of the economy which was monetarized. A monarch's seizure of large estates, as in the seizure of Church lands by Henry VIII of England, could have impacts upon production levels, with perhaps short-term disruption giving way to longer-term improvement. The imposition and enforcement of tariffs could drive up the prices of those imported goods upon which the tariffs were imposed. But these sorts of effect tended to be episodic and, given the geographically segmented nature of the economy, were sometimes only local in their effect. The state's intervention in economic life during industrialization was much greater in both scope and scale. In part this was because of the effect of the single economic area arising from state territorial consolidation. The establishment of a single area under one political authority greatly enhanced the chances of central decisions having an impact in all parts of the territory. Furthermore, as the economic barriers between regions were reduced and a single market area came into existence, the economic structure itself facilitated the flow of governmental action and decision to all parts of the territory. Given the increased infrastructural reach industrialization provided to the state (see below), the impact of state decisions was enhanced. The effect of this was increased by the way in which state elites became more aware of the increased capacity available to them to influence economic life and the perception that through conscious action they could bring about desired effects. The notion of the 'national economy', the role it played in state security and strength, and the perception that this could be changed all combined to make state elites more aware of the possibilities and consequences of influencing economic life, and therefore more willing to act in that way. During industrialization, the state was probably more engaged in economic life, and in some cases more directly and immediately engaged, than at any time in the past, except perhaps for some of the ancient states.

Industrialization and the Development of State Infrastructure

Industrialization was revolutionary. This was the most fundamental change in the mode of production since the shift to sedentary agriculture because this involved the complete reshaping of the contours of organized human life. It brought people physically together in greater numbers than hitherto and, through the modes of transport and communications that emerged, knitted them more closely together into national units. Its fundamental transformation of the contours of human society was accompanied by a revolutionary transformation of the nature of the state and its role in society. The central component of this was the massive strengthening of the infrastructural capacity of the state.

Means of communication and transport were fundamentally transformed at this time.[36] The most obvious, and public, form of this was

Table 4.1   *Railway development in Europe*

	Britain	France	Prussia/Germany	Russia	Italy
1838	864				
1848		c.3,200	2,400		
1850	10,593				
1870	24,500	17,500	19,500	12,000	6,000
1890	33,000	36,500	43,000	30,000	13,000
1910	38,000	49,500	61,000	70,000	17,000

Source: David Thomson, *Europe Since Napoleon* (Harmondsworth, Penguin, 1966), p.378.

the spread of the railways. In the second half of the nineteenth century, railway construction proceeded apace in Western Europe, tying together areas formerly separated and providing a channel the central state authorities could use to penetrate far flung parts of the country. Table 4.1 shows the extent of this development (all distances are in kilometres).

The railway provided not only an efficient means of transporting bulky, heavy items, but an effective way of despatching communications and officials from central state bureaucracies. Supplemented by the improving quality of roads, the development of networks of canals and the much later development of the internal combustion engine and the telegraph and telephone, this improved communications between central politico/administrative authorities and officials in the provinces. The reliance upon local agents with their loyalties rooted in their localities and largely cut off from external monitoring was overcome as, figuratively, the improved techniques of transport and communication strengthened the ties binding them to the centre. The degree to which this was reality in the nineteenth century should not be exaggerated. Even in a relatively small country such as Britain, which was the most highly industrialized of all, contacts between the capital and outlying regions remained for the most part extended. However, the continuing improvement in communications and transport, and the potential these gave for visits from the centre, did ameliorate the sense of distance that formerly had prevailed in relations between centre and officials.

Important in this too was the growth of literacy. Part of the social revolution accompanying industrialization was the enormous growth in adult literacy across Western Europe. This was in large part a function of the establishment of national education systems by the state; by the end of the nineteenth century a state system of education had been established in Britain and illiteracy virtually eliminated from the adult population.[37] This was complemented by the creation of a system of technical and trade education designed to equip workers for the demands of the industrial economy. The expansion of education meant the creation of a work force for the new factories and mills that, being literate, was considered to be both more dependable and more adaptable, and therefore better suited for working in the conditions of an industrialized labour force. In addition, this appealed to those pamphleteers who saw the new industrial society as producing a better, more refined type of person than had been possible earlier. For much of the population the abolition of illiteracy probably meant little more than a basic functional literacy, the ability to write their own name and perhaps to read the newspaper. However, the expansion of education also meant the creation of more people who had the literacy and numeracy skills to fill responsible positions in an expanding state bureaucracy. This meant increased record-keeping capacities. With the possibility of a large work force who could read and write fluently, the potential for the keeping of records expanded significantly. Expanded record-keeping, allied to its internal systematization, gave increased capacity for achieving consistency in decision-making and for the continuing monitoring of performance. It enabled the transmission of instructions, directives and regulations more widely and with greater reliability so that their meaning would not become transformed in the process. It thereby made bureaucratic administration possible on a much larger scale: the scope for record-keeping at the centre and the capacity for reach from the centre into the country expanded considerably.

This was part of the expansion in size of the state at this time. Michael Mann has argued that, during the nineteenth century, the state did not become 'larger in relation to its civil society' but that within the state there was a shift of resources away from military functions (because of the relatively pacific nature of that century) into civilian functions.[38] However, the situation is not that simple.[39]

The general trend shown in Table 4.2 is for an increase in the size of the state bureaucracy over the nineteenth century, including at the height of industrialization in the second half of that century, even allowing for the population increase each state experienced during this time.[40] But this increase is neither standard across the central and non-central state structures nor between countries. Only the figures for Britain and France enable us to compare the growth over this half-century in both the central and non-central spheres.

Table 4.2   *State employment of civilian personnel (in thousands, and as a percentage of the total population)*

	Central state				All levels			
	France	Great Britain	Prussia-Germany	USA	France	Great Britain	Prussia-Germany[*]	USA
1760	n/a	16 (0.26%)	n/a	n/a	n/a	n/a	n/a	n/a
1780	n/a	n/a	n/a	n/a	350 (1.29%)	n/a	n/a	n/a
1790	n/a	n/a	n/a	0.7 (0.02%)	275 (1.01%)	n/a	n/a	n/a
1800	n/a	16 (0.18%)	23 (0.37%)	2.6 (0.04%)	250 (0.91%)	n/a	n/a	n/a
1810	n/a	23 (0.24%)	n/a	3.8 (0.05%)	n/a	n/a	n/a	n/a
1820	n/a	24 (0.22%)	n/a	7 (0.07%)	n/a	n/a	n/a	n/a
1830	n/a	23 (0.17%)	n/a	11 (0.09%)	n/a	n/a	n/a	n/a
1840	90 (0.26%)	n/a	16+ (0.11+%)	18 (0.11%)	n/a	43 (0.29%)	n/a	n/a
1850	146 (0.41%)	40 (0.24%)	32+ (0.20+%)	26 (0.11%)	300 (0.84%)	67 (0.41%)	55+ (0.33+%)	n/a
1860	n/a	n/a	n/a	37 (0.12%)	n/a	76 (0.41%)	86 (0.47%)	n/a
1870	220 (0.60%)	n/a	135 (0.55%)	51 (0.13%)	374 (1.03%)	113 (0.53%)	283 (1.15%)	n/a
1880	331 (0.87%)	n/a	n/a	100 (0.19%)	483 (1.28%)	118 (0.46%)	704 (1.56%)	n/a
1890	348 (0.91%)	90 (0.32%)	n/a	157 (0.25%)	472 (1.23%)	285 (0.99%)	900 (1.70%)	n/a
1900	430 (1.10%)	130 (0.40%)	n/a	239 (0.31%)	583 (1.50%)	535 (1.66%)	n/a	1,034 (1.36%)
1910	556 (1.40%)	229 (0.64%)	n/a	389 (0.42%)	562 (1.42%)	931 (2.60%)	1700 (2.35%)	1552 (1.68%)

[*] Prussia until 1870, Germany after that date. n/a = not available
Source: M. Mann, *The Sources of Social Power. Vol. II. The Rise of Classes and Nation-States, 1760–1914* (Cambridge, Cambridge University Press, 1993), pp.806–10. In some cases, these figures differ from those cited by Mann on p. 393.

The British state grew much more rapidly than that of France, with total state employment in the former increasing 7.98 times while that of France increased 1.9 times between 1850 and 1900. Most of the British growth occurred outside the central bureaucracies, in the regions; between 1850 and 1900, central employment increased

3.25 times while that of the regions grew 15 times. This marks the professionalization of regional/local administration and the shift away from reliance upon local notables acting in an unpaid capacity just at the time when the state was seeking to increase its role in a wide variety of issue areas (see below). In France, where the rate of overall growth was lower, that growth only occurred in the central apparatus of the state; central employment increased 2.9 times while the regional bureaucracy actually shrank, becoming 90 per cent of its 1850 size in 1900. However, the French state remained substantially larger than that of Britain, although in total terms the saturation level (i.e., the proportion of bureaucrats to total population) was not much higher, except at the centre. States were clearly increasing in size during this period. This increase in size is also reflected in financial terms, as the figures for total state revenue show in Table 4.3.

Although the figures in the table are in current prices, and therefore do not control for inflation, they show that state revenues increased dramatically over the nineteenth century, thereby enabling the state to undertake more functions and to sustain a larger size than ever before. This was also a time of expanding national economies and, as Michael Mann has shown, although expanding compared

Table 4.3 *Total state revenue (in millions of relevant unit of currency)*

	Britain	France*	Prussia*	USA*
1760	9.2	259		
1770	11.4			
1780	12.5	377		
1790	17.0	472		
1800	31.6			
1810	69.2			
1820	58.1	933	96	25
1830	55.3	978		31
1840	51.8	1160	169	33
1850	57.1	1297	183	69
1860	70.1	1722		100
1870	73.7	1626	550	501
1880	73.3	2862	805	446
1890	94.6	3221	1744	584
1900	129.9	3676	2607	837
1910	131.7	4271	3732	

* The French figures for 1760–90 are in livres tournois, from 1820 in francs The Prussian figures from 1870 do not include the revenue transfers from the German government. The figure for the USA includes both federal and state revenue.
Source: M. Mann, *Sources of Social Power II*, pp.811–15.

with population size, in terms of expenditure the state was probably shrinking as a proportion of national economic activity.[41] However, the period after 1815 was a time of decreased military activity, and therefore military expenditure, with the shift of emphasis from military to civilian spending; by 1881 British civilian expenditure was greater than military expenditure.[42] This means that not only was the bulk of the state growing, but state functions were expanding, and primarily in the civilian realm.

Before looking at the increased civilian functions the state took on, this broad conjunction of industrialization and bureaucratic expansion raises an interesting issue. Charles Tilly has argued that the more commercialized a state's economy, the less extensive the administrative organization needed to tax effectively.[43] This is broadly consistent with the history of British development compared with its rivals on the Continent. However, the above analysis has shown that just when capitalist industrialization was integrating national economies and bringing them even more under the sway of commercialization, there was a major expansion in the size of the state bureaucracy. Tilly's principle requires qualification. The increased scope for taxation generated by the increasing wealth of the society, added to the advances in technology which facilitated more efficient tax collection, fuelled the expansion of state bureaucracies, both in order to maximize the tax take and to carry out the expanded functions that increased take made possible.

One of the hallmarks of the state as it developed during industrialization was the vast expansion in the civilian functions it undertook. This involved an expansion not only into new areas of activity, but also in the scope of activity undertaken in those more traditional areas of state concern. An important one of these was law and order. It was not until the eve of the nineteenth century that the leading European states created 'uniformed, salaried, bureaucratic police specialized in control of the civilian population'.[44] Prior to this, policing functions (like many low-level judicial functions) had been carried out principally by locally-based semi-professional officials who were appointed or elected by the local community. This was the norm both in the towns and villages and in the capital; the Paris police force emerged in the second half of the seventeenth century and that of London emerged in the mid-eighteenth century, while a regularized force did not emerge in Berlin until 1848.[45] The first police force with a national brief was the maréchaussée created in France in 1760, but this was mainly a highway patrol and was concerned with robbery. The first force that was established with a mandate to deal with all internal security issues was created by Napoleon in 1799. He merged and centralized the existing forces, placing them under the control of a single minister. In the following decades, all the major European states followed this example. In Britain, in 1829 the Metropolitan Police was created, replacing the existing forces in the capital; in 1835 in all incorporated municipalities, and in 1865 in all counties (and therefore the whole country) such forces were made compulsory.[46] In succeeding decades, the size of these police forces increased; for example, in London the number of officers and men increased from 3,185 in 1832 to 10,952 in 1880, while in the counties and boroughs the numbers increased from about 6,434 in 1848 to 19,706 in 1880.[47]

The structure of police forces differed in the different countries. In Britain command was decentralized and the police's formal role was quite narrow, in France command was centralized and their formal powers extensive, and in Germany command was decentralized and the powers extensive.[48] These sorts of differences reflected the historical circumstances that both preceded and surrounded the creation of the respective police forces. But what is important about the development of these forces is the way in which they contributed to the extension of state power over the population. Before the regularization of the police, public order was maintained by the sorts of semi-professional officers referred to above backed up by troops; anything involving large numbers of people or significant direct action was usually met with repressive activity by troops. This was an extraordinary response, and gave the state little flexibility in dealing with popular disturbances. The establishment of a regularized police force whose task was to exercise continuing restraint over the communities within which they worked gave the state a flexibility it formerly lacked. The establishment of the police gave the state greater flexibility because it meant that the response to law-breaking or popular disturbances could be measured and made more appropriate to the challenge. It was no longer necessary to meet infractions of order with either a local, somewhat ad hoc, constabulary or the full force of the troops. The continuing presence of an organized law enforcement force meant that some potential disturbances could be nipped in the bud, while those that did develop could be handled with a level of response that was neither too limited nor excessively heavy handed. This increased flexibility also meant an increased regularity.

The regularization of law enforcement was probably the most important consequence of the formation of national police forces. It meant that the sort of extraordinary action that was constituted by the calling in of the troops could be resorted to only in extraordinary times. Breaches of the law or the peace could be handled through the newly-developing regular procedures and arms of the state; the state could now deal with such problems as part of its normal course of functioning. The state's disciplinary function thus became routinized and rendered ordinary through the stationing of uniformed representatives of state power in the local communities. In this way the state's reach was extended both symbolically and practically much further than it was before, and its capacity to respond quickly at the local level was increased substantially. This does not mean that, from its creation, the national police force worked efficiently as the coercive arm of the state to maintain order and peace throughout the country; the military was still often involved in the maintenance of order, especially on the Continent. In many areas police forces struggled to cope and the links they had with central authorities remained looser than they were to become, but their visible presence and their activity to maintain peace and order brought the state much closer to more of the people on a continuing basis than it had ever been before.

The establishment of the police meant that, in principle, the military was no longer directly responsible for the internal order of the country, except in the direst circumstances. For the first time, a professional military force was able to direct its attention solely to protecting the country from external challenges. Its focus thereby narrowed and its professional character was enhanced. With civilian pacification no longer part of its normal remit, the military became increasingly separated from society. This trend was fuelled by the attempts of military leaders to foster a greater sense of professionalism within the military, by the attempt to give a greater sense of bureaucratization and regularity to its hierarchy, and by the impact that changing military technology was having on the way militaries functioned. This separation from society exacerbated the eternal problem of the subordination of the military to civilian leadership and the consequent danger of increasing military autonomy. Military elites tended to come from the traditional old regime elites, chiefly from among the landed nobility; even in post-revolutionary France the nobility was able to retain leading military posts through much of the nineteenth century.[49] The military leadership was therefore somewhat differentiated from the emergent civilian political leadership, which was itself being transformed by the socio-political changes under way during the nineteenth century (see below). This only served to distance the military structure even further from its civilian society. This process, and in particular the professionalization and bureaucratization of the military, had been going on since the middle of the eighteenth century, but what gave this increased potency in the nineteenth century was the withdrawal, in principle, from responsibility for domestic pacification.

The extension of the state into society more broadly through the creation of the police was also evident in a variety of other spheres of life. Mass education is one example of this. It was in the nineteenth century that the expansion of the state's responsibilities in the education area began, and those responsibilities were held to embrace the whole population. National education systems were established, and although they often took some time to capture all of the target populace, their establishment constituted a recognition by the state of the importance of education for the welfare of the country. The 1870s saw a major expansion of public education across Europe, and in the following decades these systems became 'more universally free and compulsory'.[50] As well as the system of schools, the universities also expanded. For example, in Britain, to Oxford and Cambridge were added the universities of Durham (1832), London (1836), Manchester (1851), Wales (1893), Birmingham (1900), Liverpool (1903), Leeds (1904), Sheffield (1905) and Bristol (1909). In 1871 the older universities were opened to non-Anglicans, and special colleges were opened for women. On the Continent, too, the university systems expanded, sometimes alongside special scientific institutes and academies. By the end of the century, all the European states were spending considerably more on public education than they had been at the middle of the century.

The state did not support education for education's sake. The aim was not to create a populace whose personal development could be enhanced through exposure to learning, but to ensure that the populace was imbued with the sort of knowledge that would be useful to the development of the society and the strengthening of the country. Education was seen in an instrumental fashion. An educated populace was one that could be controlled more easily, both because literacy and the ability to read enabled state instructions to be issued through the written word rather than having to rely upon word of mouth, and because education could be the vehicle for the transmission of values that contributed to popular acceptance of the status quo. Important in this regard was the post-French Revolution development of nationalism as a means of legitimation of political forms. While historically this has often been seen principally in terms of the aspirations for independent statehood represented in some of the risings of 1848, its importance right across the Continent should not be underestimated. What the unrolling of national sentiment did was to recast the vision of the past, emphasizing the national unit as the key category of historical progress at the expense of other sorts of attachments. The mythology of the nation state became supreme, as history was seen as the story of the emergence of those contemporary political units. In line with this, institutions were reshaped and traditions invented[51] in order to give the state in its current form an appearance of having always been there and having played a positive role in the society's life. The effect of this was to create an air of naturalness; subordination to the state in its current form was a natural state of affairs and was not, as some like Proudhon and Kropotkin argued, an alien imposition upon a healthy community. The projection of this sort of image was an important buttress to state power, and was something actively encouraged by the state.[52] The growth in state symbolism was one aspect of this: uniforms for state officials, the increased pomp surrounding monarchs, the reconstruction of grand state capitals, and the proliferation of representatives of state authority. But also important was the education system, because this was the channel through which much of this message passed. This was the state involved in normative pacification on a scale never before seen.

Another important element of the extension of the state's power was the regularization of movement and information flow. The development of improved infrastructures for transport and travel, particularly the railways but also the canals and roads, not only made both the transport of goods and the travel of people easier and faster than it had been before, but reinforced the state's power to regulate such movement. This was particularly important with the railways and canals, which were channels of movement that were clearly defined and invariable. They were lines of movement from one point to another, with set stopping places in between, and were therefore predictable in the pattern of movement that they imposed. This predictability meant that potentially they provided the state with the opportunity for control which would have been lacking had movement been completely unregularized. Consequently, at a time when the opportunities for travel expanded significantly, the mode whereby this occurred remained amenable to state control; indeed, the structuring of this was an important sphere of life into which formal state regulation penetrated. The establishment of a national postal service that was cheap enough for most to use [53](in Britain the penny post was established in 1840) was another important step extending the reach of the state into the lower levels of society. With its introduction, all literate people could communicate with those far away very cheaply, but only by relying upon a service provided by the state. While this too gave the state, potentially, the opportunity to monitor such communication,[54] the most important aspect of it is that this new means of communication was conducted through a state agency and, given that the post became such a crucial element in the conduct of business, rendered commerce dependent upon this aspect of state infrastructure.

The state also sought to shape the conditions of people's everyday lives. This period saw a fundamental transformation in the way in which society was organized and people's lives were conducted. The rhythm of agricultural life was replaced by the demands of factory production, and with this went the recasting of the circumstances within which millions of people lived their lives. Urban living gradually displaced that of the countryside. But in this process, the state played a central role in shaping the new conditions of life. The expanding urban environment was brought under state supervision through a range of regulations relating to things as diverse as housing and the opening hours of public gardens and liquor outlets. Major programmes of urban renewal and development were implemented, including underground water, gas and sewerage systems, street lighting, and the construction of public buildings. Regulations were introduced relating to the conditions of employment, including the health and safety of the work place,[55] and unemployment, including maximum working hours, sometimes minimum payment levels and access to relief benefits when unemployed. Labour exchanges were established to help find work for the unemployed (in 1909 in Britain). The state even sought to intervene in things that hitherto many had believed to be solely the responsibility of the individual. Education has already been noted, but important too were measures designed to improve individual health care and to regulate the number of children people had; national health insurance (paid through contributions by employer, employee and state)[56] and pensions were other measures widely adopted. The extension of state competence in these ways does not mean that, in practice, the state ruled efficiently all aspects of its people's lives; but it does mean that those lives were lived within a web of rules and regulations created by the state to provide the infrastructure of national life. And with the technological advances brought by industrialization, the state was in a much better position to be able to enforce those rules and regulations than it had ever been in the past.

It is clear that during the nineteenth century the scope of the state bureaucracy expanded significantly. Simply in terms of the numbers of people working for it, the state was very much larger at the end of that century than it had been when the century opened. But just as importantly, with the growth of literacy and the expansion of state positions, access to the bureaucracy began to open up to groups previously unable to gain entry to it. This did not yet apply to the working class, but sections of the middle class, including sons of the newly emergent industrial bourgeoisie, now found a new bureaucratic career as one of their options. As a result, the bureaucratic organic interdependence of state and society began to widen, although it would not be until the next century that this would become very broad. At the same time, the bureaucracy was becoming increasingly professionalized. In Britain this had begun in the late eighteenth century with the private ownership of office virtually ended by 1837, and more formal and professional procedures governing things such as recruitment, appointment and promotion set in place. This marked the shift from reliance upon local notables at the lower levels to salaried officials. Similar developments occurred elsewhere, but generally in Britain's wake. By 1914 in the major states of Western Europe, ownership of office had been eliminated, impersonal measurement of competence as the basis for appointment and promotion had been instituted, and the structuring of offices in departments divided by function within a single hierarchy had been achieved. The establishment of a single bureaucratic structure had been achieved in Britain, France and the USA, but not fully in Germany and Austria.[57] The state was now able to act directly on much wider sections of its population than it had ever been able to before, and now overwhelmingly through its own salaried officials rather than local notables. By the end of the century the state bureaucracy was much more firmly rooted in society than it had been in the past and, with this, the state's capacity had clearly expanded.

The sorts of developments discussed above were begun in the long nineteenth century from the French Revolution in 1789 to the outbreak of the First World War in 1914. They were developed to different degrees and at different times in the various countries of Europe, but the pattern across the Continent was the same: the expansion of the state even further into society than ever before, and in a more routinized and bureaucratic way, with the consequent large-scale displacement of the semi-autonomous corporate bodies and local notables upon which the state formerly had relied for the exercise of some of its functions. This process was to be extended quite significantly in the twentieth century.

The Social Embedding of the State

Industrialization released forces that had another major impact upon the state and its structure and processes: the creation of new classes which sought to share in the distribution of power and privilege in society. Industrialization fundamentally transformed the social structure in a way far more rapid, dramatic and far-reaching than anything in the past. Pre-industrial society had its focus in the rural areas. This was where the majority of the population lived and this was the site where the mode of economic production that both sustained and shaped society was located. Industrialization changed both of these factors. Both the balance of population and the economic centre of gravity shifted into the burgeoning towns and cities as people left (or were forced to leave) the land to go to the cities to work in the expanding industrial establishments that were located there.[58] This does not mean that the countryside ceased to be important for society as a whole; it was still the source of food and a significant proportion of the population remained resident in rural areas, but henceforth the tenor of society was set by the industrial rhythms emanating from the urban areas rather than the cyclical patterns of agricultural life. This shift in balance did not occur overnight. It was a prolonged process, but it was taking place throughout the nineteenth and twentieth centuries, at different rates in different locations. But once it began, it unleashed contradictions between the rural and urban areas which helped to shape the course of development over these two centuries. The chief form this took was the emergence of two new classes which led to the reconfiguring of the social and political contours of these societies: the capitalist owners of the means of production, or bourgeoisie, and the working class.

The sources of the industrial bourgeoisie were multiple. One study of 'the first industrialists' in Britain[59] suggests that the most important group from which the founders of major industrial establishments came[60] was those manufacturers and industrialists who were engaged in small-scale manufacturing activity, often through the 'putting out' system, that occurred prior to the major industrial upsurge. Significant proportions also came from among the merchants, traders and bankers, and from among those who worked on the land, but usually combining some farming with a non-agricultural pursuit such as mining or quarrying.[61] Only a very small proportion came from the landed classes.[62] In this sense, the overwhelming bulk of the bourgeoisie came from outside the traditional land-holding ruling group. They did not come from the disadvantaged sections of society, but from that underdeveloped middle that rested on artisanal and manufacturing production and on commerce. But in pre-industrial society, this group had been excluded from power; often despite great wealth in the hands of merchants, they stayed on the sidelines politically as power remained vested in the traditional landowning class. The emergent bourgeoisie were thus outside the political establishment. This was not only the case in Britain; throughout Europe, with the partial exception of post-revolutionary France,[63] the emergent bourgeoisie began life as political outsiders. One of the continuing themes in the nineteenth and early twentieth centuries was the struggle this group waged to gain entry into leading political circles and to displace the traditional landed class. This shift in social power was predicated on the shift in economic power associated with the course of industrial development. As the industrial sector of the economy expanded, the relative importance of the agricultural sector contracted, and with this went increased economic wealth and power on the part of the bourgeoisie. As their activity became more important for the welfare of society as a whole and as their personal and collective wealth expanded, they sought an increased say in the affairs of state. And as their wealth and power expanded, denial of this became increasingly difficult.

The working class emerged as an amalgam of those who were already working in manufacturing and the peasants who were forced off the land as a result principally of enclosures and the shift towards larger consolidated farms.[64] This class was always outside the decision-making circles of the societies of which they were part. Indeed, they were the chief domestic cause of concern for those who ruled over them. What increased their potential potency from the nineteenth century was their location in society. Two aspects of this were significant: geographical and structural. The geographical aspect consisted of the way in which industrialization brought about a concentration of the working class in the new urban centres. This facilitated the potential organization and mobilization of the working class and, added to the radicalization of their temper that was likely to flow from the harsh conditions in which many of them lived and worked, made them appear increasingly dangerous to their political and economic masters. This perception was strengthened by their structural location and in particular by the way in which, through the withdrawal of their labour, they could disrupt the economy and thereby injure the economic well-being of both the country and the owners of the enterprises in which they worked. Lacking a voice in the decision-making process and experiencing a range of grievances in their urban settings, like the bourgeoisie the working class sought to gain access to the political system.

The struggles by these two classes to gain access to the political process and the effect this had on the nature of the regime have long been recognized by scholars.[65] What has been less acknowledged has been the effect this had upon the state, and in particular its relationship with society: a broadening of the nature of interdependence, and therefore a firmer embedding of the state in society. What is crucial here has been the strategies used by these two groups in their attempts to penetrate the upper levels of the state.

The emergent bourgeoisie adopted two basic strategies for gaining access to the apex of the state. The first involved the merger of this new group with the established power holders. The best example of this was Britain, where newly-emergent capitalists sought through such means as the purchase of landed estates, the joining of private clubs and the creation of a range of personal links with traditional landowners to become accepted in establishment society. The result was a blurring of the boundaries between bourgeoisie and traditional landowners and the emergence of what has come to be called 'gentlemanly capitalism'.[66] This sort of process was only possible where the elite was relatively open and the institutions within which that elite nestled were flexible. The ability of this landed class to absorb members of the ascendant bourgeoisie, and in doing so to reshape itself in important ways, has been an important factor in both the stability of the British system and the survival in it of 'archaic' elements, such as the continuing prominence of the landed aristocracy. In other European states, this strategy of infiltration and the consequent process of absorption were less successful. In Prussia/Germany and Russia the traditional landowners generally eschewed close contact with the new bourgeoisie (although clearly there were individual exceptions), while in France[67] the power of the landed upper class was shattered by the Revolution and finally destroyed in 1830, leaving the bourgeoisie politically dominant.[68]

The second strategy adopted by the bourgeoisie right across the Continent was to seek to enter the political elite through the legislature. In the various countries across the Continent at different times during the nineteenth–twentieth centuries, political parties emerged as important public institutions. With the wave of democratic sentiment emanating from the American and French Revolutions and the shift toward elections as a mode of giving popular legitimation to governments, even if the suffrage remained restricted, political parties appeared as important elements in this new political mix. More importantly for our concerns, they were the means of gaining entry into the state legislature. As such, they were seen by the bourgeoisie as one means of penetrating the state elite. In this endeavour, the bourgeoisie was usually not sufficiently numerous to be able to go it alone, so they allied with other groups in the society. Often important in this regard was the professional middle class of the urban areas, consisting of people such as lawyers, doctors, and property-holders more generally. Within the context of a franchise that excluded the working class, this sort of alliance was often sufficient to enable the election to the legislature of representatives of this group. Not only did this constitute a means of entry to the upper echelons for some members of this group, but it constituted a symbolic tying in to the state of the interests of this group. In England this was symbolized more starkly by the way in which manufacturers entered politics at the local level through the municipal councils established after 1835 and then often set about promoting a range of municipal improvement schemes.[69] In this way they associated the functions of the state with the needs of the new urban society, with this class of new emergent capitalists acting as the mediator.

The working class did not have open to them the strategy of infiltration used by the bourgeoisie. Instead they had to rely on a different, dual fronted, approach. One arm of this was the search for election of its representatives to the legislature. In most countries the formation of explicitly working-class parties, a necessity given that no existing party sought to develop this class as a constituency, was a late development, in part because the working class was not enfranchised until quite late. Table 4.4 gives the scholarly consensus on the achievement of male and female suffrage.[70]

Table 4.4 *Achievement of the suffrage*

	Male	Female
Britain	1918	1928
France	1848	1944
Germany	1869	1918
Italy	1912	1946
Netherlands	1917	1919
Austria	1907	1918
USA	1870	1920

Source: Jan-Erik Lane, David McKay and Kenneth Newton, *Political Data Handbook: OECD Countries* (Oxford, Oxford University Press, 1991), p.111

Although parties representing the interests of the working class did not have to wait for universal male suffrage (e.g., the British Labour Party was established in 1900), they could not act effectively as legislative vehicles for working-class interests until the members of the class were able to participate fully in elections.[71] Prior to this development, other forms of organization sought to represent the interests of the workers. This was the second arm of this dual fronted approach, and comprises that vast range of organizations which emerged to in some sense represent the interests of workers. Historically the most important of these were the trade unions, but also of significance were groups such as factory committees, cooperative societies, mutual aid associations and so on. Through vehicles such as these, worker interests could be represented in different spheres: the broad industrial front, individual factories or industries, or just getting by in the normal course of life. Whatever their form, these sorts of organizations linked the working class and their interests into the broader superstructures of the society and thereby tied the working class into the political institutions of the state, with the consequent strengthening of the state's interdependence with society.

The strategies adopted by the bourgeoisie and the working class brought the state much closer to society as a whole. They established new or strengthened existing organizational linkages between some of the institutions of the state and parts of the population. These linkages may not always have been very effective in transmitting the views and interests of their constituencies into the apex of the state, but it was their success in this which determined how successful they were in integrating these new classes peacefully into the political contours of the state. In Britain the relative openness of the elite, added to the long tradition of amateur involvement in state administration, enabled this process to occur gradually and relatively peacefully. In contrast, in Germany the relative closure of both the elite and the administrative structure hindered the integration of these groups, with significant consequences for twentieth-century German development. So where these strategies were successful and the organizations thereby established acted as an integrating mechanism between state and classes, the state was drawn further into society than it had ever been. In this sense, the emergence of the bourgeoisie and working class, and their efforts to gain access to the apex of the state, reinforced the general effects of industrialization upon state development.

***

The course of industrial development during the nineteenth and early twentieth centuries thus stimulated the fundamental transformation of the state and its relationship with society. Industrial development greatly expanded the state's infrastructural reach, providing the tools which enabled state decision-makers both to penetrate society to a much greater depth and to monitor what was occurring far more effectively than ever before. The apparatus of the state increased, both in terms of its personnel and its infrastructure, and its reach into society was extended. The tyranny of geography, expressed most graphically by distance, was mitigated by the new means of transport and communication, with the result that local officials found the autonomy they had formerly enjoyed significantly reduced. It was easier for the centre to despatch instructions, exercise monitoring and generally remain in contact with its officials through these improved channels. Allied with the growing emphasis upon the professionalization of the bureaucracy, this served to counteract the tendency of local officials to identify rather more with their local regions than with the centre and to emphasize the links they possessed with the centre.

   The capacity to penetrate society more deeply was accompanied by an expansion in the sphere of active concern of the state. Generally over this period the balance of state expenditure shifted from the needs of administration to those of the provision of public facilities and services. This does not mean that state expenditure on administration declined in absolute terms, but that state expenditure as a whole increased as the economy expanded, and expenditure levels on these new areas increased faster than that on the older ones.[72] This shift of state concern marked the entry of the state into people's lives in a much more extensive and sustained fashion than ever before. Not only did it involve a structuring of their physical surroundings, but it also came to include a concern for aspects of their personal lives which injected the state into areas it had not hitherto entered. No longer was the state solely concerned with setting the general contours of society; it was now beginning to become involved at a much more personal level. In this sense, the state became more solidly entrenched in society's interstices and in the lives of its subjects than it had ever been before. But this process of state involvement at the personal level really only began in this period; it was to become more developed during the twentieth century.

Perhaps the best instance of the way in which the sphere of competence of the state expanded, and the improved infrastructure gave it the capacity to act, was in the economic sphere. During the long nineteenth century, the state became much more directly involved in the national economy than ever before. Indeed, it is during this century that the notion of a national economy took on real meaning, because it was only with the improved infrastructural links industrialism created that the diverse parts of a country could be knitted together into a single economic mosaic; it is no surprise that capitalist economic development is generally conceived in national terms. The increased capacity to affect economic life, added to the realization that the national economy was a crucial component of state power internationally,[73] encouraged state elites to seek to act to facilitate economic development. The forms this took ranged broadly, from the sorts of activity undertaken by the British state to create the conditions for industrial expansion as well as implementing policies which gave particular assistance to sectors of the emergent new economy, to the interventionist and directive policies of later industrializers such as Prussia and Russia. Although these forms of economic intervention differed, they constituted a major and sustained change in the state's approach to economic life. Now the state saw it had a continuing and effective role in national economic development as well as possessing some of the instruments to implement that role. This means that the state now saw economic policy as part of its legitimate concern, and not simply for the reasons that mercantilism had become popular earlier, but in order to promote the welfare of the society as a whole.

Furthermore, the state was projected into a new structural relationship with the economy, particularly in the British case. The state interacted cooperatively with the emergent forces of capitalism (principally the emergent bourgeoisie) to promote economic development. The more independent those capitalist forces were, the higher the level of cooperation that was necessary in the state–capitalist relationship; the less independent those forces, the greater the directive power of the state. But regardless of whether the balance of the relationship lay in cooperation between essentially autonomous entities or the direction of one by the other, the relationship of itself constituted an embedding of the state in the economy. Rather than the economy and the state being relatively insulated from one another, with the intermittent intrusion of one on the other, industrialism welded them seemingly indissolubly together. State power was dependent upon sustained cooperation with major economic actors, and this power was probably enhanced much more by cooperation with than direction of those actors.

However, this also reflects a new sort of economy. Capitalist industrialism, with its essential dynamic being one of private accumulation, needed the public authority of the state if it was to prosper. Private accumulation could be maximized and sustained only if certain costs could be shared rather than borne by one of the private actors. Chief among these were law and order, regulation, and transport and communication infrastructures, including links abroad. It made no sense for these to be constructed, maintained and monopolized by individual economic actors, even had this been possible. They had to be shared, and the state was the mechanism for achieving this. Furthermore, the emphasis upon private accumulation would, without some form of independent arbiter, lead not to the balance foreseen by pro-market ideologues, but to a process of cut-throat competition that ultimately would lead to the survival only of the most powerful. The free market without regulation cannot survive, so the development of this new form of economy, nationally-oriented, where industrialism placed significant wealth in the hands of private entrepreneurs, and where communications reduced the former ameliorating effects of distance on popular perceptions of systematic inequality in wealth, projected the state into a new position: it was indispensable to the efficient running of a capitalist economy. This point has often been made in terms of the state pacifying workers and acting as the moderator between the conflicting interests of the bourgeoisie and the working class, but to this must be added the state's centrality to the continued survivability of the market economy itself. Without the regulating and balancing role of the state, the capitalist market economy would not survive. Industrialism thus made the state central to the economy, and institutional interdependence crucial to its survival.

In these ways, during the nineteenth century the state became much more deeply embedded in society than it had ever been before. Infrastructural development and the expansion of spheres of state competence rooted the state more deeply in the society and gave its presence there a sense of normality it had formerly lacked. Both organic and institutional interdependence were strengthened. The emergence of new industrial classes seeking a share of political power generated further institutions tying the various levels of society to the state. Furthermore, the course of the struggle of these new classes for entry to the political arena also strengthened an ideology which emphasized a unity between state and society. The spread of notions of democracy meant increasing acceptance of the principle that government should be accountable to those over whom it ruled. Those who ran the state were not to be isolated from the governed but were to be continually answerable for their actions. In this way, the state itself was to be answerable to the populace within its borders. It was not to sit above society, exercising autonomous power over society, but was to be part of an integrated whole in a relationship of accountability to the other part. While such notions were not universally accepted across the Continent, even in those areas where democracy was not embraced by leading political actors, its adoption by some meant that this conception of the state and its role entered the body politic. While this paradigm did not become dominant until after the First World War, its emergence during the nineteenth century was one further force pushing the state towards greater integration with society.

All of the above factors have stemmed from industrialization, not capitalism,[74] but the fact that this process occurred under capitalist auspices has also been important for the position of the state. The principal way in which the capitalist nature of this process mattered was that it ensured that the burgeoning wealth emanating from economic development flowed largely into private pockets. Not all members of the bourgeoisie became very wealthy, but large sections of it did gain control of significant economic resources. It was the enrichment of the bourgeoisie which underpinned their challenge to the traditional landed interests noted above, but this also gave them a basis independent of the state. The accumulation of resources in private hands had always been a key to individuals and groups being able to stand up to the state and state elites, but the increased wealth emanating from industrial development added to the central place these people had in the emergent national economy, and made them a powerful force to be reckoned with in society. We do not have to accept the Marxist vision of the state as being under their control to recognize that their economic power gave them at least significant leverage against the state. Put another way, this means that the state's independence from society was even more sharply restricted by the emergence of this new and powerful group.

It is thus clear that the process of industrialization set in train the fundamental transformation of the state and its relationship with society. It gave the state greater capacity to project its power into society, but it also substantially increased state interdependence with society. This transformation was to be carried very much further during the twentieth century.

5

The Western State and the Outside World

While the development of the state has thus far been discussed in terms primarily of domestic forces, the international context has also been important. Geopolitical competition, and especially war, has often been seen as playing a significant role in state development. But the international context also includes the broader relationship between Western Europe and the rest of the world, most especially Asia. This raises the question of the non-European state and claims about both the uniqueness and superiority of the Western state form.

The states that emerged in Western Europe did not exist in a vacuum. From the collapse of the Roman Empire, the West European political units saw themselves as part of a broader geopolitical area that was united ideologically by the normative power of religion. While it may be that there is a geographical basis upon which those political units emerged,[1] it was the collapse of the Roman Empire, the weakness and limits of the Holy Roman Empire, and the rebuff to Church aspirations to rule in temporal affairs that ensured the survival of a multi-state geopolitical space in Western Europe. Rulers recognized that they were part of this area, united not only by the shared memories of a common past but, as Christianity spread across the Continent, by a normative commitment to a transcendent ideology. This was important because it provided the emergent state system with an underpinning of unity; all recognized themselves as part of a common culture area, a recognition strengthened by the rise of Islam and particularly by the Moorish conquest of Spain and the pressure that was thereby exerted upon Western Europe. This ideological unity, reflected in Latin as the common elite language in the early stages of feudalism, not only helped to create a sense of belonging but also helped to fuel the developing world of economic

149

interchange. As a normative system of values, Christianity facilitated the development of commerce by investing notions such as trust and honesty with a religious significance which was important in the absence of effective means of enforcing contracts with foreigners. Indeed, religion was a central part of society and, as a normative system of values rather than a temporal claim by the papacy, cut across international boundaries. Symbolized by the term 'Christendom', it imposed a sense of unity upon the diverse conglomeration of states that was emerging in the region.

This combination of multiple political units and overarching normative system, of diffusion and unity, was unique globally. But importantly, what it did was to create a system in which there was significant internal dynamism. With no country able to establish dominance over the region, Western Europe could not be returned to the status of empire. As the constituent states continually struggled against each other for advantage, a balance was maintained such that no state could become the permanent hegemon and thereby eliminate such struggles. But similarly, no state could opt out of this process, so that all were locked together in a dynamic relationship. While each pursued its own development path, those paths were not isolated and discrete. Their course was shaped and moulded in part by the paths pursued by their neighbours and the actions the latter took in the international arena. In this way, metaphorically, no state was an island, unaffected by its neighbours. Some, like Scotland and Burgundy, were eaten up by those neighbours; others simply had their development paths affected. But all were influenced in their formation and development by their neighbours.

The sense of regional unity was reinforced over time by the growth of inter-regional trade and commerce, especially with the economic revival and expansion of economic activity in the eleventh century. While most economic activity prior to the industrial revolution remained local in its focus, the importation of goods from outside the country was a continuing feature of life for elites throughout Europe during much of the period from the collapse of the Roman Empire. It is not possible to get a clear picture of the contribution made to economic activity in the various European states by inter-state trade at an early period because the statistics do not exist. However, in England, by the reign of Edward I (1272–1307), customs duties constituted 25 per cent of average annual royal revenue; in the reign of Edward III (1327–77) they were 46 per cent and in Richard II's (1377–99) 38 per cent.[2] While at this time customs duties were levied on all exports, especially wool, it is not clear whether the above figures also include revenues derived from the domestic transport and exchange of goods. If these figures do refer solely to inter-state trade, at least in terms of revenues generated, this was a significant aspect of economic activity. But the important point about this for the current discussion is that, over time, the scale of this grew,[3] and with that growth the channels of communication between states expanded. This point should not be misunderstood. Prior to the development of modern mass communications, most of the population most of the time remained largely oblivious to (and immune from) direct influences from outside the political unit in which they lived. However, importantly it was the elite that was most hooked in to this trade, principally because much of that trade was in luxury items for their use, and it was the elite that made the decisions about the high politics which shaped the development of the state.

The developing networks of commerce could act not only as the transporter of goods, but as the carrier of ideas. Traders and merchants could gather information about conditions in other countries and convey them back to their home rulers. This sort of activity could supplement the operations of diplomats and, once they were established, permanent missions in other states[4] in providing a continuing source of information. Through such channels, rulers learnt about what was going on in other states, and they could pick and choose what they thought were good ideas for application at home.[5] This was one way in which the development of states was shaped by other states: the borrowing of good ideas and their application. Historically states have learnt from one another, seeking to emulate what was successful and avoid what was not. Perhaps the clearest, because the most personalized, example of this was Russia when Peter I visited Western Europe to learn about their ways and then returned to his own country and sought to impose them there. But in practice this sort of thing went on all the time, as innovations in one state were transported abroad for application.[6]

Another form of influence from outside the state that had a significant impact upon state development involved the growth of international credit houses. The growth of international credit, initially through the Italian banking houses and then the Netherlands and London, and the reliance of many monarchs upon it, was a significant factor in promoting the development of internal regimes of taxation and other forms of extraction. The problem was not that international financiers adopted political positions that created difficulties for particular rulers, because financial houses generally put their commercial interests above any political concerns,[7] but that reliance upon such finance brought obligations to repay and, given that such financiers were located far from the seat of rule, they were not easily pressured. Of course monarchs could place pressure on such financial houses by implicitly threatening them with bankruptcy by non-repayment of debts; the case of Edward III's non-repayment and the consequent collapse of the Florentine bankers is an example of this. But it was more difficult for monarchs to deal with financiers located a long way away; they were more immune from royal pressure and the monarch had less influence in persuading the financier to grant him the sums requested. It was much more convenient if the monarch had the sources of such funds under his own control, and hence the stimulus to develop an internal system of taxation. Reliance upon domestic financiers was another option, but these too were less pliable than a system of taxation whose levels could be adjusted to meet royal needs. Thus the monarch's continuing need for finance and the reliance upon international financial houses stimulated the growth of domestic regimes of taxation.

War and the State

War, or geopolitical competition generally, has been seen by many authors as having played a defining part in the emergence of the modern state.[8] For Perry Anderson, the emergence of highly authoritarian states in Eastern Europe and Russia was largely a function of the challenge posed to them by the more developed Western states. An authoritarian state was necessary to tie the population to the land and thereby expand the capacity for exploitation of the country's resources, the better to meet the challenge from without.[9] Otto Hintze saw the state as a form of organization for war. Political outcomes resulted from the degree of sustained military challenge a state faced from land forces. Confronted by a continuing challenge from a large land army-based opponent, kings undercut representative assemblies and created an absolutist state based upon the army and the bureaucracy. Where such challenge was not forthcoming, and therefore a large land army did not have to be created, constitutionalist rule could survive. Such countries' reliance upon a navy rather than an army was an important factor in this.[10] Most writers who have seen war as important have emphasized the boost this gave to tax collection and to the construction of an integrated bureaucratic structure. Furthermore, this is seen as being instrumental in shaping the sort of regime that emerged. Charles Tilly argued that the kind of revenue upon which a state relied to meet geopolitical challenges determined the size and character of its politico-administrative infrastructure. He argued that the type of armed force adopted, plus the amount of military activity needed to fend off competitors, determined the amount of tax revenues necessary. Where the pool of taxable subjects was limited and the commercialization of the economy undeveloped (as in Brandenburg-Prussia), a more extensive and coercive fiscal apparatus had to be constructed. In contrast, in areas such as England where the economy was more commercialized and the tax base more readily tapped, a less intrusive and extensive apparatus was sufficient. So he believed that access to significant commercial revenues enabled a polity under sustained military pressure to avoid bureaucratization and absolutism.[11]

Michael Mann agreed with Tilly. He argued that given the increased costs of military activity from 1540 to 1660, two types of state were best placed to achieve primacy: wealthy states such as England, Holland, Genoa and Venice which could pay for and administer an army separate from domestic demands, and states such as Russia and Austria which had some wealth and a greater abundance of accessible manpower. France and Spain shared both characteristics. Mann argued that the latter of these two main types became absolutist states, relying upon the mobilization of a recalcitrant rural population through centralized bureaucracies and coercive methods to extract resources, while constitutional states such as England that were economically more developed could tax commerce and landed wealth without major bureaucratic structures.[12] They were respectively the so-called mobilization option and the fiscal option.

These views are very useful because of the way they link the development of the institutional structures of the state with the need to extract resources to defend against international competition, with war as the most extreme form of this. This is most starkly expressed in the chain of causation identified by Tilly: changes in or the expansion of land armies leads to new efforts to extract resources from the population, which leads to the development of more bureaucratic and administrative innovations, which stimulates resistance from the populace, resulting in renewed coercion, which leads to 'durable increases in the bulk or extractiveness of the state'.[13] For Tilly, war was the greatest state-building activity; state institutions were the result of rulers' attempts to obtain military resources.[14] It is clear that the conduct of war massively increased the government's need for revenue and that this increased need stimulated the development of the financial apparatus of the state.[15] Increased funds were needed not just to sustain the war effort, an enterprise that was becoming increasingly expensive over time,[16] but also to pay off the debts that hostilities inevitably induced. This need to repay the debts incurred as a result of military activity was a major factor in the finances of the feudal and early modern state, the continuation of those debts after hostilities had ended ensuring that the heightened level of resource extraction had to be maintained.[17] This means that the increased bulk of the state to which Tilly refers became a continuing factor even in times of peace. The effect of war was thus like a ratchet: as its costs increased, the state's need for extraction rose, and with it the state's infrastructure to achieve that extraction became more intrusive. This is often seen as the result of the drive of rulers to expand and rationalize the state apparatus in the face of military competition.

However, we need to be careful about this argument. It is certainly true that military conflict increased a government's costs and that, sooner or later, these had to be met through increased revenue generation, and ultimately this meant increased taxation. Certainly in the short term governments could rely upon loans, both from domestic and international sources, but these had to be repaid. So war was a major driver of increasing demands for tax revenue, but it is not clear that this always resulted in the sorts of institutional developments that have been suggested. The assumption that war and heightened geopolitical competition inevitably led to a rationalization of institutional structures is not correct. In the words of Joseph Strayer, the Hundred Years War:

> was so exhausting for both sides that it discouraged the normal development of the apparatus of the state. There was a tendency to postpone structural reforms, to solve problems on an ad hoc basis rather than by the creation of new agencies of government, to sacrifice efficiency for immediate results.

Only when wars were on a 'smaller and less devastating scale ... was there noticeable improvement in administrative techniques' in the fourteenth and early fifteenth centuries.[18]

Furthermore, as Ertman shows,[19] the onset of military competition and conflict does not necessarily lead to the construction of a more modern, rational bureaucratic structure. With the emergence of sustained geopolitical competition in Western and southern Europe in the twelfth and thirteenth centuries, these countries developed substantial bureaucratic structures that were much more complex than those of their neighbours to the east and north. However, by the fifteenth century, the 'impressive fiscal and administrative systems' developed in these states were characterized by 'a substantial loss of effective control [by the monarchy] to proprietary officeholders, tax farmers, and officeholder-financiers who viewed the state not only as an instrument of princely power but also as a source of income and social standing'.[20] Those states facing later periods of geopolitical competition, Germany, the Netherlands, Denmark, Sweden, Hungary and Poland in the fifteenth and sixteenth centuries, were able to take advantage of better techniques of administration and finance than were available earlier, greater supplies of people with the necessary expertise, and the experience of the earlier states, but the results were not consistent. While 'proto-modern' bureaucracies emerged in the German states and Denmark (and in England, which faced such geopolitical competition earlier), in Poland and Hungary patrimonial bureaucracies emerged. Thus while war did increase the development of bureaucratic structures and stimulate tax collection regimes, it did not universally lead to the rationalization of administration and the replacement of patrimonial practices by a more rationalist approach.

Care also needs to be taken in accepting the argument that war, and its increasing cost, promoted state development because it highlighted the need for protection and therefore convinced the populace, or powerful parts of it, of the utility of the bargain with the monarch of swapping protection for the payment of tax.[21] This argument presumes intentions from outcomes: because tax revenues increased at the time of war does not mean that putative tax payers saw this as a means of guaranteeing their own protection.[22] Furthermore, it is not clear why the populace would necessarily see the king located far away as better able to provide protection than the local magnate. This was especially the case if the king did not effectively control the territory. Why should people turn to a hazy power far away for their defence rather than to the local lord and his knights whose very proximity seemed to offer greater hope of salvation? Local loyalties were more likely to have been strengthened as a result of insecurity than any sense of loyalty to a central political authority. However, while the poor state of communications, and therefore the physical distance of the king and his armies, meant that this sentiment may have lasted until well into the post-feudal period, the removal of local armies under both absolutism and constitutionalism rendered this strategy of limited use. With the local powers now incapable of providing the security people craved, increasingly people began to look to the emergent centre and the king as the source of protection. In this way, geopolitical competition helped to erode localism and to stimulate the process of the centralization of power around the king.

Neither can the argument that warfare and its increasing cost and sophistication led to the national state rather than any other form of political unit because the national state could achieve efficiencies of scale be accepted without qualification. A survey of feudal and early modern Europe shows that all the units of that region faced the increasing cost and sophistication of warfare, but the political response was not uniform.[23] City-states continued to exist in Italy, the German states remained disunited, and the Hansa continued as a league of trading cities. War did not inevitably lead to the national state; the need for large territories and resources could be obviated by the increasing use of mercenaries, although this did require a substantial tax base. Moreover, the main changes in military technology often followed the centralization of power, at least insofar as we mean the consolidation of territorial rule as opposed to the infrastructural centralization of the kingdom. Certainly in France, substantial centralization had occurred prior to the major, more expensive changes in military technology.

Although war was a significant stimulus to the growth of state bureaucracies and to the collection of taxes, it alone is inadequate as an explanation for the emergence of the national state. However, war, and in particular technological change in the mode of its conduct, was important in undercutting the dyadic ties that were at the heart of feudalism. The basis of that tie was the exchange of rights over land and continuing fealty for military support of the king when required. The economic element of this tie was that such an arrangement shifted the costs of warfare away from the king and on to the magnates. Indeed the allocation of land may be seen as the king providing the means whereby magnates could raise the funds to sustain their military commitments. Those commitments were quite heavy. The cost of mounting and equipping each knight with a number of horses, assistants, armour and weapons was a major drain on the resources of the magnates, even if the terms of the feudal levy usually restricted their period of service to 40 days. But such a system relied for its rationale upon the mounted knight acting in cavalry formation. When this was undermined, the crux of feudalism disappeared.

Three factors were significant in this development. First, the unreliability of the feudal levy encouraged kings to look for alternatives. When a king called upon his vassals to gather for battle, he could never be sure that that support would arrive in a timely fashion, if at all. Furthermore, the 40-day limit on service became a restraint as the scale of warfare increased. Second, with the commercialization and monetization of the economy, many magnates sought to meet their feudal obligations through the payment of cash rather than the provision of service. This not only cut away the rationale of the feudal structure, but also provided the monarch with increased supplies of cash which he could use to employ mercenaries. With the emergence of soldiers for rent in the 1200s, a new option was available for kings to reduce their military dependence upon the magnates, and they took this opportunity with different degrees of enthusiasm. Third, there were technological developments in the mode of conducting warfare.[24] The development of the pike as a major weapon of war was an important development in the late twelfth century, because this shifted the emphasis away from the expensive mounted horseman to the cheaper infantryman. It also projected ordinary people into a central place in war rather than the rich and noble of birth. The development of the long bow, used with such deadly effect in the early part of the Hundred Years War, was another important blow to the primacy of the mounted knight. So too was the increased reliance on infantry in the fourteenth century, a reliance which increased the need for military training, and increased the size of armies both absolutely and relative to the population at large.[25]

The most important development, however, was that of gunpowder and guns. Although these had been in use from the middle of the fourteenth century, it was not until the late fifteenth century that they emerged as decisive elements in mass conflict. From that date, technological innovation and development accelerated, until the cannon became the primary weapon of large-scale engagement and of attacks upon cities. The development of the cannon as an effective weapon of attack and siege also transformed the problems of defence. The curtain walls of the castles that were so effective against mounted knights and bows and arrows were no defence against the cannon. When a defence was developed, the so-called *trace italienne*, this was very expensive. The escalation in costs that the development of cannon and its countermeasures involved made it even more difficult for small or local actors, such as individual magnates or city-states, to bear the costs of military activity. This therefore favoured those authorities with access to larger amounts of potential revenue, which meant the Crown.

This trend was accelerated by the shift in the direction of a standing army in the sixteenth and seventeenth centuries. Such a development not only reinforced the primacy of royal authority over local interests, since only the former was permitted to have control of such an army and he was able to use that force to ensure his continuing primacy, but it also aided in the bulking-up of the central state apparatus. Once a standing army was in existence, the centre had to ensure that it could be supplied with all of its needs. This stimulated the development of a central bureaucratic apparatus to both organize the new army and ensure its continued supply. It also placed increased pressure on the state treasury, and therefore upon the Crown's ability to tax its subjects more effectively. A large tax base and centralized authority, essential to the national state, were therefore encouraged by the growth of standing armies and the use of gunpowder. But it is important to recognize that these military developments did not determine the emergence of the national state. These sorts of military developments were available to all of the polities of Europe, at least in principle, and many areas did not centralize: the German states and the Italian city-states are good examples. Over time these types of polities did not prosper, and the increasing costs of military activity were one factor in this, but it was not the only one.

National Identity

Geopolitical competition was also important in the development of a sense of national identity. The origins and major stimulants of this are in dispute. For some, the development of a national market and the growth of commercial ties across the country were central to the development of a sense of national identity. Such a development clearly aided the growth of such a sentiment, but important too was the sense of the international environment and geopolitical competition. Given that warfare was a costly business and kings had to raise as much of the cash to sustain it from domestic sources as they could, it was in their interests to create a supportive attitude among the populace from whom such resources had to be gained. Appeals on the basis of dynastic rights were not a particularly effective means of mobilizing mass support. Arguments over dynastic claims to territories far away were a long way removed from the concerns of most residents of the feudal and post-feudal states, even the nobility. This was especially the case as the state shifted from being considered the patrimony of the ruler, and therefore the interests of the ruler and the state were inextricably intertwined, to being seen as an entity over which the ruler exercised temporary suzerainty. This conception of the state as no longer the personal property of the ruler undercut the rationale of appeals based on the dynastic principle and made it imperative that a new basis for generating support be developed. The form this took was to root the search for support in the development of a sense of national identity. By emphasizing the way in which all who lived within the boundaries of the state shared common national (however defined) characteristics, a basis of unity was created which did not rely upon the person of the ruler but rather on the nature of the community.

There has been much debate over the development of such a sense of national identity, and in particular over whether there are certain qualities which are inherent in a national group which give rise to such feelings, or whether it is something created from above; the phrase 'invention of tradition'[26] adequately captures this second position. While in practice both constructive efforts from above and impetus from below probably contributed to the development of national myth and identity, it is clear that elites played a central part in their emergence. Cultural elites in particular were important here, with the generation of a national literature and the projection of a national history rooted in a mythologized conception of the national past.[27] The mythology and imagery that were used in the construction of this sense of national identity assumed the location of the community within a broader geopolitical context. The story of the people was the story of a group forming themselves into a nation principally either by conquering their neighbours or by setting themselves apart from their neighbours. The nation was fired in the struggle with external opponents, its identity asserted through the rejection of claims to dominate it. Such rejections were led by great leaders, who thereby became the hero-figures of the emergent mythology and the models for the nation as a whole. The development of such a mythology was also connected with the growth of vernacular language and its replacement of local languages, dialects and those (such as Latin) that claimed a transnational currency. The growth of the vernacular language was another important cultural marker setting the nation off from those that surrounded it. But what is important here is that the growth of such a sense of national identity occurred against the process of defining oneself in distinction from those who lived beyond the borders. The sense of national self was a process of differentiation from similar national communities elsewhere. This growth of a sense of national identity (something which occurred at different times in different places) thus assumed a geopolitical context in which other such groups existed.

This is testament to the way in which there was a sense of a broad, single cultural community within Western Europe. Resting on the commonality of the legacy of the Roman Empire, sharing a common religion, until the sixteenth century bound together by the tentacles of a single church, increasingly linked by commercial connections, and swept by similar intellectual movements, Western Europe was an entity differentiated from those regions that surrounded it. It was a multi-state system within a broad cultural unity, and each of those individual political entities was affected in its development by this fact. But this region was not isolated; there were regions outside it with which it interacted. The closest was that of Eastern Europe.

The Wider World

Eastern Europe

There is no clear dividing line between Western and Eastern Europe, but at least in the feudal period the regions were marked by two distinct cultural differences. First, the East did not have a history of Roman conquest, so did not inherit directly the legacy of the Roman Empire. Second, while the West was predominantly Roman Catholic, the Christianity of much of the East was Orthodox, although Poland and Prussia were major exceptions to this. These differences were sufficient to ensure that Eastern Europe's marginal geographical location away from many of the centres of Western Europe was reinforced by the perception of it as being on the edges of the common cultural community. While at times Poland and Prussia may have been conceived as part of the European culture area, this was never really the case for Russia. Generally this region was outside the cultural parameters West European elites used to conceptualize their world.

This does not mean that the two were not linked, however. There were trade connections between the two parts of the Continent, ambassadors were exchanged, and there was a general level of social intercourse. Geopolitical competition was also present. As indicated above, one person who has emphasized this competition and seen it as important in structuring political developments is Perry Anderson.[28] Anderson seeks to explain the origins and nature of the absolutist state in Europe. In the West, he sees this as coming about as a result of the 'crisis of the nobility' in the fourteenth and fifteenth centuries, a crisis brought on by the rise of peasant opposition and the inability of the feudal structure to contain it. As a result, he argues, feudal political arrangements were deserted by the nobility, who reconstituted their class power through the absolutist state. Such a state was much more powerful than that of the feudal period, and it needed to be so in order to maintain the nobility's dominance over the peasantry. Thus Anderson sees absolutism in the West as resulting from internal factors. Turning to Eastern Europe, he argues that the emergence of absolutism there in the sixteenth and seventeenth centuries (and particularly in Austria, Prussia and Russia) was a response to the challenge posed by the newly powerful Western states. The more advanced absolutist states of the West were able to mobilize powerful military machines and thereby threaten Eastern European states. In response, the rulers of the latter imposed a 'second serfdom' upon the peasantry, centralized rule in their own hands, and created large land armies. The political forms that emerged in Eastern Europe were thus stimulated by the geopolitical challenge posed by the more powerful states of the West.

There has been significant discussion and criticism of Anderson's thesis.[29] Much of this has focused upon the nature of the absolutist state, and whether it is a revived feudal state (as Anderson claims), or whether it is capitalist in nature. This dispute was noted earlier. Of more importance now is the charge that Anderson's thesis finds difficulty in explaining the political trajectories of some countries. England and the Netherlands do not fit the Western pattern of the imposition of absolutism as a response to crisis, while Poland's developmental path shows that more than simply the challenge from the West was central to the structuring of developments; in Poland the strength of the nobility prevented the centralization of rule in the king while the primary challenge to the state's existence came not from the West, but from its immediate neighbours, Prussia and Russia. Furthermore, Anderson's thesis cannot explain variations in the power of the state over time once absolutism has been established. The waxing and waning of royal (and state) power in, for example, France and Russia, cannot be explained by Anderson's schema. But arguing that not everything stemmed from the reality of Western challenge is not to deny that that challenge had an effect upon state development in Eastern Europe. Clearly the two regions did interact at various times, and developments in Eastern Europe did have an effect upon the West; the Muslim invasion of the Balkans and central Europe is the clearest instance of this. But the influence of Eastern Europe upon state development in the West was much less than that of the West upon the East.

A World System?

There was also, of course, a broader context for West European state development, that of the globe. Developments in Europe were clearly affected by events outside that continent. For many, the best illustration of this is the way that the European region experienced military pressure from outside. The eleventh and twelfth centuries saw the crusades and the futile attempts to take the 'Holy Land' from its Muslim rulers. The Mongols reached into central Hungary in the thirteenth century, the Muslims remained in Spain until 1270 (although Granada remained under Muslim occupation until 1492), and the Turks through the Ottoman Empire remained a military threat to Central Europe until the end of the sixteenth century, and their rule extended throughout much of the Balkans into the twentieth century. The nature of the relationship between Western Europe and the rest of the world, and the influences each exerted on the other, remains a matter for debate. One pathbreaking attempt to elucidate this relationship, at least as it developed after 1450, has been given by Immanuel Wallerstein.[30]

The principal aim of Wallerstein's work is to chart the development of what he sees as an integrated supra-European world economy. He acknowledges that such economic systems existed earlier, although none was as stable and long-lasting as the capitalist one, which is the focus of his work. Importantly, too, it is not essential for his notion of the world economy that all parts of the globe are always involved in it. However, the structure of the modern world economy as he sees it is such that, over time, all parts of the globe will be encapsulated within its bounds. The capitalist world system as Wallerstein conceives of it is characterized by an economic division of labour that manifests itself in a geographical form. There are three zones, or regions: core, periphery and semi-periphery. These are tied together by world market trade in bulk commodities, comprising necessities for everyday consumption. These zones have different economic structures, different modes of labour control, different class structures, different sorts of states, and are differently rewarded by the world economic system.

The core and periphery are clearly defined zones; the semi-periphery is a kind of residual with some of the characteristics of the other two regions. The core economies are characterized by the most advanced types of economic activity: manufacturing, banking, ship-building, trading and the processing of primary produce. The periphery economies produce primary products in the technologically least sophisticated ways. In terms of labour control, the lower the skills required, the less autonomy the workers have and the more directly coercive the forms of labour control are; in the core, wage labour backed by the threat of coercion, while in the periphery, serfdom in the Old World (principally Eastern Europe) and slavery in the New World. This is reflected in the respective class structures. The core economies have a complex class structure: lord, labourer, peasant, yeoman, apprentice, artisan, merchant and professional. In contrast, the periphery has a simple structure: lord and serf or slave. These differing types of domestic economic and political arrangements led to the differential strength of states. In Wallerstein's words, 'the world-economy develops a pattern where state structures are relatively strong in the core areas and relatively weak in the periphery'.[31] The differential strength of the state is important because the strong states of the core assist in the maintenance of the system as a whole through the use of extra-economic means, increasing the flow of surplus goods and resources to the core. This thereby confirms the dominance of the core economies within the world economy.

This sort of formulation is interesting within the context of our focus upon the state and its development because of the close association it makes between the state and economic system. Core location and a powerful economy goes with a powerful state; peripheral location and a weak economy should be accompanied by a weak state. However, Wallerstein has been criticized on a number of grounds,[32] including not always being clear or consistent in the way in which he uses the principal elements of his analysis, and for adopting a teleological approach. More important for our purposes is the claim that he treats politics and the state as epiphenomenal to the economic system. In one view, the state is determined by the operation of the world market; in another view, world market opportunities and technological development possibilities determine the socio-economic structure within each country and the dominant class interests within that structure determines the state and its policies.[33] This criticism of Wallerstein has much merit, especially with regard to the first volume of his work.

Wallerstein attempts to meet this charge in his second volume[34] by relating the state and its role more closely to the nature of the dominant class. Where economic producers are more efficient, in the core, the state has less need to intervene in the world market economy than in those areas where producers are less efficient. One reflection of this is the argument that strong states are required in the periphery to maintain stringent labour controls (reminiscent of Anderson). But this leads to confusion. It seems to mean that in the core states of Western Europe, where states developed centralized institutional structures and capacities, these were reflective of the state's weakness rather than its strength, while in the periphery the development of such structures reflected state strength. Moreover, the chronology does not easily fit his argument: Bloch has shown that servile labour relations emerged in the East when the state was weak and unable to protect the peasants against the nobles, and that serfdom was undermined by the development of a strong state.[35] It is not clear, even within Wallerstein's theory, that there is a simple correspondence between location in the world economy and nature of the state; some core economies had weak states, and some peripheral economies had strong states.[36] What this shows is that location in the world economic system is not the sole determinant of the nature of the state and the power it possesses.

Wallerstein is important both for seeking to relate the state to its place in a broader economic structure and for the implication that the development of the state in Western Europe was not something that occurred in a geopolitical vacuum. However, Wallerstein's conception of the modern world system is too restricted. It is restricted in two ways: the temporal dimension of the system and his conception of it as being European dominated. These will be discussed in turn.

In this discussion, an initial issue is what is meant by world system.[37] How does a system differ from a series of essentially bilateral relations between different actors? Essential to the existence of a system is a regularized and stable pattern of interaction and exchange that embraces a range of actors in a continuing relationship. This implies a degree of integration of the parts into the whole, such that the ways in which they function as units are shaped, at least in part, by their involvement in the whole. This means that the linkages that tie the parts together must be such that change in one can affect change in others. This effect may not be immediate, but it must nevertheless be there. Such a system does not require that all parts of it be equally integrated into the whole, or that all regions of those parts are directly linked into the overarching framework. The important thing is that these units are tied together in a continuing and regular fashion, and their functioning is in part shaped by those ties. The world system of which Europe was a part consisted of four basic culture areas: Europe, principally Western Europe; the Arab Middle East which, from the seventh century, was united under Islam; India; and China. These four culture areas, all characterized by major cities and by the development of commerce within their bounds, were linked together by trade routes[38] but pursued their own trajectories of development. These were the components of the world system as it emerged, although when Wallerstein discusses the world system in his first volume, he restricts it to Europe itself.

It is impossible to pinpoint the exact date of the emergence of a world system. In part this is because of the absence of reliable data on trade and financial flows between different parts of the globe. However, it is clear that there were continuing links between the Roman Empire on the one hand and India and China on the other (the Middle East was part of the Empire). Rome was linked to Asia by the exchange of goods, and although these were primarily luxury items and this trade did not affect the vast majority of the population, it did link Roman Europe into a wider world of commerce.[39] It is not clear whether the links that did exist were sufficient to describe this as a world system, but in any case those links were substantially disrupted by the collapse of both the Roman and Chinese empires at about the same time. Northwestern Europe was now largely isolated from these Asian regions. However, southern Europe, and particularly the trading cities of Venice and Genoa, maintained some contact, if attenuated, through the intermediation of the Eastern Roman Empire centred on Constantinople and the emergent Muslim Arab civilization which took over the modern Middle East. By the thirteenth century, international trade was substantially larger than it had been in previous centuries, even if in gross terms it remained small.[40] Moreover, it was through the Muslim civilization that many advances in European culture and technology were achieved. Aristotle's works returned to Europe via Arab translators, while the thinking of major Muslim philosophers such as Avicenna, Al-Kindi and Al-Farabi entered European thinking, enriching it and driving it in new directions. Similarly many developments in medicine, science and mathematics came from this same source. The period of the so-called European 'dark ages' was actually a time of cultural flowering elsewhere on the globe. Indeed, it may not be an exaggeration to say that the seeds of the Renaissance lie in this contribution to Western thought from the Muslim world.

With the revival of economic life and commerce from the eleventh century, northwestern Europe was ready to rejoin the system that linked together the Muslim, Indian and Chinese regions.[41] With the unification of Central Asia under Mongol rule in the first half of the thirteenth century, Europe became much more closely linked into this world system than it had been earlier. The principal dynamic of this system was trade, and its vehicle was the movement of traders along the various routes that linked the four parts of the system together. Major routes linked Europe with China via the Central Asian caravan routes (often called 'the silk road'), or by sea either through Egypt, the Red Sea and Indian Ocean to India and thence China, or through the Middle East, the Persian Gulf and Indian Ocean to India and thence China.[42] These routes remained the key linkages between Europe and Asia until the Europeans' discovery of the sea routes around the Cape of Good Hope and Cape Horn at the end of the fifteenth and early sixteenth centuries.[43] The system relied upon the continued operation of these routes, and when they were ruptured, as occurred in the fourteenth century, the levels of integration generally declined. According to one student, by the early fourteenth century the increased integration of various world economies was moving in the direction of a world system:

> Linked by the Italian merchant mariner states to a vital Eastern trade that connected Asia Minor to China on the north and Egypt to India, Malaysia and China by the southern sea route, Western Europe had finally entered that trading system and, although she was not yet hegemonic, at least she was becoming a more equal partner.[44]

This system was much 'more complex in organization, greater in volume, and more sophisticated in execution, than anything the world had previously known'.[45]

Levels of integration in this world system broke down in the fourteenth century, principally because of four factors. First, the Black Death, which originated in China and spread across the continent to Europe, suppressed economic activity wherever its demographic effects were pronounced. Second, the Central Asian routes were closed due to the collapse of Mongol unity and power. Third, there was the Ming conquest of China in 1368 which ushered in a period in which the Chinese became more inward looking. The capital was moved to the north, to Beijing, and therefore a long way away from the southern routes and yet the northern routes were blocked by the collapse of Mongol power. Fourth, a vacuum appeared in the Indian Ocean region because of both the Chinese withdrawal and increased domestic disruption in India. But the breakdown in linkages did not, as Abu-Lughod suggests, mean the end of the world system; rather, the one which emerged after 1450 was not a new system but a revival of this earlier one.[46]

Levels of integration in the post-1400 world economy were higher than they were in any preceding era. Although Frank exaggerates when he says that by 1500 there was 'a single global world economy with a worldwide division of labor and multilateral trade',[47] the economic links between Europe and Asia became much more developed during this period than they had been earlier. Trade flowed around the circuit linking Europe, the Middle East, India and China, using the traditional routes noted above plus the new ones opened up by the European explorers around the Cape of Good Hope after 1498 and Cape Horn after 1522.[48] But what also flowed through these veins of intercourse was money. Especially after the entry of American silver into Europe as a result of the Spanish and Portuguese conquests in America, silver and gold became primary commodities in this international trading system. By the seventeenth century at the latest there was a world market for silver; the Mughal Empire in India was financed largely on the basis of silver, much of it brought by the Europeans, while China became a veritable silver sink as much of the silver in circulation made its way there.[49] This inflow of silver stimulated economic expansion in both India and China.[50] This economic interchange rested upon long distance trade conducted between nodes established along the trade routes. It connected an 'archipelago of towns'[51] within which commercial exchange was conducted, all of which fed into the larger circulation of goods and commodities across the continent. In many of these towns foreign merchants were resident, thereby adding a cosmopolitan flavour to them from a very early time; there had been an Arab settlement in Canton in the ninth century.[52] Trade and the quest for economic gain also brought visits by people to these foreign lands; Marco Polo is merely the most famous of such Western visitors to China. The growth of interest in Asia can be seen in Europe as the economic connections mounted, thereby providing the basis for a system that did not rest exclusively upon commerce. But even at its height, this world system linked narrow sectors of economies, at least in Europe, rather than economies as a whole; the primary imports from Asia were spices and textiles.[53] Nevertheless, the linkages between the different components of this world economic system – reflected in the presence of similar patterns of price movements and crises in all these areas[54] – make it a real system even if the points of contact between national economies and the system more broadly were much narrower than the economy as a whole.

It is also important to understand the nature of this world system in terms of political power. Wallerstein's conception is that the world system emerged as one dominated by the Europeans. Until the end of the eighteenth century, this view is clearly wrong. The world system that existed up until the industrial revolution in Europe was one in which Europe was essentially peripheral, and there was no hegemon, although China was probably the most important part. Europe was but a small peninsula on the Asian land mass, geographically remote from the Eurasian heartland, with a small population, and economically lagging behind these other areas, and certainly China, until the nineteenth century. This is not the usual picture of Europe *vis-à-vis* Asia. In economic terms, prior to the end of the eighteenth century, the Asian culture areas were predominant in terms of production, productivity, competitiveness and trade, and had appropriate technology and economic and financial institutions.[55] Estimates of global gross national product (GNP) in 1750 have more than 80 per cent of it in Asia, while throughout this period growth rates were probably higher outside Europe.[56] While technological diffusion went in both directions, it is clear that important scientific and technical developments came from China, India and the Islamic world, including things such as gunpowder, paper and printing, various metallurgical processing methods, various navigational innovations, inoculation against smallpox, and much theoretical knowledge in science and mathematics.[57] Neither was Europe more advanced in terms of the organization of economic life. The same groups to be found in European societies – manufacturers and industrialists, merchants, rentiers, financiers – were present in the societies of Asia, while the processes of finance, production and exchange were similar.[58] Since Sung times in the eleventh and twelfth centuries, the Chinese economy 'had been industrialized, commercialized, monetized, and urbanized far in excess of any other in the world'.[59] China was the driving force of this world economy, not Europe.

The problem for Europe is that while it had a strong appetite for many of the commodities that could be obtained from the East, especially spices and luxury goods such as silk and textiles, it did not have a large range of goods which were desirable in Asian markets. As a result, Europe usually had a trade deficit in its exchanges with Asia. It was not until American silver became available for Europe to use in its involvement in the world system, something that occurred in the seventeenth century, that Europe was able to become more important as a global player. The major political structures in China and India soon became dependent upon the supplies of silver that were most readily forthcoming from the Americas via Europe. Control over this resource, as well as the boost it gave to domestic economies within Europe, enabled some of the European states to expand their role in international commerce and to inject a political power dimension into it. This was to result in the transformation of the world system in the nineteenth century and its dominance by Europe. But before discussing this, we must note one other implication of the mistaken view that the earlier world system was dominated by Europe: the prevalence of the view that Asian states were backward in comparison to their European counterparts.

The Asian State

One way in which this view is shown is in the language and conceptions used to discuss Asian states. Marx used the notion of 'the Asiatic mode of production' to discuss a social formation which did not fit into his classic, teleological, schema of slave, feudal, capitalist and communist. This progression of modes of production, each superior to that which preceded it, was, for Marx and Marxists, the mainstream of human history. Each stage emerged from its predecessor and moved human society ever closer to that ultimate stage envisaged by Marx, communism. The Asiatic mode had no place in this articulation, thereby relegating Asia to the realm of backwardness that could only be made up with the assistance of the more advanced, European and American, areas.[60] Capitalism could be achieved in this area only with leadership from Europe, and until this time, Marx believed, the forces of production were traditional, backward and stagnant. The basis for the Asiatic mode of production was the absence of any form of capitalist relations and the inability of these societies to rise above the village within which production occurred. The system was seen as being stagnant.[61] Marx was clearly guilty of that Eurocentrism that has afflicted much of the Western analysis of areas outside the European culture zone.

Such a claim is also true of that other great nineteenth-century social theorist, Max Weber. Although Weber spent much time and effort studying and writing about Asian society, especially in terms of the city, religion and, in the case of China, bureaucracy, his explanation for the emergence of capitalism is purely Eurocentric. Weber's analysis is a form of European exceptionalism. What enabled Europe to be the location of the birth and development of capitalism was something specific to Europe: Protestant religion and the spirit of capitalism. In Weber's view all religions except Protestantism had a mythical, mystical, anti-rational element that prevented their followers from responding in the totally rational way that was thought to underpin capitalist development. Europe had this, Asia did not, and therefore capitalism developed in the former rather than the latter. Apart from the fact that Weber's analysis does not even hold up in its own terms – the early development of capitalist methods occurred in Catholic Italy and not every part of the Protestant world was a successful case of capitalist development – its assumption of something unique in Europe denies any role for the stimulus to European development provided from Asia. Weber's approach is classic Eurocentrism, failing to see that anything outside Europe could have helped to shape the course developments took on that continent. It also clearly denies any status to the non-European region apart from one of backwardness.

Much of the literature on the meeting of Europe and Asia from the sixteenth century has assumed a basic dichotomy. European states were modern, rational, capitalist, outward-looking and dynamic, while Asian states were traditional, religiously-oriented, peasant-based, inward-looking and stagnant. The crucial component here was the notion of 'traditionalism'. This implied that the society had not made the breakthrough to a rational, capitalist way of life but was instead mired in the traditions that reached back centuries and were rooted in the primitive conditions of village life. Even a culture that was as rich as the Chinese was seen as, if not irrational, at least arational and rooted in the past. The context of the European conquest of the non-European world was usually that of bringing civilization and progress to a backward part of the world. While Western states brought advanced technology to bear against those with whom they came into conflict, it is not accurate to see Asian societies as irrational and mired in traditional ways. Such a view clearly implied a second-class standing to these societies and their political forms compared with those of the West.

Numerous scholars have seen in the non-European civilization areas cultural reasons for the non-development of capitalism.[62] In China, the bureaucratic structure based on (and reinforced by) Confucian values was seen to be the main barrier to autonomous economic development and activity. With the bureaucracy seen as the principal path to reward, entrepreneurship was inhibited. In addition, the bureaucracy, not wanting to see the basis of its power and position undermined, consciously hindered the development of autonomous economic activity. The state was a 'capstone state', sitting on top of society but neither penetrating nor mobilizing it; all it did was inhibit development.[63] In India the caste system was seen as the principal means of structuring society, even making the presence of a central authority less necessary. The caste system had built into it a whole structure of principles governing action which, reinforced through the religion, was said to impose a straitjacket on economic activity. The state's chief task was seen to be to preserve and strengthen this system but, because of the strength of the system of values itself, the state itself was weak. The state's function, to preserve the system, meant that it did not foster independent economic activity, while its weakness meant that rulers tended to have a predatory attitude toward society, aiming to garner as much wealth as they could while in power.[64] Islamic society was seen as stagnant, dominated by a religion that was alien to capitalist principles, lacking the spark of major cities and a middle class, politically unstable because of the continual tension between urban-based would-be rulers and dissident pastoralists, and therefore rulers adopted a predatory approach to the economy in order to make as much as they could while they ruled.[65]

In all of these approaches, the state plays a role. But unlike in the West, it is not a positive role in fostering economic development. In the Islamic areas, it is neither strong enough nor disposed to promote autonomous economic activity which might lead to capitalism. In

India, the state's aim is to consolidate the existing social structure and so has no interest in fostering the sort of economic development that might disrupt that structure. In China, the state positively acts against such economic activity. But were Asian states really that different from those that emerged in Europe?

China

The Chinese state established by the Ch'in dynasty in 221 BC set a prototype of a 'tightly unified, centrally directed' kingdom[66] that, despite the rise and fall of ruling houses, remained the model for Chinese development over the following two millennia. The style of administration and of political structure that developed during the Ch'in and over the succeeding Han and T'ang periods remained to guide Chinese affairs until the institution of the republic in 1911, and even after that significant elements of continuity remained; according to one scholar, the T'ang government was the 'prototype of all subsequent imperial government'.[67] Even when external conquerors seized the throne, as the Mongols did in the thirteenth century and the Manchu in the seventeenth, they adopted Chinese styles, structures and patterns of rule. In part this was because of the enormous strength of the Chinese system, a strength that was firmly embedded in a conscious doctrine shared widely throughout the society but especially among its officialdom, Confucianism. The geographical area of the Chinese state also retained a high level of continuity. Ebbs and flows of the borders did occur at times, but over a prolonged duration the core of the Chinese state remained intact, and the state's area was much more identifiable than that of many later states in the West.

The Chinese regime was a palace regime. Power formally was centred in the palace of the emperor who led a secluded, non-public, existence serviced by an extensive palace bureaucracy. Formally absolute, the emperor's power was mediated through his officials, as in other palace systems. This did cause tensions at times between the emperor on the one hand and his officials on the other, and between household officials and those in the emergent civil bureaucracy. Indeed, one of the recurring patterns in Chinese history is of the tension between the emperor's personal officials (often eunuchs, although in the Ch'ing period, 1644–1911, they were mainly bondsmen or household slaves of the emperor)[68] and those officials in the imperial bureaucracy. There was also a tension in the role of the emperor as the prevailing Confucian ideology portrayed the imperial role as one more related to ritual than to activism, yet many emperors – especially at the start of dynasties – sought to play a more activist role. The emperor was not a war leader,[69] as in Rome, but, more like the ancient Near East, the linchpin between the terrestrial and the cosmic worlds. It was his responsibility to ensure harmony through performance of the correct rituals and the following of a pure life, not to take an active part in governing the country. This conception of the emperor, rooted in the Confucian tenets which became dominant throughout China under the Han, meant that while he was important symbolically, he was less so in a direct, ruling sense. As a result, real power lay in the hands of the bureaucracy. This remained the case even when an emperor sought to be more activist because, given the size of China, it was only through the bureaucracy that central rule could be made real in the localities.

Much more than the European states until the nineteenth century, China was a bureaucratically-run state. From the time of the Ch'in (221–202 BC), the Former Han (202 BC–AD 9) and the Later Han (AD 25–220), a complex bureaucratic structure developed to administer the country. As well as a central bureaucracy, the structure of which did undergo changes over time but which retained a high degree of continuity until imperial collapse in 1911, there was a structure of state-appointed officials which could stretch down to the district level.[70] In the second century BC there were 130,285 civil servants, excluding many of the lower ones, with 18 ranks of officials receiving a state stipend;[71] by T'ang times (618–907) the number had increased to some 150,000–160,000 officials.[72] But what made the Chinese bureaucracy different from those that emerged elsewhere, certainly at such an early time, were three characteristics that the bureaucracy acquired during T'ang times:[73]

1　Specialization. Within the central bureaucratic structure, every function had a specific official whose task it was to perform that function. This was reflected broadly in the developed, differentiated departmental structure of the central bureaucracy, and was much more highly developed than was to occur in a similar structure elsewhere for many centuries.

2　Censorate. This was a section of the central bureaucratic structure whose task was to monitor the performance of all civil servants, investigate their deficiencies and bring offenders to trial. This form of self-monitoring was meant to be a means of ensuring high standards of performance on the part of government officials.

3   Entry to the bureaucracy increasingly was becoming by competitive examination as well as the older recommendation from nobles. The examination, principally in Confucian texts, was open to all and introduced a sense of meritocracy into bureaucratic recruitment, although in practice the vast majority of places were taken by those coming from the noble landowning families. These were the best placed to be able to give their members the resources and time to study for the examinations.

These three characteristics were instrumental in the development of a bureaucratic structure that was more efficient and looked more like modern bureaucracies than anything in Europe at a similar time. What was central to this bureaucracy was the unity that stemmed from the strength of the Confucian ethic. This gave an *esprit de corps* to the officials who worked within the state civil service, and underpinned the unity and cohesiveness of outlook that characterized this structure. It was also central to the fundamental unity between the state bureaucracy and the landed nobility; the latter used their state positions to benefit their families, and those families continued to turn out sons to staff the state bureaucracy.[74] This integration made for significant levels of administrative stability over a long period of time, and despite changes of regime and emperor. Even when state unity collapsed, this structure was sufficiently strong to be able to reconstitute the state along traditional lines. It was also a major factor in sinicizing the non-Chinese Mongol (Yuan) and Manchu (Ch'ing) dynasties.

Below the centre, despite the ideological unity of the Chinese bureaucracy, the administration experienced infrastructural weakness. The ranks of appointed officialdom were highly respected state servants, but although this bureaucracy did extend into the lower reaches of society and thereby gave the state, in principle, significant reach, the centre's capacity to exercise close supervision over what happened at lower levels remained limited. Difficulties of travel and communication complicated the projection of central control. The central authorities were still dependent upon the speed at which a messenger could travel to gain information about what was happening in the far corners of the kingdom, and while they remained overwhelmingly dependent upon the reports of their local officials,[75] they were also vulnerable to the false and exaggerated reporting in which such officials often engaged. Furthermore, such local officials were usually limited to a tenure of about three years in each region, and they were therefore heavily reliant upon the cooperation of local notables for the exercise of their duties. This was especially the case given that most appointees were not natives of the regions to which they were appointed. Corruption and the use of official position for personal enrichment was normal[76] and eroded the reality of central control. So the presence of an elaborate, ideologically-unified, bureaucratic structure did not, of itself, ensure effective central control. Nevertheless, administrative centralization was more a reality in China at an early date than it was in any of the European states.

Ideologically, the state was dominated by Confucian ideology. This doctrine emphasized harmony, everything occupying its proper place and fulfilling its proper role. People owed obligations to those superior in the hierarchy, especially to the father and to the ruler. It was therefore a doctrine that underpinned a highly hierarchical society, where each person had their particular station with a set of duties and responsibilities that went with it. This applied as much to the individual peasant as to the emperor, and to all of the officials in between. This means that public life was highly ritualized, and public administration highly structured. The non-activist role of the emperor was rooted in this doctrine, his task being to ensure harmony through performance of the proper actions. His rule was by divine right; he possessed the mandate of heaven, although the doctrine was flexible here for, if an emperor was overthrown, that mandate was deemed to have passed to his conqueror. But what is most important about this ideology is the way it suffused all of society. While there were competing schools of thought, including Legalism, Buddhism and Taoism, none so embraced the official class or was as embedded in the processes of Chinese public life as Confucianism. This was an important factor in the sinicization of the population, and the integration of them into one culture group that was sufficiently strong for it to sustain itself despite the rise and fall of dynasties. The ideology thus bound political system and people together, legitimizing the former constantly through the repetition of the practices of the everyday public life of the official establishment of China.

The economy was cellular in nature, with local markets being the principal venue in which produce was sold. Prior to the T'ang (618–907), the state was little involved in economic life. The main source of revenue was taxation and income from monopolies on goods such as salt and iron, while in return it provided order, the construction of infrastructure such as roads and canals, relief from famine, and measures designed to prevent flooding. There was little sympathy for commerce within the state bureaucracy, and in T'ang times greater efforts were made to regulate trade and commerce, including prices in the markets. However, this tighter restriction collapsed along with the T'ang. Under the Sung (960–1279), the economy became much more commercialized than it had ever been. Agricultural production shifted more on to a commercial basis, big towns developed as centres of specialized craftsmen, the state sponsored the spread of technical innovation in agriculture, and metallurgy and private trade grew. Under the Ming (1368–1644), commercialization and industrialization continued, fuelled in part by the import of silver from the West,[77] but foreign trade was restricted. The first Ming emperor banned foreign travel and limited foreign trade severely, and these actions helped to close off a promising line of Chinese development. There was also a conscious policy of rejecting many paths of technological and industrial development.[78] But although under the Ming and early Ch'ing China had massive increases in production, consumption and population,[79] and China was until the middle of the eighteenth century the biggest and most important part of the world economy, the breakthrough to capitalism did not occur here.[80]

John Hall[81] seeks to explain this by arguing that it was because China was an empire and therefore a capstone state that sat atop society without penetrating or attempting to mobilize it; like all empires, it had strong blocking but weak enabling powers. He also argues that the Confucian bureaucracy continually sought to prevent the emergence of any source of power to rival its own, and therefore took measures to hinder economic development. The second of these arguments has some currency but should not be exaggerated. The state as a body and bureaucrats themselves were clearly involved in economic activity, and not just in a regulatory capacity. Many of the manufactured goods used by the state were produced by it, while the state monopolized the production and distribution of a range of commodities.[82] Officials used their offices to make money from the general course of Chinese economic life, including engaging in trade and arbitrage.[83] The economy could not have developed as it did in the face of unrelenting opposition from the state. But the officials did not favour activities such as industrialization that, in their view, would have fostered rival centres of power to those upon which they rested.[84] They were sustained in this not only by concern for their structural positions within society, but also by the Confucian tenets dictating the ordering of society. In this sense, they were cautious and conservative in their approach to industrial development, but in this they were no different from many ruling groups elsewhere. In Europe, the landed aristocracy was not uniformly in favour of industrialization either. But what was different was that in those parts of Europe which led the industrial spurt of the eighteenth–nineteenth century, the link between the landed aristocracy and those who ran the state had become much looser than it was in China. In China, these groups remained merged,[85] so that the landed base of power could use the state to sustain itself; unlike in, for example, Britain, where emergent industrialists could appeal to the state with some prospect of success. Furthermore, the Western landed aristocracy was not as united ideologically as the Chinese, and therefore it was not uncommon for some members of the former to actually join the ranks of the industrialists.

The notion of a capstone state unable to penetrate society is also problematic. One of the principal sources of power of the Chinese state was the bureaucracy, both in terms of the central administrative apparatus and the hierarchy of offices that extended out from the capital. Through the latter, the central state apparatus did penetrate society. Although this was achieved in part through local notables, with the attendant problems of conflicting loyalties and perspectives, the unity of the structure and its basic loyalty to the centre was ensured by the normative authority of Confucianism. The normative basis of the loyalty of Chinese bureaucrats was much stronger and much more systematically codified than it was for most of their European counterparts.[86] The whole process of recruitment into the state bureaucracy constituted a manifestation of organic bureaucratic interdependence; the bureaucracy was closely linked to the interests of the central group in Chinese society, the gentry. It was this link, and the resultant interdependence, that gave the state much of its power.

What this means is that if China's economic development was delayed, it was because of the interests of the ruling group, be it defined in class or status terms, not because there was something particular about the state. The Chinese bureaucratic class was not generally supportive of industrial development which threatened to transform the status quo, and it was sufficiently powerful to be able to hinder this development. Indeed, the Chinese polity does not differ greatly from those of the West discussed earlier. Certainly the detail of the structures and the ideology were different, and there was no opening for popular participation as there was developing in parts of Western Europe, but this was less a function of the nature of the state than of the strength of the ruling group. The fact that China was an empire is irrelevant. There was nothing that flowed ineluctably from China's imperial status that hindered development; it was rather the socio-political arrangements within the state that were the barrier.

India

Before its unification by the Mongols in the early sixteenth century, the modern country of India was substantially united on only one occasion, under the Mauryan dynasty in 321–185 BC. For the rest of the time, India comprised a vast number of fractious and competitive states, most of which were fluid and of relatively short duration.[87] Some states did become wealthy and powerful and enjoyed a longer-term existence, such as Chola and Vijayanagra,[88] but these were the exception rather than the rule. Not until the creation of the Mughal Empire in 1526 was India united in a substantive and relatively long-lasting state, with the collapse of this state being a result of the intrusion of the West and the assertion of British power.

The establishment of the Mughal Empire consolidated the power of Muslim rule in mainly Hindu India. Muslim rule had begun with the Turkic Delhi sultanate (*c.*1200–1526),[89] but this had embraced only northern India, while Mughal rule united both north and south. Originating as conquerors, the Mughals dominated all the leading political offices in the new state, but over time increasing numbers of Hindus entered high level state service, so the sense of being ruled by ethnic aliens did not last. Like the Chinese Empire, that of the Mughals was a palace polity. The centre of power was located in the person of the emperor but, unlike his Chinese counterpart, the emperor was expected to be a vigorous and activist leader. The Mughal emperor directly handled affairs of state himself; he was the 'driving force and the supreme co-ordinator of policy',[90] unconstrained by either a grand council of senior administrators or a household staff standing between him and political decisions. The problem with this is that it meant that the health of the system as a whole depended upon the quality, and vigour, of the emperor, and when either of these was lacking the empire's fortunes declined. Unlike in China, the emperor had no religious role. There was a court politics among senior bureaucrats and household officials, but the main source of potential instability came from the absence of a regular rule of succession. The emperor nominated his successor from among his sons, a process that often caused jockeying for position and disputes.

The administration of the state was conducted through a bureaucratic hierarchy staffed at its upper levels by imperial appointments, and at its lower levels by local appointments by lower-level officials (probably mainly the governors) and by village headmen. Thus it was a combination of a professional bureaucracy and reliance upon local notables. From early in the Mughal period, there were uniform administrative and fiscal systems. Administrative ranks had fixed salaries, but these were often paid through tax farming; many had an obligation also to provide soldiers for the imperial army if needed. Officials had no security of tenure and were moved from locality to locality on a regular basis, thereby increasing their reliance upon local notables. Although the size of the state and the standard of the communications infrastructure meant that local officials were able to exercise a degree of autonomy from the centre, the empire also had a well-developed network of reporting agents who sent messages and reports direct to the emperor. There was no codified system of law, no rights of the individual against the state, and a principle of collective responsibility on the part of the village for misdemeanours by its members.

The state did not provide the society with a wide range of services, being interested principally in warfare, order, justice and taxation. It played little role in economic life; the emperor owned numbers of magazines, workshops and arsenals, but in a highly monetized economy with a commercial sector, the state was not greatly active, except for tax collection. The state's lack of deep integration with society was prompted in part by the fact that the problems of order were solved largely through the caste system rather than state action. Castes were hereditary, endogenous social categories into which all Hindus were born.[91] Caste membership effectively defined life chances, including the occupation one could follow, who one could marry, where one could live, and the patterns of life one could pursue. The caste-based social structure was therefore self-regulating, including giving a primary role in sustaining that system to the top caste Brahmins. It was principally from this group that Hindu society took its lead. The implication of this is that, as long as the state continued to support the maintenance of this system, it would not have to become closely involved in the regulation of the day-to-day life of the populace. The Mughals recognized this when they arrived, and adapted to it.

Although the state did not have to concern itself too much with extending its tentacles into the lower reaches of Indian society, it was intent upon extracting resources from the society. At war throughout much of its life, the Mughal state needed to supplement the resources it gained through conquest by domestic sources of income. The state imposed a wide range of taxes, of which the most important was on land. Commerce was also subject to this, although mercantile activity did not generally come under close state control or scrutiny.[92] For most officials, who were *in situ* for a relatively short time, the local area was an opportunity to make profits while they were there. As a result there was little long-term investment in enterprise or development, but only short-term gain before they moved on. Moore has termed the system 'predatory',[93] yet it seems little different from, for example, contemporary France. The state was mainly intent on drawing resources from society to sustain both the war effort and the luxurious life style of the powerful, but this was not dissimilar to many contemporary states in Europe.

This was not the only factor holding back economic development: caste was also important.[94] The caste system, with its prescriptions about appropriate jobs and barriers to contact between members of different castes, imposed a rigidity upon society that did not facilitate economic development. It constrained trade, inhibited a flexible division of labour, restricted the diffusion of knowledge and invention (what Brahmins invented was considered secret), and limited competition between people. But although the caste system did impose some clear restraints on economic development, it did not prevent this from occurring; the Indian textile industry, for example, was the most important in the world until its dominance was broken by a combination of the European industrial revolution and British colonial power.[95] Furthermore, by being the main focus of loyalty and identification, caste undermined the possibility that the state could develop in this way, thereby generating a sense of instability in the state and its structures which only encouraged the predatory behaviour noted above. So while political arrangements were clearly a factor in inhibiting economic development, they were not the only factor and may even have been subsidiary to the role played by the entrenched social structure of castes.

Islam

There was no single Islamic state which, at the time of the expansion of the West, embraced all Muslims in the way that both the Chinese and the Mughal state were seen to rule over the Chinese and the Indians respectively. The main Islamic cultural area stretched from modern Turkey down through the Middle East and along the North African littoral. This area was never encapsulated by a single state. The most important were the Caliphates of the Umayyads (661–750) and the Abbasids (750–mid-tenth century), and the Ottoman Empire (1307–1918). None of these types of state had its roots deeply embedded in society, relying upon local notables for the execution of imperial rule. As the above analysis makes clear, this was not an unusual state of affairs, but in the Muslim states local functionaries seem to have been able to exercise even more local autonomy than their counterparts elsewhere, despite the fact that both Caliph and Sultan were recognized as absolute rulers in their respective states. In part this was because both were essentially conquest states, but also important was the fact that Islam provided a code for living in all respects. As a code, it was all-embracing, covering both religious and secular spheres and prescribing modes and patterns of activity for individuals, groups and society as a whole. At one level, this meant that, as in India, an intrusive state was not needed to structure the course of everyday life; this could be done by the religion. But at another it also called into question the need for a state.[96] This could be resolved in only one of two ways: the leader could be considered the vehicle of God on earth, and therefore his power would be legitimate, or there could be a division into two spheres of authority, the religious and the secular, with the latter only concerned with matters of state. In practice, both solutions were used to justify imperial power.[97]

Neither of the two most important Islamic state forms, the Caliphate or the Empire, sought to extend its roots deeply into the societies within which they were found. This is reflected in the high degree of centralization of central government operations alongside a substantial level of decentralization of local government. Both types of state were palace polities, with power concentrated in the palace of the Caliph/Sultan. In the area of activity not regulated by religious shariah law, the Caliph was supreme, bound by no established law or precedent. While in theory he was to be guided by shariah law, in matters of state this had little practical effect. The Ottoman Sultan was the supreme source of all authority, but would often be guided by the religious leaders. However, a powerful Sultan almost always received the advice he wished to hear. And while the Caliph's legal writ did not extend into the shariah sphere, where there were specific courts to deal with issues covered by religious principles, in the Empire a single court system heard matters covered by both religious and secular law. Importantly in the Empire, the laws issued by the Sultan were codified, building up a legal structure of codified law before anything similar in Europe at the time.[98] Under the Caliphate, the ulema (religious functionaries) did not constitute a formal religious establishment. They gained their authority from their learning and their religious stature and, by not possessing an office, posed a significant moral threat to the Caliph. They were the outsiders, intent only on ensuring the integrity of the religion, and could thus bring pure ecclesiastical authority to bear on the ruler. In contrast, under the Empire the ulema constituted an official religious establishment, with its elite ranks chosen by the Sultan himself. They were institutionally part of the state, and thereby compromised in any efforts they might make to roll back state power.

As with all palace polities focused upon the person of the ruler, the danger of instability in both states was high. In neither was there an established rule of succession to which all adhered. In the Caliphate, the principle developed that the ruling Caliph would nominate his successor from within the family. However, this often brought on tensions and conflicts among those not chosen. In the Empire, the choice of new Sultan often fell to the sons of the former Sultan, aided by palace cliques, in a struggle for power.[99] This sort of conflict at the top of both political structures was common because the legitimacy of the incumbent could always be contested. Furthermore, the religion could become radicalized by the emergence of a charismatic leader denouncing the effete nature of rule and calling for support to restore the society to the true way. This is linked to Ibn Khaldun's view of the cycle of Islamic society whereby desert rebellion by the tribal nomads was followed by tribal conquest of the towns, the seduction of the tribesmen by the towns, followed by another desert rebellion.[100] While it is not clear that this cyclical view of politics accurately captures the dynamics of the Caliphate, and certainly does not relate to the Ottoman Empire, it does emphasize a crucial aspect of these polities: the constant danger of turmoil and dissent. Many Caliphs came under challenge from outside the court, and many were deposed. In the Empire too, sultans were deposed; Finer provides details of nine deposed between 1402 and 1730.[101] However, unlike in the Caliphate, in the Empire there was little link between revolts in the countryside and conflict at the top. Within the elite, intrigue was fuelled by the various groups situated in the ruler's household – personal staff, eunuchs, palace guards, the harem – and by the central bureaucracy. But despite this latent instability at the top, the Ottoman Empire as a system was not unstable. This is principally because of the state bureaucracy.

The Ottoman bureaucracy, at least in the first centuries of its existence, was a well-trained, professional and reasonably efficient structure. The upper levels were staffed, at least until the early eighteenth century, either by young slaves purchased in the market or by a levy of Christian infant males who were brought to the capital, raised as Muslims and thoroughly trained for an administrative (or military) role. The lower levels were essentially self-recruiting, self-training and self-perpetuating, with sons following fathers into the service. But progression through the ranks was dependent upon passing special examinations, so the Empire had a 'rigorous system of recruitment and training'.[102] However, the members of the imperial bureaucracy were considered the Sultan's slaves, possessing no rights against him. At the time of its establishment, the Caliphate took over the administrative hierarchies inherited from the Sassanids and the Byzantines, and was therefore much more developed than that of Charlemagne's Europe.[103] Over time, though, this bureaucracy became almost an hereditary group, with many officials using their offices as means of personal enrichment. Such privatization of the state seems to have occurred on a much grander scale than in Europe and in the later Ottoman Empire.

In both states, the provinces were largely autonomous. In part this was a function of geography, but it was also due to the lack of effort on the part of central state elites to project their power into the regions. They were content to rely upon local governors, themselves reliant upon local notables, to govern the two empires. Indeed, in the Ottoman Empire, the non-Muslim areas (the 'millet') were granted local autonomy under their own political and religious leaders, with the state hardly interfering in their lives except to maintain order and collect taxes. The governors under the Empire often held the lands they ruled as fiefs, exchanging military obligations for the right to tax farm their regions. The extent of central control was much looser in these two forms of state than in any of the others noted above.

This is also reflected in the state's attitude to the economy. Islam was not, as a doctrine, hostile to either economic life or capitalism.[104]

Indeed, as noted above, many of the practices of banking and international trade developed first in the Muslim areas and many standard practices of commerce were codified in the Koran.[105] The Ottoman state took great care of the roads, there were some state enterprises in the military sphere (arsenals and dockyards), and the maintenance of order was essential for the functioning of the region's markets that were so important for the wider world, although it seems to have had little interest in regulating trade. It was also involved in various commercial endeavours, some of its conquests had commercial angles to them, and high-ranking Ottoman officials were often engaged in trading activities.[106] According to Frank,[107] these states 'made massive investments in and organized the maintenance of canals and other transport infrastructure; expanded, settled, and reclaimed arable land; ran para-state economic enterprises; made trade and other economic policy; not to mention lent military support to and promoted "national" economic interests'.[108] However, the effect of such policies was at times countered by high rates of taxation and sometimes the sequestration of assets, and these actions did not assist economic development.

So the states of the Islamic world shared many of the characteristics of their counterparts in India, China and Europe. A central court and bureaucracy sat atop a regional administration that depended overwhelmingly upon local notables. Certainly the details of these states differed, but we should not assume that at least the Ottoman Empire was a weak state. Throughout its life it was in conflict with the European powers,[109] and it retained its position until it was swept away in 1918. Militarily it was a match for whatever the European powers could throw at it for most of its life. The early Islamic polity was also the scene for cultural and scientific developments that preceded by far what was occurring in Europe at the same time. A similar point may be made with regard to the Chinese and Indian polities at different times. Yet despite the advanced nature of the cultures and many of the physical and material qualities of these societies and the contributions they made to the development of science and technology in the West, they do not appear to have exercised significant influence on political forms in the West. There are no clear and unambiguous cases of Western borrowing of Asian political practices or institutions, although the shift toward a professional and meritocratic bureaucracy did come at a time when there was increasing interest in, and knowledge about, China. Political influence seems not to have flowed from East to West. Nevertheless, these were not in any sense inferior societies to those of Western Europe; indeed, in institutional terms it may be argued that these states were at least as developed as those of Europe at many stages in their respective paths of development. But ultimately these states succumbed to European pressure. Why? Was it something about the states and their natures?

The Uniqueness of the Western State?

John Hall[110] has argued that the Chinese, Indian and Islamic polities were weaker than the 'organic states' of the West because the latter were able to send:

> deep roots into their societies... China, Islam and India created polities which acted in a zero-sum manner, being arbitrary and incapable of providing many services, and this reflected certain blockages in society. European civilisation, in contrast, produced a state which was less arbitrary and which provided a great measure of social infrastructure, and this will be explained in terms of the absence of social blockages. The former states produced, as we would expect, less total energy than did the latter.[111]

Hall then went on to argue in relation specifically to the Islamic polities that, unlike in the West where there were different states to which innovators could flee in order to escape repression at home, in an empire such escape is impossible. Furthermore, in the West, according to Hall, the state had to become more deeply rooted in society 'both because of the pre-existence of a civil society and because of the need to raise revenue to compete in war with other similarly stable states'.[112] These forced the Western states to develop infrastructure and seek to extract revenue from domestic society to sustain their military activities. Thus crucial to the explanation is the existence in the West of a multi-polar state system whereby the states were forced to rationalize their societies under the pressure of war. In contrast, the Asian states were not in a competitive geopolitical environment.

What are we to make of this line of argument? The crucial distinction Hall makes is between the agrarian empires of Asia and the multi-polar system of states in Europe. Two elements of this are crucial. First, empires did not penetrate the society very effectively and certainly not as deeply as the states of the West; and second, the absence of geopolitical competition for the Asian empires robbed them of the impetus to rationalize structures at home and encourage innovation in technological development. It is clear from what has been said above that the Mughal, Caliphate and Ottoman empires did not penetrate deeply into the societies over which they ruled. The linkages between centre and regions were weak and extended, with central power at best exercised directly only on an episodic basis. Bureaucratic organic interdependence was weak, but this was not so very different from the states of Western Europe prior to the nineteenth century. As for the Chinese Empire, relying upon a highly developed bureaucracy drawn from the society generally and held together by the discipline imposed by ideology, the Chinese state during its periods of strength probably exercised at least as much power over many of its regions as did any large European state. And this notion of size may be important. All of the Asian empires ruled over territories larger than those which constituted the basis of the European states, and therefore the infrastructural problems of exercising control were accordingly greater. But notwithstanding this, the degree of control exercised through the Chinese bureaucratic system when the dynasty was at its height was probably not qualitatively different from any European power before the nineteenth century. It is, therefore, an exaggeration to suggest that only the European state was able to penetrate society effectively. For most European states this only came about in the nineteenth century, long after European impact on the Asian empires had already begun.

The second element relates to the consequences of geopolitical location in a system of states. The argument that war stimulated state development has already been discussed. The issue is the geopolitical location of the Asian empires. It is striking that in his discussion of Islamic polities, Hall gives little attention to the most durable and powerful of these, the Ottoman Empire.[113] Throughout its lifetime, the Ottoman Empire struggled militarily in Europe, first trying to extend its domains into the centre of the continent, and then to defend those domains against challenge. Certainly it was not confronted by the militarily most powerful states of England, France and Spain (although the Empire could be a player in their politics; in the early sixteenth century, the French allied with the Turks against the Habsburgs), but its existence in the Balkans, and its control over the trade routes that traversed its territory, projected it into European affairs. It was part of the dynamic of the European multi-polar system, and therefore subject to the competition central to that dynamic. Indeed, it was that competition that finally brought about the collapse of the Empire, rather than any concerted push by

European powers specifically directed against that Empire. The Mughal and Chinese empires were not thus located. Neither was in an emergent state system in which competition and rivalry were continuing features; rather, both were clearly the dominant powers of their respective regions, with the principal challenge coming (before the Europeans) from nomads on the borders. While the relationship with such groups could become quite systematized,[114] the challenge tended to be episodic rather than sustained, and the way in which they were perceived (in the Chinese case as 'barbarians') did not stimulate self-reflection about the nature of the state and its structure.

The other side of this point about competition is the existence of different jurisdictions to which innovative or economic groups who found themselves blocked or discriminated against could escape. This clearly existed in Europe, but it is argued that it was not present in the agrarian empires of Asia. This argument is weakest with regard to the Ottoman Empire. On the fringes of Europe, those who felt disadvantaged could conceivably have escaped in the same way that people in, for example, Spain, England or France could have done. Moreover, given the lack of tight central control over the provinces in the Ottoman Empire, and especially the autonomous status of the millet, those wishing to minimize central control over them could escape to the provinces. In the provinces, their room for manoeuvre would have depended in large part upon the extent of control that the local governor and notables sought and were able to achieve. To the extent that the governor was a tax farmer, it may even have been in his interests to facilitate new economic developments. Thus the escape option appears not to have been closed off in the Ottoman Empire. Under the Mughals, the fact that local and regional power was left substantially in the hands of local authorities also provided some semblance of opportunity for escape from central oppression. In China, given the nature of the bureaucracy, this may have been more difficult, but even here the frequent occurrence of regionalism in Chinese history is evidence of the fact that lower-level officials were not the mere ciphers of Beijing. So in all of the Asian empires, while there may not have been a geopolitically-defined independent political jurisdiction to which one could escape, the looseness of central control over the localities meant that there was some prospect for escape. This means that the nature of the political states of the empires did not, in itself, constitute an insurmountable barrier to economic innovation and development.

Hall also points to the arbitrariness and predatory nature of these states in comparison with those of the West. But, as we have seen, at times Western states, or sometimes particular rulers, were both arbitrary and predatory in their dealings with society. This was not a characteristic unique to non-Western polities, but what is behind this contrast drawn between Western and Eastern polities is a contrast between the nature of the respective societies. The West is seen as a society within which organized, corporative groups were plentiful, which could act as both an intermediary between state and individuals and could impose restraints upon state behaviour. This was reflected in the corporate autonomy achieved by towns. In contrast, non-Western societies are seen to lack such intermediary and restrictive groups or, where such groups exist, they are means of constraint upon the members and of control over their actions. Islamic society is viewed as lacking groups intermediate between the individual and the state, perhaps reflecting the doctrinal position in Islam that all believers are equal before God and therefore there is no need for structured religious organization. Indian society is seen as structured according to castes, which effectively constrain the sorts of activities open to their members and lock them into set positions in the social hierarchy. In China, too, people are seen as being locked into position by the status hierarchies rooted in the traditional family structure and embedded in the Confucian ethos which dominated society.

These views are simplistic. In all three societies there were groups which united individuals engaged in particular common pursuits. The clearest example of this was in the economy, where associations of particular tradesmen, artisans and merchants were active. Certainly in India these may have been linked to the caste structure, and in Chinese and Islamic societies to family, but they were autonomous organizations along similar lines to those that emerged in the West and acting in similar ways to pursue the interests of their members.[115] However, these groups, and the notion of civil society with which they are usually associated, did not develop the sort of strength or autonomy that they did in some of the states of Western Europe, but this was purely because there was not scope for the organization of political interests in the sorts of assemblies that had developed in the West. It was not that autonomous organization did not exist in these societies; rather, the ruling elite did not allow this to take a political form. Thus such groups were not able to impose their will on the state, or to break open the closed nature of politics at the apex of the state structures. This was a real difference between these agrarian empires and the leading states of Western Europe; in the former, there was not even narrow legislative organic interdependence. This meant that the power of the central state elite was much less constrained in the Asian empires than it was in the West.

This suggests that the states formed in these major culture areas outside Western Europe were not, as a group, qualitatively different from those on the Western periphery of the continent. Certainly there were differences of detail. The Asian monarchs were less restricted even than the European absolutist monarchs by a corpus of law that had become embedded in the political process and by the entrenched nature of assemblies.[116] But notwithstanding differences of detail like this, the pre-industrial Western and the Asian states were not, as groups, radically different. All had centralized rule. All had emergent civil bureaucracies with some specialization of function, and to different degrees distinct from the ruler and his household. All relied upon the support of local notables for the administration of the country outside the capital. All sought a monopoly of force and had made substantial progress toward achieving it. And in all interdependence was not highly developed, although it was probably further developed in some of the European countries than in Asia. Prior to the growth of capitalist industrialism in the West, Eastern and Western states were, as a group, identifiable as the same sort of phenomenon: a pre-industrial, agrarian state. They were not qualitatively different types of political formations. In the eighteenth century when European contact had its devastating effect upon the Mughal Empire, both the Chinese and Ottoman empires were in the ascendant and at least as powerful as the leading states of Europe. However, ultimately European contact destroyed these empires. The Mughal Empire in India was unseated and replaced by the British Raj in the second half of the eighteenth century. The Ottoman Empire was broken up after defeat in the First World War, with some sections gaining their independence (including the Turkish heartland) and others becoming colonial appendages of the Western powers. The imperial system in China collapsed in 1911, but the country as a whole never succumbed to Western colonialism, despite the role the Western powers played in undermining that empire during the nineteenth century. In part the collapse of these empires was due to an unfortunate combination of events: their entry into a downward spiral and the increased aggressiveness of the West.

While the ultimate collapse of these states was a result of the projection of Western political and military power, this was preceded by a process of decline that had nothing to do with the conscious projection of political power into their regions by Western states.[117] From about 1400 until the middle of the eighteenth century, economic expansion occurred in the three cultural areas with which we are concerned. However, from about 1750, economic decline began to accelerate in these areas. In India, economic pressures had been coming on earlier both as a result of increased competition from European traders and Chinese manufacturers, and it was in a depleted economic state that the Mughals had to confront military aggression from the British in the 1750s. At about the same time, the Ottoman Empire went into economic decline in terms both of production and trade, once again partly due to West European competition. Similar decline took hold in China in the nineteenth century, in part due to the problems of political control during that period, but also due to the disruption to the economy caused by the British-introduced opium trade and the shift of silver in connection with that trade. This process of economic decline was accompanied by administrative decline, often associated with political disruption, in each of these empires at about the same time.

What is important about this is that, at the same time as the Asian empires were running into economic difficulties, the economies of some of the West European states were expanding significantly. This was, in part, due to their control over American silver and to the increased revenues derived from production and trade with America, and with these expanded resources they were able to buy their way into the Asian markets in a much more significant way than before.[118] This coincided with the breakthroughs leading to the so-called industrial revolution in the West. According to Frank, these breakthroughs occurred in Europe not because of any particular exceptionalism, but because of the particular economic circumstances which prevailed at the time. Europe was a high-wage/high-cost production area compared with the East, with which it was competing in various products; Britain and textiles is a clear case. Furthermore, in Europe there was labour mobility: workers could migrate to America. This meant that there were clear incentives to invest in labour-saving or energy-generating techniques. In Asia, where labour was more plentiful and the option of moving less open, there were no similar incentives. If these arguments are correct, the barrier to further economic expansion in Asia lay less with state action or culturally-imposed 'blockages' than with simple economic considerations.[119] European political dominance came about not because the Asian states were inferior to those of Western Europe, but because of the different stages these regions were in: an aggressive economically expansionist West confronted Asian states whose economies were on the decline.

The debate about why industrial capitalism emerged on a large scale in Europe and not in Asia is a large and complex one. We have only scratched the surface and need go no further into it. But what we have done is to suggest that the absence of such a development may not be due to the nature of the state in the Asian empires, although to the extent that this was part of a broader issue of cultural, social, economic and political factors, it was of course involved; rather, the state should not be seen as something qualitatively different from its counterparts in Europe. Certainly it differed from the leading states of Western Europe in the nineteenth century, but that difference is not so great if we compare either West European states in the seventeenth or eighteenth centuries, or East European states until the twentieth century. This implies an important point: it is the West European experience that is unusual, not the political formations elsewhere on the globe. Nowhere else was the combination of capitalist industrial economy and pressures for an opening of the traditional political structure (processes that were linked) present. The resultant national state form was then spread across the globe.

Colonial Globalization?

The West European state form was spread across the globe in the carry bag of imperialism. As the Spanish, English, Dutch, French and Portuguese, and later the Belgians, Germans and Americans, incorporated much of the world in far-flung overseas empires,[120] they did not see themselves as transplanting the European state form. Instead they were building political units which spanned the globe and which, although in practice highly decentralized because of the difficulties of transport, tied vast tracts of territory into the imperative of rule from an imperial centre. Political life in these colonial areas was encapsulated within structures imposed by the colonial power, even if many of the old elites retained their positions and power. The economy was restructured to serve the needs of the metropolis, either in terms of providing goods to the home country for industry or consumption, or of generating revenue through trade. Indigenous cultures often were suborned by the culture from the colonial power, backed up by the apparatus of rule set in place by that power. Not all parts of these colonial empires were closely integrated into the imperial network, but even those that were least integrated had their traditional structures undermined and transformed. This expansion of empire was a physical manifestation of the extension of competition between the European states beyond Europe. From the papal division of the new world between Spain and Portugal in the late fifteenth century, it was clear that local conflicts would now be played out on a global scale. The outcome, global colonization, represented the consolidation of a truly European world economy.

The empires represented a manifestation of globalization.[121] The parts of the empire were tied together into a system with its heart in the colonial power and the rationale of that system was the enrichment of that colonial power. In this sense, all structures and processes in the colonies were shaped by imperial imperatives, and all were part of the one system. There was not a high level of integration in the fields of culture and communication; the infrastructure simply did not permit this. The state of the infrastructure also ensured that the level of economic integration was in practice low, even if the essential dynamic of it was systemic, to serve the state at the heart of the imperial network. Similarly, the political unity was looser than a glance at the areas shaded in different colours on a map might suggest. So this was not a highly integrated, finely modulated system of globalization. Indeed, it may be argued that it was not even one system of globalization, given that each colonial empire in large part operated parallel to one another without extensive inter-connections; but the sorts of links established between imperial capital and colonial outposts certainly represent a form of globalization.

This sense of globalization was shattered by the break-up of the colonial empires in the wake, finally, of the Second World War. But what this also did was to universalize the European state form. As colonial administrators prepared to leave those colonies where they were not forced out, they left in place state structures modelled upon those at home. Where they were forced out, with no hand-over or transition time, they usually left behind colonial state structures modelled upon those at home. In any event, most nationalist leaders had been caught up in the ideas of the West. Regardless of what they embraced – nationalism, communism, liberalism and/or democracy – new national leaders almost universally took up the rhetoric of democracy, the ideal of rational bureaucratic organization, and the principles of running a modern state, all taken from the experience of their former colonial masters. Even those countries that had not been colonies, such as China, Japan, Thailand and Turkey, adopted these forms. In this way, the state form developed on the Western periphery of Europe came to dominate the globe.

Thus geopolitical competition both shaped the Western European state form's development and ensured its dominance across the globe, but this does not mean that that state form was a qualitatively different type of entity from those which emerged elsewhere. The major states that existed in Asia had many similarities to their Western cousins. But although the Western state form was not unique, at the time it came into conflict with its Asian counterparts, it was industrially and militarily more powerful. Here lay the source of Western domination of the globe throughout much of the nineteenth and twentieth centuries, a domination that was itself shaped by one of the major formative forces in the Western state, geopolitical competition.

6

The Twentieth Century:
The State Embedded?

The twentieth century saw the expansion of the state to its greatest limits, penetrating further into society and controlling more of the lives of the people who lived under it than ever before. The principal form this took in the West was the capitalist welfare state; in the East, the communist state. Linked with this was a change in the state's formal relationship with the people over whom it ruled, a change reflected in the rise of democratic politics and the designation of those people as 'citizens'. Both the development of the state and the rise of citizenship continued trends begun as a result of industrialization and discussed in Chapter 4. These changes embedded the state more firmly into society than it had ever been before and, in the welfare (but not communist) states, strengthened the ties of interdependence.

Welfare Capitalism

Rollout of the State

The notion of citizenship had, of course, been around since ancient times, but before the advent of democratic politics it had always been a socially restrictive term. It had been part of the means of exclusion of a significant section of the populace from political life, and it was only with the French Revolution that it took on a mass, national, character. But this mass character had little political substance until democratic politics transformed the political process within the state. Citizenship meant nothing if it did not mean participation in the public, political life of the state, so citizenship as a socially inclusive concept made sense only when democratic politics had expanded participation to all classes in society. This did not come uniformly in the states across the globe, and neither did it come early or quickly. However, with its onset, the relationship between state and populace was changed fundamentally. No longer were the affairs of the state considered to be relevant only to society's upper classes. Now as the citizenry, the whole adult populace had a right not just to be interested in the conduct of their governors, but to actually have a say over the decisions they made. Formally in social terms the state therefore ceased to be a class-based concept and instead became a mass concept, just as earlier it had been transformed from a royal elite concept into a national concept. In practice, of course, much of this remained symbolic, as the state frequently continued to be controlled by and to work in the interests of particular sections of society. But the symbolism was important because it melded together the interests of the state and the citizenry in an intimate fashion. The consequences of this became clear following the Great Depression in the West at the end of the 1920s and beginning of the 1930s.

The emergence of competitive politics, initially in England in the eighteenth century and then developing both depth and breadth in successive centuries as well as taking root in other countries, added to the growth of a sense of the national economy, combined to stimulate political figures to articulate programmes of national development. These did not always take the form of clearly spelled out economic programmes. More important were the political ideologies that came to structure politics and, as a consequence of the widening of the franchise, the need of those ideologies to appeal to a broad populace. Discussion of the role of the state had been a staple of political philosophers in one form or another since the time of the Greeks. But with the development of competitive politics and the gradual emergence of a mass electorate, political parties introduced this discussion into the political consciousness not just of the elites, but of a wider mass public. Such discussion was rarely framed explicitly in terms of 'the role of the state', but differing conceptions of this underpinned the positions taken by different parties on the range of policy issues with which they had to deal. By the early twentieth century, the lines of debate on the state and its role were drawn in the form noted in Chapter 1: mainstream left-wing parties favoured the expansion of state activity into areas of life it had hitherto left alone, right-wing parties favoured a much more restricted role for the state with an emphasis upon the importance of individual initiative and autonomy, while centrist parties adopted a position between these two.

The projection of the role of the state into the public, political arena was underpinned by a more expansive notion of citizenship and of the state's responsibility to its citizens. We do not have to accept Marshall's schema[1] of the unrolling of citizenship through civil to political to social rights to recognize that citizenship is not simply a political category: it implies a whole range of social and economic rights and responsibilities as well as those which inhabit the political arena. Although commonplace today, such a conception was not widely accepted in the early years of the twentieth century. What was important for the spreading of such a conception was the Great Depression. Increasingly the political imperative of gaining re-election plus the competition posed by the emergence of an alternative form of organizing society through the development of communism in the USSR (see below), stimulated the broadening of the notion of citizenship. People had a right to expect more of their government and state than simply protection. Increasingly governments came to be seen to have a responsibility not only to cope with the social effects of a disaster like the Depression, but also to take action to prevent such a development from occurring. Citizenship became multi-faceted and the state's sphere of competence greatly expanded as it came to be seen as a means for addressing problems of poverty and inequality.

The form in which this is usually discussed is the 'welfare state'. The welfare state emerged in a variety of forms (see below). Perhaps paradoxically because of its earlier reliance on local notables rather than a professionalized bureaucracy in local administration, one of the most extensive forms of the welfare state was developed in Britain.[2] While the term 'welfare state' was first used in the 1930s, the measures to which it referred actually had their roots in the British Liberal governments before the First World War. In 1908 the Asquith government had introduced old age pensions that were non-contributory and means tested, and three years later national insurance covering unemployment, accident and sickness was introduced, paid for from employers' and employees' contributions. Measures were introduced limiting rent increases and protecting tenants from eviction. These measures were extended in the 1920s with the widening of national insurance and the introduction of widows' pensions. Subsidies were introduced in the early 1920s to assist the construction of housing for working-class families. In the following decade, reflecting the experience of the Depression and the influence of Keynes's ideas on the role of government spending in fostering economic development, the social welfare net legislated by the government expanded. In 1934–35 unemployment assistance was rationalized and standardized into a single system. The state increased subsidies for slum clearance, and thereby for the provision of new housing, and expanded the scope of the ceiling on rent and interest increases and the protection for sitting tenants. But these measures were dwarfed by the massive expansion of state competence following the Second World War.

In response to the difficulties created by the Depression, in the early 1940s the British government established a commission headed by William Beveridge to enquire into post-war social services. The result was reports on social insurance (1942) and full employment (1944), which laid the basis for the post-war British welfare state. Beveridge identified five major evils: want, disease, squalor, ignorance and idleness; and five answers to these evils: social security, a national health service, the provision of housing, state education, and commitment to full employment. Initially the coalition wartime government and then, after July 1945 when the Labour Party was elected to power with a commitment to act on these proposals, successive governments built upon the earlier measures to construct the welfare state.

The 1944 Education Act re-organized the school system and provided for universal free secondary education. The 1945 Family Allowances Act provided for the payment of a universal benefit without a means test for all but the eldest child, a measure justified by the aim of relieving poverty in large families. The National Insurance Act of 1946 sought to create a comprehensive net of social security. It provided for unemployment, sickness, maternity and widows' benefits and the old age pension, funded by contributions from employers and employees with the balance coming from the state. The National Health Act of 1946 established a free medical service for all, funded by the state. It provided a free general practitioner service and medical treatment, free hospital care, and free dental and optical services, and incorporated all existing hospitals into the National Health Service. In 1948 provision was made for cash payments to those in real need. Subsidies were given to local authorities to expand the provision of housing, thereby underpinning the growth of council housing as a means of meeting the accommodation needs of the working class. In addition, the state increased its reach by expanding measures designed to regulate working conditions in private industry, to ensure healthy conditions at both work and home, and to govern conduct in public and even in private places; laws on homosexuality are a prime example of the latter. Education, health care, unemployment assistance, housing subsidies, state pensions, vocational training and transport were all areas in which the state came to play a significant part. State regulation expanded enormously.

This was a dramatic expansion of state competence into the lives of its citizens in a much more intrusive fashion than it had ever been before. The tax system became more regularized, resting principally upon a requirement, enforced by law, for employers to take from the wages and salaries of their employees the state's share of taxation before passing on the balance to the workers. In this way, income tax ceased to be something that most of the populace could avoid. This did not, of course, apply to some sections of the population, who through the nature of their wealth and income were able to avoid this sort of tax collection, but it did mean that for the overwhelming mass of the people, taxation was not discretionary. Furthermore, the introduction of many of the welfare measures noted above required a form of national registration to establish and monitor eligibility. The social welfare system delivered into the hands of the state and its functionaries a whole range of data on the citizenry which expanded the capacity of the state. The development of complex data bases on things such as taxation, welfare, saving and spending patterns, entry and departure from the country, and criminal activity (and the cross-referencing of these) gave the state expanded capacity to monitor a range of aspects of its citizens' lives.[3] In addition, the later tightening of things like welfare provisions usually took the form of demands for greater accountability on the part of recipients, thereby adding to the store of information newly available to the state.[4] Social welfare thereby gave the state a rationale and a mechanism for keeping tabs on its citizens, while the growth of technology, especially computers, increased its capacity to do so. The rationalization of the central state bureaucracy and the increasing professionalization of its staffing made this a much more efficient administrative machine, while the improvements in travel and communications technology bolstered its increasing capacity. Furthermore, the coercive arms of the state also became more effective in monitoring the citizenry. The police became more professionalized and the service, while remaining locally controlled, was integrated more closely into a national system through improved technology and cooperation. But perhaps more importantly, the intelligence arms of the state, on the basis of the continuing struggle against the communist challenge reflected in the Cold War, took increased interest in the affairs of its citizens. Indeed, the perceived perils of the international environment encapsulated within the Cold War confrontation justified greater state monitoring of the activity of its citizens. The state was much more invasive in the lives of its citizens than it had ever been in the past.

This expansion of state competence rested heavily upon taxation revenues and the improved capacity the state had to gather such income. But in Britain it was also linked to the nationalization of various aspects of the economy. Although in the post-Second World War period this was mainly associated with the Labour Party,[5] the process of creating state national entities actually began under Conservative-dominated governments in the 1920s and 1930s: in 1926 the Central Electricity Board and in 1933 the London Passenger Transport Board were created, while in 1927 the BBC and in 1939 the British Overseas Airways Corporation were nationalized as autonomous public corporations. But the main wave of nationalization occurred under the post-war British Labour governments.[6] In 1946 the Bank of England, Cable and Wireless, civil aviation and coal were nationalized, in 1947 inland transport and electricity, in 1948 gas, and in 1949 iron and steel[7] were nationalized.

While this process was in part seen in terms of generating income to sustain the expanding welfare state, its principal driver as far as its proponents were concerned was ideological: the conviction that the state had a positive role to play in structuring the lives of its citizens in a way that would both improve their welfare and increase equality. The effect of this was to inject the state even further into the economy than it had been in modern times except perhaps for the period of the Second World War. No longer was the state simply setting the broad direction of economic development and providing minimal regulation designed to assist the private sector in pursuing that course; now the state was actively regulating private economic activity while at the same time being directly involved in economic production, distribution and exchange through its own economic arms. The bulk of the economy remained in private hands, although subject to state regulation, but the state did play a crucial and direct role in the actual functioning of the economy through both the nationalized sectors and regulation.

The welfare state developed generally across the Western world. Not only in Britain but in much of continental and Nordic Europe, and in the Anglophile democracies – the USA, Canada, Australia and New Zealand – variants of the welfare state developed. There have been a number of types of welfare state. For Esping-Anderson, there have been three types: conservative-corporatist, liberal and social democratic.[8] Huber and Stephens distinguish between four types: Christian democratic, liberal, social democratic and wage earner welfare states.[9] Others have distinguished the welfare states of Europe along geographical lines: Nordic, Anglo-Saxon, Continental and Mediterranean.[10] The distinctions between these different types of welfare state are based principally upon the mix of types of welfare payments and recipients, but the precise details are less important for us than the fact that they all represent a significant expansion of state activity into society. Even in states such as the USA, where welfare provision and state direct involvement in economic life were more restricted,[11] the state became a much larger actor in economic life than it had been at any time in the past. A reflection of the state's expanded role is to be seen in the growth in government spending as a proportion of gross national product (GNP). Between 1950 and 1973, this rose from 27.6 per cent to 38.8 per cent in France, 30.6 per cent to 42 per cent in West Germany, 26.8 per cent to 45 per cent in the UK, 34.2 per cent to 41.5 per cent in the Netherlands, and 23 per cent to 35.8 per cent in the USA.[12] According to the Organization for Economic Cooperation and Development (OECD) figures, the mean for the period 1960–90 of public expenditure as a proportion of gross domestic product (GDP) for selected countries was as follows: USA 35.7 per cent, Japan 30.4 per cent, Britain 46.6 per cent, France 48.4 per cent, Germany 47.7 per cent, Italy 44.9 per cent, and Sweden 64 per cent.[13]

The essence of the welfare state was expanded interdependence with society at all levels, rendering the state much more embedded within society than it had been historically. With the consolidation of democracy as the paradigm throughout the industrialized West, the legislative arms of the state were structured to enable much broader social access than at any time before in the state's history. As the suffrage widened, educational levels rose, political parties developed and knowledgeable public opinion about politics emerged, legislative chambers took on a more diverse class composition. Particularly important here was the role of parties seeking to represent the working-class and possessing trade union affiliations because these became the vehicles for the entry of working-class representatives into national politics. Nowhere did national legislatures become the exact mirror of society. Wealth and access to wealth was everywhere a factor shaping access to legislative office, and all legislative organs remained gender-unbalanced, with women grossly underrepresented among legislators. Youth and ethnic minorities also had poor representation. But although national legislatures remained predominantly white, male, middle-aged and middle class, the level of legislative organic interdependence was much higher than it had been in the past. This was reinforced by the increased linkages that developed between citizens and the political system more generally. Participation in national elections is one marker of this, but also important was citizen involvement in non-government organizations active in public affairs, ranging from local citizens' action groups to highly targeted pressure groups. This sort of involvement in public life expanded considerably during the twentieth century. While involvement in this sort of activity was class-sensitive (with the middle class much more likely to be involved than the working class), it nevertheless tied a significant proportion of the populace into the political process and to the institutions involved in it. Similarly at the local government level, as barriers to involvement (such as the property franchise) fell away, the organs of local governance ceased to be the preserve of local notables alone. The modern welfare state enjoyed levels of legislative organic interdependence much higher than at any time in the state's history.

Bureaucratic organic interdependence also increased dramatically during the twentieth century. One measure of this was the increased size of state bureaucracies. Between 1950 and 1980 the proportion of government employees in the national work force in Western Europe grew from 11 per cent to 23 per cent, and in the USA from 9.7 per cent to 15.2 per cent;[14] in 1986 in Britain, some 26.1 per cent of civilian employees were in the public sector.[15] This dramatic expansion of the state bureaucracies vastly increased the bulk of the state within society. It also became, like the legislature, more socially accessible, as rising education levels and the shift to merit rather than breeding as the criterion for selection and advancement opened up this sector of employment to wider sections of society. This enhanced organic interdependence. The elimination of the farming of functions and its replacement by bureaucratic arms to implement state policy throughout the society also served to strengthen bureaucratic organic interdependence. Important here too were the increased levels of routinization of performance within the bureaucracy. As both its size and responsibilities expanded, the patterns of its work became regularized and the linkages between its different levels became stronger. The development of technology, including things such as telephones, fax and computers, was particularly important in tying the apparatus together and helping to ameliorate the effects of distance. Part of the increased professionalism of the bureaucracy was that it was no longer seen as a path to personal enrichment; this was replaced by a stronger sense of its public service function. The state bureaucracy thereby became more efficient than it had been in the past, and this strengthened the development of its interdependence with society. So too did the replacement of local notables and amateurs by full-time professional civil servants in local government. The state bureaucracy was rooted much more firmly in society than it had ever been in the past.

Important in this also was the range of new tasks the state took on. The welfare state built upon the expansion in state functions that had occurred in the nineteenth century, so that by the second half of the twentieth century the state's sphere of competence had become very wide-ranging. In addition to its established role as law-giver, regulator, keeper of the peace and defender, the state became a major provider of services in areas as diverse as health, child minding, education, employment, re-training, communications, banking, insurance, social welfare, aged care, housing, transport, and economic production. In those countries where the welfare state was most extensive (such as Sweden and Britain), there was barely a field of public interest where the state was not involved. Its involvement in these various fields projected the state into the lives of its citizens in a direct and immediate fashion; not only was a significant proportion of the populace dependent upon the state for their employment, but they also relied upon it for a range of goods and services which they required for the conduct of their lives. In this sense, the state was directly embedded in the immediate living conditions and circumstances of its citizens.

Even in those areas where it was not a direct provider of goods and services, other providers were reliant upon the continuing cooperation and functioning of the state and its organs. For example, the provision of health care by private providers was often interlaced with state involvement in the supply of some medical services through such means as the public hospital system or the drug supply regime, while privately-operated transport systems (such as bus lines) often had to interact with public systems in order to be effective. In this sense, the state became intertwined with the private sector, with both relying upon the other to service the demands made upon them. Institutional interdependence was thus highly developed. The state worked with private entities to ensure the delivery of goods and services to citizens. There were many different forms such interdependence could take: contracting-out, joint enterprises, special coordinating organs to manage and regularize relations between state and private bodies, secondment of officials, investment, the provision of financial assistance (e.g., tax breaks, loans, subsidies, grants, foreign exchange controls) or state incentives for performance, the pursuit of policies such as protectionism to bolster a private entity's position in the domestic marketplace, absorption of public risk, and the involvement of private sector actors in the design of public policy. In these sorts of ways, the state could work with private sector actors to produce outcomes desired by both.[16]

State involvement with the economy, and in particular its private sector, was also stimulated by military exigencies. The demands made by the Cold War, reflected in the drive to maintain improving levels of defence/attack preparedness and the technological nature of much of this development, tied parts of the private sector economy into the state military imperative. Much of the supply of military equipment was carried out by private providers, working on the basis of government contracts. Such providers tended to build up substantial research and development operations to parallel their production activities, with much of this oriented towards satisfying the state's defence needs. While talk of a 'military-industrial complex' may in many cases have been exaggerated, the defence industry sector was closely interlinked with the state. For the major protagonists in the Cold War, this sector was one of the central driving forces of the economy.[17]

This type of state involvement in economic life differed from what went before in the range of issue areas it encompassed, in the depth to which it projected the state into society, and the form in which it was manifested. The range of issue areas has been noted above. The depth of state penetration is reflected in the way in which state activity became central to the conduct of the lives of its citizens. In the sense that civilized life was always dependent upon the maintenance of law and order, the state was always central. But this changed in the course of the nineteenth and twentieth centuries, reaching its height after 1945 when the state became central not just for maintenance of the broad structures sustaining social life, but for many of the elements that directly structured individuals' daily lives: their health, education of their children, income support, the cost of much they had to buy, the availability of different types of food, travel to work, what they could read, watch and listen to, how they would be cared for in old age; all these became areas of state concern. The state was thereby embedded within the vital interstices of society, crucial not just to the ordering and general functioning of society, but to its patterns of activity at the micro level. Furthermore, the state's activities were regularized and routine; it cooperated with other actors and acted independently within society in a routine and systematic fashion, as its infrastructural reach was contained within routinized institutions and norms. The level of organic interdependence of state and society far exceeded that in earlier periods, and embedded the state deeply within the basic needs of the society and its members.

Rollback of the State

The welfare state was not a static, unchanging entity. In Britain, as early as 1951 the principle of a completely free medical service was compromised with the introduction of charges for dentures and spectacles, while over the succeeding decades successive governments tinkered with the system. However, such changes did not substantially reduce the state's penetration of society. But policy changed in the 1970s–80s, following the breakdown of the broad cross-party agreement on the welfare state. Within the context of increasing fiscal crisis in the wake of the 1973 oil price shock and the continuing popular resistance to high taxation levels (the historical trend of reluctance to pay high taxes except in war time), the increasing costs to the budget that the welfare state involved, added to the rise in the Anglo-Saxon world of a vigorous ideology which saw the state as having little role to play in social life (an ideology most directly associated with Margaret Thatcher in Britain and Ronald Reagan in the USA), this cross-party agreement collapsed. The dry wing of the Conservative Party, led by the Prime Minister, embarked on a programme of 'rolling back the state' through a process of divesting the state of many of the assets which it had built up over the years.[18]

Initially (1979–83) the government sought to privatize a number of major enterprises seen as peripheral to government activity by converting them into companies and selling shareholdings to private investors. Among these were British Aerospace, Cable and Wireless, Britoil, BP and the National Freight Corporation. At the same time, it introduced a programme of selling council houses to sitting tenants, thereby privatizing the housing market. In a second wave of privatization beginning in the early 1980s, the government moved to include major utilities in the programme. British Telecom and British Gas were privatized in 1984 and 1986, alongside the selling of such concerns as Enterprise Oil, Sealink Ferries, Jaguar Cars, British Airways, and the final slices of Cable and Wireless, Britoil and British Aerospace. The third wave of privatization embraced virtually all types of activity that remained in the public sector. As well as privatizing such major enterprises as Rolls-Royce, British Steel, Rover cars and a further slice of BP, the government privatized the water industry, regional electricity distribution companies, electricity generating companies, British Coal and British Rail. By the 1990s, the public involvement in industry had shrunk considerably. The government also sought to introduce privatizing measures in the health system and education.[19]

As well as this programme of transferring ownership out of public hands and into private, the government also pressed forward on a plan to inject private elements into the remaining operations of government. The chief form in which this was achieved was by the opening-up of the activity of government bodies to private competition. This was sought primarily through the introduction of competitive tendering as a compulsory modus operandi, with in-house providers having to compete with commercial firms for the provision of services, and through imposing upon such bodies citizens' charters which sought to make them directly answerable to those they served. Citizens were transformed into customers as government instrumentalities were summoned to treat them on a commercial basis. The relationship between citizen and state was thereby transformed. Rather than offering a service which it was the responsibility of the state to provide, which was the philosophy underpinning the welfare state, the state was now in the business of selling its products to its customers. In a wide range of areas, from the collection of garbage to the provision of power, the state withdrew from the positions it had occupied in the three decades following the end of the Second World War.

Such contracting-in and its reliance upon private agents bears some similarities to the earlier dependence upon notables and farming of functions, but it also differs in that rather than being a reaction to infrastructural weakness, it was a conscious attempt to deconstruct the state, at least in part. The rollback of the state's functions was massive, even if it left intact a central state bureaucratic machine that was still very large and a dominating force in society; the extent of state involvement at the end of the twentieth century still significantly surpassed the corresponding level at the beginning of the century. Such a process of rollback occurred in all of the welfare states. Conservative, Labour and Social Democratic governments were all active in rolling back the state by cutting back on welfare measures, usually in the form of undermining the universality principle but also through a form of the privatization of the provision of services, and withdrawing from involvement in economic activity. The degree to which such measures were implemented differed from country to country, with New Zealand suffering from a particularly extreme form of government rollback, but the trend was the same everywhere: the expansion of state competence earlier in the century was reversed in the final two decades of the twentieth century. But in many countries it was much less vigorous than in Britain. In the words of one study, 'in all but two countries ... cuts in entitlements were quite modest; the basic contours of the system of social protection remained intact'.[20]

A combination of reasons motivated this rollback. One was the short-term budgetary consideration (privatization provided a significant but temporary injection of funds into the state budget), but more important was the general philosophical position that the state should not be involved directly in the functioning of the economy. Not only was such activity seen as being alien to the 'proper' role of the state, but it was also seen as having a negative effect on the economy. The state was widely characterized as being inefficient, or at least as less efficient than private enterprise, and although such an argument was one-sided and partial, it was able to capture the central ground in the debate. The effect of this was the conviction that private enterprise could do things better than the state, and could provide services more cheaply and efficiently than the state, thereby giving its customers better service at lower cost. Furthermore, it was argued that the presence of the state in the economy was crowding-out the private sector, making it unnecessarily difficult for private enterprise to prosper since it was competing on an unequal basis with private sector providers. Linked with this was the view that state enterprise, plus the widespread provision of social services, in some way undercut the development of an 'enterprise culture' and instead embedded a 'welfare mentality' in people that made them more intent on seeking a handout than working independently to overcome their own problems. Even many of those who supported continued state involvement believed that the state had taken on too much, had become 'overloaded', and thereby lost the capacity to play an effective directing role in society.

It is clear from this brief summary that the privatization programme was highly ideological in nature, in the sense that, at base, it rested on assumptions about what the 'proper' role of the state should be. It was precisely this ideological nature of the programme that enabled it to gain a dominant position in British public discourse, so much so that even the Labour Party came to see in privatization the answer to many pressing problems. In this way, the rollback of the state came to dominate the public agenda, with both major sides in politics wedded to it. Even when the need for state regulation became apparent to ensure continued standards of service and safety in such areas as water supply and rail transport, where the private companies had squeezed safety and maintenance considerations in the quest for commercial gain, the dominance of the privatization paradigm was not shaken in the major parties. Many others in the community opposed this drive for privatization, but they were unable to shake the hold this paradigm had gained on the political mainstream. The Western state in the twentieth century thus experienced these two major waves, one taking it further into the society than it had ever been before, the other leading to its withdrawal back to a position closer to its nineteenth-century counterpart. From being a major provider of services and a driver of economic development, in many countries it became more a safety net of last resort and a light regulator of economic activity.

Clearly the level of state involvement in the economy was much greater under the welfare state at its height than it was before or since. Such involvement occurred in all spheres of economic activity: financing, production, distribution and exchange. It was also dominant in the sphere of service and welfare provision. The problem for the welfare state was that, simply put, the proceeds of the state's involvement in productive activity did not match the demands generated by its growing responsibilities, especially in the welfare sector. The nationalized industries, most of which came to suffer from the blight of excessive size, were caught between governmental demands for reduced costs and popular demand for low-cost services, with the result that their longer-term viability was always in question in the absence of increased government funding. Many of these seem also to have lacked the industrial plans and managerial talent to make their way in these circumstances, and although they may have been no worse managed than many private enterprises, their failings were both reflected in the state budget's bottom line and were a matter of public debate. Furthermore, successive governments generally did not have well-developed, clear and effective industry policies with which they could assist private enterprises to function in the market. As a result, government policy was often counterproductive, something that became of central importance when the post-war long boom ended in the early 1970s.

East Asian Welfarism

It was precisely at this time, when the welfare state was facing diffi-culties, that another model of state involvement in the economy came to the fore. This was the example of the so-called 'tiger economies' of East Asia, especially Japan, South Korea and Taiwan. The expan-sion and success of these economies in the last decades of the twentieth century was directly linked to the substantial role played by the state.[21] In these countries, the state sought to work in partner-ship with private enterprise in order to restructure and direct the economy. State policies of protection, financial support (e.g.; alloca-tion of foreign exchange, tax and credit subsidies, tariff exemptions, loans and direct investment) and disciplining of the labour market were the key to the East Asian success, but this combination of poli-cies differed from similar attempts in the West in two important ways. First, the Asian states provided selective rather than across the board support. They chose specific areas (e.g., semi-conductors, motor cars) rather than individual firms for support, with the result that state support could promote the activities of more than one firm in a particular sector. Second, support was given subject to strict per-formance criteria, usually defined in terms of the achievement of export targets. In these ways, the state did not seek to displace the market, but to shape it and to stimulate some actors involved in it. This strategy also differed from that common in the West through the more highly developed nature of the institutional interdependence evident between state and economic actors. A network of bodies, organizations and practices was developed tying particular state organs into their policy constituencies.

The important thing about this, however, is the dynamic whereby they operated. The situation was not one where the state dictated to its potential private sector partners, but one in which negotiation, dis-cussion and bargaining ensued, with the result being a decision that reflected a substantial degree of consensus. State and private sector partners could use this structure to work out common positions and policies, with both sides playing a positive role in the generation of an effective programme. In this way the state was deeply embedded in the policy constituencies and was thereby able to direct an industry policy that had support from within industry and was also likely to be of benefit to that industry. This was thus a cooperative partnership, much more soundly rooted in the private economy than that of the welfare state.[22]

The provision of welfare was also structured differently in the East Asian states compared with those of the West. An important factor here was the tradition of corporate welfare or enterprise paternalism whereby enterprises took on responsibility for a range of welfare measures for their workers, especially in Japan and Taiwan. The most frequently remarked-upon type of this was so-called 'lifetime employment' in Japan whereby enterprises retained employees even when their particular jobs had disappeared. Such enterprise paternalism was supported by the state. This is consistent with the fact that the state's approach to welfare arose out of its concentration upon driving economic development. Deyo summarizes this point well: 'Developmental states, whose governments have attempted systematically to restructure their economies by directly influencing investment decisions in targeted industries, are prone systematically to implement development-enhancing social measures.'[23] Because of the paucity of their natural resources, these states were heavily reliant upon the value-adding character of their work forces, and this encouraged them to invest in areas such as education, housing and social security in order both to pacify the work force and to improve its productivity. In Japan in particular there has also been a policy of state support for potential losers from the development policy fostered by the state.[24] Thus broad-based social support measures have been directly associated with the state's development goals, thereby embedding both those goals and the state within society more broadly.

While organic interdependence was structured in the same broad fashion in the welfare states and the East Asian development states, with professional multi-class bureaucracies and legislatures based on a broad franchise, institutional interdependence in the economy was structured differently. In the development states of East Asia, the state was a leading partner with the private sector in shaping the market and determining economic success within it. In the welfare states, the state played a role along with the private sector in shaping the market, but it was also a much more direct and active participant in the economy through the large range of economic activity in which its subsidiaries were engaged. In both forms of interdependence, large parts of the market remained beyond state control. This was the major contrast with the model for organizing society that challenged the welfare state in the second half of the twentieth century: communism.

The Communist Challenge

The Totalist Aspirations of Communism

The historical importance of the rise of communism, centred initially in the USSR and later also in China, was not that this constituted simply another case of would-be hegemonic states struggling for primacy (albeit in this case on a global scale), but that communism presented itself as an alternative means of organizing society to the model that had developed in the West. This was not, therefore, simply a struggle for political control, but for ideological primacy, for the dominance of a particular model of social organization. Intrinsic to this was the role of the state.

The founders of the Soviet state were motivated in part by the writings of Marx and the image he had of a future society in which the forms of oppression and exploitation evident under capitalism would be eliminated. Although his image of communism was not fully worked out, Marx seemed to envisage a society in which the state ceased to exist as a political machine independent of the people. The state would, in the famous phrase, 'wither away'.[25] However, once the Bolsheviks had seized state power, with the exception of some groups within middle and upper levels of the Communist Party in the first five years or so of the regime's life,[26] they were committed to the construction of a new state form on the ashes of the former Russian Empire. The sort of state they constructed was historically unique in two senses: first, it was a party state, and second, it had totalist aspirations and soon gained the technology to go a considerable way towards realizing those aspirations. Both of these characteristics were adopted by those communist states that came into existence in the period immediately after the Second World War.

The notion of a party state means that this was a state in which power was vested permanently in a ruling party, the Communist Party. The state possessed the full panoply of institutions that comprised modern Western states: legislature, executive, bureaucracy, court system, police, military and border forces. But all of these institutions were systematically penetrated by the party, in the sense that a dominant role in these bodies was played by party members, and a party member's primary responsibility was to obey party rules and instructions. At every level of the state system, from national through regional to local, state bodies had within them party cells which exercised control over party members. The party members exercised control over the state bodies, thereby ensuring that those bodies were by and large the cipher of the party. There have been disagreements between scholars over the degree to which non-party bodies could act independently of the party, but until the last part of the 1980s, such independence could only occur at the margins. The party ran the country through the state bodies, with state institutions lacking independence from the party.

Totalist aspirations were embedded in the emergent system virtually from the start. One of the terms used most commonly to describe the USSR was 'totalitarian',[27] meaning a system in which control over the populace and society more generally was total. Used as an ideal type, totalitarianism was useful because it emphasized the way in which the system was geared for the exercise of totalist control over society. However, all too often, observers used the term as a description of Soviet reality, when in practice the sort of control exercised by the political authorities was anything but total.[28] Nevertheless, it is probably true that, with the single exception of Nazi Germany at the height of its power, the degree of control that the Soviet regime was able to exercise over its society was far greater and more extensive than the power exercised by any other regime in history. The basis upon which this power and control rested was the Communist Party. The party was conceived as a monolithic structure, tied together by tight organizational discipline and fervent ideological commitment. In structural terms, the party was a hierarchical organization with party bodies at all levels strictly subordinate to the higher organs, culminating in practice in the Politburo (between 1952 and 1966 called the Presidium) at the all-union (Soviet) level. Instructions emanating from the central bodies of the party were mandatory for all party members and organizations, although clearly in practice there was some scope for lower-level party organs to interpret those instructions in ways relevant to their immediate conditions. But such scope was highly restricted and, given that the failure to satisfy higher-level commands could lead to expulsion from the party (and at times to worse penalties, including death), there was a strong incentive to adhere precisely to the instructions received from above. Many have used the epithet 'military' to characterize the nature of the discipline demanded of party members, and this description is appropriate. Highly centralized and highly disciplined, the party was a powerful organizational machine at the heart of the Soviet system.

What gave the claims for totalism credence was the organizational network throughout Soviet society that the party constituted. In every work place throughout the country where there were at least three party members, there was a party organization. In every government department, factory, farm, shop, military unit, ship, academic institute, university and school, a party organization was active. While the precise duties of a party member changed during the life of the system, those duties were essentially of two types. First, party members acted as a control mechanism, with responsibility for monitoring the performance and views of their immediate work colleagues. While the emphasis upon this changed over time, this remained an essential task of the party member. Second, party members had a proselytizing role, with the duty both of spreading the party's ideological message to non-members and of enthusing them with the spirit and commitment to work harder to achieve the country's/party's objectives. Because party members were themselves subject to strict party discipline, and because they were to be found in all of the organizations of Soviet life, they were a crucial means for party leaders to exercise monitoring and control over the Soviet populace. The party was therefore a powerful organizational tie uniting all parts of the society with the central component of the political system.

The organizational discipline of the party was enforced by a series of bodies developed over the life of the system, possessing the capacity to bring a delinquent party member to heel and, if necessary, have that person expelled from the party. More broadly in society, the party's control was enforced through various organs of the state. As in Western states, paramilitary and police forces were active in ensuring citizen compliance to the law, with the military available as a back-up if needed. But in the communist states, there was heavier reliance than in most non-communist states on the security apparatus. Established barely two months after the foundation of the regime, the Soviet security apparatus functioned as an effective weapon in the hands of Soviet leaders desiring the removal of political and other sorts of opposition. The use of this apparatus as such a weapon was less widespread and indiscriminate during the post-1953 period than it had been before that time, but even during this later period the activities of the security organs were a potent organizational force in ensuring civil compliance. This was backed up throughout the entire life of the system by a network of labour and incarceration camps separate from the prison system, a factor that served to emphasize for Soviet and other citizens the extraordinary nature of the power wielded by the security forces. In addition, the justice system was not a neutral player in Soviet society. It was clearly controlled by the party, with the result that it largely functioned as a means of consolidating party control. Certainly it dealt with the ordinary run of criminal activity present in any society, but it also ensured that dissent against the Soviet regime gained little ground. Its task was not to deal independently with cases brought before it, but to ensure that Soviet stability was not threatened. In this sense, the whole of the administrative-judicial system in the USSR was part of the control mechanism focused in the political power of the party.

Central to the power of the Soviet system was also ideological power. The Soviet state claimed to rest upon a basis of adherence to the ideological tenets of Marxism-Leninism. It claimed its legitimacy from following the precepts of this system of thought,[29] which it was believed would lead to the creation of a communist system. Based upon a belief that the ideology provided a key to understanding the laws of history, and therefore constituted a scientific guide to decision-making, the commitment to Marxism-Leninism was central to the attempt to construct a communist society. The extent to which this commitment to the ideology was genuine has been a matter for debate since early in the regime's life, but in terms of the issue of control with which we are currently concerned, this question is irrelevant. What is crucial is that the regime's official espousal of a legitimating ideology and the concern for orthodoxy in it created a straitjacket for ideas that forced out any hint of heterodoxy. Any deviation from the officially-sanctioned ideological path was met with retribution. This drive for orthodoxy extended right through society. Through an official system of censorship, backed up by what became almost an institutionally-entrenched self-censorship, the regime exercised tight control over all aspects of intellectual life, debate and discussion. All media outlets, including newspapers, radio and television stations and publishers were either owned directly by the state or by one of the official organizations which were in turn controlled by the party. There was no independent sphere of public discussion and debate. The tertiary education and research sectors were tightly controlled by the party, while the state-run primary and secondary education system was an effective vehicle for imparting the regime's values. All forms of entertainment functioned under the watchful eye of the party, subject to the ideological and political controls exercised by that body. This meant that the society lacked independent institutions which could sustain an autonomous culture of ideas.

One area where this was particularly clear was that of ethnicity. The USSR comprised more than 100 different national groups with their own languages, cultures and histories. The official attitude to these different groups changed over time, ranging from vigorous Russification through a tolerance for some measure of national diversity. But there was never any official sanction for real autonomy on the part of these groups, and neither was there any deviation from the principle that the population of all parts of the Soviet Union were Soviet citizens. There was no such thing as Russian citizenship, or Ukrainian citizenship or Uzbek citizenship; ethnic identity was subordinated to Soviet identity. Citizenship was thus used as an inclusionary mechanism, a means of embracing the diverse races and cultures of the country into one single identity. But it was also a means of exclusion. Denial of Soviet citizenship to anyone left them adrift, without a formal attachment and without right to the range of benefits and entitlements available to Soviet citizens (see below). The notion of Soviet citizenship was also exclusionary in the sense that it rendered national diversity irrelevant in official politically symbolic terms. In practice, ethnic difference was to be politically crucial in the collapse of communism, but in terms of the functioning of the Soviet state, it was not to be mobilized in a political way. This is reflected in the way in which all of the national cultures, especially the non-Slavic, were reconfigured to fit into the prevailing symbols and categories of 'socialist realism', the official doctrine governing cultural expression throughout much of the life of the regime. National identity and national cultures were thereby subsumed under the standardized picture projected by the regime, lacking the autonomy of expression that was vital for their continued growth and health.

Thus cultural life in the Soviet Union was highly controlled by the political authorities. Both the categories within which discussion could be couched and much of the content of those categories were shaped and moulded by official fiat, while the institutional vehicles through which cultural life flowed were controlled by the party. An effective monitoring mechanism functioned to ensure continuing obedience to the official line. For most of the life of the regime, there was no room for independent discussion and dissident ideas, and when these did emerge, the regime reacted swiftly and usually violently.

If the Soviet state's penetration of the cultural sphere was extensive, it was no less so in the social sphere. The basis upon which this rested was collective ownership. From the time of agricultural collectivization and forced pace industrialization at the end of the 1920s and the start of the 1930s, virtually all property was in the hands of the state or one of the official organizations. Individuals were able to own small plots of land upon which they could grow vegetables and, for those living in the towns, put up a summer cottage, but everything else was in public ownership. All of the institutions of which the economy consisted, including the factories and farms, and all major forms of transport, storage and distribution were publicly owned. Housing was also in public ownership. Officially no one was self-employed; all worked for bodies controlled by the state. There was therefore no independent economic sphere within which individuals could build up their resources and thereby gain autonomy from the state. Instead because the state and its agencies was the single employer, all were reliant upon it for their continued livelihood.

This was manifested most clearly by the way in which the state was the provider of a very wide range of public services. State subsidies kept food, liquor, rent, utilities and public transport prices low. Education and medical care were basically free, while old age and other pensions were non-contributory. Holidays in state sanatoria were heavily subsidized. There was no unemployment insurance, because in theory the state provided jobs for all. The Soviet system at its peak in the 1960s provided cradle to grave social welfare as well as employment to all of its citizens. The citizen's dependence upon the state was overwhelming, given the absence of independent resources. The state was highly intrusive into the lower reaches of society, shaping the lives of its citizens in a multitude of ways: where they worked, what they were paid, how much they had to pay for the necessities of living, what they were allowed to read and see, and how they could spend their leisure, were all within the realm of state concern; hence it was called by some a 'dictatorship over needs'.[30]

As should be clear from the above, the state was also the decisive force in the economy. With all parts of the economy under direct state control (except for the private plots and the produce markets that developed on the basis of these in the large cities), it should not be surprising that the state should be the main driver of economic development. Through a highly centralized planning mechanism, central state officers directed the development of the economy in all of its aspects. Five-year plans were enacted from 1927 (except from 1959 to 1965 when there was a seven-year plan). These were documents that encapsulated within them targets for all the production units of which the economy consisted, along with plans about the provision of the necessary raw materials to achieve those targets. They were very detailed, embracing all aspects of economic activity, including supply and production levels, wage rates and pricing levels. They were the means through which the state's central planners sought to drive the economy forward. They constituted the nucleus of the administered economy. This was an attempt to replace the operation of market forces by state direction, to ensure the adequate supply of all needs not through the independent operation of some hidden hand, but by the direction of the state. Through this state ownership and direction of the economy, the state entered much further into the economic life of the community than any state hitherto had done. It was here that the state's totalist credentials were most manifest.

The Limits and Decay of Communist Totalism

However, this picture of the state with an effective reach deep into all areas of society needs to be moderated by an appreciation of the limits of this. It is clear that the society was not totally controlled; people were not automatons, criminal and dissident activity did occur, and state control was not omnipresent. While the extent of the effectiveness of the state's reach varied from period to period, there were always areas into which its control did not extend very effectively. The development of the dissident movement in the 1960s, and the fact that it took until the early 1980s to snuff it out, is one striking reflection of the limits of state power. The state's ability to control the movement of people could always be evaded by individuals seeking to travel independently; the memoirs of Boris Yeltsin's early life provide a good instance of this.[31] All people were not constrained in what they could think, and free and open discussion often occurred around the kitchen table in individuals' flats.[32] And as the Soviet Union approached its end, the informal economy became vital to many people's livelihood.[33] Thus there were limits to the state's capacity to control the society, but this should not blind us to the extent of state control; it was probably much greater in the Soviet regime than it had been in virtually any other form of organized society, with the possible exception of Nazi Germany.

The limits of state power, illustrated above, need to be explained. Here the distinction between infrastructural and despotic power is useful. While the infrastructure of Soviet control was highly developed, the task it was set was enormous. If the aim was to establish as close to total control as possible over the entire territory of the USSR, state infrastructure had to be much more highly developed than it was throughout the life of the Soviet regime. The Soviet communications network was throughout much of this period adequate for the centre to maintain a monitoring brief on what went on in most parts of the country. However, much of this monitoring was at a high level of generality, and there were many regions that were not subject to close and continuing monitoring. Control and monitoring rested fundamentally upon lower-level functionaries, but this was a source of weakness in the overall structures because of the incentive structure embedded in the system. Given that the overall rationale for the system was the achievement of communism and everything was rationalized in terms of that end, effectively what was important was the ends rather than the means by which those ends were achieved. The Soviet system was teleological in nature, and therefore all activity had to be justified in terms of that teleology.

For people at lower levels of the hierarchy, this created a problem. They were under continual pressure from above to meet the plan targets they were set and to carry out the instructions they were given. Failure to satisfy higher-level expectations could have implications for one's career and, in the 1930s, even for one's survival. This meant that lower-level functionaries had a strong incentive to satisfy their superiors, while the latter were usually not too worried about how this was done. As a result, lower-level functionaries often found it to be in their interests to operate in ways not consistent with the formal and official power structure. The most usual form of this was the formation of local cliques which used official bodies to achieve their own ends but which were little constrained by those bodies or the rules that governed them. Such local cliques often established their own control in the areas over which they ruled, running them as fiefs independent from Moscow.[34] The official structure was thereby undercut by these informal power centres, with the central authorities usually able to remove individual cliques and their leaders, but unable to prevent such things from reforming. The Soviet power structure was therefore in practice much more cellular and less centralized than it seemed.

Another characteristic of the Soviet power structure was the tension within it between organizational and personalist norms. The organizational norms were embedded in the formal rules governing the functioning of state and party institutions: state constitution, party rules, various administrative regulations and decrees. These specified a set way of operating, emphasizing collective leadership, regularity of meetings and the formality of processes. In contrast to this were personalist norms, which stemmed from the prominent place in party history held by individuals. Both Lenin and Stalin were able to play much more activist and influential roles in the conduct of party life and politics than seemed to be provided for in the formal rules that were meant to govern these things. Indeed, under Stalin, it is no exaggeration to speak of a system that was designed around the personal needs and idiosyncrasies of the leader. Subsequent leaders, Khrushchev, Brezhnev and Gorbachev,[35] all sought to exercise a dominant leadership style. This does not mean that the Soviet regime was one in which personal dictatorship was the norm; rather, it means that beside the collectivist, routine-oriented norms of organizational life, there was also a tradition of dominant leaders who strained against such collectivist principles. This tradition was replicated at lower levels, with the clique leaders being their means of realization. The result was that the system was not able easily to generate routine operating norms which unambiguously structured internal political life: the emphasis on organizational routine was in constant tension with that on personal leadership and on the demand for performance.

Far from being a smoothly functioning power mechanism, the Soviet structure was one in which the dictates of central control were mediated through a cellular structure characterized by ambiguous operating norms. The system was therefore unable to develop the sort of infrastructural power that was necessary to extend the tentacles of the state in a regularized fashion into all corners of the society to the extent suggested by the regime's aspirations. Rather than functioning in a smooth, routine fashion, the system was subject to the personal foibles of its leaders at all levels. The central state certainly had the capacity to intervene in society in a major and little constrained way, but this was more episodic than continuing; its capacity for continuing monitoring and management remained limited. The power it could exercise was therefore more despotic than infrastructural, more reliant upon the mobilization of exertion and will than upon the smooth functioning of organizational structures.

Of course the organizational structures did function after a fashion, and in some areas at some times produced effective local administration, but the system as a whole was always wracked by its organizational tensions: organizational administrative norms did not sit well beside personalist aspirations. This tension was to be significant in the fall of communism.

Many factors contributed to the collapse of the communist regime in the USSR, but central to it was the inability of the country to reform its economy. During the 1970s the Soviet economy slowed down considerably. It was no longer possible to seek to promote extensive growth as in the Stalinist model by throwing more resources at economic trouble spots, because those resources were already being highly stretched. The arms race with the USA was by this time placing increasing strains on the economy and, with growth stalling, the surpluses for increased economic stimulus were not available. The only real option available to the Soviet leaders, other than tightening the belt and trying to ride out the difficult times, was reform. But in the Soviet system, the introduction of significant reform relied on the presence of a leader or leaders able and willing to press for such a change. The tension between the organizational and personalist norms meant that it was really only from within the latter that significant change was likely to come. The routinized patterns associated with the organizational norms were status quo oriented and unlikely to produce major change or upheaval. Throughout Soviet history major change had been associated with dominance of the personalist over the organizational norms, reflected in the clear primacy of a predominant leader. During the 1970s, the leading position was occupied by Leonid Brezhnev, who for much of this decade was ailing and whose priority seemed to be simply to see out his term in office. None of his lieutenants was in a position to be able to counter the resultant sense of drift at the top while, at lower levels of the party, this was probably the period in which local cliques were at their most powerful ever in the party's life.[36] Many of them were too concerned with managing their own local affairs, and often lining their own pockets, to worry about the national interest and questions of economic reform.

This sense of drift was maintained into the mid-1980s, until the rise to supreme power of Mikhail Gorbachev. The almost seven years during which Gorbachev led the USSR was a perfect illustration of the disastrous effects of the tension that existed at the heart of the Soviet power structure between organizational and personalist norms. Gorbachev saw the need for major change and, from 1986 began to drive through a complex, and developing, programme of reform, which by 1989 had become a programme for the transformation of the regime.[37] It must be acknowledged from the outset that Gorbachev's programme for change was not well thought out in advance. If its main planks were political reform, economic restructuring and the reworking of foreign policy, then Gorbachev neither implemented these in the most logical sequence nor introduced the different elements of these in a sequence designed to maximize their chances of success. Neither the overall programme nor its constituent elements was well conceived. This is partly a result of the immensity of the task Gorbachev had taken on and the fact that there were no pioneers upon whom he could rely for advice or guidance; but it was also a function of the tension between organizational and personalist norms within the overall structure.

In his struggle to bring change to the USSR, Gorbachev was confronted by opposition at both the central and regional levels of the political structure. At formal meetings of party and state institutions, his opponents sought to stand in the way of Gorbachev's proposals. For much of the time the argument was not about whether changes were necessary, but the type of changes needed and the speed with which they should be introduced. Such opposition often frustrated the reform proposals, but it was never strong enough to halt them entirely. It was, however, one factor in the increasing radicalization of those proposals. As time passed and there was little positive change as a result of his measures, Gorbachev became increasingly more radical in the solutions he espoused. However, one effect of this process of radicalization was to turn lukewarm supporters of his efforts into critics and opponents, so that even though Gorbachev was able generally to triumph over his opposition, the decline of one group usually presaged the emergence of another. As a result, the central leadership was never sufficiently united to be able to agree upon and push through a coherent programme of change. Neither did Gorbachev ever feel himself in a position whereby he could unilaterally override his opposition and introduce the measures he believed necessary. He was always looking to compromise in order to carry his colleagues with him, with the result that his programme was often reduced to measures that were much more limited than they needed to be.

However, Gorbachev also faced opposition from below. If Gorbachev and his supporters were to bring about significant change in the USSR, they needed to be able to ensure that decisions taken at the centre were implemented throughout the country. This meant that they had to be able to rely upon lower-level political organs to carry out decisions made at the centre. As noted above, this was a continuing problem for the Soviet system; even under the heightened centralism of the Stalin period, lower-level party organs were a law unto themselves in day-to-day matters.[38] But the problem for Gorbachev was even worse than this. Many of the measures he sought to introduce, particularly those that were part of the campaign for 'democratization', were contrary to the interests of lower-level office-holders. These measures were designed to make such officials more accountable, both to their hierarchical superiors and to their local constituents. In this way they threatened to make life more complicated and difficult for these officials. Not surprisingly, there was significant opposition from lower levels of the party. Gorbachev only increased the opposition of many of these officials by trying to mobilize the Soviet populace into the struggle for reform through the campaign for glasnost, or openness. Despite changes in personnel, the exhortation of popular support, and the attempt in 1990 to create an alternative power apparatus in the presidency, Gorbachev was never able to command an effective political machine to carry his changes to the country. The cellular nature of the Soviet power structure meant that, to be successful, he needed to gain the support of most of those cells, and this he was unable to do.

This means that the highly centralized Soviet power structure was, in practice, much less coherent and disciplined than the model and much of the writing on the USSR suggests. It was a structure that was unable successfully to carry through major change late in the twentieth century. Despite the immensity of its earlier achievements and its capacity to bring about fundamental change to the country as a whole, it could not manage the consequences of that change. It could industrialize quickly, and at considerable cost, but it could not manage effectively the consequences of that industrialization. The pressures for pluralization in society, the need for improving and expanding social welfare measures, the need to compete with a militarily more powerful rival, and the requirement to manage a complex industrialized society, was a combination the unreformed Soviet power structure could not handle, and neither could it handle the need for change in its own modus operandi. Thus while external pressure and the need to compete with the capitalist West was a significant factor in the collapse of communism, it was essentially the internal contradictions of this state which were its undoing.

However, it is important to be clear about what happened here. The multi-national Soviet state collapsed with the fragmentation of the USSR into 15 independent states. But what really fell apart was the federal arrangement which had tied the Soviet republics into the centre. In all of these former Soviet republics/new states, with the possible exception of Tajikistan which slipped into civil war, the local Soviet power structure generally was retained. In most cases the legislature was partly reshaped in a more democratic direction,[39] but the bureaucratic structures of the state (government ministries, coercive arms, judiciary) remained in the new political conditions with relatively minor changes. This is because, despite the inefficiencies of the Soviet structure, the individual bureaucratic hierarchies had a high degree of organic interdependence with the populace. In the legislative and especially the bureaucratic sphere, Soviet institutions were deeply embedded within the Soviet populace. What hindered their performance was less a sense of isolation from the population (although there was a Soviet official bureaucratic manner which was alienating for people having to deal with it) than the norms and principles that governed its internal working. This means that although the Soviet regime fell in 1991, taking with it the multi-national superstructure, the essential organs of the state remained broadly intact, embedded as they were in the essential needs of the society, to provide the framework for the newly-independent post-Soviet states.

Capitalist Success, Communist Failure?

This raises the issue of the survival of the Western capitalist state and the failure of its communist rival. This turns on the capacity of the two types of state to handle major challenges to their normal modus operandi, challenges which can easily be transformed into challenges to the very existence of the state itself. Much of the literature on communism emphasized the strength of the communist state, especially in contrast with what was seen as the comparative weakness of the state in the West. However, this judgement rested upon a misperception about the nature of the state and how best to judge its power. The communist state was considered to be very powerful because of the extent of the change it was able to implement in Soviet society. Writers looked at the fundamental transformation of Soviet society from an agrarian-based peasant society in the 1920s to the superpower of the

1970s, noted the central role of the state in bringing this about through agricultural collectivization and forced pace industrialization, and concluded that the Soviet state was exceptionally powerful. Part of the reason for this power was believed to lie in the state's autonomy, in the fact that it was not captured by any group in society, and was therefore able to exercise the power over society needed to bring about these dramatic social changes.

The role the Soviet state played in bringing about the transformation of Russia clearly marks it out as a powerful actor possessing high-level capacity to achieve its aims. However, as argued in Chapter 1, state capacity is dependent upon the nature of its linkages with society, including the development of institutional and organic interdependence. While the principle of the communist system was to penetrate all corners of society, the ethos of the most important organ of that system, the communist party, was to maintain a self-contained, disciplined existence. Only party members were allowed to participate in party meetings (although this principle was violated for some time under Khrushchev), and members were subject to party discipline before that of the state; indeed, party members were immune from state prosecution unless prior approval was received from the party. The party saw itself as a disciplined vanguard, and so although it was meant to penetrate society in all of its parts, there was always to be a wall between it and surrounding society. It was not to melt into or merge with society. The party was something citizens could go to for assistance, but this was never seen as them asserting their rights; rather they were seeking favours. The sense of separateness from society was much greater here than it was for state organs in the West. Furthermore, there was limited institutional interdependence in the economic sphere. In the USSR, the linkages between the state and the economy were administrative and controlling as the state sought through its own institutions to provide for all of its citizens' needs. This was administrative control, not a cooperative partnership; domination, not interdependence.

In addition, the sort of connectedness central to institutional and organic interdependence can only occur if there are organized social forces with which to connect. But one of the principles of communist society was that there was to be no organization independent of the party-state. The sorts of social forces with which the state could connect were therefore either non-existent or very weak in communist society. The result of this is that the Soviet state lacked the finely-grained linkages into the community that would enable it to manage the complexity of an industrial society and to effectively implement its policies. Thus while the Soviet state may have had significant levels of organic interdependence, in practice it lacked the connectedness to make it really powerful and to enable it to surmount the challenges that confronted it at the end of the twentieth century; it had high despotic power and low infrastructural power, reflecting weakly developed institutional interdependence and domestic norms of operation that ensured its organs were not always highly responsive to demands from the centre. In contrast, the capitalist state in the West was designed to maximize the connectedness with society while the society itself was awash with the sorts of social forces with which the state needed to connect. The diversity of society, the wealth of organized social forces in all spheres of activity, and the willingness of the agents of the state to interact with those forces ensured that the conditions existed for the state powerfully to embed itself in the society and thereby strengthen its stability. The private basis of the economy was clearly very important for this, but so too was the diversified nature of the state. Strongly developed interdependence was central to capitalist democracy. This was crucial to the greater capacity of Western capitalism when challenged by communism.

No Third Way

If, throughout the second half of the twentieth century, the main challenge was between the so-called 'First World' (the capitalist West) and the 'Second World' (the communist East), then the 'Third World' did not offer a viable alternative model for society- and state-building.[40] The Third World comprised a large number of states, mostly ex-colonies of the European powers, which had gained their independence in the post-Second World War period. They were generally struggling to develop their economies, usually seeking to industrialize in one form or another. The state and its nature varied considerably in these countries, but none had the infrastructural reach and development of the most advanced states of the West. Indeed, many of these states, especially in Africa, were termed 'broken-backed' states because of their excessive weakness. Some, like that of Zaire under Mobutu, were little more than cliques of gangsters using state office to line their own pockets. But even when states were not noticeably corrupt, were quite stable and able to pursue a coherent development path, such as India, they were not models except for those which were more corrupt, less stable and less able to pursue such a development path. It is by no means clear that such states are temporary phenomena on the international scene, or that they will develop into replicas of the most advanced Western states, but it is clear that they are not held up as models for others to emulate. With the collapse of communism, and perhaps the exception of Islamic fundamentalism in its different forms, the only model still generally seen as viable lies in some variation of the Western state form.

The twentieth century thus witnessed the greatest extension of state infrastructural power in its history. The welfare state became solidly embedded in society, active in all spheres of life and rooted in the needs of its citizens. Its democratic structure also tied the state into the populace politically. The organic and institutional interdependence characteristic of the welfare state made it by far the strongest and most stable political structure on the globe during the second half of the twentieth century. In contrast, the communist state sought administrative and organizational control over society, which gave that state the appearance of great strength, but in practice this appearance hid significant weakness. The modern, twentieth-century state was unique in its penetration of society. It was not clear, however, how such a state would survive the new challenge of globalization.

7

State Capacity in a Globalized World

In the second half of the twentieth century, the modern state seemed to have become the dominant form of organization on the globe. All states, including former imperialists, former colonies and those never engaged in the imperial adventure, seemed to be adopting the broad outlines of the state as it developed in Western Europe. Even the communist states shared many of the forms of the Western liberal democratic state. But in the last decades of the twentieth century, the nature of the ongoing process of globalization changed. Instead of being associated with the territorial state, it became deterritorialized, and thereby has been seen by many to threaten the state's very existence. Thus just when it had appeared to become dominant, the state appeared under mortal threat. How real are such fears?

By the end of the twentieth century, globalization was seen by many as the dominant force on the globe. Yet globalization is not a new phenomenon; it has been occurring since ancient times. However, during the twentieth century, its nature changed, principally under the impact of technology. If the essence of globalization as a phenomenon is that it erases the significance of national borders,[1] prior to the twentieth century this had been a dual, even ambiguous, process: the national borders, and therefore formal national identity, of many political units were rendered less important, but that of others was strengthened. The reduction in the number of political units in Europe between 1500 and 1900 is one example of this; the development of the colonial empires is another. This form of globalization was essentially territorially-centred. Its clearest expression was the expansion of the territorial sovereignty of some states at the expense of others. This is the classic expression of imperialism. During the second half of the twentieth century, a territorially-centred globalization continued in train, but rather than taking an imperial form, with decolonization we saw the spread of the independent state form across the globe. But more important was the emergence of a new strand, deterritorialized in nature and resting overwhelmingly upon the development and growth in power of modern technology. Deterritorialized globalization was different from what had gone before because not only did its logic not assume territory divided along political lines into states, it actually worked to overcome such divisions. The growth of this was facilitated by two political developments, the break-up of the European colonial empires and the collapse of communism; both empire and communism segmented the putative global system. Thus a tension developed within globalization between these two strands, one reinforcing aspects of the established state, the other working to undermine it. Most scholars who have conducted work on globalization have seen only the latter aspect, and have emphasized the malign consequences for the state that globalization represents.

In this view, globalization is undermining the state. By removing the boundaries of states as real physical barriers to the ebb and flow of commodities, power and ideas, globalization has significantly reduced the sovereign power of states. One clear statement of this view, albeit one which emphasizes the economic at the expense of other strands of globalization (see below) asserts: 'the impersonal forces of world markets, integrated over the postwar period more by private enterprise in finance, industry and trade than by cooperative decisions of governments, are now more powerful than the states to whom ultimate political authority over society and economy is supposed to belong'.[2] The state's loss of control over what happens inside its borders is seen, in the more extreme views of globalization, to render the state irrelevant or, more moderately, to significantly reduce its power and role. How accurate is this view?

Economic Globalization

Globalization is not monolithic; it comprises a range of different processes. These may be seen in terms of three principal strands: economic, political and cultural/ideological. In the view of most observers, the economic is primary.[3] There are three principal elements of economic globalization: the internationalization of production, the freeing of world trade, and the globalization of financial transactions.[4] The internationalization of production takes place principally through the activity of transnational corporations (TNCs). These are bodies which, while having their headquarters in one state, have production and/or distribution units in other states. Decisions are made within the TNC on the basis of the global performance of the company and, it is argued, with little regard for national economies.[5]

The development of TNCs seems to have occurred in two basic phases. First, the production units outside the country in which the company is headquartered serve the market in the country in which they are found; for example, an Australian branch of an automobile company headquartered in the USA will produce cars for the Australian market. Second, a division of labour is instituted within the TNC so that, for example, different parts of the car will be produced in branches of the TNC located in different parts of the world, but the car will be assembled in the national plants. The second is a much more integrated form of internationalized production, but both phases are seen as posing a major challenge to the state because of the power and resources at the disposal of the TNC. By the mid-1980s, offshore production by TNCs was greater than the total volume of inter-state exports, while by 1992 TNC sales were 37.5 per cent larger than the total volume of world trade.[6] Of the 100 largest economic entities, 50 are TNCs.[7] The decisions made in corporate headquarters about where to invest or where to withdraw investment from can have major consequences for national economies in terms of the balance of payments, employment, economic growth and even survivability.[8] These sorts of decision are made with the best interests of the corporation, not the country, in mind, and this in the view of many gives the TNC the upper hand in dealing with states. Given the consequences of such decisions, TNCs are able to play states off against each other in terms of things such as investment climate, tax regimes, production costs and infrastructural support. The role played by TNCs is thus seen as denying to states the power to decide what sort of economic activity is conducted within their borders and under what conditions. It also underlines the capitalist nature of economic globalization.[9]

The second element of economic globalization is the freeing-up of world trade and the decline of protection with the development of a special international regime, the World Trade Organization (WTO), to police it. During the 1990s global free trade became the international watch word of international economics. Under the banner of free trade, and driven by the belief that free trade would enrich all by making for much more efficient economic production, distribution and exchange, countries across the globe reduced their tariff barriers and cast their producers on to the free market, sometimes with negative domestic short-term consequences. Mirroring the philosophy of the nineteenth-century free traders, supporters of this development saw the withdrawal of the state from the economic process as enhancing the efficiency of that process. But unlike in the nineteenth century, the expansion of free trade has been taken up internationally and pushed by all of the largest trading nations, so rather than being presented as a weapon specifically designed to further the economic interests of the already dominant trading state, it has been presented as bringing benefit to all.

One aspect of the growth of free trade has, paradoxically, been the development of trade blocs within which protection has been either drastically reduced or completely eliminated. The North American Free Trade Agreement (NAFTA) is a recent example of this. Such blocs, which effectively involve the denial of entry on favourable conditions to states which are not members of the blocs, are exclusivist in their intent, designed to promote the interests of the member states through the promotion of free trade within the bloc. However, not everyone sees this sort of development as positive. In the view of one critic, such blocs are:

> little more than giant trade groups whose purpose is to increase the flow of commerce. They do this by eliminating government regulations and ignoring international frontiers. Their purpose is to make international governments irrelevant. What is novel about them, and a telling mark of their power, is that they have enlisted governments to do this work for them. Governments are being reduced to the role of traffic cops, ensuring that everyone follows the regulations that are, of course, written by and for the most powerful corporations.[10]

Even if this criticism is exaggerated, it is clear that by surrendering protection, states give up much of the capacity to structure their trade profiles.

The third element of economic globalization is the globalization of financial transactions. Two things have been important here: the floating of the currency and the introduction of electronic funds transfer. The breakdown of the Bretton Woods agreement meant a widespread shift away from fixed exchange rates towards floating exchange rates.[11] This means that currency values were calculated by the financial markets on the basis of comparisons with other currencies rather than in relation to holdings of gold bullion. Currency rates thereby became more unstable and less amenable to state policy. The financial markets became more important as the determinants of currency values. The effect of this was compounded by the electronic transfer of funds, something that was reliant upon the international computer network as discussed below. The electronic transfer of funds encourages the direction of capital into speculative activity rather than production; it results from currency trading rather than investment, production, consumption or trade. In this sense, it is totally mobile, because it is not rooted in any form of productive activity located in a fixed spot. It is virtual currency.[12] With transactions able to be conducted in a few seconds, vast amounts of capital could be shipped around the globe, in and out of national economies, at the behest of those who worked in the markets. The size of such capital flows is enormous. According to one study,[13] the total value of financial assets traded in global markets in 1992 was twice the gross domestic product (GDP) of the 23 richest industrial countries, while the daily international transactions on average exceed the total gold and currency reserves of all members of the International Monetary Fund (IMF). Such capital flows occur independently of the wishes of national governments. National economies are now at the mercy of the international markets, their very liquidity under potential threat by the capacity of others to move funds around at will. The days of the need physically to transfer bullion have been replaced by the swift flight of funds at the press of a computer button.

Economic globalization has thus, in some versions, rendered the state redundant. No longer can political authorities exert much power in the economic sphere, their national economies are no longer under their control, and those economies have been effectively withdrawn from the societies and sets of social relations within which they sat.[14]

Political Globalization

The second strand of globalization is political. This sees the boundaries of states being undercut by political developments. An important element in this argument actually predates the 'globalization debate' and focuses upon the development of armaments and weaponry. This argument emphasized the state's capacity to control whatever happened within its borders as a central determinant of how state power was conceptualized. When that capacity was reduced, so the state's sovereignty was reduced. The development of gunpowder, and in particular of the cannon, marked an early form of the erosion of this capacity because an opponent could now cause military damage within a state's territory from outside that territory. The state's response was to develop the notion of a territorial sea limit set at the distance a cannonball could fly from a ship-mounted cannon. This may have maintained the fiction of state sovereignty for island states such as Britain, but it was of no use to countries with land borders. However, historically the border areas had always been least under central control, so the development of cannon did not substantially change this situation. What did bring about change was the development of aircraft and their use, initially in the First World War but with more devastating effect in Spain, Abyssinia and the Second World War, for military purposes. Given the much greater range of aircraft compared with the cannon, and the development of bombs of increasing magnitude that could be dropped by these aircraft with devastating effect, they were a much more serious challenge to state sovereignty. They meant that the front line of warfare was no longer the sole location of direct and open conflict. Now the whole country, including the capital, was subject to enemy attack without the need for land invasion. The response to this was the use of aircraft in a defensive capacity. All states with any pretensions developed an air force as an essential buttress to its claims to national sovereignty.

Subsequently the ground shifted with the development of the next generation of weapons, both in term of delivery systems and warheads. During the Second World War, the Nazi regime developed the V1 and V2 rockets. These were effectively pilotless flying bombs and could be combated only by destroying their launch sites. These ushered in the missile age. In addition, towards the end of the war, the Americans developed the atomic bomb, which used energy created by nuclear fission to produce an explosion that was much more powerful and deadly than a conventional bomb. This ushered in the nuclear age. In the post-1945 world, these two developments, missiles and nuclear warheads, were combined to produce the nuclear weaponry under whose shadow the world has lived since.

The development of nuclear and missile technology took warfare and its conduct into a new realm in two ways. First, the destructive power of nuclear weapons was such that people could envisage not just the elimination of whole peoples, but of the world itself. Even if such fears were exaggerated, and given the stockpiles of nuclear weapons maintained by the main protagonists it is not clear that they were, nuclear weapons gave the capacity to inflict crippling damage on an enemy in a very short space of time. Previously, the destruction of a people and its culture had required armed men on the ground establishing control and then seeking to implement genocidal policies. This was not something that was achieved easily. In contrast, the releasing of a few nuclear weapons could achieve similar results (and with the development of the neutron bomb in 1977 which killed people but left property intact, potentially even more satisfactory results for an aggressor) in a much shorter time period and with seemingly less effort. The capacity to inflict unacceptable damage thus seemed to be rendered much easier than it had been in the past. Second, there did not seem to be any effective defence against missile attack. Passive defence through shelters was impractical for all except a very few, and there did not seem to be any way of intercepting all of the missiles potentially launched before they landed. Although the USA under Ronald Reagan tried to develop a space-based nuclear shield and this aim has been revived under George W. Bush, it is not clear that it will be successful. Even taking out the missiles before they were launched did not seem a practical solution because of the accuracy that would have been needed and the protection that was afforded such sites.

The effect of these two factors was heightened in many people's minds by the fear that non-state actors could gain control over nuclear weapons (and other weapons of mass destruction, such as biological warfare) and further challenge the security provided by states. The attack on the USA by al Qa'eda in September 2001 was vivid realization of this fear. The development of nuclear technology and its application to military purposes seemed to pose a clear threat to individual states' survival. But it is not clear that it posed a threat to the state's survival (see below).

In the view of Martin Shaw,[15] nuclear weapons were one aspect of a wider phenomenon which 'overcame the classic nation-state', the outcome of the Second World War. This produced two superpowers which consolidated around themselves alliance blocs of states. By entering those blocs, states were said to have lost substantial military-political autonomy. For these states, national borders were no longer defensive borders, while national decision-making became in some areas subordinated to broader bloc concerns. While these were much more voluntary processes and looser structures in Western alliance systems than in the Soviet bloc, the subordination of individual states (although much less so the two superpowers than the other members of the alliances) to trans-national concerns was evident.

The functioning of bloc/alliance structures is one way in which states voluntarily surrendered some of their sovereign decision-making power, with the circumstances of the different alliance structures determining how much of this they lost. Another form of this, pointed to by many as the harbinger of state erosion, is the range of international agreements, regulations and regulatory bodies to which states bind themselves. International treaties, conventions and law comprise normative principles which the signatory states acknowledge and profess to use to shape their behaviour. In many cases, such normative documents are backed up by institutions designed in many cases specifically to ensure their implementation: United Nations (UN) specialized agencies, the General Agreement on Tariffs and Trade (GATT) and the WTO are some of the most important. The network of regulation resting upon such international organizations, covering areas as diverse as human rights, environmental protection, weapons systems and the use of force, clearly restricts the state's room for manoeuvre. Particularly important here has been the practice that has emerged of individuals and groups challenging the decisions of domestic authorities in international jurisdictions.

Another common political constraint upon the state has been seen to be the shift towards world government. Such arguments for world government have been around for centuries, but they seemed to take a significant step forward with the establishment of the League of Nations in 1920. This attempt at international regulation was clearly seen to have failed with the outbreak of war in Spain and Abyssinia in the 1930s. It was replaced by the UN in 1945, but this too failed to act as a replacement for the state. Both bodies assumed the centrality of state sovereignty, and therefore had to adjust to the state rather than bringing about the erosion of the state as the primary actor on both the international and domestic stages. More significant in the eyes of those who looked towards the demise of the state was the formation of the European Economic Community. This body, which from its foundation has expanded both its membership and the competence of its internal organs, is seen by many as a means for the internationalization of contemporary nation states. The central organs of the (now) European Union – or EU – have expanded their competence along with the gradual integration of various aspects of national life in the member states. The creation of a common currency (the euro), which 12 of the member states adopted on 1 January 2002, was widely heralded as a significant step on the way to the full integration of these economies, and the countries within which those economies resided. However, the capacity of the EU to coordinate and mobilize the military potential of its members remains limited, as the reaction to the wars in Yugoslavia in the early 1990s demonstrates. Nevertheless for many, from the perspective of the end of the twentieth century, the EU appears as the most likely vehicle for the elimination of states and their replacement by a trans-national agency.[16] The difficulties of achieving this should not, however, be minimized (see below).

To match the development of more overarching political structures superimposed on the state, some have seen a parallel development of so-called global civil society.[17] While the concept remains somewhat amorphous, it embraces the development of a global public sphere populated by an emergent public opinion, and a range of international non-governmental organizations (NGOs). The former relies principally upon the sorts of communications technologies discussed with regard to the third strand of globalization below, and constitutes a public arena within which the actions of states (and other actors) come under scrutiny and criticism. The latter comprise a wide range of different sorts of NGOs, both profit-seeking and not-for-profit bodies, coalitions, social movements and cultural–religious groups. Interacting with states, domestic actors and the emergent international public sphere, these bodies cover the gamut of interests in the causes they espouse and the aims they pursue. Bodies such as Amnesty International, Greenpeace, the International Football Federation (FIFA), the Red Cross and Red Crescent, plus TNCs such as News Limited and IBM pursue their concerns on the international stage, interacting as equals with states and impinging upon the freedom of movement and decision possessed by states. By projecting this international civil society, such bodies constitute the same sort of constraint upon the state as the emergence of domestic civil society did in nineteenth-century Europe. So politically, too, globalization is seen as a force undermining the traditional authority of the state and constraining the actions it is able to take.

Cultural/Ideological Globalization

The third strand of globalization, cultural/ideological, is also seen to undercut the state's position, this time by destroying the control it formerly could exercise over the cultural life of its citizenry. A number of elements have contributed to this.

The development of transport has had an impact on the porosity of state borders. The second half of the twentieth century was characterized by the peaceful mass movement of peoples on a scale hitherto almost unprecedented. Furthermore, with the exception of the waves of refugees that have been similar to earlier centuries, this movement has not been in response to military conflict. World travel has become a leisure time activity for millions of people from wealthy states, while business travel has expanded exponentially. What made this possible was the development of fast and efficient means of transport. The growth of air travel revolutionized inter-continental travel; what formerly took weeks by ship could now be achieved in a day. The growth of air travel, and its increasing level of affordability, opened up the long distance movement of people in a completely new way. It was now possible for people to spend leisure time outside their countries of residence, experiencing new things and becoming acquainted with different cultures and peoples.

Similar considerations operated with regard to railways for countries with land borders. The fact that railways could only follow the pathways determined by where the tracks were laid and the expense of laying tracks meant that usually there were very few tracks crossing national borders. This meant that they were always vulnerable to state inspection. This consideration applied less to the motor car. Most countries sharing land borders had a proliferation of roads, lanes and tracks which people could use to cross the border. The state could maintain checks on major road crossings, something which was in principle made easier by the development of freeways and autostrada, but it could not physically check every potential crossing point. This was, of course, always the case. In earlier centuries, the borders were even more porous. However, in those centuries when the modes of transport were much slower and developed roads far fewer in number, this was not a significant problem. With the development of the automobile and its post-war proliferation, border crossing became physically much easier for those who lived in all parts of the state, not just those people along the borders. The increased mobility provided to increasingly wide sections of the populace in many countries exacerbated this problem of border surveillance for the state. The flow of people unchecked by state authorities was made increasingly possible, and the porosity of the borders thereby increased. However, it is also true that improved means of transport have lengthened the state's reach. Through the use of automobile and air transport, the central state authorities are able to move state officials, both civilian and police/military, around the country much faster and more efficiently than they were able to do before. As such, the state's infrastructural reach has been extended, including its capacity to move officials to trouble spots, including border crossing points. So while the technology of transport has increased popular mobility, it has also strengthened state capacity.

Significant, too, has been the growth of communications. Radio and television, both invented early in the twentieth century (radio 1901, television 1926), became dominant influences in society in the second half of the century. They transformed the populace's access to information, rendering literacy no longer the barrier to such access that it had been earlier. As the technology developed and became cheaper, radios spread throughout society. This provided the state with a new and effective means of communicating with its populace and an important vehicle for the broadcast of propaganda. During the Cold War, it was also used as a means of seeking to go over the heads of hostile governments and appeal directly to their population. Both sides used the radio waves in an attempt to subvert their opponents, although there is no evidence that such activity was particularly successful. However, its prospects were widely appreciated, with the result that the establishment of an external radio service became common among states. Television also became a dominant medium, with its impact probably being greater than radio because it combined visual impact with audio. This too could act as an important tool of propaganda for states although, unlike radio, it could not easily be used to project one state's message far beyond the borders of another state. At least, this was the case until satellite technology was introduced.

Initially radio and television were restricted to national networks. They broadcast to markets that were essentially defined in national (or sub-national or regional) terms. However, with the introduction of satellite and cable technology and the formation of large media companies with international aspirations, all of this changed in the 1990s. Alongside the national networks, the people of many countries were able to gain access to international channels. The most prominent of these has been CNN, but also important in different parts of the world have been the BBC and Sky Channel. Relying upon satellites which provided broadcast footprints that took no account of national borders, the international media companies were able to spread their programmes and their messages to people who, a mere decade earlier, had been well out of reach. Suddenly local regulation of broadcasting was less effective in shaping what people watched. Furthermore, the diversity of offerings that came with this technology gave the consumer a significantly wider variety of choices than had been available only with the national network. This development was significant for the way in which it could shape people's perceptions of what was going on across the globe. News and current affairs were presented by these international companies not from an internationalist perspective, but essentially from the national perspective of the host country of the broadcaster. For the most part this was the USA and Britain. Moreover, the main language of discourse was English. In this way, international broadcasting and television threatened to erode states not simply by nullifying the effect of state borders, but by transforming the indigenous culture of the country through the imposition of foreign perspectives and language.

The development of modes of inter-personal communication has also been important. This gave ordinary people a much greater capacity to talk to people not only in the next village but also on the other side of the world. Although the telephone was invented in 1876, it was the twentieth century, and especially the second half of that century, that saw it transform personal life styles. In 1923 the first trans-Atlantic call took place, while four years later the first commercial two-way service between Britain and the USA was established. In succeeding decades, telephone technology advanced such that, by the third quarter of the century, it was sufficiently inexpensive to enable most private homes in the industrialized world to possess a handset and, given the expansion of the telephonic network across the globe, to talk to anyone virtually anywhere a telephone system existed. The introduction of long-distance direct dialling, and therefore the removal of the need to go through an operator to connect calls, gave greater flexibility to telephone users and also complicated state attempts to monitor calls. From the 1970s, with the switch away from land lines to satellite technology, greater flexibility was introduced into the system, and this eventually made possible the mobile phone, which enabled people to make and receive calls in many more parts of the world than those served by the earlier generation telephone technology. The monitoring of calls remained possible with satellite-based mobile phone communication, but it was technically much more difficult and expensive than had been the case when reliance was upon landlines.

Even more difficult for the state to monitor was the growth in the 1990s of a new mode of communication based upon the international computing network. This was electronic mail, or email. This mode of communication was available to anyone who had access to a computer that, in turn, had access to the Internet (see below). It was virtually instantaneous and, except for the price of the equipment and connection, costless. It enabled people on opposite sides of the globe to converse almost in real time and, because of the speed of its transmission, it was difficult to monitor, at least at the time it was being done. First the telephone and then email liberated a state's populace from many of the communications constraints that earlier states had been able to impose. The checking of mail deliveries either at a central collection and distribution point or at the border, for example, was no longer an adequate means of monitoring personal communications; the telephone and email rendered the art of letter writing obsolete in the industrialized countries. However, we should be careful not to exaggerate the impact of email in particular because of the fact that most people on the globe lack access to it (see below).

The spread of email rests upon, and is symbolic of, the most important new type of information delivery and communication that developed in the 1990s. This is the Internet. Comprising an international electronic network with computers the key points of access, the Internet is a vast resource of information that can be tapped into and a powerful weapon for both the transmisson and discovery of information. Consisting of millions of different sites that can be accessed from anywhere on the globe that has a computer linked in to the network, the Internet constitutes a force that seemingly floats independently of existing states. As a medium of information and exchange, it enables individuals and groups to interact largely outside state control. While some states have sought to regulate what is transmitted (e.g., pornography) and control Internet access, and they have been able to do this by, *inter alia*, limiting access to computer equipment and even conducting spot checks on displayed and stored material, once the computer links are established, continuing systematic monitoring is much more difficult. Furthermore, although the Internet is not restricted to the English language, most sites have been in English, and in the minds of some this threatens a form of cultural imperialism by displacing indigenous languages as the normal form of discourse, at least for this form of communication.

It is this computer-based revolution in communications that has most marked this phase of globalization as distinct from earlier phases. Its speed, extent and multiple points of access mean that the Internet is a means of communication autonomous of states and, largely, undirected. The Internet is potentially a significant source of power, combining as it does high-level technology with virtually unlimited sources of information, and cannot be controlled from a single source. In this sense, it is 'decentred' and 'deterritorialized'.[18] It enables the transmission of both information and of virtual money without concern for the state and its interests.

The Limits of Globalization

The combined effect of these forces for globalization has been seen by some to be overpowering the state, rendering it irrelevant, and creating a homogenized world.[19] It is feared that with the expansion of the communications media, especially the internationalization of news and entertainment and the growth of the Internet, indigenous cultures will be undermined and replaced by a standard product, emanating from the north Atlantic culture area and using English as its mode of discourse. As evidence for this, people point to the way in which English has modified other languages through the exportation into them of loan words, phrases, sayings and even concepts; pronunciation has also taken on a standardized, north American, form. National myths, heroes and history are being overwhelmed by the standardized figures coming from, principally, American popular culture. The dress of teenagers has taken a common form, with the reversed baseball cap symbolic of this. National perspectives are displaced by an orientation with its source in the north Atlantic culture area, while the values pulsating through the programming are redolent of the sort of consumer capitalism dominant in the USA.

Similarly there is a fear that, with the interlocking of national economies into a global super-economy, national differences will disappear, along with national sovereignty. As the logic of global capitalism grinds remorselessly on, market principles will govern economic life; national economies will merge and become alike as none will be able to create the sorts of potential barriers to economic activity that would make them less competitive with other parts of the emerging whole. The economies will not, of course, become exact replicas because the law of the market will determine where particular goods are produced, but all will be interlocked into a single economic organism. This merging of the economies will be underpinned by the free flow of capital. With national borders irrelevant, capital will flow to those areas where it can be most profitably used. The world will become a single market for capital, labour and goods, and the needs of that market will overwhelm the sorts of more limited concerns generally attached to sovereign states. Regulation will be undertaken not by states but by international bodies whose remit will ignore state boundaries and state sovereignty.

How realistic is this picture?

In answering this question, it is important to see the limits of globalization, at least insofar as those limits existed around the turn of the millennium. The distinction between internationalization and globalization is useful here. Internationalization refers to a process of increasing interdependence between states and economies, but this is a process in which the national units maintain some autonomy and identity, and are able to act unilaterally in defence of their interests. Globalization involves the meshing together of the national units into a single system, so that those units cease to have an autonomous existence and function only as a part of the whole. In the former, national policies are viable; in the latter, they are futile.[20] While the difference here is one of quality, crucial in it is the nature, quality and quantity of the linkages between the units. The greater the number of linkages and the deeper (in terms of embracing all aspects of the type of activity in question) they are, the more the situation will approach one of globalization and will transcend internationalization.

The nature of the linkages that have emerged between national units in the last part of the twentieth century is both extensive and deep, but we should not exaggerate this. There is a clear politico-geographic dimension to globalization. It is a process predominantly of the developed North, with the South much less integrated into it. Much of the world, including most of Africa, Latin America, the former USSR, the Middle East (excluding Israel) and large parts of Asia are at best only weakly linked into the network that has the Organization for Economic Cooperation and Development (OECD) countries at its heart, and in some cases there are virtually no linkages at all. Furthermore, even within the OECD countries, there are regional differences; for example, northern Italy is much more closely linked in than southern Italy, southern Norway more than the northern part of the country. By the early 1990s, around 84 per cent of international trade and 90 per cent of investment occurred in the OECD countries.[21] The reverse side of this is that both trade and investment have become highly regionalized; intra-regional (e.g., within the EU or the Association of South East Asian Nations (ASEAN) countries) trade has become the dominant trend in Europe and Asia and has been increasing in North America.[22] In political terms, the OECD countries as a group have taken more of a leading role in the international arena, especially in those areas bound by international regulations, than the countries of the South, although the difference is probably not great. There is a greater difference in the ideological domain, because the southern countries tend to be less developed technologically and poorer than the northern states. A much larger proportion of the population of the southern countries has no regular access to a computer or to the telephone and certainly much less than their counterparts in the North, and they rarely travel internationally. Radio and television are more widespread, and therefore can potentially act as nodes of the international communications industry, but even these are much less ubiquitous in many countries of the South than they are in the North. Clearly the sorts of linkages of which globalization consists are much more important in the developed North of the OECD states than in the South.

Even in the North, where globalization is more advanced, there are limits to it. While the contemporary period is one of significant economic openness, it is not clear that it is substantially more open than those years leading up to 1914. If levels of state interdependence are measured in terms of trade or capital flows as a proportion of gross national product (GNP), contemporary levels are about the same as for this earlier period; contemporary levels of labour mobility and military dependence are lower than for the earlier period.[23] Where the contemporary period does differ from the earlier one is in the technology that enables both an extra dimension of interdependence and a speed in the movement of large sums of capital which potentially constitutes a significant source of destabilization for states. This technological dimension renders the contemporary period qualitatively different from its predecessor. But there are still limits, even within OECD states. Despite the internationalization of their economies, countries with the largest economies still do most business on the domestic market. For example, in the USA, Americans produce 88 per cent of the goods they buy, while those sectors of society barely involved in international trade employ 82 per cent of American workers. The three largest economies, the USA, Japan and the EU, each have 12 per cent or less of GDP composed of exports,[24] which means that up to 90 per cent of production remains for the domestic market. In the OECD states, most domestic investment comes from domestic savings, not the capital of other states.[25] This does not, of course, deny the enormous impact of the internationalization of finance, but even here it is not clear that economic globalization has been sufficient to produce the consequences attributed to it.

One of the principal assumptions about economic globalization is that it would bring about a standardization of national economies,[26] but there is much evidence for a lack of this. Structurally, the capitalism of the USA remains different from those to be found in the UK, France, Japan and Korea, and they are different from each other; in terms of financial patterns, for example, the USA depends upon capital imports, the EU does not, and Japan exports capital.[27] Of course, it may be that the elimination of structural differences between different types of capitalism may take a significant time to occur, but even so one would expect there to be some substantive evidence of it; yet the nature of the corporations, the role of trade unions and the place of the state remain significantly different in all of these leading industrialized states. Furthermore, the expected narrowing of differences in major policy areas has not occurred. National tax regimes are not converging,[28] global factors are not having a standard impact upon the welfare regimes of states[29] and, despite the pressure, protection has not been completely abandoned in favour of free trade. Even the USA, the loudest supporter of free trade, has retained restrictive policies on the import of some types of primary produce, essentially to satisfy a domestic constituency. In the area of labour policy, the period of globalization has seen the unprecedented development in many of the old European states of a multi-national work force with heightened levels of labour immigration in the last decades of the twentieth century.

The cost of money has not converged in the sense that national price differentials for loan and equity capital remain significant, while national differences in savings and investment rates remain considerable.[30] Despite the 2001 linking of the French, Dutch and Belgian stock markets in a new market called Euronext, national stock markets still generally continue to function and, while they are clearly affected by international developments, their primary concern is domestic; company stocks remain listed overwhelmingly on national markets, although this is not the case for bond, currency and futures markets, thereby reflecting a dualism in the financial markets.[31] The three most important markets, New York, London and Tokyo, do not act in a coordinated, or even a consistent, fashion. In reality, the impact of globalizing tendencies upon national economies differs depending on the nature of those economies. The impact upon a highly industrialized economy will be different from that upon an economy resting overwhelmingly upon the export of primary produce, which will be different again from that resting on the development of high technology, and from that which takes minimal part in the international trading system at all. This means that the impact of these tendencies will be differential depending upon the national economic basis (see below). It also means that the gap between North and South is likely to be maintained, since the nature of the economies in the two regions is very different. It is thus simplistic to see economic globalization as a force making for the early standardization of the globe.

Neither is it clear that the arguments for political globalization are as compelling as their proponents suggest. The development of nuclear technology has been very costly and for a long time the major nuclear protagonists sought to maintain a monopoly on it. The largest arsenals have been maintained by the two pre-1991 superpowers, the USA and Russia (as the successor state to the USSR), with smaller stocks of nuclear weapons being held by the UK, France and China. By the end of the century, the number of states possessing nuclear weapons had grown, including at least Israel, India, Pakistan and perhaps Iraq. Such weapons may also have fallen into the hands of non-state groups, although this remains uncertain. For most of the century, though, nuclear weapons were in practical terms almost a monopoly of the superpowers and their immediate allies.[32] This means that while nuclear weapons seemed to threaten the sovereignty of the majority of states on the globe, they may have actually strengthened the position of the states possessing nuclear weapons. But it was not as clear cut as this. During the Cold War, much of the globe sheltered uncertainly under one or other of the main protagonists' nuclear umbrellas. It was never clear which countries were definitely covered by realistic guarantees of nuclear protection on the part of either the USA or USSR. However, there was sufficient ambiguity about this effectively to deter the use of nuclear weapons against a range of non-nuclear states. The basis for this was the sort of defence the superpowers had constructed to defend themselves from their counterpart. Acknowledging that effective military defence against nuclear attack was probably impossible, at least given current technology, both sides worked on a strategy of deterring the other. This involved building up such a large nuclear arsenal that, even if a nuclear attack was sustained, there would be sufficient weaponry left to inflict unacceptable damage upon the opponent. This strategy, based on assumptions about 'mutual assured destruction', was one factor in preventing the use of nuclear weapons even when the Cold War was at its height. This unwillingness to use nuclear weapons, and the growth in a sense of the impossibility (both ethically and practically) of using them, means that in practical terms the challenge they seemed to pose to both individual states and to the existence of the state itself was blunted.

It is not clear that alliance structures or the regulation involved in international agreements have posed a new type of restriction upon states. Alliance systems and international agreements have existed in the past, and all have been transitory. Indeed, what was commonly seen as one of the most solid alliance systems of all, the Warsaw Treaty Organization, has now broken up. Furthermore, the majority of sovereign states were not members of the two main alliance systems of the Cold War. The situation may be more serious for the future of the states in the EU, but even here we should not exaggerate. The path to unity thus far has been long and hard, with local nationalism continuing to obstruct what some have seen as the inexorable march of EU integration. But while the role played by existing national governments under a more tightly integrated and larger EU remains unclear, we should not assume that a fully integrated EU represents the disappearance of the state. It is important not to confuse the conception of the state with contemporary individual states. While the individual states of the EU member countries may decline in importance, although they would probably maintain some necessary functions even if there was a much higher level of integration, the political form that is the EU may also constitute a state. Thus the development of an EU state, if it occurs, would only be another step on the road of the decline in the number of political units on the European continent that has been going on for centuries. Thus the EU does not necessarily represent the decline of the state, although it may mark the emergence of the mega-state.

In the cultural/ideological sphere, there is significant evidence of a continuing lack of homogenization. National populations are becoming more diverse as many states in the OECD turn to immigration and the widespread use of foreign guest workers to provide labour for their economies. This occurs, broadly, under state control. Similarly the movement of people across the globe also remains largely within the control of the state. This flow of people in much larger numbers than ever before has been accommodated within the existing state structures. Given the infrastructure required to sustain an international airline industry, and in particular the need for airports with facilities for aircraft to land, refuel and be repaired if necessary, the access of aircraft to a state can generally be regulated with little difficulty. Airports constitute choke points through which airline passengers are channelled into a country, and thereby give the state the opportunity to regulate the access and egress of people into and from its territory. Through the mechanism of passports and visas, states can regulate visitors coming by air and thereby continue to determine who comes in and who does not.

The growth of international telecommunications has not destroyed national broadcasting networks. Sometimes protected by national policies regarding local content but also responding to local demand, television and radio in the OECD countries retain a distinct domestic bias. Local programming, content and orientation remain the key planks of national broadcasting companies. Even the development of cable television has promoted new avenues for local programming alongside the transnational channels. Local news programmes are not displaced by those beamed from CNN or the BBC. Similarly the presumed standardization of taste reflected in charges about the 'McDonaldization of the world' has run up against cultural differences. The need to be guided by kosher rules in the making of hamburgers and the resistance encountered in different parts of the world to the US-inspired Barbie doll are instances of this trend.[33] And although English may be becoming the international language of business, there is no evidence that it is becoming the language of everyday intercourse in non-English-speaking societies.

The development of global communications has certainly led to the spreading of a form of Anglo-American culture into parts of the world formerly shielded from it; one has only to visit the former communist states to see evidence of this. However, the technology that underpins this is not monolithic; it is neither controlled from a single centre nor immune from local capture. Indeed, one of the chief characteristics of the computer-based communications network is that it is accessible not just in a passive fashion but in an active fashion from all parts of that network. Anyone with a linked computer, and the knowledge of how to do it, can not only access what is already on that network, but can post their own material. Individuals and groups can establish their own sites on the web, and thereby communicate with others in whatever language and for whatever purpose they see fit. Thus while much of the mainstream traffic may fit into this homogenizing model, there is a whole level of communication that facilitates the expression of difference and diversity.

It provides a means for groups that wish to either maintain or develop a sense of group identity separate from those that currently prevail to do so. In this sense the growth of computer-based communication and culture development is ambiguous in its effects. While it may promote the spread of Anglo-American cultural forms, it also gives the opportunity for the growth of other cultural forms, erosive of any attempt at the imposition of cultural standardization on the globe. This reflects the fact that while globalization may promote a general process of homogenization or standardization, it also promotes localism. As Held and McGrew argue,[34] globalization is dialectical, not unilinear, promoting opposing tendencies: integration and fragmentation, universalism and particularism, homogenization and differentiation.

Indeed, to see globalization as a single force is mistaken. Globalization as a tendency consists of a number of forces which, although they intersect and intertwine, are essentially separate; it is multi-stranded and driven by discrete but intersecting logics. For example, cultural forces may be sustained by economic forces, but they are different both among themselves and from the economic forces. While it is the combined impact of globalization forces upon which many focus, in practice it is the individual operation of each which produces the whole. And this individual operation may have different and contradictory effects. This is evident in the discussion above about the way in which computer-based communications may be liberating for small groups. In the operation of these forces, room is created between them within which forces hostile to (or at least not promoting) globalization can find room for development, growth and manoeuvre. This capacity is strengthened by the contradictory nature of some of these forces themselves, how they may promote both homogeneity and difference. Within the space thereby created, independent actors may act in ways designed to achieve their own ends but in conflict with the trends of globalization. Indeed, local opposition to the forces of globalization may be nurtured within these spaces and their actions may have wide-ranging effects. The action of terrorists in flying aircraft into the World Trade Centre in New York and the Pentagon in Washington in September 2001 is an illustration of how this can happen.

The State and Globalization

The spaces between the forces for globalization also provide room within which the state can function. There is much that the forces of globalization do not encompass but which still need regulation.

A prime example is in the economic sphere, where globalization has involved the free movement of trade, investment and capital, but not labour; states still control who may work within their boundaries and under what conditions. The opening-up of such room for the state is reinforced by the way in which globalization promotes fragmentation, particularism and differentiation. This ensures the existence of communities that are locally-based and oriented, and these require the sort of order, regularity and predictability that can only come from the presence of a political authority. The lives of people will continue to be lived locally; globalization may continue to structure the macro-universe within which such lives will be lived, but the immediate conditions of such existence will require local regulation. This the state can provide. And this is essential for the continued functioning of the major struts of globalization. In all spheres – economic, political and cultural/ideological – the forces of globalization rely upon the activities of people. They cannot function without the actions of those who drive them: the futures dealers and currency speculators, the international bureaucrats and the media celebrities and technicians all rely upon the local communities within which they live.

The people who work in the institutions of the emergent globalized world have to get to work each day; they need to be secure in their ability to travel about the streets, to acquire food and those other necessities of life. The continuing capacity of the state to provide this security is crucial. Even if the boundaries of states are becoming less important given the transnational nature of capital and goods, the task at the heart of the state's rationale, the provision of security in all of its contemporary forms, remains central.[35] Indeed, it may be that the perceived operation of impersonal globalizing forces will generate an increased sense of uncertainty and danger among people, which could stimulate powerful pressures for states to act to heighten security for their citizens. Similarly, much of the other infrastructure that goes with a civilized way of life is dependent upon the state and its capacity to maintain the structures of that way of life: law and order, transport, education, health care will continue to be needed, and much of this can only be provided at the local level. The state provides what one writer has called the 'necessary conditions for social existence'.[36] The local roots of the state, reflected in its capacity to continue to provide the struts of a regular collective life style, will ensure that it continues to have an important role in the face of the forces of globalization.

It is not only the spaces within globalization that create the room for state action, however. The forces of globalization themselves rely directly upon the state for their ability to function. Markets, NGOs, media companies and all the other institutions that propel globalization need to have some guarantees that they will not be subject to criminal or terrorist attack. The state remains the best placed organization to ensure that, as shown by the response to the 11 September attacks on the USA. It was left to the government to respond to this and to deal with it. But more importantly, states are also crucial in the operation, and sometimes success, of these organizations. For example, the operation of TNCs is often heavily dependent upon states. TNCs generally remain disproportionately located and active in their 'home states' and reliant upon them for some of the means whereby they function: law and order, the stabilization of property rights, communications infrastructure, preparation of labour supply (through education and training), and economic support.

Such support comes in a variety of forms and has differed substantially in different countries. In Japan, major companies have benefited from the government's push for national coordination of the industrial and export effort. This has involved a range of industrial policies involving differentiated tax rates or conditional subsidies for key (usually export) sectors, public shouldering of the risk of innovation, and coordination of technological upgrading between firms.[37] In the USA, government contracts have been an effective form of state assistance, but important also has been the sense of security companies have gained in operating abroad in the belief that the US government will intervene on their behalf with local governments if this is thought to be necessary. The construction of NAFTA, and the access this has given to the whole North American continent, is another instance of a political structure set in place through state action which benefits major US-based companies. The US government has also been central to decisions about who may buy a major US export, defence-related equipment. In Europe, the EU framework gives substantial support to local companies, yet this is a framework resting upon and continually reshaped by the member states. In addition, in a globalized world, size will be important. Not all companies operating in a global market need to be large in size; some will be able to fill niche markets and thrive on this. However, for those that hope to make a major play in the global market, access to significant relevant resources will be important. In this regard, states can be a positive, value-adding factor. Given the resources available to states, should they choose to throw those resources behind one or a number of 'national' companies, they can significantly increase the resource base and therefore commercial weight of those companies. In this way, through strategic decisions, the state can facilitate the trading of its national companies and help them to grow into major players. Thus the companies which are at the heart of globalization, both in its economic and cultural/ideological strands, rely upon their respective states not only for their basic conditions of existence, but for their very capacity to pursue global strategies. States help to structure the way globalization operates.

Different states have different capacities to do this. The OECD countries, with higher levels of technological development and richer economies, are best placed to do this, and among these, the USA seems particularly well situated. The USA has shown both its capacity and will to structure developing globalization in ways that will advantage its interests. US policy in the last half of the twentieth century combined regulation at home with the championing of free mobility of capital abroad so as to shape the conditions of the global market in a way advantageous to US interests.[38] The USA has been willing to support this with military threat, and use, if necessary. The capacity of the American state to act in this way was facilitated by the large number of TNCs which are based within its borders. Other OECD states which are the homes of TNCs have followed similar policies of support, albeit usually without the military back-up. But even those states in which TNCs are not based are able to bargain and negotiate with TNCs for entry and access to their resources. TNCs are not as mobile as many had thought. They cannot always easily and cheaply transfer their operations from one state to another in the quest for more attractive operating conditions. Bargains must be struck with local states, and these are not always unambiguously in favour of the TNC. States are not helpless before the TNCs. They are, in principle, able to play TNCs off against each other because international business is not monolithic. The different companies have their own interests, and while all share an interest in the peaceful regulation of the societies in which they function, when it comes to specific operating conditions their interests can diverge. This divergence, added to the state's formal right to decide who operates on its territory, a right embedded in international law and strongly supported by all states, gives all states scope to deal with the TNCs. The capacity to do this differs, and this relies not just on the wealth of the national economy and the sorts of resources the state can mobilize, but upon the state's relationship with society (see below).

The state is crucial to the future development of globalization in another way. Like all markets, the emergent global market requires regulation. Much of this regulation has come through bodies especially established for this purpose, such as the IMF, GATT and the WTO. Although these bodies have been able to gain some autonomy from states, states have remained the major players in their operations. They have thus been the vehicle through which states have sought to structure and regulate the international economy. Perhaps even clearer in this regard is the G7, and maybe the annual Davos economic summit, which has operated in a somewhat ad hoc fashion to bring about international coordination of fiscal and monetary policies.[39] States have shown a capacity to come together jointly to structure international developments; trade blocs are another manifestation of this.[40] There is no reason to believe that this will not continue to be the case.

Globalization is also dependent upon states in the same way that the domestic market economy is dependent upon the state: for its legitimacy. The operation of the market naturally leads to inequality. This is the essential dynamic behind the operation of market forces. In the twentieth century the state has played a role in moderating the effect of this, both through regulation and the evening out of inequality through the provision of assistance to those who are in difficulties as a result of the operation of market forces. This was the principal, structural, purpose of the welfare state: to provide state support for those who suffered as a result of market competition. This amelioration of the effects of the market was an important factor in the popular acceptance of it and its broader basis of popular legitimacy. The blunting of the political power of the radical left in OECD countries is in part a reflection of this. Such a process of legitimation will be just as essential in a globalized market and, because the negative effects of market competition will be felt locally, it is at this level that ameliorative action will be necessary. This is the sphere that the state will manage: too low level for micro-administration by globalizing forces, but directly relevant to the lives of much of the globe's populace. In this sense, through the provision of government welfare and support services (or the coordination of such non-government services), states will underpin economic globalization and help to clothe it in a veneer of legitimacy. In so doing, they will be playing an important role in the stabilization of the system, and one that flies in the face of the neo-liberal rhetoric that generally has underpinned globalization.

Central to the state's capacity to maintain both the structures sustaining the local community and those underpinning the forces of globalization is the relationship it possesses with the broader society of which it is part. Where it is embedded in the society, functioning in cooperation with social forces and adding value to their actions (in other words, where institutional and organic interdependence are strongly developed), the state will remain relevant, including in the economic sphere. As the examples of the East Asian states prior to the 1997 crash show, when the state works hand in glove with industry, it can play an important role in shaping the course of national development. There is no reason why it cannot continue to play this positive role. Indeed, as indicated above, in a global economy, the survival of many nationally-based economic actors may depend upon the extra resources and flexibility that the state can bring to their operations. In this sense, the impact of globalization may make the state even more important for economic life than it has been in the recent past. It is appropriate to recall in this light that the contemporary state remains more interventionist in society than at any time in its history except for the height of the post-1945 welfare state and the communist experience.

However, the state also retains strong roots in the local. The globalization of culture will not eliminate the localism of national and regional cultures. Such cultures are carried in all the pores of the society, from its buildings and geographical layout through its names to its domestic points of reference. While identity remains important to people, it is likely that they will continue to look to the local rather than the transnational.[41] The continuing importance of local culture and history is clearly evident in the bloody events in the 1990s in places such as the former Yugoslavia, Rwanda, Kalimantan and Chechnya. While Huntington may not be correct about his civilizational fault lines,[42] he is on sure ground when he emphasizes the continuing importance of cultural values and outlooks. It has been within a localized environment that people have grown up and gained their basic orientations, and it is unlikely that a trans-national identity will be able easily to displace that. If the state remains relevant to that identity, if it continues to reinforce that identity through such things as the education system and the provision of services, and if it remains part of that identity through the continued succouring of the national culture, it will continue to meet a need for its citizens.

Crucial to this is the state's ability to retain the strong links into the society that developed in the twentieth century. Through highly developed institutional interdependence it must remain closely in touch in a positive way with the variety of constituencies in society, because only if it does this will it remain relevant to people's lives and effective in the economic sphere. This may involve the greater development of some of its institutional structures at the expense of others, and therefore could mean some restructuring of the state apparatus, if it is to remain solidly embedded in the society. But it must also ensure that through strengthened ties of organic interdependence, its primary politico-administrative institutions remain solidly rooted within society. This is best achieved through the opening-up of state structures and an expansion of participation within them. The transformation of political systems into more genuinely widespread systems of popular involvement, giving people a meaningful role in the structure that governs them, will strengthen the state and increase its capacity to continue to play a meaningful role in a globalized world. Strengthening democracy is the key to greater organic interdependence and to a more solidly-based state structure. Thus, as throughout its history, the state's capacity to act effectively will remain reliant upon the levels of its interdependence with society.

Implicit in the above discussion of interdependence is the notion that the impact globalization has on particular states will be shaped by the institutions of those states.[43] This has also been referred to in passing when it was noted that the type of economy a state has will be important for the effect globalization has. The impact globalization has will be very different in a state where many economic institutions are linked into the global economy compared with one where there are few institutions thus linked. This is also important for the ability of states to shape the operation of the global forces themselves, as discussed above. But what is also important here is the nature of the institutions. Those societies in which dominant institutions, not just of the state but of civil society as well, are flexible and open to new ideas, function in a cooperative fashion, and are both willing and able to change if needed, are likely to be the best placed in dealing with the challenges of globalization. State bodies must be able to mould their activities in order both to give a lead to domestic actors and to add value to their actions, as well as to interact positively with forces from outside the state. Business must be able to rework its modes of functioning to attune them to the challenges of globalization. Non-governmental organizations must be sufficiently flexible to be able to interact with their global counterparts and to play a part on the global stage. The same point applies to all organizations and groups within society. Indeed, it can be seen too in individuals; they must be educated and trained to be able to make their way in a changing world, and those states with populations that are skilled, mobile and wealthy are likely to be more receptive to globalization. States in which the principal institutions are either characterized by this sort of flexibility or can soon attain it will be affected by, and be able to respond to, globalization in a far more effective fashion that those in which the institutions lack those characteristics. The state's domestic configuration will therefore help to shape both the impact of globalization on society and its response to globalization. Indeed, this configuration, and in particular the nature and flexibility of its institutions, may be more important than size and the resources at a state's disposal; witness the collapse of Soviet communism, the survival of the welfare state, and the continued preponderance of American power in a globalizing world.

Part of this flexibility of institutions is their ability to change. A state's institutional contours may undergo transformation as part of its interaction with globalization. Historically, the pattern of institutions of which the state has consisted and the sorts of functions that it has fulfilled have not been static; both have undergone significant change, as this book has shown. There is no reason why that dynamic will not continue, with globalization being an important factor in shaping institutional change. Part of a state's response to globalization may be alteration in the structure and function of some of its constituent parts. State capacity in different sectors of national life may change, with the state's role being wound back in some and expanded in others. Indeed, this has already happened. In this way, the state is being transformed just as it has in the past when faced with new challenges. This will pose a particular challenge to state elites, who must manage this change. They will have to make the hard decisions about how best to cope with the changing environment,[44] and they will have to sell what may not be very popular changes to their populations. For example, the advantages accruing from globalization will not outweigh the disadvantages in all societies, regardless of the rhetoric otherwise. The operation of the laws of the market in the absence of an effective regulatory body will lead to increased inequality and, for some societies, economic difficulty. More efficient production in one area will mean the closure of less efficient production, and therefore unemployment, in another. It is likely that advantages in one sector will generate advantages in others, and thereby compound the growing inequality. The level of interdependence between state and society, and in particular organic interdependence realized through a democratic political system, will be central to how this question is worked out. It will enable such decisions that need to be taken to possess the sort of popular legitimacy that is central to the success of any public policy. It will also inject the state into the centre of the whole process of globalization and its intermediation with domestic society. This means that the state will continue to have a crucial role in the structuring of domestic life, despite the views of those who would like to see it otherwise.

The twentieth century thus posed the greatest threat to the state in its history. In the first part of the century, two logics faced each other across the globe, and both sought to transcend the state. The functioning of capitalism and communism were both seen as being best realized through the transcending of the state. For communism, the achievement of the ultimate society required the disappearance of the state as a separate entity above society. For capitalism, the free movement of goods required the removal of state barriers to such a development, and therefore the loss of state economic sovereignty. However, in the conditions of challenge and competition between capitalism and communism, rather than being transcended, the state form was reaffirmed; political elites sought to build both communism and capitalism within state forms. And in both cases, the state's power and position were strengthened. With the collapse of communism, the tie between capitalism and the state seemed less immediate. Capitalism has been the driving force behind globalization, and to the extent that the latter threatens the state, that threat is capitalist-driven. However, in practice, globalization relies upon the state for its sustenance. As the repository and regulator of the local, the state safeguards the necessary basis upon which globalization rests and helps to sustain some of those forces making for globalization, while also functioning between the strands of globalization to attend to those areas globalization does not regulate. But it can only be successful if it is characterized by well-developed institutional and organic interdependence, a combination which seems most likely in a regime of political democracy. This means that globalization will not lead to the elimination of the state. The latter may have to work in some different ways and state capacity may be transformed and in some areas reduced, but the state has been adjusting to the operation of international forces for centuries, and there is no reason to believe that, despite the nature of the current challenge, it will be able to adjust any less well this time around.

The *Longue Durée* of the State

The challenge posed by globalization and the capacity of the state to resist that challenge highlights the central factor distinguishing the modern state from its pre-industrial precursors: the rooting of state capacity in an organic relationship with society. Prior to the so-called industrial revolution in the West in the eighteenth–nineteenth centuries, the infrastructural capacity of the state was very weak. The state lacked the institutional means of penetrating society to any great depth, relying overwhelmingly upon the farming of state functions and upon the often questionable loyalty of local notables. Even when states had grand structures at the centre, they were generally not highly embedded in the society. In this sense, most pre-industrial states approximated to the capstone model, even if this model exaggerated the weakness of state links with the society. With low levels of both organic and institutional interdependence and an undeveloped bureaucratic structure, such states relied much more on despotic power than they did on infrastructural power. This changed with the industrial revolution.

Industrialization and the associated transport, communications and cultural (especially educational) revolutions, enabled the construction of the sort of state infrastructure that would permit the effective institutional penetration of society. Bureaucracies consisting of salaried, professional officials, based on written record-keeping and instructions, and held together by the new modes of communication and transport, could now project central power in an institutional fashion far beyond the state capital. The machinery of state could actually extend into the society to a considerable depth, thereby projecting state infrastructural power throughout the community. The institutional nature of this structure gave the state both increased bulk and better prospects for effective communication. However, as the example of the communist state shows, a bureaucratic structure penetrating society does not alone ensure either state effectiveness or survival. What is crucial is the dominance of infrastructural power in the domestic functioning of the bureaucracy, and the embeddedness of the state in the society. The former, domestic infrastructural power within the state machine, comes about principally through the routinization of the functioning of the state machine along rationalist bureaucratic lines. The latter, embeddedness, comes about through the construction of particular sorts of linkages with society and its actors.

Without a bureaucratic structure extending into society, the state could not become embedded. But for this to be achieved, this structure has to enjoy both organic and institutional interdependence. The combination of these two types of interdependence ensures that the state is rooted in the fabric of the society: demographically it is socially (and often increasingly ethnically) inclusive, institutionally it is intertwined with non-state actors in the performance of its functions. Achievement of this sort of situation requires a state that is relatively open, flexible and highly differentiated, but it also requires a society that is itself sufficiently differentiated and developed, with a variety of autonomous social actors with whom the state can interact. A culture supporting widespread involvement in public activities is also necessary for the required interaction between state and society to develop. These conditions of both state and society did not, historically, develop everywhere, but once they had become established in a few countries of the West, their example leached out ultimately to embrace the rest of the globe. It is this relationship between state and society, characterized by organic and institutional interdependence leading to a high level of embeddedness, that makes the modern state unique. It is also the single most important factor in ensuring that the state continues to have a central role to play in a globalizing world.

Notes and References

1 The Modern State

1. To use the phraseology that has now become somewhat trite. See Peter B. Evans, Dietrich Rueschemeyer and Theda Skocpol, *Bringing the State Back In* (Cambridge, Cambridge University Press, 1985).
2. This neglect was never shared by their continental colleagues.
3. Max Weber, *Economy and Society. An Outline of Interpretive Sociology* (Berkeley, CA, University of California Press, 1978, eds. Guenther Roth and Claus Wittich), Vol. 1, p.56.
4. Much of the following discussion builds on the views to be found in Gianfranco Poggi, *The State. Its Nature, Development and Prospects* (Cambridge, Polity Press, 1990), ch.2; John A. Hall and G. John Ikenberry, *The State* (Milton Keynes, Open University Press, 1989), ch.1; Patrick Dunleavy and Brendan O'Leary, *Theories of the State The Politics of Liberal Democracy* (London, Macmillan, 1987), ch.1; and Andrew Vincent, *Theories of the State* (Oxford, Basil Blackwell, 1987), ch.1.
5. The modern state is not concerned for the spiritual welfare of its citizens, and neither is it run by an official with major religious responsibilities. This is despite the fact that, for example, in the UK the queen remains the head of the established church, while people holding ecclesiastical office may also enter the representative arm of the state. Iran in the last two decades and Afghanistan in the last decade of the twentieth century are exceptions to this generalization.
6. S.E. Finer, *The History of Government from the Earliest Times. Volume 1. Ancient Monarchies and Empires* (Oxford, Oxford University Press, 1997), p. 3.
7. To use the words of Eric Hobsbawm and Terence Ranger, *The Invention of Tradition* (Cambridge, Cambridge University Press, 1983).
8. J. Dunbabin, *France in the Making, 843–1180* (Oxford, Oxford University Press, 1985), p.277.
9. Dunleavy and O'Leary, *Theories of the State*, pp.331–2.
10. On realism, see the classic Hans J. Morgenthau, *Politics Among Nations* (New York, Alfred A. Knopf, 1948). For a discussion of realism and neo-realism, see John A. Hobson, *The State and International Relations* (Cambridge, Cambridge University Press, 2000), ch.2.
11. Dunleavy and O'Leary, *Theories of the State*, p.329.
12. For example, see the discussion in Kenneth Dyson, *The State Tradition in Western Europe* (Oxford, Martin Robertson, 1980), pp.139–43, and the discussion in Hobson, *The State*, ch.3. Many pluralists (see below) hold this view.

13. Elman R. Service, *Origins of the State and Civilization. The Process of Cultural Evolution* (New York, W.W. Norton, 1975).
14. Robert L. Carneiro, 'A Theory of the Origin of the State', *Science* 169 (1970), pp.733–8. Also Robert L. Carneiro, 'Political Expansion as an Expression of the Principle of Competitive Exclusion', in Ronald Cohen and Elman R. Service (eds), *Origins of the State. The Anthropology of Political Evolution* (Philadelphia, PA, Institute for the Study of Human Issues, 1978).
15. K. Wittfogel, *Oriental Despotism: A Comparative Study of Total Power* (New Haven, CT, Yale University Press, 1957). There is also a hint of this sort of approach in Crone's view of the state being associated with the construction of monumental religious architecture: Patricia Crone, 'The Tribe and the State', in John A. Hall (ed.), *States in History* (Oxford, Basil Blackwell, 1986), pp.48–77.
16. Otto Hintze, 'Military Organization and the Organization of the State', *The Historical Essays of Otto Hintze* (New York, Oxford University Press, 1975, trans. Felix Gilbert), pp.178–215.
17. For example, Gaetano Mosca, *The Ruling Class* (New York, McGraw-Hill, 1939, trans. Hannah D. Kahn, edited and revised by Arthur Livingston).
18. For example, see Robert A. Dahl, *Polyarchy. Participation and Opposition* (New Haven, CT, Yale University Press, 1971). This view is also present in the classic Joseph Schumpeter, *Capitalism, Socialism and Democracy* (London, Allen & Unwin, 1944).
19. Morton H. Fried, *The Evolution of Political Society. An Essay in Political Anthropology* (New York, Random House, 1967) and Morton H. Fried, 'The State, the Chicken, and the Egg', in Cohen and Service, *Origins of the State*, p.36.
20. Ludwig Gumplowicz, *The Outlines of Sociology* (Philadelphia, PA, American Academy of Political and Social Science, 1899); Franz Oppenheimer, *The State* (New York, Free Life Editions, 1975, originally published 1909); and Herbert Spencer, *Principles of Sociology* (New York, Appleton-Century-Croft, 1897).
21. Karl Marx and Friedrich Engels, 'The Manifesto of the Communist Party', in Karl Marx and Friedrich Engels, *Selected Works* (Moscow, Foreign Languages Publishing House, 1951), Vol. 1, p.35. On the Marxist theory of the state, see Bob Jessop, *The Capitalist State* (Oxford, Martin Robertson, 1982), and Bob Jessop, *State Theory. Putting Capitalist States in their Place* (Cambridge, Polity Press, 1990).
22. Friedrich Engels, *The Origin of the Family, Private Property and the State* (Moscow, Foreign Languages Publishing House, 1954). In earlier work, Engels gave a more rounded view of the origins of the state, invoking military factors, the emergence of surplus product, population growth and increased contacts between agricultural communities. These had to be coordinated by a small group of officials. In Engels' view this functional power was gradually transformed into exploitative power and the state: Friedrich Engels, *Anti-Duhring* (Moscow, Foreign Languages Publishing House, 1954).

23. For a celebrated debate within Marxism over the role of the state and its basis, see Ralph Miliband, *The State in Capitalist Society* (New York, Basic Books, 1969); Nicos Poulantzas, *Political Power and Social Classes* (London, New Left Books, 1973, trans. Tim O'Hagen); 'Poulantzas on the Capitalist State', *New Left Review* 82 (November–December 1973), pp.83–92; Nicos Poulantzas, 'The Capitaist State: A Reply to Miliband and Laclau', *New Left Review* 95 (January–February 1976), pp.65–83; and Nicos Poulantzas, 'The Problems of the Capitalist State', in Robin Blackburn (ed.), *Ideology in Social Science* (New York, Vintage Books, 1973), pp.238–53.

24. Karl Marx, 'The Eighteenth Brumaire of Louis Bonaparte', in Marx and Engels, *Selected Works*, pp.225–311, esp. pp.303–11. For a discussion of Bonapartism, see Ralph Miliband, *Marxism and Politics* (Oxford, Oxford University Press, 1977), pp.74–90.

25. See this approach in Ellen Kay Trimberger, 'State Power and Modes of Production: Implications of the Japanese Transition to Capitalism', *The Insurgent Sociologist* 7 (Spring 1977), pp.85–98 and Ellen Kay Trimberger, *Revolution From Above· Military Bureaucrats and Modernization in Japan, Turkey, Egypt, and Peru* (New Brunswick, Transaction Books, 1978).

26. Michael Mann, 'The Autonomous Power of the State: Its Origins, Mechanisms and Results', in Hall, *States in History*, pp.109–36.

27. Mann, 'Autonomous Power', p.109; emphasis in original.

28. See Theda Skocpol, *States and Social Revolutions. A Comparative Analysis of France, Russia, and China* (Cambridge, Cambridge University Press, 1979), esp. p.32.

29. Scholars have defined this type of relationship in particular policy spheres in different ways: 'embedded autonomy', 'interactive embeddedness' and 'governed interdependence'. Respectively, Peter Evans, *Embedded Autonomy. States and Industrial Transformation* (Princeton, NJ, Princeton University Press, 1995); Leonard Seabrooke, *US Power in International Finance. The Victory of Dividends* (Basingstoke, Palgrave, 2001); and Linda Weiss, *The Myth of the Powerless State Governing the Economy in a Global Era* (Cambridge, Polity Press, 1998).

30. Mann, 'Autonomous Power', pp.109–36. The definitions are on pp.113, 114 and 116.

31. Michael Mann, *The Sources of Social Power. Volume 1. A History of Power from the Beginning to AD 1760* (Cambridge, Cambridge University Press, 1986).

32. One useful way in which this has been conceptualized is by Owen Lattimore. He argued that there were three radii of extensive social organization which remained relatively invariate until fifteenth century Europe: (a) geographically most extensive was military action which included areas pacified and included within the state and those from which tribute was obtained; (b) civil administration, or the state, which was less extensive; (c) economic integration, which could encompass every level from the village to the state to the broader region. See Owen

Lattimore, *Studies in Frontier History* (London, Oxford University Press, 1962), pp.480–91 and 542–51.

33. One qualification to this is the way in which people may obey the law in the absence of a supervising official. This type of situation is akin to the argument above for economic power. But when it comes to positive administrative activity (as opposed to simply setting rules and watching people obey them), the presence of officials or of an administrative network is essential.

2 The Ancient State

1. S.N. Eisenstadt, *The Political Systems of Empires. The Rise and Fall of the Historical Bureaucratic Societies* (New York, The Free Press of Glencoe, 1963), pp.10–11.
2. Joan Oates, *Babylon* (London, Thames & Hudson, 1986, rev.edn), p.25.
3. Aage Westenholz, 'The Old Akkadian Empire in Contemporary Opinion', in Mogens Trolle Larsen (ed.), *Power and Propaganda. A Symposium on Ancient Empires* (Copenhagen, Akademisk Forlag, 1979), p.109.
4. J.N. Postgate, *Early Mesopotamia. Society and Economy at the Dawn of History* (London, Routledge, 1992), pp.34–5.
5. The sources are scantier for this region than for Egypt, Greece and Rome, with much of the detail subject to argument.
6. On unification and the establishment of the first Egyptian state, see Michael Rice, *Egypt's Making. The Origins of Ancient Egypt 5000–2000BC* (London, Routledge, 2000) and Katharine A. Bard, 'The Emergence of the Egyptian State (c3200–2686BC)', in Ian Shaw (ed.), *The Oxford History of Ancient Egypt* (Oxford, Oxford University Press, 2000), pp.61–88.
7. For earlier, see W.G. Runciman, 'Origins of States: The Case of Archaic Greece', *Comparative Studies in Society and History* 24, 3 (July 1982), pp.364–77.
8. Paul Millett, 'The Economy', in Robin Osborne (ed.), *Classical Greece 500–323 BC* (Oxford, Oxford University Press, 2000), p.30.
9. This thesis is rejected by S.E. Finer, *The History of Government. I. Ancient Monarchies and Empires* (Oxford, Oxford University Press, 1997), pp.111–12. For works advocating early 'primitive democracy', see T. Jacobsen, 'Primitive democracy in Ancient Mesopotamia', *Journal of Near Eastern Studies* 2 (1943), pp.159–72 and 'Early political development in Mesopotamia', *Zeitschrift für Assyriologie* 52 (1957), pp.91–140; also Henri Frankfort, *Kingship and the Gods. A Study of Ancient Near Eastern Religion as the Integration of Society and Nature* (Chicago, IL, University of Chicago Press, 1948), pp.215–20.
10. Michael Mann, *The Sources of Social Power. Volume 1. A History of Power from the Beginning to AD 1760* (Cambridge, Cambridge University Press, 1986), p.99.

11. Michael D. Coogan (ed.), *The Oxford History of the Biblical World* (Oxford, Oxford University Press, 1998), chs 4 and 5.
12. Finer, *History I*, p.113.
13. For one study that does not emphasize this, see William W. Hallo, *Origins. The Ancient Near Eastern Background of Some Modern Western Institutions* (Leiden, E.J. Brill, 1996), ch.vi.
14. Finer, *History I*, p.116.
15. Postgate, *Early Mesopotamia*, pp.263–6.
16. The chief exception to this principle was Sparta which had a dual monarchy, but even here political power was mainly in the hands of the citizenry.
17. For surveys of other poleis, see Michael Grant, *The Rise of the Greeks* (New York, Charles Scribner's Sons, 1978), and Roger Brock and Stephen Hodkinson (eds), *Alternatives to Athens. Varieties of Political Organization and Community in Ancient Greece* (Oxford, Oxford University Press, 2000).
18. Only in Athens during its most radical democratic period was citizenship extended to landless people.
19. Rosalind Thomas, 'The classical city', in Osborne, *Classical Greece*, pp.52–60.
20. John V.A. Fine, *The Ancient Greeks. A Critical History* (Cambridge, MA, Belknap Press, 1983), p.395, ch.10.
21. Magistrates who required specific professional knowledge were elected, including the generals who commanded the military. There were some posts too important to be devoid of human choice.
22. A.H.M. Jones, *Athenian Democracy* (Oxford, Basil Blackwell, 1964), pp.99–104. Also Fine, *Ancient Greeks*, pp.396–400.
23. For a study of the importance of gift-giving in Greece, see Paul Veyne, *Bread and Circuses. Historical Sociology and Political Pluralism* (London, Allen Lane, 1990), ch.II. Also see M.M. Austin, 'Society and Economy', in D.M. Lewis, John Boardman, Simon Hornblower and M. Ostwald (eds), *The Cambridge Ancient History. Volume VI. The Fourth Century*, 2nd edn (Cambridge, Cambridge University Press, 1994), pp.548–50.
24. Aristotle, *The Politics* (Harmondsworth, Penguin Books, 1962, trans. T.A. Sinclair), pp.159–61.
25. See the argument in W.G. Runciman, 'Capitalism without classes: the case of classical Rome', *The British Journal of Sociology* 34, 2 (June 1983), esp. pp.164–77.
26. Finer, *History I*, p.396.
27. For the development of its membership, see Andrew Lintott, *The Constitution of the Roman Republic* (Oxford, Oxford University Press, 1999), pp.68–72.
28. Before Sulla a senator had to belong to the equestrian order, and therefore possess landed property worth 400,000 sesterces. Sulla added 300 members to the existing 300 and made entry dependent upon occupation of the quaestorship. Caesar made many of his supporters senators, and by 45 BC the size of the body had risen to 900. Under the triumvirate it was more than 1,000, until reduced to around 600 by Augustus.

For a discussion of the wealth of one senator, Pliny the younger (a senator from the late 80s until his death in *c.* AD 112 and therefore after the republican period), see Richard Duncan-Jones, *The Economy of the Roman Empire* (Cambridge, Cambridge University Press, 1974), ch.1.

29. E. Badian, *Publicans and Sinners. Private Enterprise in the Service of the Roman Republic* (Ithaca, NY, Cornell University Press, 1972).

30. A.H.M. Jones, *The Roman Economy. Studies in Ancient Economic and Administrative History* (Oxford, Basil Blackwell, 1974, ed. P.A. Brunt), pp.117–18.

31. A third, the Comitia Curiata, had primarily religious functions. Most of the original functions of this body were subsumed within the functions of the Comitia Centuriata.

32. Lintott, *Constitution*, pp.55–61.

33. The higher census classes (i.e., the richest property-owners), which numerically were the smallest, had the largest number of centuries, while all of those without property (the proletarii) were enrolled in a single century.

34. This number stemmed from 241 BC. Prior to that date there were fewer tribes. See Lintott, *Constitution*, pp.50–5.

35. The term *concilium plebis*, or assembly of the plebians, was used for meetings of plebeians alone: Lintott, *Constitution*, p.53. Formally this had merged with another body, the Comitia Populi, in 376 BC: T.J. Cornell, 'The Recovery of Rome', in F.W. Walbank, A.E. Astin, M.W. Frederiksen and R.M. Ogilvie (eds), *The Cambridge Ancient History. Volume VII, Part 2. The Rise of Rome to 270BC*, 2nd edn (Cambridge, Cambridge University Press, 1989), p.341.

36. It was acting as the concilium plebis when it elected the tribunes of the plebians. Both the tribunes and aediles were civic officials, the former to protect the privileges of the plebeians against encroachment by others, the latter shared these functions but also had responsibility for maintenance of the fabric of the city, roads and buildings.

37. Lintott, *Constitution*, chs 7 and 8.

38. Consuls and praetors could have their authority extended if the former were engaged in military activity at the time it ran out: Lintott, *Constitution*, p.113.

39. Although this principle was breached, for example during the Punic War and in 104 BC.

40. The number grew over time. See Lintott, *Constitution*, p.107.

41. For Pompey's use of the tribunes to further his political ambitions, see Ronald Syme, *The Roman Revolution* (Oxford, Oxford University Press, 1956), ch.2. Finer disputes the role of clientage: Finer, *History I*, pp.416–21.

42. Oswyn Murray, 'Introduction', Veyne, *Bread and Circuses*, p.xx.

43. Veyne, *Bread and Circuses*, p.208.

44. Veyne, *Bread and Circuses*, p.213.

45. Finer, *History I*, p.387.

46. M.I. Finley, *Politics in the Ancient World* (Cambridge, Cambridge University Press, 1983), p.65.

47. David C. Braund, 'Introduction', in David C. Braund (ed.), *The Administration of the Roman Empire 241BC–AD193* (Exeter, University of Exeter Press, 1988), p.1.

48. On the governorship during the late Republic, see John Richardson, 'The Administration of the Empire', in J.A. Crook, Andrew Lintott and Elizabeth Rawson (eds), *The Cambridge Ancient History. Volume IX. The Last Age of the Roman Republic, 146–43 BC* (Cambridge, Cambridge University Press, 1994), pp.572–91.

49. Badian, *Publicans and Sinners*, and Max Weber, *Economy and Society. An Outline of Interpretive Sociology* (Berkeley, CA, University of California Press, 1978, ed. and trans. Guenther Roth and Claus Wittich), ch.11.

50. Jones, *Roman Economy*, pp.151–85. Also see Margaret Levi, *Of Rule and Revenue* (Berkeley, CA, University of California Press, 1988), ch.4. For the view that the contracting-out of such public tasks for multi-year periods reflects the fact that each administration held office only for a year, see Tenney Frank, *An Economic Survey of Ancient Rome. Volume 1. Rome and Italy of the Republic* (Paterson, Pageant Books Inc., 1959; first published 1933), p.148.

51. Badian, *Publicans and Sinners*, pp.16–21.

52. For his typology of regime types, see Finer, *History I*, pp.34–59.

53. On Assyria, see Paul Garelli, 'L'état et la légitime royale sous l'empire assyrien', in Larsen, *Power and Propaganda*, esp. p.320. This was not the case in the Persian Empire: Finer, *History I*, p.292.

54. Mogens Trolle Larsen, 'The Tradition of Empire in Mesopotamia', in Larsen, *Power and Propaganda*, p.83.

55. Egyptian kings were only called 'pharaoh' from the Amarna period and the reign of Amunhotep IV/Akhenaten, *c*.1350–1334 BC, but will be designated as such throughout.

56. With the exception of Peribsen and Khasekwemy (who adopted a different deity) every king of the early dynastic period bore the title of Horus and therefore claimed to be that god's earthly embodiment; see I.E.S. Edwards, 'The Early Dynastic Period in Egypt', in I.E.S. Edwards, C.J. Gadd and N.G.L. Hammond (eds), *The Cambridge Ancient History Volume I, Part 2. Early History of the Middle East*, 3rd edn (Cambridge, Cambridge University Press, 1971), p.35. For a discussion of the changing conception of kingship in the Late Period, see B.G. Trigger, B.J. Kemp, D. O'Connor and A.B. Lloyd, *Ancient Egypt A Social History* (Cambridge, Cambridge University Press, 1983), pp.288–9.

57. Trigger *et al.*, *Ancient Egypt*, p.77.

58. Finer, *History I*, p.157.

59. For a description of the administrative structure at the time of the Eighteenth Dynasty, see William C. Hayes, 'Egypt: Internal Affairs from Tuthmosis I to the Death of Amenophis III', in I.E.S. Edwards, C.J. Gadd, N.G.L. Hammond and E. Sollberger (eds), *The Cambridge Ancient History. Volume II, Part 1. History of the Middle East and the Aegean Region c1800–1380BC*, 3rd edn (Cambridge, Cambridge University Press, 1973), pp.353–63. Similar structures seem to have existed in the Middle Kingdom.

60. The pharaoh was usually able to get his way over any opposition from bureaucrats, priests or the army. Indeed, a 'national' standing army (based on conscription) was not established until the Middle Kingdom; it became influential in the New Kingdom when it was used for imperial expansion.

61. Veyne, *Bread and Circuses*, pp.324–34.

62. Although Augustus was considered a god in some Eastern parts of the Empire (Finer, *History I*, p.545 and Veyne, *Bread and Circuses*, pp.306–21), until 218 when Elagabalus was acknowledged as a god while he lived, this status was usually conferred on emperors only after they died. This changed when Constantine made Christianity the official religion of the Empire.

63. See the discussion in Hugh Last, 'The Principate and the Administration', in S.A. Cook, F.E. Adcock and M.P. Charlesworth, *The Cambridge Ancient History. Volume XI. The Imperial Peace, AD 70–192* (Cambridge, Cambridge University Press, 1936), pp.399–408.

64. M. Grant, *The World of Rome* (London, Sphere Books, 19–74), p.109.

65. This tendency was strengthened by the practice which had emerged by the time of Marcus Aurelius of stationing soldiers in their home areas, thereby giving them an incentive to support local candidates for emperor.

66. Michael Grant, *The Climax of Rome* (London, Phoenix, 1988; first published 1968), pp.49–51.

67. See Fergus Millar, *The Emperor in the Roman World (31 BC–AD 337)* (London, Duckworth, 1977), ch.III.

68. On the Julio-Claudian court, see Andrew Wallace-Hadrill, 'The Imperial Court', in Alan K. Bowman, Edward Champlin and Andrew Lintott (eds), *The Cambridge Ancient History. Volume X. The Augustan Empire, 43BC–AD69*, 2nd edn (Cambridge, Cambridge University Press, 1996), pp.283–308.

69. Last, '*The Principate*', pp.426–33.

70. By the fifth century the civil service amounted to more than 30,000 people, but this was not a large number for such a large political unit: Jones, *Roman Economy*, p.129.

71. This was sometimes, as in the later Assyrian Empire, accompanied by the deportation of sections of the native population believed to be troublesome. See J.A. Brinkman, 'Babylonia Under the Assyrian Empire, 745–627 BC', Larsen, *Power and Propaganda*, p.234 and Postgate, *Early Mesopotamia*, p.41.

72. Finer, *History I*, p.221.

73. Larsen, *Power and Propaganda*, p.83.

74. Postgate, *Early Mesopotamia*, ch.15.

75. Finer, *History I*, pp.225 and 295.

76. On the late Assyrian Empire, see Postgate, *Early Mesopotamia*, p.216.

77. Mann, *Sources of Social Power I*, pp.111–12.

78. K.W. Butzer, *Early Hydraulic Civilization in Egypt. A Study in Cultural Ecology* (Chicago, IL, University of Chicago Press, 1976), ch.5 and p.109.

79. See William C. Hayes, 'The Middle Kingdom in Egypt. Internal History from the Rise of the Heracleopolitans to the Death of Ammenemes III',

in Edwards *et al.*, *Cambridge Ancient History*, I/2, pp.468–72 and Stephen Seidlmayer, 'The First Intermediate Period (c2160–2055BC)', in Shaw, *Oxford History*, pp.131–2.

80. Gae Callender, 'The Middle Kingdom (c2055–1650BC)', in Shaw, *Oxford History*, pp.174–5.

81. Finer, *History I*, p.162.

82. Paul John Fraudsen, 'Egyptian Imperialism', in Larsen, *Power and Propaganda*, pp.175–6.

83. Finer, *History I*, p.532. On the cities, see Jones, *Roman Economy*, chs 1 and 2, and Joyce Reynolds, 'Cities', in Braund, *Roman Empire*, pp.15–51.

84. Veyne, *Bread and Circuses*, p.42.

85. Braund, 'Introduction', p.7.

86. Peter Garnsey and Richard Saller, *The Roman Empire. Economy, Society and Culture* (London, Duckworth, 1987), pp.34–6.

87. The expanding system of roads was crucial for maintaining contact and was an effective means of communication: Caesar and his army travelled 800 miles in eight days, while the news of Nero's death reached Spain 332 miles away in seven days: Grant, *World of Rome*, p.48.

88. The establishment of colonies and their settlement by veterans was also an important factor here. This was begun under Marius and continued until the time of Hadrian.

89. Grant, *Climax*, p.72.

90. For an argument that 'Supralocal exchange systems existed long before the rise of civilizations', see K. Ekholm and J. Friedman, ' "Capital", Imperialism and Exploitation in Ancient World Systems', in Larsen, *Power and Propaganda*, p.42. For the argument that the Mesopotamian temples played an important part in commerce by providing a site where the different parties could reach their agreements (and thereby constituting a guarantee of those agreements) and in generating a sense of trust, see Morris Silver, *Economic Structures of the Ancient Near East* (London, Croom Helm, 1985), pp.7–18.

91. Also see Susan Pollock, *Ancient Mesopotamia* (Cambridge, Cambridge University Press, 1999), ch.5.

92. For a critique of the original temple state thesis, see Benjamin Foster, 'A New Look at the Sumerian Temple State', *Journal of the Economic and Social History of the Orient* xxiv, iii (1981), pp.225–41. For one view emphasizing the control over land exercised by the temples during the time of the Third Dynasty of Ur, see Henri Limet, 'Le rôle du palais dans l'économie néo-sumerienne', in Edward Lipinski, *State and Temple Economy in the Ancient Near East I* (Leuwen, Department Orientalisk, 1979), pp.245–7. For a view which sees the temples as much less important, see Silver, *Economic Structures*, ch.3.

93. The temples also produced goods for commercial purposes and provided for their workers from the produce of their estates; excess land was leased to tenants. Postgate, *Early Mesopotamia*, p.115.

94. For an argument about the development of specialization in the economy, see Pollock, *Ancient Mesopotamia*, ch.4.

95. Finer, *History I*, p.114, Mann, *Sources of Social Power I*, p.87. On land ownership, see Silver, *Economic Structures*, pp.92–102.

96. Silver, *Economic Structures*, chs 5 and 6.
97. For example, see J.N. Postgate, 'The Economic Structure of the Assyrian Empire', in Larsen, *Power and Propaganda*, pp.193–221, and Johannes Renger, 'Interaction of Temple, Palace, and "Private Enterprise" in the Old Babylonian Economy', in Lipinskı, *State and Temple I*, pp.249–56. For an argument that in Neo-Babylonian times land generally was held by those who cultivated it, see M.A. Dandamayev, 'State and Temple in Babylonia in the First Millennium BC', Edward Lipiński, *State and Temple Economy in the Ancient Near East II* (Leuwen, Departement Orientalisk, 1979), p.592. On different categories of land-holding, see Postgate, *Early Mesopotamia*, pp.183–7.
98. Postgate, *Early Mesopotamia*, pp.219–21.
99. Mann, *Sources of Social Power I*, pp.146–54.
100. Trigger *et al.*, *Ancient Egypt*, p.81.
101. For a cautious statement of this for the Old and Middle Kingdoms, see Butzer, *Hydraulic Civilization*, p.88.
102. In the Old Kingdom, trade was a royal monopoly, with no clear distinction in the Egyptian mind between trade and tribute: Paul Johnson, *The Civilization of Ancient Egypt* (New York, Harper Collins, 1999; first published 1978), p.43.
103. Trigger *et al.*, *Ancient Egypt*, pp.325–6.
104. Finer, *History I*, p.185.
105. Butzer, *Hydraulic Civilization*, p.88 and Jac J. Janssen, 'The Role of the Temple in the Egyptian Economy During the New Kingdom', Lipinski, *State and Temple II*, p.509.
106. Finer, *History I*, pp.192–6. Although, in the words of one author, 'Egypt during much of the Old Kingdom was a centrally planned and administered state, headed by a king who was the theoretical owner of all its resources and whose powers were practically absolute.' See Jaromir Malek, 'The Old Kingdom (c2686–2125 BC)', in Shaw, *Oxford History*, p.102. This may exaggerate the degree of central control.
107. On taxation, see Hayes, '*Egypt*', pp.381–5. On private merchants during the time of Rameses II (1290–1224 BC), see Sılver, *Economic Structures*, pp.135–6.
108. Finer, *History I*, p.195.
109. On gift-giving and reciprocity, see Patricia Springborg, *Royal Persons. Patriarchal Monarchy and the Feminine Principle* (London, Unwin Hyman, 1990), ch.13.
110. Many granaries found from the Middle Kingdom were said to be privately owned: Butzer, *Hydraulic Civilization*, p.88.
111. Mann, *Sources of Social Power*, p.112.
112. For an argument that the emergence of the polis at the end of the eighth century was shaped fundamentally by population increase and the expansion of trading activity, see David W. Tandy, *Warriors into Traders. The Power of the Market ın Early Greece* (Berkeley, CA, University of California Press, 1997).
113. For Athenıan provisions for resolving commercıal disputes and protecting its citizens acting abroad, including in trade, see R.J. Hopper,

Trade and Industry in Classical Greece (London, Thames & Hudson, 1979), pp.110–17. In Millett's words, Greek maritime trade was characterized by 'fragmentation and remoteness from state control': Millett, 'The Economy', p.42.

114. M.I. Finley, *The Ancient Economy*, 2nd edn (London, Penguin Books, 1985), pp.155 and 165. Unlike other poleis, Athens was able to build up a cash reserve; elsewhere public finances were more hand to mouth: Millett, 'The Economy', p.38.

115. Austin, 'Society and Economy', p.545.

116. On the range of taxes, see Jones, *Athenian Democracy*, pp.152–6. Taxes on sales, auctions, imports and exports were common; private wealth was sometimes also taxed: Austin, 'Society and Economy', p.544.

117. Finley, *Ancient Economy*, pp.117–18. Banks seem to have emerged in the mid-fifth century, but to have been mainly involved in money exchange rather than accumulation or lending: J.K. Davies, 'Greece After the Persian Wars', in D.M. Lewis, John Boardman, J.K. Davies and M. Ostwald (eds), *The Cambridge Ancient History. Volume V. The Fifth Century BC*, 2nd edn (Cambridge, Cambridge University Press, 1992), p.24.

118. Davies, 'Greece', p.302. Much economic activity was motivated less by purely economic concerns than by status, citizenship and the style of a 'respectable' life. Non-citizens could not own land while citizens were not involved in commercial, artisanal or financial activities.

119. Badian, *Publicans and Sinners*, p.33. On the working of these public companies, see Badian, *Publicans and Sinners*, ch.iv. For the argument that with senators able to hold shares in public companies, at least by the middle of the first century BC, the distinction between the functions of government and of public contracting had broken down, see Badian, *Publicans and Sinners*, pp.103–4.

120. Even when owners lived on the land, the practice of the wealthy owning a number of geographically dispersed estates rendered an owner effectively absentee on parts of his land.

121. Jones, *Roman Economy*, ch.21. Very large estates were common throughout Roman history, especially in the Late Empire. For one discussion, see Richard Alston, *Aspects of Roman History AD14–117* (London, Routledge, 1998). On large estates existing during the Republic, see C. Nicolet, 'Economy and Society, 133–43BC', in Crook *et al.*, *Cambridge Ancient History*, IX, pp.617–18.

122. Finley, *Ancient Economy*, p.22.

123. For an argument that 'the whole Roman Empire was integrated into a single monetary economy', based upon the concentrations of coin minted between 200BC and AD400 found in different parts of the Empire, see M.K. Hopkins, 'Taxes and Trade in the Roman Empire (200 BC–AD 400)', *Journal of Roman Studies* 70 (1980), pp.101–25; citation from p.112. For a critique of this, see Richard Duncan-Jones, *Structure and Scale in the Roman Economy* (Cambridge, Cambridge University Press, 1990), pp.38–42.

124. Despite the view of Runciman, 'Capitalism without classes'.

125. For some figures, see Jones, *Roman Economy*, pp.114–15.
126. Badian, *Publicans and Sinners*, p.51.
127. Jones, *Roman Economy*, p.119.
128. In addition, there was often widespread bribery of electors: Veyne, *Bread and Circuses*, pp.219–32.
129. Murray, 'Introduction' p.xix.
130. Veyne, *Bread and Circuses*, p.6. However, cities and municipalities could and did receive gifts from wealthy citizens, often those who ran these entities. Such gifts usually took the form of the financing of public works. For the study of privately-funded public building in one town, Thugga, over three centuries, see Duncan-Jones, *Structure and Scale*, pp.178–82.
131. For one discussion of imperial gift-giving, see Fergus Millar, *The Emperor in the Roman World (31BC–AD337)* (London, Duckworth, 1977), ch.iv. Also Veyne, *Bread and Circuses*, ch.iv. Similarly investment in land was less a matter of economic calculation designed to generate economic returns than for prestige reasons. See the discussion in Finley, *Ancient Economy*, pp.112–20 and Runciman, 'Capitalism without classes', pp.161–2. On the role of honour more generally, see J.E. Lendon, *Empire of Honour. The Art of Government in the Roman World* (Oxford, Oxford University Press, 1997).
132. For one discussion, see Grant, *Climax*, pp.44–9. Although Constantine took important steps to halt this process, an end to it did not occur until the end of the fifth century in Constantinople, by which time Rome had fallen: Grant, *Climax*, p.56.
133. Mann, *Sources of Social Power I*, p.278. Also see the discussion in Garnsey and Saller, *Roman Empire*, pp.88–95.
134. Garnsey and Saller, *Roman Empire*, p.87.
135. Although it did stimulate private ship-owning and operation because the grain was shipped in private vessels: Garnsey and Saller, *Roman Empire*, p.88.
136. Jones, *Roman Economy*, pp.131–2. This was particularly marked following the state's expansion under Diocletian.
137. For the lack of interest on the part of city authorities in commercial matters, see Jones, *Roman Economy*, pp.46–8.
138. Finley, *Ancient Economy*, p.53.
139. For the varieties of tax imposed throughout the provinces, see Duncan-Jones, *Structure and Scale*, ch.12, and Jones, *Roman Economy*, ch.8.
140. Finley, *Ancient Economy*, p.96. This tax on land produced more than 90% of the late Empire's revenue and was a combined tax on land and a poll tax: Jones, *Roman Economy*, p.83. For a discussion of the way the poor carried the burden while the rich were often able to avoid it, see Jones, *Roman Economy*, p.133.
141. Garnsey and Saller, *Roman Empire*, p.24.
142. Grant, *World of Rome*, p.86.
143. Jones, *Roman Economy*, ch.21.
144. Peter Garnsey and C.R. Whittaker, 'Trade, Industry, and the Urban Economy', in Averil Cameron and Peter Garnsey (eds), *The Cambridge Ancient History. Volume XIII. The Late Empire, AD 337–425* (Cambridge, Cambridge University Press, 1998), pp.316–17.

145. Grant, *Climax*, p.48.
146. F. Oertel, 'The Economic Life of the Empire', in S.A. Cook, F.E. Adcock, M.P. Charlesworth and N.H. Baynes (eds), *The Cambridge Ancient History. Volume XII. The Imperial Crisis and Recovery AD 193–324* (Cambridge, Cambridge University Press, 1939), p.272.
147. See the excellent discussion in Patricia Crone, *Pre-Industrial Societies* (Oxford, Basil Blackwell, 1989).
148. Crone, *Pre-Industrial Societies*, pp.55–6.
149. The notion of empire, and its relationship with the state, is problematic. Empire usually implies very large size and domination by one group (ethnically or territorially defined) over others. But neither of these is unique to empires, and even in the traditional empires the distinction between rulers and ruled was not always clearly demarcated in primordial terms. In this book, empire will be treated as a form of state. For discussions of empire, see Finer, *History I*, pp.8–9; Eisenstadt, *Political Systems*; and Dominic Lieven, *Empire The Russian Empire and its Rivals* (London, John Murray, 2000), ch.1.

3 The Feudal and Early Modern State

1. Charles Tilly, 'Reflections on the History of European State-Making', in Charles Tilly (ed.), *The Formation of National States in Western Europe* (Princeton, NJ, Princeton University Press, 1975), p.26.
2. See the argument in Michael Hechter and William Brustein, 'Regional Modes of Production and Patterns of State Formation in Western Europe', *American Journal of Sociology* 85, 5 (1980), pp.1,061–94. For the argument that feudalism was more developed in Western than Eastern Europe because of the differential mixes of the legacy of the Roman Empire and Nordic–Germanic bands, see Peter Gourevitch, 'The International System and Regime Formation. A Critical Review of Anderson and Wallerstein', *Comparative Politics* 10, 3 (April 1978), p.428.
3. W.M. Ormrod and Janos Barta, 'The Feudal Structure and the Beginnings of State Finance', Richard Bonney (ed.), *Economic Systems and State Finance* (Oxford, Oxford University Press, 1995).
4. S.E. Finer, *The History of Government. II. The Intermediate Ages* (Oxford, Oxford University Press, 1997), p.82.
5. G.B. Adams, 'Feudalism', *Encyclopaedia Britannica*, 11th edn (London, 1910), x, p.302, cited in Finer, *History II*, p.867
6. Finer, *History II*, p.865; emphasis in original.
7. Michael Mann, *The Sources of Social Power. Vol. 1. A History of Power from the Beginning to AD 1750* (Cambridge, Cambridge University Press, 1986), p.392.
8. The loss of the lands in France was crucial to the development of a separate sense of England, which was in turn important for the later development of a sense of national identity.
9. Perry Anderson, *Lineages of the Absolutist State* (London, Verso, 1974), p.15.

10. Thomas Ertman, *Birth of the Leviathan. Building States and Regimes in Medieval and Early Modern Europe* (Cambridge, Cambridge University Press, 1997), pp.161-3.
11. For a comparative study, see Samuel Clark, *State and Status. The Rise of the State and Aristocratic Power in Western Europe* (Montreal, McGill-Queen's University Press, 1995), esp. chs 1 and 3.
12. Gianfranco Poggi, *The State. Its Nature, Development and Prospects* (Cambridge, Polity Press, 1990), pp.37-9.
13. Hechter and Brustein, 'Regional Modes', p.1,087.
14. Hechter and Brustein, 'Regional Modes', pp.1,077-8.
15. On the nature of vassalage and of this process, see Marc Bloch, *Feudal Society. 1. The Growth of Ties of Dependence* (London, Routledge & Kegan Paul, 1962, trans. L.A. Manyon), 1, Part iv.
16. For a survey discussion of the argument about commercialization undercutting feudalism, see John Hatcher and Mark Bailey, *Modelling the Middle Ages. The History and Theory of England's Economic Development* (Oxford, Oxford University Press, 2001), ch.4.
17. For a discussion of the shift from feudal dues to rents in the context of the fourteenth century crisis, and the different geographical patterns of this, see Immanuel Wallerstein, *The Modern World-System. I. Capitalist Agriculture and the Origins of the European World-Economy in the Sixteenth Century* (New York, Academic Press, 1974), pp.86-116.
18. On towns and their role, see Charles Tilly and Wim P. Brockmans (eds), *Cities and the Rise of States in Europe, A.D. 1000 to 1800* (Boulder, CO, Westview Press, 1994); John Merrington, 'Town and Country in the Transition to Capitalism', *New Left Review*, September–October 1975, pp.71–92; Fernand Braudel, *Civilization and Capitalism. 15th–18th Century. Volume 1. The Structures of Everyday Life. The Limits of the Possible* (London, Fontana, 1985, trans. Sian Reynolds), pp.510–14; and Charles Tilly, *Coercion, Capital, and European States, AD 900–1990* (Oxford, Basil Blackwell, 1990). Also the classic Henri Pirenne, *Medieval Cities* (Garden City, New York, Doubleday, 1925, trans. Frank D. Halsey).
19. Mann, *Sources of Social Power I*, pp.433-4.
20. Mann, *Sources of Social Power I*, p.379.
21. The Holy Roman Empire was not a realistic challenger to national power.
22. In Finer's words: 'By the death of Edgar in 975, England, in stark contrast to France, was recognized at that time by its ruling strata, if not by its population, as a single *regnum* ... Thenceforward aristocratic reaction against the Crown was to seek privileges or to command the whole, but *not* to return to the Heptarchy' of Saxon kingdoms: Samuel E. Finer, 'State- and Nation-Building in Europe: The Role of the Military', in Tilly, *Formation*, p.113. On early English monarchy, see Ann Williams, *Kingship and Government in Pre-Conquest England* (London, Macmillan, 1999) and Sir Frank Stenton, *Anglo-Saxon England* (Oxford, Oxford University Press, 1971), ch.xv.
23. Ertman, *Birth of the Leviathan*, p.24.
24. The situation in England is succinctly captured in Harding's comment about William I: 'The relationship which the king established with

ecclesiastical landholders was from the first one of public authority, not private lordship, and this spread by way of dispute-settlement to laymen': Alan Harding, *Medieval Law and the Foundations of the State* (Oxford, Oxford University Press, 2002), p.131.

25. For the argument that this represented the organizing capacity and solidarity of the Norman aristocracy as a whole, see Robert Brenner, 'The Agrarian Roots of European Capitalism', in T.H. Ashton and C.H.C. Philpin (eds), *The Brenner Debate. Agrarian Class Structure and Economic Development in Pre-Industrial Europe* (Cambridge, Cambridge University Press, 1987), p.255.

26. The administrative jobs undertaken throughout the country following William's accession were farmed: Marc Bloch, *Feudal Society. 2. Social Changes and Political Organization* (London, Routledge & Kegan Paul, 1962, trans. L.A. Manyon), p.430.

27. Finer, *History II*, p.901.

28. Finer, *History II*, p.901. This was the Danegeld.

29. This is the basic argument of Hillay Zmora, *Monarchy, Aristocracy and the State in Europe 1300–1800* (London, Routledge, 2001). Also see Brenner, 'Agrarian Roots', p.257.

30. The king often sought to centralize power in his own hands by shifting functions from those institutions where his control was more problematic to those of his personal household.

31. Joseph R. Strayer, *On the Medieval Origins of the Modern State* (Princeton, NJ, Princeton University Press, 1970), pp.28–9.

32. For a discussion of this in both England and France, see Harding, *Medieval Law*, esp. ch.5. Also on the importance of law, especially in the sense of it providing an infrastructure of administration and rule, see Harold J. Berman, *Law and Revolution. The Formation of the Western Legal Tradition* (Cambridge, MA, Harvard University Press, 1983).

33. Strayer, *Medieval Origins*, p.41.

34. Finer, *History II*, p.915.

35. Reinhard Bendix, *Kings or People. Power and the Mandate to Rule* (Berkeley, CA, University of California Press, 1978), pp.199–200.

36. Funds from the domainal lands were significantly reduced by the loss of the Duchy of Normandy in 1204, thereby pushing the English Crown to rely further on taxation. Paradoxically, the capture of Normandy and its revenues by the French king reinforced reliance upon domainal revenues and therefore eased the pressure to seek expanded taxation powers: Ormrod and Barta, 'The Feudal Structure', pp. 66–8.

37. Strayer, *Medieval Origins*, p.43.

38. Finer, *History II*, p.919.

39. Ertman, *Birth of the Leviathan*, p.172.

40. G.R. Elton, *The Tudor Revolution in Government. Administrative Changes in the Reign of Henry VIII* (Cambridge, Cambridge University Press, 1962). The measures undertaken by the Tudors were more a re-organization of existing resources than a major restructuring: Mann, *Sources of Social Power I*, p.475.

41. Ertman, *Birth of the Leviathan*, p.180.

42. The farming of customs was abolished in 1671 and of excise in 1683: Patrick K. O'Brien and Philip A. Hunt, 'England, 1485–1815', in Richard Bonney (ed.), *The Rise of the Fiscal State in Europe, c.1200–1815* (Oxford, Oxford University Press, 1999), p.73.

43. On the decline of the power of magnates to dominate local politics under the Tudors, see Richard Lachman, *Capitalists in Spite of Themselves. Elite Conflict and Economic Transitions in Early Modern Europe* (Oxford, Oxford University Press, 2000), pp.109–10. Early Tudor kings brought members of the gentry into the Privy Council rather than the landed magnates, thereby strengthening the influence of the former at the expense of the latter: Zmora, *Monarchy*, p.53.

44. Colin Mooers, *The Making of Bourgeois Europe* (London, Verso, 1991), pp.155–9.

45. Ertman, *Birth of the Leviathan*, pp.23–5.

46. Ertman, *Birth of the Leviathan*, p.68.

47. Strayer, *Medieval Origins*, p.65.

48. Gianfranco Poggi, *The Development of the Modern State. A Sociological Introduction* (London, Hutchinson, 1978), p.52.

49. A.R. Myers, *Parliaments and Estates in Europe to 1789* (London, Thames & Hudson, 1975).

50. Ertman, *Birth of the Leviathan*, p.167. Burgesses and knights of the shires first gained representation in de Montfort's Parliament of 1265, but it was not until 1295 that this became standard practice. Finer, *History II*, p.1,039.

51. Some have called the Tudor kings absolute monarchs because of their wide discretionary powers, including the ability directly to raise some revenues, to modify the impact of existing statutes, to implement justice through their own courts outside the common law system (the Council and Court of Star Chamber), and to exercise some control over the local administration. But they remained fundamentally reliant upon the Parliament. See the discussion in Finer, *The History of Government. III. Empires, Monarchies and the Modern State* (Oxford, Oxford University Press, 1997), pp.1,335–6. Any prospect the Crown had of creating an independent basis of power through the retention of Church lands seized in the reformation was undercut by the need to sell those properties (which amounted to about 25% of the country) in order to pay off debts incurred in the recent French wars and to generate support for the Reformation: Lachman, *Capitalists*, pp.102–5.

52. Finer, *History II*, p.1,041.

53. On commercial elements and the Parliament, see Clark, *State and Status*, p.99.

54. Strayer, *Medieval Origins*, p.49.

55. Finer, *History II*, p.925. The parlement was, therefore, unlike the English Parliament which exercised legislative and administrative as well as judicial functions.

56. Finer, *History II*, p.928.

57. Clark, *State and Status*, pp.34–6.

58. Brenner, 'Agrarian Roots', pp.258–9.

59. Clark, *State and Status*, p.39.

60. The number of officials working for the king increased from about 7,000–8,000 in 1515 to about 80,000 in 1665: Winfried Schulze, 'The Emergence and Consolidation of the "Tax State". 1. The Sixteenth Century', in Bonney, *Economic Systems and State Finance*, p.268. The vast bulk of growth in the French bureaucracy was at the non-central levels.

61. Ertman, *Birth of the Leviathan*, p.90.

62. Ertman, *Birth of the Leviathan*, p.103. As Ertman says (p.110), this constituted a hollowing-out of the state.

63. This was needed because of the Crown's continuing need for more funds. Kings became beholden to financiers with ready access to cash, and from 1556 it became common for the state to borrow from its own officials, with financiers often being given state office on the understanding that they would lend money to the government. As well as financiers in the strict sense of the term, the handling of royal finances was dominated by businessmen whose main aim was to increase their own wealth, even at the expense of the Crown. For a review of the sorts of businessmen who became involved over the two hundred years before the revolution, see J.F. Bosher, *French Finances 1770–1795. From Business to Bureaucracy* (Cambridge, Cambridge University Press, 1970), pp.6–10. Also see Julian Dent, *Crisis in Finance: Crown, Financiers and Society in Seventeenth Century France* (Newton Abbott, David & Charles, 1973). Much of the public debt in the sixteenth century was financed by the nobles, something that helped to bring them closer to the state and turned the state into a source of wealth for them. In the seventeenth century, nobles provided much of the capital upon which private financiers relied: Zmora, *Monarchy*, pp.58–61 and 88.

64. Although it also created a means of tying those sections of the traditional nobility that benefited from venal office-holding to the royal state: Mooers, *Making of Bourgeois Europe*, pp.51–2. For the view that the funds venality generated strengthened the state's coercive capacity, see Wallerstein, *Modern World-System I*, p.138.

65. Lachman, *Capitalists*, p.122. Office-holding usually also involved exemption from taxation, a salary, and ennoblement through the newly established noblesse de robe.

66. Bosher, *French Finances*, p.16.

67. Clark, *State and Status*, p.44.

68. Donna Bohanan, *Crown and Nobility in Early Modern France* (Basingstoke, Palgrave, 2001), p.33.

69. Finer, 'State- and Nation-Building', p.126.

70. In the mid-sixteenth century, the total fiscal burden of France was four times that of England, in the early seventeenth century 13 times, and in the middle of the seventeenth century 13.6 times. The French population was about four times that of England: Finer, 'State- and Nation-Building', p.128.

71. The reverse also applied. The financial difficulties the magnates experienced in the fourteenth century enabled the king to expand his control through the development of the bureaucracy: Wallerstein, *Modern World-System I*, pp.28–9.

72. These included a rejection of the consultative role of the Estates-General and some centralization and regularization of finances: Bohanan, *Crown and Nobility*, pp.35–8.
73. Finer, *History III*, p.1, 285.
74. There had been a temporary stabilization in the latter part of Henri IV's reign (1589–1610), but this was upset by the struggle surrounding Louis XIII's infancy and the regency of his mother, Marie de Medici. For some limitations on Richelieu's success in centralizing, see Zmora, *Monarchy*, p.88.
75. Finer, *History III*, p.1,318.
76. For an excellent discussion of the centre's problems in overcoming magnates' power at the local and provincial levels, see Lachman, *Capitalists*, pp.118–28.
77. Ellen Meiskins Wood, *The Pristine Culture of Capitalism. A Historical Essay on Old Regimes and Modern States* (London, Verso, 1991), p.27.
78. This view is therefore more complex than that of Ertman, who sees the outcome as a result of the type of assembly and the role it played.
79. Zmora, *Monarchy*, pp. 68–75.
80. For the classic study of the development of a set of norms that was part of this process, see Norbert Elias, *The Civilizing Process. Volume 2. State Formation and Civilization* (Oxford, Basil Blackwell, 1982; first published 1939).
81. This both established royal primacy and disestablished many lesser nobles.
82. Mann, *Sources of Social Power I*, p.463, and Brenner, 'Agrarian Roots', p.257.
83. Strayer, *Medieval Origins*, p.101.
84. Strayer, *Medieval Origins*, p.106.
85. Poggi, *Development*, pp.67–8. On the court as a partnership between king and nobles, see Zmora, *Monarchy*, p.82.
86. Zmora, *Monarchy*, p.82.
87. On sale of office as a means of integrating the feudal nobility into the absolutist state, see Anderson, *Lineages*, pp.33–7. On the emergent bourgeoisie using the same process to buttress its position and strengthen its links with the nobility, see Mooers, *Making of Bourgeois Europe*, pp.56–64.
88. Clark, *State and Status*, p.116.
89. Michael Mann, *The Sources of Social Power. Vol.II. The Rise of Classes and Nation-States* (Cambridge, Cambridge University Press, 1993), p.452.
90. Mann, *Sources of Social Power II*, p.453.
91. Mann, *Sources of Social Power II*, pp.479–80.
92. Mooers, *Making of Bourgeois Europe*, p.50.
93. Mann, *Sources of Social Power I*, pp.480–1.
94. Theda Skocpol, *States and Social Revolutions. A Comparative Analysis of France, Russia, and China* (Cambridge, Cambridge University Press, 1979), p.48.
95. It was originally founded as a private company in 1694. Also see Zmora, *Monarchy*, pp.92–3.

96. Fernand Braudel, *Civilization and Capitalism. 15th–18th Century. Volume 2. The Wheels of Commerce* (London, Fontana Press, 1985, trans. Sian Reynolds), pp.526–42.
97. This had not happened on a large scale earlier despite the Crown's heavy reliance upon private financiers. Following Edward III's reneging on his debts to private financiers, these people were reluctant to lend to the Crown. This prevented them from entering the state apparatus, as they had in France, before the seventeenth century: Ertman, *Birth of the Leviathan*, p.171.
98. Benedict Anderson, *Imagined Communities. Reflections on the Origin and Spread of Nationalism* (London, Verso, 1983).
99. Strayer, *Medieval Origins*, p.109.
100. By the early seventeenth century, at least in England and France, trade treaties were appearing that assumed a national entity and that economic activity should serve its interests: Liah Greenfeld, *The Spirit of Capitalism. Nationalism and Economic Growth* (Cambridge, MA, Harvard University Press, 2001), pp.37–58 and 116–53. According to Greenfeld, 'by 1600, the existence in England of a national consciousness and identity, and as a result, of a new geo-political entity, a nation, was a fact': Liah Greenfeld, *Nationalism. Five Roads to Modernity* (Cambridge, MA, Harvard University Press, 1992), p.30.
101. For the argument that the notion of the king's two bodies (i.e., a distinction between the 'body natural' and the 'body politick', between king as man and king as king; this was a conception that implied the continuation of the state even when the king died) was a doctrinal mechanism which, *inter alia*, effectively linked the king with the nobility while providing a way for the latter to defend themselves against overweening royal power; see Bohanan, *Crown and Nobility*, p.28. The classic study is Ernst H. Kantorowicz, *The King's Two Bodies. A Study in Mediaeval Political Theology* (Princeton, NJ, Princeton University Press, 1957).
102. Anthony Giddens, *The Nation-State and Violence. Volume Two of A Contemporary Critique of Historical Materialism* (Cambridge, Polity Press, 1985), p.94.
103. Giddens, *The Nation-State*, p.94.
104. Finer, *History III*, p.1,478.
105. For a good discussion of Germany and Italy, see Hendrik Spruyt, *The Sovereign State and its Competitors. An Analysis of Systems Change* (Princeton, NJ, Princeton University Press, 1994), pp.109–48.
106. This is the basic argument of Spruyt, *The Sovereign State*.
107. John Bell Henneman Jr, 'France in the Middle Ages', in Bonney, *Fiscal State*, p.103.
108. Henri Pirenne, *Economic and Social History of Medieval Europe* (London, Routledge & Kegan Paul, 1972; first published 1936), p.87.
109. W.M. Ormrod, 'England in the Middle Ages', in Bonney, *Fiscal State*, p.34.
110. The lack of a distinction between public debt and the personal debt of a king is reflected in the fact that creditors would go bankrupt when kings who were heavily indebted to them died without repaying the

loans: W.M. Ormrod, 'The West European Monarchies in the Later Middle Ages', in Bonney, *Economic Systems and State Finance*, p.159.

111. Ormrod and Barta, 'The Feudal Structure', pp.66–9 and 72, and Henneman, 'France', p.113.

112. This growth is reflected in the fact that in sixteenth century England, 35 per cent of state expenditure came from the royal estates and other forms of Crown property, while by the early 1700s this was only 5 per cent. O'Brien and Hunt, 'England, 1485–1815', pp.60–1. There was also considerable reliance upon borrowing, either from external or domestic sources. For one study of this, see Martin Korner, 'Public Credit', in Bonney, *Economic Systems and State Finance*, pp.507–38.

113. For studies of taxation, see the collections of essays in Bonney, *Economic Systems and State Finance* and Bonney, *Fiscal State*.

114. The first modern income tax in England was not imposed until 1799: O'Brien and Hunt, 'England, 1485–1815', p.75.

115. The taille was made permanent in 1439: Schulze, 'Emergence and Consolidation', p.266.

116. For discussion of the fairs of Champagne, see Janet L. Abu-Lughod, *Before European Hegemony. The World System A.D.1250–1350* (New York, Oxford University Press, 1989), pp.51–73.

117. Richard N. Britnell, *The Commercialization of English Society 1000–1500* (Manchester, Manchester University Press, 1996), p.27.

118. Britnell, *Commercialization*, pp.11 and 15–17.

119. Britnell, *Commercialization*, pp.26–7.

120. Mann, *Sources of Social Power I*, p.423. Although private mints in France were not closed down until the fourteenth century, and the last ecclesiastical mint in England was closed in 1543–44. There were no uniform weights and measures until the nineteenth century.

121. Fernand Braudel, *Civilization and Capitalism. 15th–18th Century. Volume 3. The Perspective of the World* (London, Fontana Press, 1985), pp.289–90.

122. On the development of a national market in England and France, see Braudel, *Civilization and Capitalism 3*, ch.4.

123. Peter Musgrave, *The Early Modern European Economy* (London, Macmillan, 1999), pp.95–7.

124. For an argument about the role of states as economic stimulators and actors in this way in the sixteenth to eighteenth centuries, see Wallerstein, *Modern World-System I*, p.133.

125. Schulze, 'Emergence and Consolidation', p.262.

126. Schulze, 'Emergence and Consolidation', pp.270 and 278. Indeed as late as the eve of the Revolution, France did not have a state budget, a centralized treasury system, centralized accounting of revenue and expenditure, or centralized monitoring of debt. On attempts to bring greater regularization about the time of the Revolution, see Bosher, *French Finances*.

127. Following John U. Nuf, *Industry and Government in France and England 1540–1640* (Ithaca, NY, Cornell, 1957), p.59.

128. The Elizabethan Poor Laws can be seen as part of this attempt to regulate the life of the urban population in the wake of the disturbances following on from the enclosures of the sixteenth century.

129. Tilly, *Coercion*, pp.119–20.
130. States had for a long time been involved in the production of some material for war: Tilly, *Coercion*, p.118.
131. From the time of Henry VI nearly 50 per cent of public revenues came from foreign trade, within which wool was the most important: M.N. Pearson, 'Merchants and States', in James D. Tracy (ed.), *The Political Economy of Merchant Empires. State Power and World Trade 1350–1750* (Cambridge, Cambridge University Press, 1991), p.93.
132. Wallerstein, *Modern World-System I*, p.263. This may have been one factor in the French drive to strengthen the state.
133. Linda Weiss and John Hobson refer to three types of economic development: militarized agrarian in France, militarized capitalist in England, and militarized feudal in Prussia: Linda Weiss and John M. Hobson, *States and Economic Development A Comparative Historical Analysis* (Cambridge, Polity Press, 1995), pp.64–8.
134. See Richard Bonney, 'Early Modern Theories of State Finance', in Bonney, *Economic Systems and State Finance*, pp.176–83.
135. Robin Briggs, *Early Modern France 1560–1715* (Oxford, Oxford University Press, 1998), pp.65–6.
136. Mercantilism was not simply a tool of absolutist rulers to generate capital to support their rule (Poggi, *Development*, p.78); it was also implemented by constitutional states such as Britain.
137 Braudel, *Civilization and Capitalism, 3*, p.287.
138. O'Brien and Hunt, 'England, 1485–1815', p.54. Prior to this, funds were raised independently for defence in the cities, boroughs and shires. It was also from this time that a single authority had overall responsibility for receiving and accounting for royal revenues.
139. In the Nine Years War (1689–97), the British and Dutch were able to pressurize Spain and Austria to join an economic blockade of France: Richard Bonney, 'The Eighteenth Century. II. The Struggle for Great Power Status and the End of the Old Fiscal Regime', in Bonney, *Economic Systems and State Finance*, p.320.
140. For this judgement, see Briggs, *Early Modern France*, pp.66–9. Colbert sought, among other things, to reduce domestic tolls and imposts, to improve transport, to organize traders into trading companies, to regulate industry through inspectors and controls, and to impose high tariff barriers against the Dutch.
141. O'Brien and Hunt, 'England, 1485–1815', p.60.

4 The State, Capitalism and Industrialization

1. Capitalists were a major source of funding for state loans: Charles Tilly, *Coercion, Capital, and European States, AD 990–1990* (Oxford, Basil Blackwell, 1990), pp.85–6. Also see the argument in Ellen Meiksins Wood, *The Origin of Capitalism* (New York, Monthly Review Press, 1999), chs 4 and 5.
2. Janet L. Abu-Lughod, *Before European Hegemony. The World System A.D.1250–1350* (New York, Oxford University Press, 1989), pp.115–16.

3. Perry Anderson, *Lineages of the Absolutist State* (London, Verso, 1974), pp.17–40. Direct quotations from pp.18 and 42. Also see Colin Mooers, *The Making of Bourgeois Europe* (London, Verso, 1991), ch.4; Christopher Hill, 'The Transition from Feudalism to Capitalism', *Science and Society* 4, xvii (Fall 1953), pp 348–51; and V.G. Kiernan, 'State and Nation in Western Europe', *Past and Present* 31 (July 1965), pp.20–38.

4. Immanuel Wallerstein, *The Modern World System I. Capitalist Agriculture and the Origins of the European World Economy in the Sixteenth Century* (New York, Academic Press, 1974), pp.157–62, and *The Modern World System II. Mercantilism and the Consolidation of the European World Economy, 1600–1750* (New York, Academic Press, 1980), pp.32–3. For a review of theories about the emergence of capitalism, see Richard Lachman, 'Origins of Capitalism in Western Europe: Economic and Political Aspects', *Annual Review of Sociology* 15 (1989), pp.47–72. On absolutism, see pp.60–4.

5. For example, Friedrich Engels, *The Origin of the Family, Private Property, and the State* (Moscow, Foreign Languages Press, 1954).

6. Charles Tilly, 'War Making and State Making as Organized Crime', in Peter B. Evans, Dietrich Rueschemeyer and Theda Skocpol (eds), *Bringing the State Back In* (Cambridge, Cambridge University Press, 1985), pp.169–91.

7. On the notion of industrialism, see Anthony Giddens, *The Nation-State and Violence. Volume Two of A Contemporary Critique of Historical Materialism* (Cambridge, Polity Press, 1985), pp.138–9. Giddens discusses the relationship between capitalism and industrialism in ch.5.

8. Michael Mann, *The Sources of Social Power. Volume 1. A History of Power from the Beginning to AD 1750* (Cambridge, Cambridge University Press, 1986), p.481.

9. Alan McFarlane, 'The Cradle of Capitalism: The Case of England', in Jean Beachler, John A. Hall and Michael Mann (eds), *Europe and the Rise of Capitalism* (Oxford, Basil Blackwell, 1988), p.201.

10. This is a variant of Weiss and Hobson's difference between market-promoting strategies and unplanned market influence: Linda Weiss and John M. Hobson, *States and Economic Development. A Comparative Historical Analysis* (Cambridge, Polity Press, 1995).

11. For an argument emphasizing the importance of a national market, see Ellen Meiskins Wood, *The Pristine Culture of Capitalism. A Historical Essay on Old Regimes and Modern States* (London, Verso, 1991), ch.6. Important in this was the dissolution of medieval rigidities like the guilds and sumptuary laws, which the state was active in achieving.

12. Mann, *Sources of Social Power I*, p.462.

13. State enforcement of property rights was essential for the development of capitalism and, in North's view, the 'rise of the West': Douglas C. North and Robert Paul Thomas, *The Rise of the Western World. A New Economic History* (Cambridge, Cambridge University Press, 1973),

14. Weiss and Hobson, *States and Economic Development*, p.81.

15. Weiss and Hobson, *States and Economic Development*, p.95.

16. Weiss and Hobson, *States and Economic Development*, pp.114–15.

17. For a stimulating discussion of the split between financial and industrial capital in Britain, see Geoffrey K. Ingham, *Capitalism Divided? The City and Industry in British Social Development* (London, Macmillan, 1984); also Martin J. Wiener, *English Culture and the Decline of the Industrial Spirit 1850–1980* (Harmondsworth, Penguin, 1992, originally published 1981), pp.128–9.

18. Weiss and Hobson, *States and Economic Development*, pp.117–21.

19. Weiss and Hobson, *States and Economic Development*, pp.124–6. Britain did not turn to free trade until about 1860 when all imported manufactured goods gained entry without duties and only 48 items remained on the customs list. Tariffs were reduced generally from 1830. For the period after this, see John M. Hobson, *The Wealth of States A Comparative Sociology of International Economic and Political Change* (Cambridge, Cambridge University Press, 1997), ch.4.

20. This proceeded principally through parliamentary enactment. Between 1720 and 1779 there were 1,139 acts bringing about enclosure, and from 1793 to 1815 there was a further 2,000: Mooers, *Making of Bourgeois Europe*, p.167.

21. E.J. Hobsbawm, *Industry and Empire* (Harmondsworth, Penguin, 1969), p.233.

22. Barry Supple, 'The State and the Industrial Revolution 1700–1914', in Carlo M. Cipolla (ed.), *The Fontana Economic History of Europe*, Vol. 3 (London, Collins, 1973), p.340.

23. Hobsbawm, *Industry*, p.239.

24. For the argument that the nature of British imperialism was rooted in the particular contours of emergent British industrial society, a society within which the dominance of traditional landed interests remained largely in place through the emergence of so-called 'gentlemanly capitalism', reflecting the coming together of landed and capitalist interests, see P.J. Cain and A.G. Hopkins, *British Imperialism 1688–2000*, 2nd edn (Edinburgh, Pearson, 2002).

25. On this, see for example, Frank Longstreth, 'The City, Industry and the State', in Colin Crouch (ed.), *State and Economy in Contemporary Capitalism* (London, Croom Helm, 1979), pp.157–90; Y. Cassis, 'Bankers in English Society in the Late Nineteenth Century', *Economic History Review* 38, 2 (1985), p.210; and Ingham, *Capitalism Divided?*

26. Derek Sayer, 'A Notable Administration: English State Formation and the Rise of Capitalism', *American Journal of Sociology* 97, 5 (March 1992), pp.1,405–7.

27. Sayer, 'A Notable Administration', p.1,406.

28. In France the balance was reversed, especially under Napoleon when the state was used actively to promote economic development and hinder that of Britain. Protectionism was introduced in 1791, internal tariffs and guilds were abolished, a navigation act was introduced in 1793, five years later neutral vessels were prohibited from landing British goods in France, and in 1806–7 a continental blockade was mounted. In addition, the state was used to subsidize industry: church properties were transferred cheaply to manufacturers, the development of new

machinery derived from British models was encouraged and subsidies were given for the installation of such machinery.

29. The classic statement is Alexander Gerschenkron, *Economic Backwardness in Historical Perspective* (Cambridge, MA, Harvard University Press, 1962).

30. See, e.g., Supple, 'The State'. The communist states of the twentieth century could also be added to this list. They will be discussed in Chapter 6.

31. For an excellent discussion of Russian development at this time which disputes aspects of the Gerschenkron thesis but provides evidence for the extent of state involvement in the economy, see Hobson, *Wealth*, ch.3.

32. These had been reduced in the middle of the century but were increased again towards its end. A similar pattern occurred in France.

33. Including the sponsorship of credit banks to provide loans.

34. Hobson, *Wealth*, p.74 and Weiss and Hobson, *States and Economic Development*, pp.93–5.

35. For example, at times the Tsarist state actually restrained industrialization. See the discussion in Weiss and Hobson, *States and Economic Development*, pp.109–10.

36. For one study of transport, see T.C. Barker, 'Transport: the Survival of the Old beside the New', Peter Mathias and John A. Davis, *The First Industrial Revolutions* (Oxford, Basil Blackwell, 1989), pp.86–100.

37. Pauline Gregg, *A Social and Economic History of Britain 1760–1965*, 5th rev. edn (London, George G. Harrap, 1965), p.228. For a discussion of the introduction of this system, see chs xi and xxiv.

38. Michael Mann, *The Sources of Social Power. Volume II. The Rise of Classes and Nation-States, 1760–1914* (Cambridge, Cambridge University Press, 1993), pp.360–1.

39. Mann, *Sources of Social Power II*, p.392.

40. In each country, the proportional increase in state employment 1820–1910 far exceeded the increase in population; the state became bigger relative to the population at this time. For population figures, see Angus Maddison, *The World Economy: A Millennial Perspective* (Paris, OECD, 2001), p.241.

41. Mann, *Sources of Social Power II*, pp.366–8.

42. Mann, *Sources of Social Power II*, pp.375–7. Mann suggests that in 1760 about 25 per cent of state expenditure was devoted to civilian matters, rising to 75 per cent in 1900.

43. Tilly, *Coercion*, pp.88–9.

44. Tilly, *Coercion*, p.76.

45. On the Metropolitan Police and its predecessors, see Stanley H. Palmer, *Police and Protest in England and Ireland 1780–1850* (Cambridge, Cambridge University Press, 1980), pp.76–9. For a comparative study of the French and British experiences, see Clive Emsley, *Policing and its Context 1750–1850* (London, Macmillan, 1983). For the Prussian experience, see Emsley, *Policing*, pp.99–103.

46. This had happened earlier in Ireland. By 1822 the Irish Constabulary was compulsory in all counties. For one history, see T.A. Critchley,

A History of Police in England and Wales (London, Constable, 1978). For some comparative work, George L. Mosse (ed.), *Police Forces in History* (London, Sage, 1975).

47. Palmer, *Police and Protest*, p.558.
48. David Bayley, 'The Police and Political Development in Europe', in Charles Tilly (ed.), *The Formation of National States in Western Europe* (Princeton, NJ, Princeton University Press, 1975), pp.330–41. For a discussion, *inter alia*, of the police role in politics, see Hsi-Huey Liang, *The Rise of Modern Police and the European State System from Metternich to the Second World War* (Cambridge, Cambridge University Press, 1992).
49. See the discussion in Mann, *Sources of Social Power II*, pp.419–36.
50. In the words of David Thomson, *Europe Since Napoleon* (Harmondsworth, Penguin, 1966), p.364.
51. To use the terminology of an excellent set of essays on this topic, Eric Hobsbawm and Terence Ranger (eds), *The Invention of Tradition* (Cambridge, Cambridge University Press, 1983).
52. The fusing of state and nationalism first occurred in France following the Revolution.
53. Formerly the postal service had been carried by coach internally, which was slow and not always reliable; neither was it cheap.
54. This possibility existed even before the introduction of a national postal service because the carriage of letters by coaches was subject to checking by state agents.
55. State inspectors to monitor the labour code were created in Britain in 1833, Prussia 1853 and France 1874.
56. The first comprehensive system of social insurance was established in Germany in the 1880s. Britain borrowed the German model in 1911.
57. Mann, *Sources of Social Power II*, pp.471–2.
58. Or perhaps more accurately in some cases, in the towns that grew up around new industrial establishments.
59. Francois Crouzet, *The First Industrialists. The Problem of Origins* (Cambridge, Cambridge University Press, 1985), pp.147–51.
60. This is calculated both in terms of their fathers' occupations and their own current occupations at the time of the founding of the enterprise.
61. According to Crouzet, 29.2 per cent of these first industrialists had fathers who worked as manufacturers and industrialists, 23 per cent as merchants, traders and bankers, and 21.7 per cent on the land: Crouzet, pp.147–51.
62. Crouzet found (pp.147–51) that only 8.8 per cent came from the upper class, landed peers, landed gentry, and army and navy officers.
63. On France, see Mooers, *Making of Bourgeois Europe*, pp.73–83.
64. There are many studies of the formation of the class. See the classic, E.P. Thompson, *The Making of the English Working Class* (Harmondsworth, Penguin, 1968).
65. For example, see Barrington Moore Jr, *Social Origins of Dictatorship and Democracy. Lord and Peasant in the Making of the Modern World* (Harmondsworth, Penguin, 1967) and Dietrich Rueschemeyer, Evelyne Huber Stephens and John D. Stephens, *Capitalist Development and Democracy* (Cambridge, Polity Press, 1992).

66. For example, see P.J. Cain and G. Hopkins, 'Gentlemanly Capitalism and British Expansion Overseas. I. The Old Colonial System, 1688–1850', *Economic History Review* 2nd series, XXXIX, 4 (1986), pp.501–25; M.J. Daunton, ' "Gentlemanly Capitalism" and British Industry 1820–1914', *Past and Present* 122 (February 1989), pp.119–58; Martin J. Wiener, *English Culture and the Decline of the Industrial Spirit 1850–1980* (Harmondsworth, Penguin, 1985); H.L. Malchow, *Gentlemen Capitalists. The Social and Political World of the Victorian Businessman* (Stanford, CA, Stanford University Press, 1992). For a critique of the notion of 'gentlemanly capitalism', see Geoffrey Ingham, 'British capitalism: empire, merchants and decline', *Social History* 20, 3 (October 1995), pp.339–54.

67. The emergent bourgeoisie did, through the purchase of office, enter the same ranks as the traditional nobility and even acquire noble titles prior to the Revolution, but this route was closed off by the Revolution.

68. For an argument about the French Revolution that discusses the notion of a bourgeois revolution and essentially dismisses it, see George C. Comninel, *Rethinking the French Revolution. Marxism and the Revisionist Challenge* (London, Verso, 1987). For a counter view, see Mooers, *Making of Bourgeois Europe*, pp.64–73. Comninel argues that although there were no boundaries between the pre-revolutionary nobility and the bourgeoisie, there was tension between them because the bourgeoisie was the class of property and state offices without the privileges of noble status, while the nobility stood for those privileges. However, approaching 1789, the nobility split between the constitutionalists and those who wanted to repossess the powers of the state through the Estates-General. The revolution was therefore a result of an intra-class dispute over the powers of the state: Comninel, *Rethinking the French Revolution*, pp.197–9. For Wallerstein, bourgeoisie and aristocracy were overlapping groups rather than different classes: Immanuel Wallerstein, *The Modern World System III. The Second Era of Great Expansion of the Capitalist World Economy, 1730–1840s* (New York, Academic Press, 1989), pp.34–53 and 100. For a brief summary of how the bourgeoisie benefited from the Revolution, see William Doyle, *The Oxford History of the French Revolution* (Oxford, Clarendon Press, 1989), pp.407–9.

69. Allan Cochrane, 'Industrialisation and Nineteenth Century States', James Anderson (ed.), *The Rise of the Modern State* (Brighton, Wheatsheaf, 1986), p.76.

70. It is difficult to get a precise date for universal suffrage because of the way in which various sorts of restrictions on voting remained. Common were property qualifications, differential age limits, and the continuing disenfranchisement of minorities. For an interesting argument (and some different dates) about the role of the working class in bringing about democratic political forms, see Goran Therborn, 'The Rule of Capital and the Rise of Democracy', *New Left Review* 103 (May–June 1977), pp.3–41. The dates come from p.11.

71. This point ignores the argument as to whether the parliamentary representatives actually represented the class interests of the workers or not.

72. This was, of course, helped by the comparative international peace on the European continent between 1815 and 1914.
73. This was related to the fact that Europe constituted a competitive system of states. This is discussed in Chapter 5.
74. Consequently Hintze's view that the rise of capitalism and the rise of the state were two sides of the one process is only partly correct: Otto Hintze, 'Economics and Politics in the Age of Capitalism', *The Historical Essays of Otto Hintze* (Oxford, Oxford University Press, 1975, ed. Felix Gilbert), p.452.

5 The Western State and the Outside World

1. See the discussion in E.L. Jones, *The European Miracle. Environments, Economies and Geopolitics in the History of Europe and Asia* (Cambridge, Cambridge University Press, 1981), chs 1 and 6.
2. Michael Mann, 'State and Society, 1130–1815: an analysis of English State Finances', in Michael Mann, *States, War and Capitalism* (Oxford, Basil Blackwell, 1988), p.89.
3. On the growth of trade, see Philip D. Curtin, *Cross Cultural Trade in World History* (Cambridge, Cambridge University Press, 1984).
4. Permanent diplomatic representation began in the Italian states after 1450, but was disrupted by the Reformation. It resumed after 1600. France had 22 ambassadors in 1660 and 32 in 1715, while in England William III (1689–1702) appointed 80 during his reign and Anne (1702–14) 136: Martin van Creveld, *The Rise and Decline of the State* (Cambridge, Cambridge University Press, 1999), p.134.
5. For an example of a French observer sent to England to negotiate a trade contract reporting back about the nature of English financial administrative processes, see Fernand Braudel, *Civilization and Capitalism. 15th–18th Century. Volume 2. The Wheels of Commerce* (London, Fontana Press, 1985), p.526.
6. This also took place in the economic sphere, as tradesmen moved to other political jurisdictions either to escape persecution or make their fortunes. For example, in the late sixteenth century, Dutch and Flemish craftsmen were persuaded to go to England to teach their skills to local tradesmen. The borrowing of banking techniques from Italy is another instance.
7. On the role of financiers, see Braudel, *Civilization and Capitalism 2*, pp.532–7.
8. For a critique of some of these theories, see Thomas Ertman, *Birth of the Leviathan. Building States and Regimes in Medieval and Early Modern Europe* (Cambridge, Cambridge University Press, 1997), pp.3–4.
9. Perry Anderson, *Lineages of the Absolutist State* (London, Verso, 1974).
10. Otto Hintze, 'Military Organization and the Organization of the State', *The Historical Essays of Otto Hintze* (Oxford, Oxford University Press, 1975, ed. Felix Gilbert), pp.178–215. Hintze's generalization is intriguing but does not explain all cases; for example, Poland was

confronted by large land armies in both Prussia and Russia, but its political structure was anything but absolutist.

11. Charles Tilly, 'War Making and State Making as Organized Crime', in Peter B. Evans, Dietrich Rueschemeyer and Theda Skocpol (eds), *Bringing the State Back In* (Cambridge, Cambridge University Press, 1985), pp.169–92. For a more extended analysis, see Charles Tilly, *Coercion, Capital and European States, AD 990–1990* (Oxford, Basil Blackwell, 1990). Tilly identified three modes of development: the coercion-intensive mode where 'rulers squeezed the means of war from their own populations and others they conquered, building massive structures of extraction in the process', such as Brandenburg and Russia; the capital-intensive mode where 'rulers relied on compacts with capitalists – whose interests they served with care – to rent or purchase military force, and thereby warred without building vast permanent state structures' as in the city-states and the Dutch Republic; and the capitalized-coercion mode where 'rulers did some of each, but spent more of their effort than did their capital-intensive neighbors on incorporating capitalists and sources of capital directly into the structures of their states. Holders of capital and coercion interacted on terms of relative equality', such as in France and England: Tilly, *Coercion*, p.30. Infrastructural power was weak in the coercion-intensive path and strong in the capital-intensive. For the argument that the type of military force a state had affected the political form, see S.E. Finer, 'State- and Nation-Building in Europe: The Role of the Military', in Charles Tilly (ed.), *The Formation of National States in Western Europe* (Princeton, NJ, Princeton University Press, 1975).

12. Michael Mann, *The Sources of Social Power. Vol. 1. A History of Power from the Beginning to AD 1760* (Cambridge, Cambridge University Press, 1986), pp. 456, 476, 479. Brian M. Downing, *The Military Revolution and Political Change. Origins of Democracy and Autocracy in Early Modern Europe* (Princeton, NJ, Princeton University Press, 1992) agrees with Mann about the implications of the nature of resource extraction for the type of political structure, adding two other sources of income to those identified by Mann: wealth from conquered territories, and foreign subsidies.

13. Charles Tilly, 'Reflections on the History of European State-Making', in Tilly, *Formation*, p.73.

14. Tilly, 'Reflections', p.74.

15. For a study of English finances which brings out the impact of war on state budgets, see Michael Mann, 'State and Society, 1130–1815: An Analysis of English State Finances', in Mann, *States, War and Capitalism*, pp.73–123. More broadly, see Hillay Zmora, *Monarchy, Aristocracy and the State in Europe 1300–1800* (London, Routledge, 2001), pp.55–61.

16. For one discussion of this during this time, see Linda Weiss and John M. Hobson, *States and Economic Development. A Comparative Historical Analysis* (Cambridge, Polity Press, 1995), ch.2; also Mann, *Sources of Social Power I*, p.426. For figures on the changing size of the military in Europe over the 1470–1814 period, see Angus

Maddison, *The World Economy: A Millennial Perspective* (Paris, OECD, 2001), p.81.

17. Mann, *Sources of Social Power I*, p.430. Tilly argues that also important in this was that war gave officials new capacities to extract resources and take on new activities, and it revealed new problems needing state attention: Tilly, *Coercion*, p.189.

18. J.R. Strayer, *On the Medieval Origins of the Modern State* (Princeton, NJ, Princeton University Press, 1970), p.60. Neither did reliance on mercenaries have the same sort of impact on the state as reliance upon a national army. The latter required the provision of arms, uniforms and general upkeep, and is therefore more likely to have an administrative impact than reliance on mercenaries who provided their own means.

19. Ertman, *Birth of the Leviathan*, pp.27–30.

20. Ertman, *Birth of the Leviathan*, p.28. For the argument that war and the need for finance could weaken the position of the king in relation to other elites, including financial and traditional landowning elites, see Richard Lachman, *Capitalists in Spite of Themselves. Elite Conflict and Economic Transitions in Early Modern Europe* (Oxford, Oxford University Press, 2000), pp.105–6.

21. See Tilly, *Coercion*.

22. Hendrik Spruyt, *The Sovereign State and its Competitors. An Analysis of Systems Change* (Princeton, NJ, Princeton University Press, 1994), pp.84–6.

23. Spruyt, *The Sovereign State*, pp.82–4.

24. For one discussion of this, see William H. McNeill, *The Pursuit of Power. Technology, Armed Force, and Society since AD 1000* (Chicago, IL, The University of Chicago Press, 1982), ch.3.

25. Mann, *Sources of Social Power I*, p.428.

26. Eric Hobsbawm and Terence Ranger (eds), *The Invention of Tradition* (Cambridge, Cambridge University Press, 1983).

27. For a stimulating study of this process in England, see Philip Corrigan and Derek Sayer, *The Great Arch. English State Formation as Cultural Revolution* (Oxford, Basil Blackwell, 1985).

28. Anderson, *Lineages*.

29. For example, Michael Hechter, 'Review Essay: Lineages of the Capitalist State', *American Journal of Sociology* LXXXII (March 1977), pp.1,057–74; Theda Skocpol and Mary Fullbrook, 'A Review of Perry Anderson's Passages and Lineages', *The Journal of Development Studies* XIII (April 1977), pp.290–5; Peter Gourevitch, 'The International System and Regime Formation. A Critical Review of Anderson and Wallerstein', *Comparative Politics* 10, 3 (April 1978), pp.419–38.

30. See the three volumes, Immanuel Wallerstein, *The Modern World-System I. Capitalist Agriculture and the Origins of the European World Economy in the Sixteenth Century* (New York, Academic Press, 1974); *The Modern World-System II. Mercantilism and the Consolidation of the European World Economy, 1600–1750* (New York, Academic Press, 1980); and *The Modern World-System III. The Second Era of Great Expansion of the Capitalist World Economy, 1730–1840s* (New York, Academic Press, 1989).

31. Wallerstein, *Modern World-System I*, p.355. 'Strong' is defined in terms of 'strength vis-à-vis other states within the world-economy including other core-states, and strong vis-à-vis local political units within the boundaries of the state. In effect, we mean a sovereignty that is *de facto* as well as *de jure*. We also mean a state that is strong vis-à-vis any particular social group within the state' (emphasis in original), p.355.

32. For some critiques, see Theda Skocpol, 'Wallerstein's World Capitalist System: A Theoretical and Historical Critique', *American Journal of Sociology* 82, 5 (1977), pp.1,075–90; Aristide R. Zolberg, 'Origins of the Modern World System: A Missing Link', *World Politics* 33, 2 (January 1981), pp.253–81; and Gourevitch, 'International System'. For a defence of Wallerstein against his critics, see Daniel Garst, 'Wallerstein and His Critics', *Theory and Society* 14, 4 (1985), pp.469–95.

33. See respectively Zolberg, 'Origins', and Skocpol, 'Wallerstein's World Capitalist System'.

34. See the discussion in Garst, 'Wallerstein and His Critics'.

35. Gourevitch, 'International System', pp.425–6.

36. Gourevitch, 'International System', p.423.

37. For a discussion of what he calls world economies, all of which have a capitalist city at their heart, see Fernand Braudel, *Civilization and Capitalism 15th–18th Century. Volume 3. The Perspective of the World* (London, Fontana Press, 1985).

38. Abu-Lughod discusses these in terms of eight interlinked subsystems. For a useful map showing how she conceives of their relationships, see Janet L. Abu-Lughod, *Before European Hegemony. The World System A.D. 1250–1350* (Oxford, Oxford University Press, 1989), p.34.

39. Curtin, *Cross Cultural Trade*, ch.5.

40. See the discussion in Abu-Lughod, *Before European Hegemony*, pp.10–11.

41. For a discussion of the development of trade, see Curtin, *Cross Cultural Trade*, chs 6–9. For an emphasis on the 'interconnections' between people on different parts of the globe, see Eric R. Wolf, *Europe and the People Without History* (Berkeley, CA, University of California Press, 1982), ch.2.

42. For a discussion of the world system at this time, see Abu-Lughod, *Before European Hegemony*.

43. There is evidence that Arab seafarers had actually cicumnavigated Africa some time before this, but the route was not used as a means of linking Europe with the East, and was not even known about by Europeans.

44. Abu-Lughod, *Before European Hegemony*, p.124.

45. Abu-Lughod, *Before European Hegemony*, p.353.

46. For a study of the 1400–1800 world system, see André Gunder Frank, *ReOrient: Global Economy in the Asian Age* (Berkeley, CA, University of California Press, 1998). On this point, see p.xix. Also see K.N. Chaudhuri, *Asia before Europe: Economy and Civilisation of the Indian Ocean from the Rise of Islam to 1750* (Cambridge, Cambridge University Press, 1990).

47. Frank, *ReOrient*, p.52.
48. The route around the Cape of Good Hope was the more important for trade, and it certainly had an impact upon the continuing use of the Central Asian route.
49. Frank, *ReOrient*, pp. 132, 142 and 147.
50. Frank, *ReOrient*, pp.158–62.
51. Abu-Lughod, *Before European Hegemony*, p.13.
52. Abu-Lughod, *Before European Hegemony*, p.200. On the sixteenth–seventeenth century chartered companies (the English and Dutch East India Cos, the Muscovy Co., the Hudson's Bay Co. and the Royal Africa Co.) as precursors of modern transnational corporations, see Ann M. Carlos and Stephen Nicholas, ' "Giants of an Earlier Capitalism": the Chartered Trading Companies as Modern Multinationals', *Business History Review* 62, 3 (1988), pp.398–419.
53. Maddison, *The World Economy*, p.84.
54. Frank, *ReOrient*, ch.5; and Jack A. Goldstone, 'East and West in the Seventeenth Century: Political Crises in Stuart England, Ottoman Turkey, and Ming China', *Comparative Studies in Society and History* 30 (1988), pp.103–42.
55. Frank, *ReOrient*, p.166.
56. Frank, *ReOrient*, 171–2. For different figures, but with Asia still 2.5 times the size of Europe, see Maddison, *The World Economy*, p.263. According to Maddison (p.42), GDP per capita in China was surpassed by that of Europe about 1250, although of course the population of China was much greater.
57. For a summary and survey, see Frank, *ReOrient*, pp.193–204. On China, see the magisterial Joseph Needham, *Science and Civilization in China* (Cambridge, Cambridge University Press, 1954). On India see G. Kuppuram and K. Kumudamani, *History of Science and Technology in India* (Delhi, Sundeep Prakashan, 1990).
58. Frank, *ReOrient*, p.213.
59. Frank, *ReOrient*, p.219.
60. This notion of backwardness ran right through the followers of Marx, becoming particularly acute when communist revolutions occurred in two countries that were seen as the archetypes of the backward state: Russia in 1917 and China in 1949.
61. It should be noted that Marx was inconsistent in his characterization of Asia. As well as the points noted in the text, he also acknowledged that Chinese purchasing power had stimulated European markets, and that Oriental despotism was necessary to manage large-scale irrigation projects, a situation that does not fit easily with the view of production as being restricted to the village: Frank, *ReOrient*, pp.14–15.
62. For a stimulating treatment which, while ultimately assuming European superiority, acknowledges the complexity of economic life in the major Asian empires, see Braudel, *Civilization and Capitalism 2*, pp.113–34 and Braudel, *Civilization and Capitalism 3*.
63. John A. Hall, *Powers and Liberties: The Causes and Consequences of the Rise of the West* (London, Penguin, 1985), ch.2.
64. Hall, *Powers and Liberties*, ch.3.

65. For example, see Brian Turner, *Marx and the End of Orientalism* (London, Croom Helm, 1986), p.81; David S. Landes, *The Unbound Prometheus. Technological Change and Industrial Development in Western Europe from 1750 to the Present* (Cambridge, Cambridge University Press, 1969). For a discussion of this view, see Hall, *Powers and Liberties*, ch.4.

66. S.E. Finer, *The History of Government. I. Ancient Monarchies and Empires* (Oxford, Oxford University Press, 1997), p.473.

67. S.E. Finer, *The History of Government. II. The Intermediate Ages* (Oxford, Oxford University Press, 1997), p.743.

68. S.E. Finer, *The History of Government. III. Empires, Monarchies, and the Modern State* (Oxford, Oxford University Press, 1997), p.1,135.

69. Although some did play this role.

70. Although 'Mandarin officials, always non-natives', were usually only appointed as far as the county level: Vivienne Shue, *The Reach of the State. Sketches of the Chinese Body Politic* (Stanford, CA, Stanford University Press, 1988), p.97.

71. Finer, *History I*, p.508.

72. Cited in Finer, *History II*, p.749.

73. Finer, *History II*, pp.746–57.

74. Landed families financially supported a male heir or heirs who studied for the exams to enter state service. Once they had gained official position, they were expected to expand the family fortune. Given the absence of primogeniture, this was crucial for the long-term future of the family. In Shue's words, 'the gentry embodied the mutual interests and interdependence of the imperial state and the agrarian elite': Shue, *The Reach of the State*, pp.86–7.

75. At a very early date, the Chinese bureaucracy worked on the basis of written reports.

76. Shue, *The Reach of the State*, pp.97–100.

77. Finer, *History II*, pp.808–9.

78. Jones, *The European Miracle*, p.203.

79. Frank, *ReOrient*, p.108.

80. According to Huang, the conditions to facilitate the development of capitalism did not exist in late Ming China. He argues that money was scarce, legal protection for businessmen absent, interest rates high, and the banking system underdeveloped. Roadblocks on trade routes, state purchase orders and forced contributions, a near monopoly on the use of the Grand Canal by the state, and the state's active participation in manufacturing, are all seen as hindering the activities of merchants and entrepreneurs. Potential business investment was undermined by the security and status of land ownership, tax exemptions for those who had bought official rank, and the non-progressive nature of land tax: R. Huang, *Taxation and Governmental Finance in Sixteenth Century Ming China* (Cambridge, Cambridge University Press, 1974), pp.318–19. For the view that virtually all of the institutions necessary to enable state and private capitalism to exist were in place in Sung and Yuan times (960–1328), see Abu-Lughod, *Before European Hegemony*, pp.330–7.

81. Hall, *Powers and Liberties*, ch.2. For an explicit argument about the state standing in the way of economic development, see Dwight Perkins, 'Government as an Obstacle to Industrialization: The Case of Nineteenth Century China', *Journal of Economic History* 27 (1967), pp.478–92.

82. M.N. Pearson, 'Merchants and States', in James D. Tracy (ed.), *The Political Economy of Merchant Empires. State Power and World Trade 1350–1750* (Cambridge, Cambridge University Press, 1991), pp.67–8.

83. On the blurred boundary between private trade and state activity, see Abu-Lughod, *Before European Hegemony*, p.318. During the Ch'ing period the emperor himself was active in economic life: he held a monopoly of the ginseng trade, played a major role in the copper trade, took a share of revenues from customs and the salt monopoly, and had his own armouries and factories for silk and other textiles. He was also able to place his retainers in key economic posts: Finer, *History III*, p.1,136.

84. On the gentry engaging in mercantile activity but not progressing to manufacturing capitalism, see Shue, *The Reach of the State*, p.94.

85. According to Wickham, 'One development during the whole of Chinese history that is now increasingly clear is the slow political absorption of the landed aristocracy in the state': Chris Wickham, 'The Uniqueness of the East', in Jean Baechler, John A. Hall and Michael Mann (eds), *Europe and the Rise of Capitalism* (Oxford, Basil Blackwell, 1988), p.74. Also Shue, *The Reach of the State*, ch.3.

86. Shue, *The Reach of the State*, ch.3 gives an interesting argument and comparison.

87. For a survey of this period, see Romila Thapar, *A History of India*, Vol. 1 (Harmondsworth, Penguin, 1966).

88. Thapar, *History of India*, chs 9 and 14.

89. Thapar, *History of India*, ch.12.

90. Finer, *History III*, p.1231.

91. Movement from one caste to another was very rare.

92. For a study of the Mughal Empire's relationship to the economy, see Pearson, 'Merchants and States', pp.52–61. The state did provide incentives for bringing new land into cultivation and did try to restrict the movement of peasants in areas where the frontier was still open.

93. Barrington Moore Jr, *Social Origins of Dictatorship and Democracy. Lord and Peasant in the Making of the Modern World* (Harmondsworth, Penguin, 1966).

94. What follows relies upon Hall, *Powers and Liberties*, ch.3. Also see Jones, *The European Miracle*, p.193. For a view which questions this, see Braudel, *Civilization and Capitalism 3*, p.504.

95. See the discussion of the Indian economy in Braudel, *Civilization and Capitalism 3*, pp.498–511.

96. According to Hall, it even led to a distrust of political power itself: Hall, *Powers and Liberties*, pp.88–9.

97. Finer, *History II*, p.668.

98. Finer, *History III*, p.1,198.

99. For an argument about the way in which the sons of the Sultan were treated and the effect this had on the production of a line of 'effete and degenerate incompetents', see Finer, *History III*, p.1,172. Also see Jones, *The European Miracle*, p.186.
100. Hall, *Powers and Liberties*, pp.93–6.
101. Finer, *History III*, p.1,181.
102. Finer, *History III*, p.1,184. See pp.1,181–4 for the discussion upon which this is based.
103. Finer, *History II*, p.671.
104. See the discussion in A.L. Udovitch, *Partnership and Profit in Medieval Islam* (Princeton, NJ, Princeton University Press, 1970).
105. Abu-Lughod, *Before European Hegemony*, pp.217–24.
106. Palmira Brummett, *Ottoman Seapower and Levantine Diplomacy in the Age of Discovery* (Albany, NJ, State University of New York Press, 1994), pp.176–9.
107. Frank, *ReOrient*, p.206.
108. For the argument that between 900 and the fifteenth century the state in Egypt was heavily involved in the economy, including production, see Abu-Lughod, *Before European Hegemony*, pp.226–36. For arguments that the Ottomans virtually ran a command economy, see B. McGowan, *Economic Life in Ottoman Europe: Taxation, Trade and the Struggle for Land, 1600–1800* (Cambridge, Cambridge University Press, 1980), and Hahil Inalcik, *The Ottoman Empire: Conquest, Organization and Economy* (London, Variorum Reprints, 1978). This view seems exaggerated.
109. The Ottoman Empire was engaged in war for 270 of the years between 1400 and 1789: Finer, *History III*, p.1,164.
110. Hall, *Powers and Liberties*, pp.31 and 102–3. The argument is also found in abbreviated form in John A. Hall and G. John Ikenberry, *The State* (Milton Keynes, Open University Press, 1989), ch.3.
111. Hall, *Powers and Liberties*, p.31.
112. Hall, *Powers and Liberties*, p.102.
113. And when he does, he uses the notion of empire, meaning capstone state, to explain weakness in economic dynamism: Hall, *Powers and Liberties*, pp.107–9.
114. Thomas J. Barfield, *The Perilous Frontier. Nomadic Empires and China, 221 BC to AD 1757* (Oxford, Basil Blackwell, 1989).
115. For example, see the comment: 'Both inside and outside India, Tamil, Bengali and Gujerati merchants formed closeknit partnerships with business and contracts passing in turn from one group to another, just as they might in Europe from the Florentines to the Lucchese, the Genoese, the South Germans, or the English': Braudel, *Civilization and Capitalism 3*, p.486.
116. Finer, *History III*, pp.1,455–60.
117. This discussion follows Frank, *ReOrient*, ch.6.
118. For this notion of buying themselves in, see Braudel, *Civilization and Capitalism 3*, p.491.
119. On this see Mark Elvin, *The Pattern of the Chinese Past* (Stanford, CA, Stanford University Press, 1973), p.300. Also see Mark Elvin,

'Why China failed to create an endogenous industrial capitalism: a critique of Max Weber's explanation', *Theory and Society* 13, 3 (May 1984), pp.379–91.

120. The Russian Empire was not an overseas empire but a geographical extension of the state itself, hence its omission from this list.

121. For a discussion of various aspects of the historical dimension of globalization, see A.G. Hopkins (ed.), *Globalization in World History* (London, Pimlico, 2002). For a typology of archaic, proto, modern and post-colonial, see pp.3–11.

6 The Twentieth Century: The State Embedded?

1. T.H. Marshall, *Citizenship and Social Class* (Cambridge, Cambridge University Press, 1950).

2. For a recent study, see Michael Sullivan, *The Development of the British Welfare State* (London, Prentice-Hall, 1996).

3. This is in addition to the commercial data bases established to underpin the credit revolution.

4. For a discussion of the increased surveillance capacity, see Stephen Gill, 'The Global Panopticon? The Neoliberal State, Economic Life, and Democratic Surveillance', *Alternatives* 2 (1995), pp.13–16.

5. In 1954 the Atomic Energy Authority was established and in 1971 the collapse of Rolls-Royce led to its nationalization by the Conservatives.

6. Similar developments occurred on the Continent. See the discussion in Martin van Creveld, *The Rise and Decline of the State* (Cambridge, Cambridge University Press, 1999), pp.358–61.

7. Iron and steel were denationalized in 1953 and renationalized in 1967.

8. Gosta Esping-Andersen, *The Three Worlds of Welfare Capitalism* (Princeton, NJ, Princeton University Press, 1990).

9. Evelyne Huber and John D. Stephens, *Development and Crisis of the Welfare State. Parties and Policies in Global Markets* (Chicago, IL, University of Chicago Press, 2001), p.87.

10. Tito Boeri, 'Does Europe Need a Harmonised Social Policy?', Thirtieth Economics conference of the Austrian national bank, Vienna, 13–14 June 2002, p.3.

11. On the development of the American welfare state, see Theda Skocpol, *Protecting Soldiers and Mothers. The Political Origins of Social Policy in the United States* (Cambridge, MA, The Belknap Press, 1992); Edward D. Berkowitz, *America's Welfare State. From Roosevelt to Reagan* (Baltimore, MD, The Johns Hopkins University Press, 1991); and Margaret Weir, Ann Shoal and Theda Skocpol (eds), *The Politics of Social Policy in the United States* (Princeton, NJ, Princeton University Press, 1988), esp. Part 1.

12. Van Creveld, *Rise and Decline*, pp.361–2.

13. Cited in Richard Rose and Rei Shiratori (eds), *The Welfare State East and West* (Oxford, Oxford University Press, 1986).

14. Van Creveld, *Rise and Decline*, p.361.

15. Figures are based on Gavin Drewry and Tony Butcher, *The Civil Service Today* (Oxford, Basil Blackwell, 1988). For a longer term view, see Geoffrey K. Fry, *The Growth of Government. The Development of Ideas about the Role of the State and the Machinery and Functions of Government in Britain since 1780* (London, Frank Cass, 1979) and R.G.S. Brown and D.R. Steel, *The Administrative Process in Britain* (London, Methuen, 1970).

16. Sometimes this could in practice be more an uneasy cohabitation than a fruitful partnership, often because the state lacked an effective industry policy and a well considered plan for the long-term management of the economy.

17. For one useful study, see Dan Smith and Ron Smith, *The Economics of Militarism* (London, Pluto Press, 1983).

18. For an excellent short discussion of the process of privatization in Britain, see Harvey Feigenbaum, Jeffrey Henig and Chris Hamnett, *Shrinking the State. The Political Underpinnings of Privatization* (Cambridge, Cambridge University Press, 1999), ch.3. The remainder of this paragraph is based on this source.

19. For example, common methods used in welfare included the introduction of means tests, substitution of tax credits for direct transfer payments, inclusion of welfare payments in income for tax purposes, changes in eligibility criteria, introduction of part or full payment for some services, and the cancellation or reduction of subsidies: van Creveld, *Rise and Decline*, p.365.

20. Huber and Stephens, *Development and Crisis*, p.2.

21. There are numerous studies of these states. For example, Alice H. Amsden, *Asia's Next Giant. South Korea and Late Industrialization* (New York, Oxford University Press, 1989); Richard P. Appelbaum and Jeffrey Henderson (eds), *States and Development in the Asian Pacific Rim* (Newbury Park, CA, Sage, 1992); Robert Wade, *Governing the Market. Economic Theory and the Role of Government in East Asian Industrialization* (Princeton, NJ, Princeton University Press, 1990); Linda Weiss, *The Myth of the Powerless State. Governing the Economy in a Global Era* (Cambridge, Polity Press, 1998); Linda Weiss and John M. Hobson, *States and Economic Development. A Comparative Historical Analysis* (Cambridge, Polity Press, 1995).

22. See the analysis in Weiss, *Myth*, ch.3.

23. Frederic C. Deyo, 'The Political Economy of Social Policy Formation. East Asia's Newly Industrialized Countries', in Appelbaum and Henderson, *States and Development*, p.298.

24. Significant resources have been directed into agriculture, structural adjustment for declining industries, employment support, and small business: Weiss, *Myth*, pp.158–61.

25. The most famous Marxist analysis of this was Vladimir Lenin's *The State and Revolution*, written in 1917 and published the following year.

26. On the diversity of views in the initial years of Soviet power, see the standard studies, Leonard Schapiro, *The Origin of the Communist Autocracy. Political Opposition in the Soviet State: First Phase, 1917–1922* (New York, Frederick A. Praeger, 1965); Robert Vincent Daniels, *The Conscience of the Revolution. Communist Opposition in*

Soviet Russia (New York, Simon & Schuster, 1960); Robert Service, *The Bolshevik Party in Revolution 1917–1923. A Study in Organisational Change* (London, Macmillan, 1979).
27. The classic works are Carl J. Friedrich and Zbigniew K. Brzezinski, *Totalitarian Dictatorship and Autocracy* (Cambridge, MA, Harvard University Press, 1956) and Hannah Arendt, *The Origins of Totalitarianism* (London, André Deutsch, 1986, first published 1951).
28. For one study showing the absence of such control within the party structure itself, see Graeme Gill and Roderic Pitty, *Power in the Party. The Organization of Power and Central-Republican Relations in the CPSU* (London, Macmillan, 1997).
29. The actual basis of legitimation was far more complex than this, but it is the ideological element of the state's legitimation programme that provided the driving force for the following discussion.
30. Ferenc Feher, Agnes Heller and Gyorgy Markus, *Dictatorship Over Needs* (Oxford, Basil Blackwell, 1983).
31. Boris Yeltsin, *Against the Grain. An Autobiography* (London, Pan Books, 1990, trans. Michael Glenny), pp.25–8.
32. See a good discussion of the importance of this in Geoffrey Hosking, *The Awakening of the Soviet Union* (London, Heinemann, 1990), ch.4.
33. David Lane, *Soviet Economy and Society* (Oxford, Basil Blackwell, 1985), pp.64–7.
34. For fuller discussions of this, see Graeme Gill, *The Origins of the Stalinist Political System* (Cambridge, Cambridge University Press, 1990) and Gill and Pitty, *Power in the Party*.
35. Andropov and Chernenko were both in office for too short a period to really confirm a leadership style, although the indications were that Andropov sought to be a dominant leader in the mould of his forebears.
36. On this latter point, see Gill and Pitty, *Power in the Party*.
37. For this distinction, see Graeme Gill and Roger Markwick, *Russia's Stillborn Democracy? From Gorbachev to Yeltsin* (Oxford, Oxford University Press, 2000), ch.3.
38. Gill, *Origins*.
39. See Graeme Gill, *Democracy and Post-Communism. Political Change in the Post-Communist World* (London, Routledge, 2002).
40. For the purposes of this argument, the situation of the avowedly neutral states (such as Switzerland, Finland and Austria) will be ignored. They can, in any case, be lumped together with the West in terms of their levels of social development and forms of society.

7   State Capacity in a Globalized World

1. There are numerous definitions of globalization, but most focus on the quality captured by Tabb, who defined it as 'the process of reducing barriers between countries and encouraging closer economic, political, and social interaction': William K. Tabb, 'Progressive globalism: challenging the audacity of capital', *Monthly Review* 50, 9 (February 1999), p.1.

According to Shaw:

> [globalization] is not simply or mainly either an economic or a recent historical phenomenon, indeed not a single process at all. It can be defined as a complex set of distinct but related processes – economic, cultural, social and also political and military – through which social relations have developed towards a global scale and with global reach, over a long historic period.

Martin Shaw, 'The state of globalization: towards a theory of state transformation', *Review of International Political Economy* 4, 3 (Autumn 1997), p.498.

2. Susan Strange, *The Retreat of the State* (Cambridge, Cambridge University Press, 1996), p.4.
3. For example, K. Ohmae, *The End of the Nation State* (London, Harper Collins, 1996); M. Horsman and A. Marshall, *After the Nation State* (London, HarperCollins, 1994); Joseph A. Camilleri and Jim Falk, *The End of Sovereignty? The Politics of a Shrinking and Fragmenting World* (Aldershot, Edward Elgar, 1992). For some studies of the way globalization curtails the competence and effectiveness of national economic policies, see J. Frieden, 'Invented Interests: The Politics of National Economic Policies in a World of Global Finance', *International Organization* 45, 4 (1991), pp.425–53; G. Garrett and P. Lange, 'Political Responses to Interdependence: What's Left for the Left?', *International Organization* 45, 4 (1991), pp.539–65; Peter Gourevitch, *Politics in Hard Times* (New York, Cornell University Press, 1986); R. O'Brien, *The End of Geography* (London, Routledge, 1992); C. Webb, 'International Economic Structures, Government Interests, and International Co-ordination of Macro-economic Adjustment Policies', *International Organization* 45, 3 (1991), pp.309–43.
4. See David Held and Anthony McGrew, 'Globalization and the liberal democratic state', in Yoshikazu Sakamoto (ed.), *Global transformation: Challenges to the state system* (Tokyo, United Nations University Press, 1994), p.64 for a discussion which sees the first and third of these elements as independent.
5. For one discussion of TNCs, see Strange, *Retreat of the State*, ch.4.
6. Ian Clark, *Globalization and Fragmentation. International Relations in the Twentieth Century* (Oxford, Oxford University Press, 1997), p.184.
7. Jerry Harris, 'Globalization and the Technological Transformation of Capitalism', *Race and Class*, 40, 2/3 (October 1998–March 1999), p.26.
8. Foreign direct investment (FDI) has increased enormously in the latter part of the twentieth century, with some seeing it as more important than international trade as a generator of international growth. Between 1983 and 1990, FDI is estimated to have grown at an annual average of 34 per cent, and to have reached a gross figure of US$2 trillion by 1992: Clark, *Globalization*, p.184.
9. For the argument that globalization is 'the latest episode in perpetually restructuring capitalism', see Don D. Marshall, 'Understanding

Late-Twentieth Century Capitalism: Reassessing the Globalization Theme', *Government and Opposition* 31, 2 (Spring 1996), p.195.

10. Ronald Steel, 'A New Realism', *World Policy Journal* xiv, 2 (Summer 1997), p.5.

11. This was initiated by the August 1971 US decision to withdraw from the Bretton Woods fixed exchange system and adopt a programme of wage and price controls.

12. Peter F. Drucker, 'The Global Economy and the Nation State', *Foreign Affairs* 76, 5 (September–October 1997), p.162.

13. Harris, 'Globalization', p.23.

14. See the discussion in Eiko Ikegami, 'Democracy in an Age of Cyber-Financial Globalization: Time, Space and Embeddedness from an Asian Perspective', *Social Research* 66, 3 (Fall 1999), pp.887–914. She argues that the re-embedding of the economy in society can be brought about through democracy.

15. Shaw, 'The state of globalization', pp.500–1.

16. For an exaggerated argument about the spread of federal institutions and principles in Europe, see Daniel J. Elazar, 'From statism to federalism: a paradigm shift', *International Political Science Review* 17, 4 (October 1996), pp.417–29.

17. For example, John Keane, 'Global Civil Society?', Globalization and Its Challenges, Conference, University of Sydney, 12–14 December 2001.

18. See the analysis in Michael Hardt and Antonio Negri, *Empire* (Cambridge, MA, Harvard University Press, 2001).

19. For an argument about the way in which common rationalized organizational and social forms have become universalized, principally through the borrowing of these by states from a common 'world society', see John W. Meyer, John Boli, George M. Thomas and Francisco Ramirez, 'World Society and the Nation State', *The American Journal of Sociology* 103, 1 (July 1997), pp.144–81. On homogenization, see Kenneth N. Waltz, 'Globalization and Governance', *PS: Political Science and Politics* 32, 4 (December 1999), p.694.

20. Paul Hirst and Grahame Thompson, *Globalization in Question* (Cambridge, Polity Press, 1996), p.185.

21. Linda Weiss, *The Myth of the Powerless State. Governing the Economy in a Global Era* (Cambridge, Polity Press, 1998), p.176.

22. Weiss, *Myth*, pp.176–7.

23. On this issue, see Waltz, 'Globalization and Governance', p.695; Josef Joffe, 'Rethinking the Nation-State; The Many Meanings of Sovereignty', *Foreign Affairs* 78, 6 (November–December 1999), pp.122–7; Stephen D. Krasner, *Sovereignty: Organized Hypocrisy* (Princeton, NJ, Princeton University Press, 1999); Daniel Verdier, 'Domestic Responses to Capital Market Internationalization Under the Gold Standard, 1870–1914', *International Organization* 52, 1 (Winter 1998), pp.1–34.

24. Waltz, 'Globalization and Governance', p.696.

25. Weiss, *Myth*, p.179.

26. But even if there is to be a convergence, is this necessarily a result of globalization? Historically, states have modelled themselves on more

successful states, so any convergence may be a function of conscious choice to emulate rather than the operation of globalization forces.

27. Waltz, 'Globalization and Governance', p.695. For a view about the increasing convergence of capitalism, see Strange, *Retreat of the State*, p.75.
28. Comments by John Hobson, 'Globalization and Its Challenges', Conference, University of Sydney, 12–14 December 2001. This is despite the operation of tendencies towards tax reform reducing the marginal rates on high income earners so as to attract the foreign and retain domestic ones in a world in which the freeing up of capital movement has made it more mobile. The reduction of such marginal rates has often been funded by cuts in welfare spending.
29. Comments by M. Ramesh, 'Globalization and Its Challenges', Conference, University of Sydney, 12–14 December 2001.
30. Weiss, *Myth*, pp.178–9.
31. Weiss, *Myth*, p.179.
32. China does not fit this generalization, but it has not sought to use its nuclear capability for military ends.
33. Robert J. Holton, *Globalization and the Nation State* (London, Macmillan, 1998), p.60.
34. Held and McGrew, 'Globalization', p.59.
35. Notwithstanding the growth of private security companies.
36. Michael Mann, 'Has globalization ended the rise and rise of the nation state?', *Review of International Political Economy* 4, 3 (Autumn 1997), p.474.
37. Linda Weiss, 'Governed interdependence: re-thinking the government–business relationship in East Asia', *The Pacific Review* 8, 4 (1995), pp.607–12.
38. See the analysis in Leonard Seabrooke, *US Power in International Finance. The Victory of Dividends* (Basingstoke, Palgrave, 2001).
39. Holton, *Globalization*, p.70.
40. Also see the discussion of the Basle Accord in Seabrooke, *US Power*, chs 5 and 6.
41. For an argument that loyalty to a state is no different from loyalty to an employer, see Strange, *Retreat of the State*, p.72.
42. Samuel P. Huntington, *The Clash of Civilizations and the Remaking of World Order* (New York, Simon & Schuster, 1996).
43. For an argument about the importance of institutions, see Weiss, *Myth*. Also see Mann, 'Has globalization ended'. For an argument that the international system poses different sorts of economic constraints depending upon a state's mix of resources, see David M. Rowe, 'World Economic Expansion and National Security in Pre-World War I Europe', *International Organization* 53, 2 (Spring 1999), pp.195–231.
44. For the view that 'the withdrawal of the state from regulatory and social welfare functions in the interests of capital mobility and "competitiveness" in the world market – is the product of policy choices, not the working out of natural laws …', see Ellen Meiksins Wood, 'Modernity, postmodernity or capitalism?', *Review of International Political Economy* 4, 3 (Autumn 1997), p.558.

Index

absolutism 90, 98–9, 100–1, 104,
113, 116–17, 156, 161–2,
189, 272
Abu-Lugod, Janet 115–16, 167
Abyssinia 231, 233
aediles 42, 43, 44, 262
Afghanistan 257
Akkadian Empire 34, 47
Alexander the Great 34, 35
Anderson, B. 102
Anderson, Perry 116, 152,
161–2, 164
Aristotle 166
Assembly, Athenian 37–8, 39
Assyrian Empire 48, 52, 53
Athens 34, 35, 36–40, 45, 62,
69–70, 261
Augustus 41, 49, 50, 51, 56,
261, 264
Australia 199, 228
Austria 108, 138, 143, 153, 161, 277
autonomy 4, 12–22
Avicenna 166

Balkans 162, 186
Belgium 191, 242
Beveridge, William 197
Bloch, M. 164
Bodin, Jean 103
Bolsheviks 210
bourgeoisie 116, 123–4, 125,
139–40, 141–2, 146, 147, 282
Braudel, F. 112
Brezhnev, L I. 218, 219
Britain 99, 103, 117, 118–24, 125,
126, 128, 129, 130, 131, 132,
133, 137, 138, 139–40, 141, 143,
144, 145, 146, 177, 178, 180,
189, 190, 196–206, 231, 237,
242, 243, 257, 277, 279, 281

bureaucracy 3–4, 16–17, 19, 32, 38,
45–6, 47–8, 48–9, 52–8, 68, 70,
71, 73, 80–97, 99, 101, 103, 104,
115, 123–4, 129–35, 138, 144,
152–6, 170, 172–8, 179, 183,
186, 198, 194–210, 255, 288
Bush, George W. 232

Caligula 50
Caliphate 181–5, 186
Canada 199
capacity 1, 22–32, 33, 71–2, 73,
104, 113, 115, 138, 223
Capetian dynasty 83, 92
capitalism 28, 63–6, 115–24,
146–8, 162–4, 169–94, 194–210,
222–4, 239–40, 242, 254, 288
capstone state 171, 176–8, 255
Caracalla 51, 66
Carneiro, R.L. 9
Carthage 34, 46
caste system 171, 179–80, 188
Castile 74
censors 42, 43
Charles VII 92
Chechnya 251
Ch'in dynasty 172, 173
China 19, 63, 165, 166, 167, 168,
169, 170, 171, 172–8, 181, 184,
185, 186, 187, 188, 189, 190,
193, 210, 243, 287, 288, 289
Ch'ing dynasty 172, 176, 289
Chola 178
Church 7, 73, 74, 81, 86, 114, 126,
149–50, 160
citizenship 36–7, 38, 40, 47, 55,
56, 68, 69–70, 194–5, 196, 205,
214, 261
city states 3, 33, 34, 35–47, 48, 58–9,
68, 69–70, 104, 115–16, 156, 158

civil war, English 102, 110
Claudius 51
Cleisthenes 37
coercion 5, 119, 121, 133–4,
   212–13, 277, 284
Colbert, J.-B. 112, 277
Cold War 199, 203, 236, 243–4
Comitia Centuriata 42, 49, 50, 262
Comitia Tributa 42, 49, 50
communications 31, 45–6, 52–7,
   68, 82–97, 99, 120, 127–9,
   136–7, 144, 146, 151, 201–2,
   213–14, 230, 234–9, 241, 244–6,
   255, 265, 281
communism 1, 11, 28, 196, 210–24,
   254, 255, 287
Communist Party of the Soviet Union
   210–13, 220, 221, 223
Constantine 51, 264, 268
Confucianism 171, 172–8, 188
constitutionalism 98, 99–102,
   104, 156
consuls 42, 43, 44, 49, 64, 262
council, Athenian 37–8, 39

Delhi sultanate 178
Denmark 155
dictator, Roman 43
Diocletian 51, 52, 57, 63, 66, 67
Domitian 66
Deyo, F.C. 209

Eadred 77
early modern state 73–114
Eastern Europe 115, 152,
   160–2, 163
economy 58–68, 69, 79–80,
   104–14, 115–48, 150, 160–93,
   194–225, 227–30, 239–40,
   241–3, 247–51, 289, 290
education 135–6, 200
Edward I 85, 150
Edward II 77
Edward III 150, 152, 275
Egypt 33, 34, 35, 47, 48–9, 53–5,
   57, 58, 59–61, 68–72
elitism 10
embeddedness 12–22, 23, 32, 33,
   36, 40, 45, 46, 47, 57, 58–68,

71–2, 84–97, 100, 104, 113,
   114, 127–48, 186, 194–225,
   247–56
emperor, Chinese 172–3
emperor, Roman 49–52, 55–7, 64
emperor, Mughal 178–9
empire 33, 34, 47–58, 59–61,
   176, 269
Engels, Friedrich 10, 258
England 74, 76–7, 80, 82–91,
   92, 95, 96, 97, 98, 99–100,
   101, 102, 104, 106, 107, 108,
   109, 110–11, 112, 113–14,
   115, 118, 150, 153, 155, 161,
   186, 187, 191, 195, 269,
   270, 271, 272, 275, 276,
   283, 284
Eridu 34
Ertman, T. 155
Esping-Anderson, G. 200
Estates General 92
Etruscans 34
European Union 233–4, 240, 241,
   242, 244, 248
external context 5, 15–16, 120–1,
   149–93, 226–56

Farabi, Al- 166
feudalism 34, 73–114, 149, 156–7,
   160, 269
Finer, S.E. 47, 61, 94, 182
France 7, 14, 77, 80, 82, 83–4, 87,
   88, 91–7, 99, 100, 101, 102,
   104, 107, 108, 109, 110–13,
   113, 114, 117, 119, 120, 128,
   130, 131, 133, 138, 140, 142,
   143, 153, 156, 162, 180, 186,
   187, 191, 200, 242, 243, 269,
   271, 274, 275, 276, 277, 279,
   281, 282, 283, 284
Francis I 94
Frank, A.G. 167, 184, 190
French Revolution 80, 103, 113,
   136, 138, 142, 194, 282
Fried, M.H. 10

General Agreement on Tariffs and
   Trade 233, 250
Genoa 153, 165

Germany 1, 103–4, 115, 125, 128,
    130, 131, 133, 138, 141, 143,
    144, 145, 153, 155, 156, 158,
    160, 161, 162, 191, 200, 211,
    217, 231, 281, 284
Gerschenkron, A. 126
Geta 51
globalization 191–3, 225,
    226–56, 294
Gorbachev, M.S. 218–21
Greece 33, 34, 35, 36–40, 45, 46,
    61–2, 66, 68–72

Habsburg Empire 73, 115, 186
Hall, John 176–8, 185–9
Han dynasty 172, 173
Hanseatic League 73, 74, 104,
    111, 156
Held, D. 246
Henry II 85
Henry III 77
Henry VIII 99, 102, 126
Hintze, Otto 9, 152, 283
Hobson, John 125–6
Holy Roman Empire 73, 82,
    104, 149
Huber, E. 200
Hundred Years War 92, 154, 157
Hungary 88, 155, 162
Huntington, S.P. 251

Ibn Khaldun 182
India 165, 166, 167, 168, 171,
    178–80, 181, 184, 185, 186, 187,
    188, 189, 190, 224, 243, 290
industrialization 28, 115–48,
    194, 255
interdependence 12–22, 23, 32, 33,
    36, 40, 45, 46, 57, 58–68, 71–2,
    84–97, 100, 104, 113, 114, 138,
    186, 194–225, 247–56
interdependence, institutional 19,
    21, 23, 32, 47, 58–68, 104–14,
    194–225, 247–56
interdependence, bureaucratic organic
    19–22, 23, 32, 36, 45, 46, 47,
    49, 57, 58, 68, 71–2, 73, 90–1,
    104, 113, 114, 138, 186, 201–2,
    209–10, 223–4, 252, 256

interdependence, legislative organic
    20–2, 23, 32, 36, 40, 47, 57, 58,
    68, 71–2, 73, 90–1, 104, 113,
    114, 189, 200–1, 209–10, 223–4,
    252, 256
internationalization 240
International Monetary Fund 250
Internet 238–9
Iraq 243
Islam 149, 162, 165–6, 168, 171,
    180–5, 186, 187, 188, 189, 190
Israel 240, 243
Italy 104, 115, 128, 143, 151, 152,
    156, 158, 170, 200, 240, 283

Japan 193, 200, 208–10, 241,
    242, 248
John, King 77

Kalimantan 251
Keynes, J.M. 196
Khrushchev, N.S. 218, 223
Kindi, Al- 166
kingship 36, 45, 47, 49, 53,
    75–80, 82, 84–97, 98–9, 100–1,
    103, 117
Kropotkin, P.A. 136

Larsa 34
law 38, 48, 49, 53, 55, 63, 77–9,
    85–6, 87, 91, 92, 99, 100, 117,
    118–19, 146, 182, 189
League of Nations 233
legitimation 25–6, 36, 39, 40, 47,
    48, 49, 69–70, 89, 103, 113,
    172–8, 181, 250–1, 275
Lenin, V.I 218
liberalism 9, 12
liturgy 39, 44, 46
Louis XI 109
Louis XIII 95, 274
Louis XIV 95, 97
Lucius Verus 51

Macrinus 50, 57
magistrates, Athenian 36–8
Magna Carta 77, 84, 90
Mann, Michael 24, 29, 59, 80, 129,
    131, 153

Marcus Aurelius   51, 57, 66, 264
Marshall, T.H.   196
Marx, Karl   10, 14, 169–70,
    210, 287
Marxism   9, 10, 12, 115, 148,
    169–70, 287
Mauryan dynasty   178
Maximian   51
Maximinus   66
Mazarin, J.   95
McGrew, A.   246
mercantilism   102, 112–13, 117,
    119, 122, 145, 277
Mesopotamia   30, 34, 35–6, 39,
    40, 45, 46, 47–8, 52–3, 58–9,
    68–72
military   24, 29, 38, 46, 50–1, 56,
    65, 70–1, 77, 79, 100, 102, 103,
    133–5, 152–8, 180, 184, 203,
    231–3, 243–4, 285
Ming dynasty   167, 176, 288
Mobutu, S.S.   28, 224
Monaco   3
Mongols   162, 166, 167, 172,
    174, 178
Montfort, Simon de   84, 90
Moore, B.   180
Mughal Empire   167, 178–80, 181,
    186, 187, 190

Napoleon   133, 279
nation state   6
national identity   6, 102–3, 136,
    158–60, 214, 251, 269, 275
Netherlands   143, 151, 153, 155,
    161, 191, 200, 242, 277, 284
New Zealand   199, 206
NGOs   3, 234, 248
nightwatchman state   11
Nippur   30
nobility   44, 49, 52, 53–5, 59, 68,
    71, 74–99, 100–1, 102, 105,
    107, 116, 139–42, 156–7, 159,
    174, 177
Normans   76–7, 82–3
North American Free Trade
    Agreement   229, 248
Norway   240
nuclear weapons   231–3, 243–4

officials   3–4, 16–17, 19, 30–1, 49,
    52–7, 63, 75, 80–97, 99, 101–2,
    123–4, 172–8, 179
organic state-building   73, 84–91
origins of the state   9, 10
Ottoman Empire   115, 162, 181–5,
    186–7, 190
overarching state-building   73, 91–7

Pakistan   243
palace polity   47, 57–8, 172,
    178, 181
Parlement de Paris   91–2
Parliament, English/British   86,
    88–91, 92, 96, 97, 98, 99, 100,
    104, 106, 107, 115, 117, 279
parliaments   88–90, 100–1,
    200–1, 272
party-state   210–13
Persian Empire   34, 48, 53
Peter I   151
Philip IV   91
Poland   88, 155, 160, 161–2
police   121, 132–4
political parties   4, 142, 195, 200
Portugal   191, 192
power   7, 22–32
power, despotic   23–4, 217–19, 224
power, economic   24, 26–9, 30, 32,
    71–2, 227–30, 241–3, 247,
    247–51
power, ideological   24, 25–6, 30, 32,
    71–2, 81, 174–8, 213–15, 234–9,
    244–6
power, infrastructural   23–4, 32, 45,
    49, 70, 71–2, 73, 81, 104,
    127–48, 217–19, 224, 247–56
power, political   24, 29–32, 71–2,
    230–4, 243–4
praetors   42, 43, 44, 262
privatization   204–8
Proudhon, P.J.   136

Qa'eda, al-   232
quaestors   43

Reagan, Ronald   204, 232
realism   8
Richard I   86

Richard II 77, 150
Richelieu, Cardinal 95
Rome 33, 34, 35, 36, 40–6, 47,
    49–52, 55–7, 58, 62–7, 68–72,
    73, 149, 150, 160, 165, 173
Russia 78, 115, 125, 128, 141, 145,
    151, 152, 153, 161, 162, 243,
    284, 287
Rwanda 251

Scandinavia 88
Senate, Roman 41–2, 49, 50, 55,
    56, 57, 58, 63–4, 261
Septimius Severus 51, 57, 66
Service, E.R. 9
Shaw, Martin 232
society 4, 12–22, 32, 45, 52, 58–68,
    71–2, 127–48, 172–85, 194–225,
    247–56
South Korea 208–10, 242
sovereignty 4–5, 7
Spain 102, 117, 149, 153, 162, 186,
    187, 191, 192, 231, 233, 277
Sparta 35
Stalin, J.V. 218, 221
Stephens, J.D. 200
Strayer, Joseph 84, 102, 154
suffrage 142–3, 282
Sumer 35, 48, 69–70
Sung dynasty 169, 176, 288
Sweden 155, 200, 202

Taiwan 208–10
Tajikistan 222
T'ang dynasty 172, 173, 176
taxation 13, 45, 46, 60, 62, 65,
    66, 70, 75, 81, 85, 86, 89, 90,
    92, 93, 95, 96, 99, 100, 101,
    106–8, 113, 121, 125, 132,
    152–4, 155, 156, 158, 179,
    180, 198, 208, 242, 267, 268,
    271, 276, 296
territory 5–6, 7, 15, 29, 74, 103,
    116, 118, 226–7, 230–1
Thailand 193
Thebes 35
Thatcher, Margaret 204
Tiberius 50

Tilly, Charles 132, 153–4, 284, 285
totalitarianism 211–12
trade routes 166, 167, 286, 287
Trajan 57, 67
transnational corporations 228, 234,
    248, 249
tribunes of the plebeians 42, 43, 50,
    262
Trimberger, E.K. 14
Turkey 189, 193

United Nations 233
Ur 34
Uruk 34
USA 130, 131, 138, 191, 199, 200,
    201, 204, 219, 228, 231, 232,
    237, 239, 241, 242, 243, 245,
    248, 249
USSR 196, 210–24, 243

Vatican 30
venality of office 87, 93–4, 99,
    102, 138
Venice 108, 120, 153, 165
Vijayanagra 178

Wallerstein, Immanuel 162–4,
    165, 168
war and state development 120–1,
    152–8
Wars of Religion 95
Wars of the Roses 84
Weber, Max 2–7, 8, 10, 170
welfare state 11, 194–210
William I 82, 96, 108, 270
Witte, Sergei 125
Wittfogel, K. 9
working class, industrial 140–1,
    142–4, 200, 201, 282
world system 162–93
World Trade Organization 228,
    233, 250

Yeltsin, Boris 216
Yuan dynasty 174, 288
Yugoslavia 234, 251

Zaire 28, 224

CPSIA information can be obtained at www.ICGtesting.com
Printed in the USA
LVOW132147180712

290691LV00004B/10/A

9 780333 804506